WORKS BY FRANCES WINWAR

→»» • «««←

Biographies

THE HAUNTED PALACE: A *Life of Edgar Allan Poe*

OSCAR WILDE *and the Yellow Nineties*

WINGLESS VICTORY (D'Annunzio and Duse)

THE IMMORTAL LOVERS (Elizabeth Barrett and Robert Browning)

THE SAINT AND THE DEVIL (Joan of Arc and Gilles de Rais)

THE LIFE OF THE HEART (George Sand and Her Times)

AMERICAN GIANT (Walt Whitman and His Times)

POOR SPLENDID WINGS (The Rossettis and Their Circle)

THE ROMANTIC REBELS (Byron, Shelley and Keats)

FAREWELL THE BANNER (Coleridge and the Wordsworths)

Novels

THE LAST LOVE OF CAMILLE

THE EAGLE AND THE ROCK

THE SENTIMENTALIST

GALLOWS HILL

PAGAN INTERVAL

THE GOLDEN ROUND

THE ARDENT FLAME

Translations

THE DECAMERON OF GIOVANNI BOCCACCIO

History

PURITAN CITY: THE STORY OF SALEM

THE LAND OF THE ITALIAN PEOPLE

Art Monograph

RUOTOLO: MAN AND ARTIST

The Haunted Palace

A LIFE OF

EDGAR ALLAN POE

BY

Frances Winwar

And travellers, now, within that valley,
  Through the red-litten windows see
Vast forms, that move fantastically
  To a discordant melody,
While, like a ghastly rapid river,
  Through the pale door
A hideous throng rush out forever
  And laugh—but smile no more.

HARPER & BROTHERS PUBLISHERS, NEW YORK

Winwar, Frances
    The haunted palace; a life of Edgar Allan Poe.
[1st ed.] New York, Harper [1959]

396 p. illus. 22 cm.

Includes bibliography.

1. Poe, Edgar Allan, 1809-1849.   i. Title.

PS2631.W57   928.1   58-12457 ‡

Library of Congress

DEDICATION

->>> • <<<-

To

My Cherished Friends

Dora and John Koch

For Their Encouragement and

Inspiration

CONTENTS

—≫≫ • ≪≪—

vii

PART FOUR

A group of illustrations follows page 152.

Part One

CHAPTER I

-»» • «&-

Actors in Young America

THE ship *Outram,* Captain Davis, was pulling into the harbor of Boston on the 3rd of January, 1796. After a voyage of nearly two months the passengers were eager to catch their first glimpse of what, for many of them, would be their adoptive land. Even after the spectacular hurly-burly of the port of London, Boston's eighty quays and moles, with the great length of Long Wharf stretching out from State Street, offered a sight to make them gasp. Often as many as a hundred sail could be counted lying at two or three wharves alone, ready to slip into their devoted element, as one of the papers put it.

Still, even the most aesthetic of sights cannot keep the mind from returning to its immediate concerns. As the *Outram* neared port the natural, if unspoken, query of the emigrating navvies as of the group of actors scanning the new horizon was one of bread and butter. What opportunities would the New World offer? What welcome would it give them? For the laborers and artisans the reply held hope, thanks to the needs of the rapidly expanding country. For the ladies and gentlemen of the theater the welcome of Puritan Boston remained an unresolved question. It had not been so long ago in England itself that Puritan opposition to plays had subjected actors to a whipping at the cart's tail. New England, a Puritan stronghold, had no doubt carried over Puritan prejudices as well as Puritan virtues.

Among the passengers who landed that day were an attractive woman, Mrs. Elizabeth Arnold, her young daughter, a Miss Green and a Mr. Charley Tubbs, who seemed to form a congenial group. Two days later the *Massachusetts Mercury* informed Boston that Mrs. Arnold hailed from the Theatre Royal, Covent Garden, and that both she and Miss Green had been engaged for the Boston Theatre by Mr. Powell. "Each of the ladies are tall and genteel," commented the reporter, letting grammar lapse in his admiration—"have an expressive countenance—And move with Symetry unequalled. Mrs. Arnold is about in her four and twentieth year." Her daughter Elizabeth, or

3

Betty, was a large-eyed, curly-headed sylph of nine. Mr. Charley Tubbs, though mentioned, was not especially remarked. "They will be valuable acquisitions to our Theatre, and we anxiously hope they will be engaged," the reporter concluded, returning wistfully to the tall and genteel ladies who, if they read the notice, must have fervently echoed, "Amen."

After a struggle of nearly a century, following the passage of various acts to prevent the performance of stage plays, the theater-loving minority of Boston had succeeded in erecting the first dramatic playhouse in the city. Many brave efforts had been made before that, the latest in 1792 when, in the muddy reaches of Boston's Broad Alley, a stable had been equipped with benches and a stage and euphemistically named the New Exhibition Room.

The plays were announced in the handbills as edifying lessons, Otway's *Venice Preserved* suffering a sea-change into a rich and strange moral lecture in five parts, "in which the dreadful effects of conspiracy will be exemplified." Shakespeare's *Hamlet* and *Romeo and Juliet* also underwent similar disguises.

Nevertheless, Governor Hancock, one of the most vigorous enemies of the theater, was not fooled, and the sheriff was soon sallying forth with a warrant. The young hotheads of the city promptly retaliated by tearing down the portrait of the Governor from its place of honor in front of the stage box and trampling upon it. The State Arms suffered the same treatment. "An open assault upon the laws and Government of the Commonwealth!" protested Governor Hancock before the Legislature, which had prudently met in Concord, because of both the row and a sudden outbreak of smallpox in Boston. Somehow the New Exhibition Room was the sole casualty, for in the spring of 1793 it was taken down.

However, many who had survived the smallpox succumbed to the lure of the theater. Gradually legal opposition, in the form of the prohibitory law in the statute books, became a dead letter. The audience that had enjoyed the edifying lectures clamored for more. On the plea that the theater was a great instructor through the works of genius of every age, public-spirited citizens raised a subscription for the erection of a playhouse. At last, under the management of Charles Stuart Powell, the Boston Theatre, a handsome two-story brick edifice with a columned portico, opened its doors on the 3rd of February, 1794. Robert Treat Paine wrote the inaugural prologue, eloquently declaimed by the manager himself in the robes of Apollo. An English cast performed *Gustavus Vasa* and a trifle entitled *Modern*

Antiques. Unfortunately, at the end of the first season the management pleaded bankruptcy.

Mr. Powell evidently recovered his forces, for the theater reopened its doors to new plays and imported talent. Perhaps because he appreciated the drawing power of looks as well as of art, he engaged for his 1796 season the two English actresses whose movements had so entranced the *Mercury* reporter.

Mrs. Arnold had a little over five weeks to refurbish her repertory. Then, on the 12th of February, 1796, she made her debut as Rosetta in the comic opera *Love in a Village.* The *Mercury* reporter was not disappointed. "We have had the pleasure of a complete fruition," he wrote in the issue of February 16, "in the anticipation of the satisfaction a Boston audience would receive from the dramatic abilities of Mrs. Arnold. The theatre never shook with such bursts of applause. . . ."

It continued shaking appreciatively to Mrs. Arnold's talents as she recited, sang, laughed and wept in a variety of roles ranging from comedy and farce to melodrama and tragedy. At the close of the Boston season, in the middle of May, she set out with Betty and other members of the troupe to awaken New England towns to the Thespian art.

It was in Portland, Maine, early in June, that Betty, dignified as Miss Arnold in the announcements, emerged as a singer at one of the vocal concerts for which Mr. Charley Tubbs furnished the pianoforte accompaniments. The response to the programs was sufficiently encouraging for Mrs. Arnold and Mr. Tubbs to announce an acting company of their own on the 17th of November, 1796, in Portland's *Eastern Herald and Gazette of Maine.* Incidentally the article disclosed an event of more personal nature: "Mrs. Tubbs, late Mrs. Arnold of the Theatre Royal. . . ."

When or where Mrs. Arnold married her pianoforte player, history does not disclose. It may have been in Portland or in Boston, or perhaps even in England before the departure of the *Outram.* There is also an element of uncertainty in her first marriage, if, indeed, she was the Elizabeth Smith who, according to the records of St. George's Church in London, married a Henry Arnold on the 18th of May, 1784.[1] At any rate, Mrs. Arnold appears to have been left a widow in 1790.

[1] See Arthur Hobson Quinn, *Edgar Allan Poe,* p. 2, who prints the record. One of the peculiarities of this record, however, is that, although the two witnesses wrote their names, both Elizabeth Smith and Henry Arnold merely made their marks, an implication of illiteracy which would scarcely be compatible with

According to the press of the day, the Tubbs theatrical venture met as gratifying a success as the frigid Puritan temperament and an improvised stage could afford. It was the precocious Miss Arnold, however, who on the opening night captivated the public as the delightful flirt, Biddy Bellair, in Garrick's *Miss in Her Teens*. "Her powers as an actress would do credit to any of her sex of maturer age," commented a critic who, nevertheless, warned the ladies to stay away till they were certain that their ears would not be offended by expressions of obscenity and profanity.[2]

For several weeks the Tubbs company offered a varied repertory, Miss Arnold proving her versatility by playing girl or boy, maiden in her teens or spoiled child. Like a faithful barometer the friendly critic indicated her progress. "The beautiful Miss Arnold whose powers as an actress command attention," he wrote on December 12. Again, after a brief mention of Mrs. Tubbs, he rhapsodized: "The powers of her daughter . . . astonish us. Add to these her youth, her beauty, her innocence and a character is composed which has not, and perhaps will not again be found on any theatre." [3] Such demolition of grammar argues for the sincerity of the writer's feelings.

Still, in spite of the attractions of mother and daughter, the company's cashbox did not thrive, even after several benefits. Moreover, the Maine winter exhibited all its rigors which the new year did not promise to allay. Packing up their properties, Mr. and Mrs. Tubbs, with Miss Arnold, joined John Sollee's acting troupe which was making its way south, after a few performances in New York's John Street Theatre and a sojourn in Philadelphia. An outbreak of yellow fever, however, altered Mr. Sollee's plans and his Boston and Charleston Comedians went their separate ways, arranging to meet in South Carolina for the theatrical season there.

Throughout the winter Mrs. Tubbs and her daughter acted and sang, Miss Arnold never failing to charm with the vocal novelty "The Market Lass." Mr. Sollee also found roles for Mr. Tubbs in farce and comedy. Before long Mr. Tubbs, who had no relish for inferior parts, joined an offstage intrigue with two other disaffected actors, Mr. Edgar and Mr. Whitlock. By the following spring the

a career that required the memorizing of England's classical drama. If, according to the *Mercury* reporter, Mrs. Arnold was in her twenty-fourth year in 1796, she would have been twelve years old at the time of her marriage—unless Mrs. Arnold employed her prerogative as woman and actress to lop off a lustrum or so from her age.

[2] *Eastern Herald and Gazette of Maine,* Nov. 28, 1796.

[3] *Ibid.,* Dec. 12 and 22, 1796.

group had seceded and formed a new company with Mr. Edgar in charge. Mrs. Tubbs and, of course, Miss Arnold, were the chief feminine assets. Indeed, Betty had recently acquired new dignity with her first Shakespearean role, the boy Duke of York in *Richard III*. How many in the audience caught the pathetic overtones in the recitation of the slight girl with the overlarge eyes?

> Grandam, one night, as we did sit at supper,
> My uncle Rivers talk'd how I did grow
> More than my brother: 'Ay,' quoth my uncle Gloucester,
> 'Small herbs have grace, great weeds do grow apace:'
> And since, methinks, I would not grow so fast,
> Because sweet flowers are slow and weeds make haste.

Betty did not grow apace, yet her frail body and her young mind soon had to sustain parts beyond her years. The company performed in Wilmington, North Carolina, as well as in Charleston, where, because of the feeling which the split in the dramatic ranks had aroused, the press was largely unfavorable. Mr. Sollee's estimate of Mr. Tubbs, whom he blamed for the disruption, was terse: "A vermin."

Early in the spring of 1798 what remained of the Edgar-Tubbs Troupe set out for Philadelphia and Wignell's New Theatre Company, housed in a temple with a Grecian porch and massive wings and capable of holding two thousand persons. Alas, the newcomers were not to tread its boards. They arrived only to find the New Theatre about to close because of the spread of the dreaded "Yellow Jack" which that year was to take more than three thousand lives. In the group with Mr. Tubbs and Miss Arnold was only one other actress, a Mrs. Snowden, who had been a member of the Charleston Company.

No mention whatever appears of Mrs. Tubbs after her recital of the 2nd of May, 1798, with her husband and daughter. Whether she died in Charleston and was laid in a common grave or whether she succumbed to the fever in Philadelphia and there found her narrow bed in the potter's field, the records do not say. Soon the name of Mr. Tubbs also faded from the programs and the press. Perhaps he met the same fate as his wife. The death of mere players was of too little note to be recorded.

With both her mother and her stepfather gone, the eleven-year-old Betty was looked after by Mrs. Snowden. Indeed, the current of her life was not greatly altered by her loss. She traveled from city to city with the small troupe. She recited, danced in an occasional ballet and, in December of 1799, sang her part in *A Monody on the Death of General Washington*. It must have been a spectacular performance if it resembled the commemorative ceremony thus announced in the Boston Theatre: *"A Monody on the death of General Washington,* by Mrs. Barrett, in the character of the *Genius of America* weeping over the tomb of her beloved *hero*. With a solemn March of Officers, drums, Fifes, Band of Music, Soldiers with Arms and Colors reversed, forming a Grand Processional Dirge. . . ." [4]

Little by little, as Betty matured, she sustained important roles, though she was best liked in such parts as Little Pickle in *The Spoiled Child,* certainly more in keeping with her years.

The spring of 1800 found the players in Philadelphia with Mr. Wignell's Company, which was soon increased by the engagement of a new comedian, Charles Hopkins, a young man whom versatility, or perhaps necessity, shuttled about in diverse roles. Later in the season it was joined by another actor, Luke Usher. In the propinquity enforced by the common life of the group emotional entanglements inevitably developed. Mrs. Snowden soon became the wife of Mr. Usher.

Husband and wife now watched over their self-assumed charge, the lovely child who began attracting more attention as she grew into a still lovelier girl. She remained small, but her rounded figure in its short-waisted Empire gowns had a sylphlike grace while her face, framed in its curls, well became such parts as that of Cupid in *Cymon and Sylvia*. The Ushers had much to do guarding so alluring a flower against the stage-door bees.

The danger, however, lay within their group. Charles Hopkins fell in love with Miss Arnold and in the summer of 1802 the fifteen-year-old girl became his wife. Marriage did not alter the general routine of their lives. The comings and goings continued from city to city—from Baltimore to Philadelphia, to Norfolk, to Richmond, to any town that offered a playhouse and a fair audience. One may wonder if, during the Baltimore season, that summer of 1802, a stage-struck law student, David Poe, had seen and admired the versatile young actress? Certainly he missed no theatrical performance in his home town, while awaiting the moment when he would throw Blackstone overboard in favor of the stage.

Shortly afterward, in Richmond, Mrs. Hopkins and her husband joined the Virginia Players with whom they toured for the next two years. Then, in the summer of 1804, the company had an addition in a good-looking youth, still too much of a novice to be called an

[4] *Memorial History of Boston,* Vol. IV, p. 367.

actor: David Poe, shy, with sensitive features, and about twenty years old. So far he had played nothing but minor parts, after he had chosen between the solidity of Blackstone and the hazards of Thespis. He still played with such diffidence that the audience became uncomfortable. However, a critic who saw him for the first time found a few things in his favor. "His voice seems to be clear, melodious and variable; what its compass may be can only be shown when he acts unrestrained by timidity. . . . On the whole, we think that if the young gentleman has a passion for histrionic fame he may promise himself much gratification." [5]

The passion for histrionic fame David Poe indeed possessed. Unfortunately his was the tragedy of ambition without genuine talent. That he had taste and discrimination is evidenced by the fact that he did best in Shakespeare's rolling lines, though only in such parts as Donalbain in *Macbeth,* Tressel, an attendant to Lady Anne in *Richard III,* and, as an exception, Don Pedro in *Much Ado about Nothing.*

Probably his first performance with Betty Hopkins was in *Speed the Plough* and his most ambitious role that of George Barnwell in the tragedy of that name. He was an excellent dancer, and by way of a divertissement to some ponderous play he and Mrs. Hopkins would delight the public in an allemande or a Scottish strathspey. In short, David was no worse, though perhaps no better, than many a secondary actor of his day.

Eventually he had his moment of triumph when he enacted young Norval in *Douglas,* by John Home, dubbed the Scottish Shakespeare on the strength of his verse and the floods of tears which his melodramatic plot had been unsluicing for several generations. Lady Randolph, whose role had contributed to Mrs. Siddons' fame, had been Lady Douglas before her second marriage into which she had entered on the conviction that her lord and her son had been killed. When the scene opens, Lady Randolph has a caller, a young shepherd who introduces himself, to the unaccountable rapture of the audience, with the words:

> My name is Norval; on the Grampian hills
> My father feeds his flocks . . .

At his heels comes Old Norval, ostensibly his parent, who has prudently taken along the gold chain the boy had worn, when the shepherd had come upon him years earlier. Instantly Lady Randolph recognizes the chain and cries:

[5] C. C. Carpenter, *Charleston Courier.*

My son! My son!
I am thy mother and the wife of Douglas!

At this the audience invariably broke into sobs and kept on sob-
bing throughout the plot whose villain, Glenalvon, convinces Lord
Randolph that his lady is having an illicit affair with the young
stranger. In the end Young Norval kills the evil Glenalvon, but not
before the villain has run him through. The youth has hardly expired, breathing poetry to the end, when Lady Randolph is heard
shrieking, as she plunges over a cliff.

Young Norval's role suited to admiration David Poe's weak yet
appealing good looks. It is to be hoped that at least for the one
performance he gave in his native Baltimore he managed to prove
himself a prophet, if only to his family.

The players went on to Richmond. There, after a brief but unspe-
cified illness, Mr. Hopkins died on the 26th of October, 1805. He
may have succumbed to an epidemic, for two more members of the
company followed him within a few weeks.

The depleted troupe, nevertheless, remained in Richmond, where
Mr. Hopkins' eighteen-year-old widow was given a benefit to recoup
her resources. She and David Poe now appeared more frequently
together, and for her final night, toward the end of March, 1806, she
chose to play the part of Lady Randolph in his favorite *Douglas*.

It was difficult for a young actress to avoid the pitfalls of her
kind of life without the protection of a husband. By this time, however, propinquity had worked its spell. Some time during the first
ten days of April, Mrs. Elizabeth Arnold Hopkins became the wife
of David Poe, in Richmond.[6] There had been no precipitous haste,
for an interval of six months had elapsed between Mr. Hopkins'
demise and his young widow's marriage.

The nomadic life continued—a week in Philadelphia, a few engagements in the summer theater at Vauxhall Garden, in New York.
Young Norval had his allotment of cheers and jeers from his unin-
hibited audiences, and Mrs. Poe her generally favorable, if tepid,
press. That autumn Betty once again met the Ushers, who lost no
time in procuring an engagement for their young friends with the
Boston and Charleston Players.

The Boston Theatre, while still on Federal Street, was not the
same whose boards, according to the rhapsodic critic, Mrs. Arnold
had shaken, for the original building had burned down in 1798. It
was rebuilt the same year, Mr. Bulfinch the architect receiving high

---

[6] Marriage bond discovered by Professor A. H. Quinn, *op. cit.*, p. 23.

praise for "the interior arrangements." Among these same arrangements the Poes made their debut in Thomas Morton's popular comedy, *Speed the Plough*. This time the critic was of a different breed from the enthusiast of Mrs. Arnold's day. The parts of the hero and heroine had been more ably sustained before on those boards, he said, but he granted that Mr. Poe had a manly voice. Of the talents of Mrs. Poe he was magnanimously disposed to judge favorably.

There was no enthusiasm and, at best, only restrained approval of the young actors during the three years that they held the Boston stage, except for a few excursions south. From the criticisms one gathers that Mrs. Poe was an appealing and versatile actress whose efforts, in such parts as Cordelia and Juliet, were not quite up to the mark. However, the critic of the *Emerald* conceded that Mrs. Poe had one asset, and that of no mean value. She did not mutilate the language of Shakespeare. He also found her *the delight of the eye.*

In fairness to the valiant young actress one must consider that often she had to sustain her roles against such redoubtable actors as James Fennell and Thomas Cooper, famous for their tragic force. Mrs. Poe was more in her element in plays of a lighter vein which gave her the opportunity to romp and flirt and dance, when she would compensate for her want of depth by the grace of her fairylike beauty.

The kindly editor of the *Boston Gazette,* in announcing a benefit for the Poes in the issue of March 21, 1808, inadvertently struck at the core of the young actors' deficiencies: "If industry can claim from the public either favor or support, the talents of Mrs. Poe will not pass unrewarded. . . . We hope, therefore, when . . . the talents of both Mr. and Mrs. Poe are put up for public approbation, that that public will . . . not discountenance virtuous industry . . . but will stretch out the arm of encouragement." Unhappily, virtuous industry without genius has never sufficed for the creation of art.

The Poes often had need of public appeals, as the lot of actors, except for the greatest, was at best precarious. Since the age of nine Betty had scarcely been off the stage except for an interval of a few weeks in the winter of 1807 when, perhaps on the 30th of January of that year, or possibly a few days later, she had given birth to her first child. The boy received a superabundance of names: William Henry Leonard Poe. It was the sole luxury his parents could afford. Their makeshift lodgings were scarcely suitable for bringing up a child. Their earnings did not permit the expense of a nurse. Incidental engagements, to eke out their scant savings, often took them far from home.

Mrs. Poe had no relatives with whom she could leave her infant, and David Poe had alienated his family by giving up the respectable career of the law and marrying an actress.

"My parents were so indignant," wrote David's sister Maria, "that they *could* not forgive him, consequently we knew nothing about her until after the birth of their first child, and as it was the first grandchild of my parents, they were forgiven and taken home to their hearts and house." [7]

Maria Poe, who was a girl of seventeen when Betty and David Poe arrived in Baltimore to leave their baby with his grandparents, found her sister-in-law a lovely little creature and doted on her for the aura of unreality which the stage imparts. They were indeed taken into the hearts of General David Poe and his wife, but they could enjoy the hospitality of the house for only a short time, since the theater called them. Little Henry's stay was to be of much longer duration. No doubt at first he had been left with his grandparents as a temporary expediency, to tide the parents over a difficult period, for occasionally they sent small sums for their child's maintenance. Gradually, as the allowance ceased, little Henry's provisional stay became a permanent adoption.

Meanwhile, on the 19th of January, 1809, Betty Poe had given birth to another son, also in Boston. She called him Edgar.

[7] Mrs. Maria Clemm to Mrs. Whitman in "Poe and Mrs. Whitman" by James A. Harrison and Charlotte F. Dailey, *Century Magazine,* January, 1909.

CHAPTER II

-»» • «<-

Ancestors

INTELLECTUAL snobbery would foist aristocratic antecedents upon those who achieve greatness, and when such antecedents cannot be established, as with so supreme a genius as Shakespeare, the *reductio ad absurdum* is attained by wild theories that his plays were written by Lord This and Sir That—even by Queen Elizabeth—but *never* by Will Shakespeare, the son of a tradesman.

In the case of Edgar Poe biographers have endeavored with extraordinary diligence to trace a suitable romantic ancestry. "The name of Poe," solemnly wrote William F. Gill, "is an old Italian name, and the minutest genealogical research finds it antedating the River Po, which, it is presumed, followed the original spelling of the princely family from which it is named." [1] The presumption, unfortunately, is wholly unwarranted by dispassionate history, which derives the name of the river from its original designation, the Latin Padus. Nonetheless, pursuing his theory, Gill carries the Italian Poes from their pleasant valley to the north of France, from France through England and Wales, and thence to Ireland, "where from their isolated position and other causes, they retained for a long period their hereditary traits." [2]

Miss Mary E. Phillips, while also adhering to the Italian beginnings, adds: "It is all but certainty that the poet's ancestors were a branch of the Powell family of County Armagh, Ireland, amongst which were counted not only bards but princes. . . ." [3] To give a deeper indigo to the blue blood of the Poes, Miss Phillips mingles some ichor from the maternal strain. "Genealogy records the family of Arnold as having its origin 'amongst the ancient princes of Wales, trailed in from Latin landings.' " [4]

[1] William F. Gill, *The Life of Edgar Allan Poe.*
[2] *Ibid.*
[3] Phillips, *Edgar Allan Poe, the Man.*
[4] *Ibid.*

13

Whether or not the Poes gave their name to the Italian river or whether Betty Arnold's family trailed in from Latin landings, there is one reliable voice for the possibility of Italian antecedents for the Poes, again that of David Poe's sister Maria, who recalled: "I have often heard my Father say his Father was of Italian descent and their name was originally spelled Po like the river Po in that country." [5]

In the early years of the nineteenth century when Maria, who was born in 1790, heard her father make these remarks, Edgar had not yet come into the world, so that the good General could not be accused of fabricating romantic origins for his grandson. One can therefore assume that in all likelihood there had been an Italian strain in the Poe family. Certainly the adult Edgar Poe had something unusual, if not exotic, about his looks, which were often remarked upon as foreign. He himself stressed this exoticism in the various self-portraits in his tales.

Whatever his antecedents, none can question his first biographer's assertion that the family of Edgar Poe was one of the oldest and most reputable in Baltimore.[6] The Poes hailed from Dring, Cavan County in Ireland, where a farmer, David Poe, tended his acres and made a fair living. Of his three sons the firstborn, John, proved adventurous and in 1750 sailed for America with his wife, Jane McBride, and his six-year-old son, David. After a few years in Pennsylvania they sought the milder climate of Baltimore, where the family firmly established itself.

The early years of struggle in a new country are always obscure. John Poe may have set up a shop as wheelwright, but if he did it was not for long, as he died in 1756. His son, David, however, succeeded in making such a thriving business of it that by 1776 he could afford a large advertisement in a Baltimore journal, announcing his removal to ampler quarters on Market Street, where he continued as usual to make and repair all sorts of spinning wheels, clock reels, weavers' spools and similar objects. He had cogent reasons to solicit trade. His beautiful young bride, Elizabeth Cairnes, was about to bear him a child, a function she was ably to perform at least seven times.

David Poe was an ardent Whig, a libertarian and a patriot. When William Goddard, the editor of the *Maryland Journal,* in which Mr. Poe had inserted his advertisement, wrote a political article slandering George Washington, he was one of the group, if not the ring-

[5] Mrs. Clemm to Mrs. Whitman, *Century Magazine,* January, 1909.
[6] R. W. Griswold, *Memoir.* Vol. I, *The Works of the Late Edgar Allan Poe.*

leader of the party, that drove Goddard out of town, as they had earlier ousted Robert Christie, the royal sheriff.

During the Revolutionary War David Poe became assistant quartermaster general, a post for which his patriotism and his vigorous nature fitted him. He served with courage and loyalty, and with a dedication which made him deprive himself and his family to supply the army. At a ball in honor of La Fayette in 1781, the General seemed much preoccupied. "How can I enjoy this gaiety," he said, "while so many of my poor soldiers are in need of clothes?" There was one man to hear, and a small army of women to do his bidding.

La Fayette never forgot that it was Quartermaster General David Poe who had supplied him with money from his own savings, money which the government never repaid; and that Mrs. Poe, with her own hands, had cut out five hundred pairs of pantaloons which she distributed among volunteer seamstresses to sew for the soldiers. A less tangible, yet as eloquent a proof of General David Poe's patriotism lay in the names of two of his five sons—John Hancock and George Washington Poe.

The old fighter never let his arms rust. As late as 1814, when the British were threatening to invade Baltimore, the septuagenarian carried his gun to good purpose at the Battle of North Point, and though he was not really entitled to being called "General," General he had been and General he remained to all who knew him.

The directory of Baltimore in its laconic statistics traced his rise through the years. In 1786 he was listed as owning a dry goods store. In 1790, according to the Census, his family consisted of five free white males of sixteen and over; four free white males under sixteen; two free white females and four slaves. In 1807 he was inspector of fish. From 1810 on he appeared simply as "Gentleman." In short, General David Poe had lived a useful and honorable life which had won the respect of his fellow citizens.

He was therefore mortified when young David, to whom he had given the best education available at the time, formed a Thespian Club with a few other stage-struck boys and, instead of poring over torts and briefs, shook the rafters in declamations from the old dramatists. David's marriage to an actress gave the final blow to the old man's ambitions for his son. His grief and disappointment, however, were assuaged by the little grandson in his care.

Meanwhile the *Boston Gazette* was announcing on the 9th of February, 1809: "We congratulate the frequenters of the Theatre on the recovery of Mrs. Poe from her recent confinement. . . . This charming little actress will make her reappearance tomorrow evening as Rosamunda in *Abaellino the Great Bandit.*"

The play was an adaptation of A. H. D. Zschokke's popular romance which had appeared in 1794 and had played upon the then startlingly new theme of dual personality. As its highly spiritual and engaging heroine Mrs. Poe had one of her most sympathetic parts.

The Boston sojourn and the brief years of comparative security for the young actors were drawing to a close—but not before a flash of glory for Mrs. Poe, in six thrilling appearances with the current sensation, John Howard Payne, who was assailing the cultural bulwarks of New England for the first time. Advertised for publicity reasons as Master Payne, the youth was eighteen years old but, with his small frame and clear rosy skin, he looked younger. The son of a schoolmaster at East Hampton, he had left for New York at fourteen, to help support the family by working as clerk in the countinghouse of Grant and Forbes.

Not long after his arrival, the sophisticated metropolis was charmed by the appearance of a tiny magazine that called itself the *Thespian Mirror,* and revealed a talent and lightness of a rare sort. The initial number came out late in December, 1805. Others, issued the following year, made Payne famous throughout the land when it was discovered that he, the knowledgeable and sprightly editor, was a lad in his early teens.

At first no one would believe that a mere boy could have written the incisive criticisms of Cooper, Hodgkinson and the rest, not to mention the variety of wit and information on the literary as well as the dramatic scene. His admirers were to marvel even more when, spurred on by success, he attempted something more ambitious. Whenever he could, after his day's clerking, he would go to the Park Theatre, whose portals opened at five-thirty to a double and, sometimes triple, bill, through which he would sit, enchanted and emulous. Then, for a week, he spent the evenings at home, letting the quills fly on the foolscap. By the end of that time he had composed a five-act comedy, *Julia, or the Wanderer.*

It was lively, gay, and delightfully amusing. With it under his arm he went to the manager of the Park Theatre. On the night of February 7, 1806, it played to an appreciative audience, though the press shied at what it considered indecorous incidents. Payne was then four months from his fifteenth birthday.

Nature had not stinted in her gifts. Besides literary facility she had given Payne a charming presence and a sweet voice. Soon the youth was besieged by the various cities for recitals, which he had been giving in a small way, after the appearance of the *Thespian Mirror.* Now, however, he became the rage. "His voice is music itself," chanted the *Philadelphia Port-Folio* of February 4, 1806. "This miraculous youth possesses a person . . . well-proportioned and graceful; a large blue eye of the most unusual sweetness and expression and a complexion of the most susceptible delicacy." Lest the reader imagine Payne a Cyclops, that large blue eye was merely a stylistic affectation of the era, which found the singular number more genteel than the plural.

Meanwhile, thanks to a group of patrons who had appointed themselves the guardians of so shining a light, Payne had been admitted to Union College, Schenectady. The lad's mind, however, dwelt more upon the flickering oil lamps of the footlights than on the scholar's midnight urn. Soon he was indulging in his chosen art on the stage of the Union College auditorium in the drama *Pulaski,* whose heroine, Lodoiska, he portrayed in flowing garments. After this exhibition he became the idol of the institute which, however, soon found it difficult to hold him. His mother's death, in June of 1807, and the needs of the orphaned family decided him, and he returned to the public stage.

At first he recited and sang, as before. Then, on February 24, 1809, he became a full-fledged actor in the inevitable but, for him, appropriate role of Young Norval, at the Park Theatre. Now, in Boston, with the wistful young Mrs. Poe to support him, John Howard Payne attempted the most challenging role of English tragedy, *Hamlet.*

The melancholy Dane had been portrayed before on the American stage, but never by an American. Conscious that he was establishing tradition, the youth was spurred on to do his best. In Mrs. Poe he, who had always required that the female counterparts should be given to persons as small of figure as himself, found the perfect Ophelia.

For Elizabeth Poe it was a time of excitement and exaltation. She had never had so inspiring a partner as the youth who might have been her twin physically as well as in that spiritual quality which emanated from his sensitive features. She became a passionate and credible Juliet to his Romeo and both made a pair of impulsive, rash and beautiful young lovers. She was Palmyra in *Mahomet,* Irene in *Barbarossa,* Sigismunda in *Tancred and Sigismunda.* In Kotzebue's *Pizarro* she was Cora, the Priestess of the Sun who, for love, violated her vestal vows. In each of the dramas which she and Payne had to make so intensely real, she kissed and embraced the youth— though observing all the stage proprieties of the day—and believed the illusion of his Zaphna, his Selim, Tancred and Rolla.

It was not until Payne's benefit, on the 17th of April, 1809, that *Hamlet* was at last performed. Never had Boston seen so stirring a Prince nor so pathetic an Ophelia. By now the two were so completely attuned to each other that the merely adequate performances of the rest—David Poe had the part of Laertes—appeared even more indifferent than they were.

David had been none too happy about his reviews. In the meantime he had gone down South to borrow money from his Baltimore cousins, the George Poes, only to come back soured by their rebuffs. He was drinking to allay the worries and frustrations that had begun to persecute him. As it was, he had justification enough to seek forgetfulness. At home as well as on the boards he had the subsidiary role as breadwinner. Indeed, if he had not been the husband of the charming Mrs. Poe, he might not have been on the stage at all. The criticisms of his acting, if favorable, were hardly more than lukewarm. In unfavorable, they attained brutality. Sometimes the critics, professional and lay, vented their feelings then and there in jeers and personal abuse. Certainly, so far as he was concerned, it was not with regret that he contemplated leaving Boston for New York. Betty's final burst of success, thanks to Master Payne, did not help to make matters any pleasanter for the ineffectual husband.

With his flair for the dramatic, young Payne had not been content to rest on his laurels after his stirring performance as Rolla in *Pizarro,* played on Mrs. Poe's benefit night, on April 19. At the close of his regular engagement he gave a double spectacle. The opening drama was his adaptation of Kotzebue's *Lovers' Vows,* in which, as usual, he and Mrs. Poe played the leading parts. It was followed by a spectacular production, described as a grand operatic drama in three acts: *Lodoiska, or the Captive Princess,* with Mrs. Poe playing and singing the title role. It was the part which Payne himself had performed at Union College, though then the drama had been known as *Pulaski* and had been given without benefit of lyrics. These, and the rest of the musical numbers, were Payne's tribute to his leading lady's vocal merits.

The season over, Powell's company disbanded and the Poes set out for the South. There could have been little besides their costumes or "dresses," as they were called, that Betty and David Poe took away when they left their Boston lodgings with their son Edgar, five months old. Betty, however, had a little jewel box, in which she kept such occasional gifts as actresses customarily received, and a small sketch of Boston Harbor, in which she had set down the view that had first struck her as a child of nine. She called it *Morning, 1808.*

As the season at the Park Theatre did not begin until September, Betty may have given recitals here and there, under the aura of her recent performances with the miraculous youth, to supplement the family's meager savings. Perhaps the Poes also paid a visit to their Baltimore relatives and their son Henry. They were in New York, however, for the opening performance on September 6—Monk Lewis' *The Castle Spectre,* whose Gothic horrors had caught a whole generation, including young Shelley, who had stayed up many a midnight setting down horrid fantasies of his own in imitative zeal.

The Park Theatre had undergone extensive remodeling within the past several years and now was perhaps the handsomest playhouse in New York. A great crystal chandelier hung from the lofty ceiling, while the lowest tier of boxes, decorated in blue and gold, was illuminated at intervals by smaller lusters hanging from gilt brackets over the cornice. In front, an immense oval mirror reflected the glittering audience in the first row. Altogether the Park Theatre accommodated nearly three thousand persons, a thousand more than Philadelphia's great playhouse. The devotees, however, missed one picturesque tradition, discarded in the remodeling—the critics' huge box, known as "the Shakespeare," in the center of the second tier, facing the stage. This lack was compensated for by the majestic colonnade in the lower lobby, lighted by crystal lamps between the columns, against a background of mirrors.

It was not Payne with whom Betty was playing now, but Mr. Cooper, the actor-manager himself, who had shared the Boston season with her and David in 1807. She was his Ophelia in the performance of *Hamlet* on the 11th of September, while David doubled as Rosencrantz and Bernardo. She was also Rosamunda to Cooper's Abaellino several nights later; but somehow the thrill she had known with Payne was not there. It was obvious that Great Roscius, as Mr. Cooper was called, to distinguish him from Payne, Young Roscius, was jealous of the prodigy and had set out to expose his immaturity by enacting the same parts.

David, meanwhile, continued in his unimportant roles, as Hassan, a Negro slave, in *The Castle Spectre,* Malcolm in *Macbeth* and, finally, one of his most important parts, that of Captain Cypress in *Grieving's a Folly.* If the Boston critics had been cruel, their New York brethren were savage in their attacks. Something about David's nervous, faulty delivery, his unconquerable diffidence, stirred up the latent cruelty which the human animal seems to have, in common with the brute, in the tendency of the strong to attack the weak. The critic of *Rambler's Magazine* gave him no quarter and seemed almost to be seeking some slip of the tongue, some awkward gesture, or even a peculiarity in the make-up, as a pretext for his vicious reviews. Soon he had tagged on the hapless actor the nickname of Dan Dilly, because Poe had not known the right stress and the Italian pronunciation of Dandoli, in *Abaellino*.

"This man was never destined for the high walks of the drama," he wrote. "A footman is the extent of what he ought to attempt. . . . His person, voice and non-expression of countenance, all combine to stamp him—*poh! et praetera nihil.*" [7]

It was not the first time that the name was to serve as the butt for punsters to ridicule, as the *Rambler's* critic further demonstrated in some macaronic French verses entitled, with an obvious coarse pun, "*Sur un POE de Chambre.*" The subject this time was David Poe's drinking, and the verses closed with:

> Son père était pot
> Sa mère était broc
> Sa grand mère était pinte.[8]

David had begun to seek solace in the bottle in the early spring of 1809 when, on his visit to Baltimore, his cousin George Poe had commented upon it. He resorted to it more often after young Payne's season at the Boston Theatre with Betty when he, David, had been shown up by contrast in all his inadequacy. At times he had had to be replaced for indisposition, a polite stage euphemism for overindulgence in drink. Now, in New York, while Betty was drawing the plaudits of the audience and the press, he found himself viciously attacked for shortcomings which, unfortunately, he could not but admit. In his frustration he sought the by now habitual remedy.

On the 19th of October he played his usual Captain Cypress in *Grieving's a Folly* and was scheduled to repeat it two days later. Once again indisposition made it impossible for him to appear. Whether he had really been ill or whether intoxication had prevented him, the patrons sitting round the ornate tiers of the Park Theatre never saw him more, nor did he ever perform again on any stage.

The valiant Betty, however, kept on playing her infinite variety, from Jessica in the *Merchant of Venice,* to Little Pickle, a part which had made the humorless *Polyanthos* critic in Boston snort:

[7] *Rambler's Magazine,* Vol. I, p. 27.
[8] *Ibid.,* p. 88.

"We never knew before that the Spoiled Child belonged to that class of beings termed hermaphroditical. . . ." [9]

Throughout the season, which lasted until the middle of January, 1810, Mrs. Poe appeared on an average of four times a week, most often in the leading role. Besides learning new parts, she had the care of her infant son, Edgar, and now also the responsibility of her unemployed, ailing and self-tormented husband, whose hurt pride was not healed by the knowledge that he was dependent on her. The month's imposed vacation, when the Park Theatre closed until the beginning of the new season in February, was far from being a holiday for the little family.

For Betty, however, there was the joy of anticipation in another series of appearances early in March with Payne, whose benefit, that same January, had brought him $1,408 in Mr. Placide's Company in Richmond, and whose Hamlet had gained him almost as much. He was exciting, he was famous and inspiring to play with. The theater itself was charged with a strange vitality at the impact of so thrilling a personality. Yet the very anticipation that quickened Mrs. Poe could only have brought new anguish to her husband and deepened his sense of futility, increased by actual ill-health in a tubercular tendency aggravated by drink.

At the Park Theatre Payne once again conquered. From the 5th of March, 1810, through the 9th, Mrs. Poe shared in the ovations that greeted him. Once more, in spite of the jealous rift between him and Mr. Cooper, supported by the manager's hangers-on, the strings of carriages extended for blocks all up and down Park Place. Long before curtain time the boxes were already tenanted by the butlers of the finest families, each servant soberly dressed, with his right arm circled above the elbow by the white band of a carefully folded serviette. They were holding the reserved seats for their masters. Excitement and anticipation hung upon the air.

Once again Betty was Cora, the Priestess of the Sun. She was Payne's Ophelia, she was his impassioned Juliet. For a few rapturous days she glowed in the aura of the prodigy's success. Then again came the routine performances in uninspired and uninspiring plays.

At home the situation was aggravated as David, in his enforced idleness, in the grip of his sense of failure, was more often drunk than sober. Inevitable frictions arose between the successful, attractive wife and the husband, gnawed by his sense of futility, tormented by the insecurity of his position, both as male and as provider, jealous

[9] *Polyanthos,* March, 1807.

of younger and triumphant men—all potential rivals in the accepted intimacies of the stage.

Through this distressing period Mrs. Poe took care of the baby Edgar in the intervals when the theater closed, and fulfilled her engagements during the season, often supplementing them with vocal recitals.

Then, in July of 1810, David Poe vanished. No certain trace of him has ever been found to establish his movements or even the time or place of his death.

Did David Poe abandon his wife? Did he die in some dismal purlieu of New York and end on the dissecting table or the potter's field? Did he go to Norfolk, as an obscure undated clipping indicates, and there breathe his last, on October 19, 1810? Or was it in December, 1811, that he died, as unsubstantiated tradition maintains? [10]

Whatever the truth of the matter or the circumstances of David Poe's death, whenever it may have occurred, it is indisputable that for some potent reason he disappeared from the life of Elizabeth Poe in July of 1810, when she was in her fourth month of pregnancy. Naturally, in that situation, any woman would have expected solicitude and affection from her husband. What could have compelled David Poe to leave her, if he was still alive? Was it despair at his inability to support his family? Was it an aggravation of his consumption which made him seek the shelter and care of relatives? But in that case his wife would have joined him. Had there been a rift between them, caused by jealousy, which precipitated his desertion? A packet of letters which Betty was to treasure and which remained as a rueful inheritance to her children may have held the secret. In any case the separation between Mrs. Poe and her husband was final.

Since Betty had not been re-engaged by the Park Theatre, perhaps because of her pregnancy or because she belonged to the Payne, versus the Cooper, faction, she left New York and joined Mr. Placide's company of Virginia Players, which was about to begin its tour of the South. Whatever her thoughts, her regrets, perhaps even a sense of having failed her insecure and ailing husband, she had to face the realities of existence. She did so, bravely.

Through part of August and September Mrs. Poe was acting in

[10] From a letter to the author from Professor Thomas Ollive Mabbott: "Poe's father, according to a Baltimore tradition that reached me from Mr. Howard in 1954, 'was a widower only two days.' This is the kind of thing people remember. . . ." However, there is a letter from an unchallengeable source which would indicate that David Poe may still have been alive in 1813. See p. 31.

CHAPTER III

The Orphans

Y, with the disappearance of his mother, the closest being
hood world and the source of all the security and tender-
d ever known, Edgar found himself among strangers—
ersolicitous in their anxiety to allay his bewilderment, yet
strangers. Even Rosalie, his only companion, had been
him.

ystery of death was explained to him in the usual fictions
adults to reach the much underestimated intelligence of
apable by the age of two of mastering speech, of asserting
d of exercising reason and imagination—Edgar's impres-
still have remained, indelibly, in his mind. There the image
r would linger as long as he lived: in the rare moments
uld put him to bed; in her sorrow at having to part with
e him with strangers. He would remember her as a gay,
te in a place full of flickering lamps and recall the happy
lause if, often, also of hisses. There would be the shadowy
father, too, a pale handsome man, often sick and cross,
ometimes be away for days and who finally disappeared
Edgar would also recall the long, wearisome journeys
ge and clumsy theatrical scenery, his mother holding the
in her lap, while he crouched at her feet on the deck of
ling south.

y, because of his growing awareness, Edgar would re-
n her last days, lying on a shabby lodging-house bed, in
re room. Then there were the final and most enduring
hich death, even if unrecognized as death, stamps upon
ver: the stony fixity of the beloved face; the sunken
rrible stillness and, in those ruder days, the undisguised
ption. All these left their scar on the infant mind.

sical world, however, expanded and, perhaps for the
is life, grew stable. He was taken to live in a large,

26

Richmond. She then went on to Norfolk, where, on the 20th of December, 1810, she was delivered of a daughter whom she called Rosalie. Strangers tended her in the Forrest House, where the child was born; neither David nor any members of the Poe family came to see her, or to offer assistance. David's disappearance from her life seems to have been a decisive break, whose reasons may have been known or surmised by the family. Certainly his vanishing at that particular time threw a cloud on the advent of Rosalie, whose legitimacy from then on was held in question.

Mrs. Poe no sooner recovered than she was on her way with her two infants to join Mr. Placide's company in Charleston. No one knows who took care of Edgar, by now a lively two-year-old, and the newborn Rosalie. No doubt during the performances Betty left them with some other actress for whom she may have done the same service, or probably she engaged some elderly woman to take care of them. Such a nurse was indeed seen a year later in Norfolk, "a very nice old woman, plump, rosy and goodnatured," who used to soothe the children with sops dipped in gin, to make them strong. There was talk that this woman was in reality Mrs. Tubbs, which is an untenable assumption. Certainly the Shakespearean actress from the Theatre Royal would never have called her little grandson "Hedgar." [11]

With her departure from the Park Theatre, the days of glory for Elizabeth Poe ended. There were no more Juliets and Ophelias with John Howard Payne, no performances with Cooper or Fennell. She played her old romping parts that always pleased, and added new ones—Sheridan's Lydia Languish and Lady Teazle. It was as if, now that her life had taken a tragic turn, she was condemned to laughter.

For some time her delicate organism, flawed by tuberculosis, had been failing. Childbearing and the hardships of theatrical life, with its exacting hours and its demands upon the emotions, had also taken their toll. There was, moreover, the incessant worry of making a living for herself and her children by an art which in America had not as yet captured a wide following and which many still considered immoral.

Nevertheless, the slight, small figure continued to trip across the changing stages; the rippling voice laughed and sang; the expressive face molded itself to gaiety which, more often than not, belied the emotions of the heart. Now, with increasing frequency, the papers carried appeals to rouse public interest in the young actress on pleas other than those of art. The last appeared in the *Richmond Enquirer*

[11] Weiss, *The Home Life of Poe.*

on the 29th of November, 1811: *"To the humane heart. On this night Mrs. Poe,* lingering on the bed of disease and surrounded by her children, asks your assistance and *asks it perhaps for the last time.* The Generosity of the Richmond Audience can need no other appeal. . . ."

Since the 11th of October, when she was last seen on the stage of the Richmond Theatre, Mrs. Poe had been too ill to make an appearance. She had come for the season, which began in August, and had taken lodgings for herself and her children near the old Indian Queen Tavern, later known as the Washington, a place frequented by stage folk for its nearness to the theater. She acted as long as her strength lasted. After her benefit, on October 9, she played only once more and then took to her bed.

All the while her little son and her baby daughter were with her, hearing her cough and moan, witnessing her tears at the knowledge that she must soon leave them. To Rosalie's infant senses her mother's suffering could have conveyed little. But on the aware, sensitive mind of her intelligent three-year-old son, the sights and sounds of the sickroom, which he and Rosalie had perforce to share, the mother's despair and anguish, the gradual change in the familiar face, must have left their unforgettable mark.

The tragic, real-life last act of the dying actress and the pleas of the press had touched the hearts of the good ladies of Richmond, some of whom visited the sickroom and brought aid, as well as sympathy. Among them were Mrs. John Allan, the wife of a Scottish merchant, and her friend, Mrs. William Mackenzie. But alas, the frail young actress whose fevered eyes seemed to devour her face, was soon beyond their ministering. At twenty-four she had lived her full cycle, known triumph and love, borne children, suffered tragedy as well as portrayed it. She was now ready for the ultimate experience. It came, on Sunday the 8th of December, 1811. "By the death of this lady," said the friendly Richmond press, "the stage has been deprived of one of its chief ornaments."

Her children had been deprived of much more—the love and care she was able to give them, the sense of home that her presence managed to create in the dingy lodgings she could afford, most of all the security of the family tie, already slackened by the disappearance of the father.

The charity of Richmond did everything possible for the friendless dead and for her orphaned children. Most prominent of all were the Allans and the Mackenzies. On Monday morning the two women came to the room where Mrs. Poe had been laid out for burial.

Mrs. Allan took the little boy by th for a last look at his "sleeping" mo Mrs. Mackenzie followed, with Ro members of Mr. Placide's company from the little orphans whom they h

The burial of Mrs. Poe was no the prejudices of the times agains on the seemliness of burying an a Allan, however, a firm character congregation, won out and the ear only a few months since had bee somest women in America," [12] was ground. Still, as if in dread that other dead, they laid away the c the eastern wall.

Such bigotry was not limited to York, a well-known house of C services for an actor and scorn church around the corner" wh of thing.

John Allan had still anothe of the few possessions which M whom the Mackenzies took int jewel box, though its content food and shelter. For the little her starving heart, he kept a n of Boston Harbor on the back my little son Edgar, who sho birth, and where his mother friends."

There was also a packet

[12] *Norfolk Herald,* July 26, 181

solid house at Richmond's Main and Thirteenth Streets, over the general store of Ellis and Allan, tobacco merchants and dealers in everything marketable—from tuns of the golden leaf to that other profitable merchandise, black slaves, whom the partners would send out for hire or, occasionally, sell outright.

Mrs. Allan would have preferred a more fashionable neighborhood, but her husband, who had just entered his thirties, was ambitious, had a sharp eye for profit, and wished to be sure of the ground under his feet before making a move. He had come to America from Ayrshire, Scotland, as a lad of fifteen, to work under his uncle, a well-to-do merchant, William Galt, who had been serving Richmond for several decades. Young John Allan profited so much by his experience that by the time he was twenty he felt prepared to enter commerce on his own account. With his cousin, Charles Ellis, who had also clerked in William Galt's establishment, the shrewd Scotsman established the junior firm of Ellis and Allan, each partner furnishing half the capital, a thousand pounds sterling.

Three years later John Allan married one of the most beautiful young women in Richmond, Frances Keeling Valentine. She and her sister Anne had been orphaned in their early years, but when they reached what was considered the age of discretion—Frances was eleven and Anne twelve—they appeared in Hustings Court and chose John Dixon, a Richmond printer, as their guardian. They went to live in his household and it was with his blessing that, in 1803, Frances, nineteen years old, made what was considered an excellent match by marrying the promising nephew of the wealthy Mr. Galt. Because the two sisters had been inseparable Anne, or Miss Nancy, soon joined the young household as a permanent member.

In Thomas Sully's portrait of Mrs. Allan one sees a face of a perfect oval, with wide-set, thoughtful eyes under delicately shaped dark brows. The forehead, broad and high, is framed in wispy ringlets, escaped from the classical coiffure with the central part, adopted by the Empire which had set the style in Europe and in the New World. The nose, straight and well formed, was worthy of the gentle mouth with its arched upper lip. A classical aura, emphasized by the artist, permeates the whole, together with a sense of melancholy, almost of unhappiness, radiating from the eyes.

Whatever may have been the sorrows which Frances Allan at the time concealed, one was the unfulfilled longing for a child of her own upon whom to lavish her affection. As far as the world knew, her marriage had been a happy one but for this lack. Her social position was enviable. Her husband, though not yet the very rich man he was to become, enjoyed respect. He was handsome, too, with a kind of hawk-like sharpness about the beaked nose and keen eyes that seemed to appraise one as they peered from under the craggy brow with its thatch of dark, closely crinkled hair. A hint of humor lifted the corners of his wide mouth, though the smile verged on a sneer, while the outthrust lower lip bespoke truculence as well as strength.

When Frances Allan took home Edgar Poe in her hired hack, she was twenty-seven years old and her husband a virile thirty-one. Though their seven years of marriage had proved sterile, it did not mean that they would never have children. This, at least, was the reasoning of John Allan, whose proliferating prowess had already borne fruit—unknown to his wife—in a boy, Edwin, by a Mrs. Collier of Richmond. Meanwhile he was willing to have Mrs. Allan find solace for her frustrated maternity in the orphan of the little actress.

As it happened, all of Richmond was soon called upon to open heart and hand to the victims of one of the cruelest calamities that had ever befallen it. On the night after Christmas, 1811, while the audience was sitting in fascinated horror during the performance of *The Bleeding Nun,* a greater horror broke out with the cry of "Fire!" The stage chandelier had somehow started the blaze and soon the theater was filled with smoke while flames began spurting out of the windows and through the roof. There were no fire escapes down the steep sides of the three-story building, and the stairs were so narrow that the people, in their panic, were caught in a dense mass. Some jumped out of the windows and died in their fall. Others, near the exit, managed to make their way to the open, their clothes in flames, their faces scorched. When it was possible for rescuers to enter the pyre, those who were lying unconscious were carried out and laid on the ground of Theatre Square, suddenly become an improvised hospital. Altogether seventy-two persons perished, among them the Governor of Virginia and a number of children. What remained of Mr. Placide's company carried away scenes more harrowing than any they had ever enacted.

The Allans, with Edgar, had been spending the holidays at Turkey Island as the guests of one of Mr. Allan's friends. On their return they found a city in mourning and every family engaged in works of charity. Joseph Gallego, the wealthy flour merchant, an acquaintance of theirs, had lost a relative in the fire. Little George Dixon, whom they knew, also perished in it. If John Allan had entertained any thought of relinquishing the orphan of Mr. Placide's leading actress, the wholesale charity of his neighbors would have shamed him. Thus tragedy, for once, was on Edgar's side.

To the child the physical change in his circumstances was fairy tale come true. For the first time he knew the security of home, and such a home, with two women looking after him—Ma and Miss Nancy, as he was taught to call them. Then there was Pa, who would come up from the store for his meals, and there were the Negro servants in their own part of the house, which often rang to the song and laughter of warm, husky voices. Also, there was the store itself, an Aladdin's realm to the marveling child. First, one breathed the rich smell of tobacco and spices and coffee and the strong tang of leather, and the warm whiff of corn and wheat, rice and all kinds of grain in long-eared sacks, or in great heaps on the floor. Back of the dry goods counter, on the broad shelves, bolts of fine serges or India prints, silks and velvets, madras and linen and the finest batiste, lay one against the other, like colorful books—and indeed each could have told a story of a far journey it had had to travel to reach Mr. Allan's store in Richmond.

If, as he grew older, Edgar overheard the conversation of Pa and Uncle Galt, or of the people who came in to buy, he would have learned of the trouble a certain Napoleon Bonaparte had been making for the merchants in the far-off waters round Europe. He would have heard of Napoleon's quarrels with England, of the Peninsular Campaign, and of Lord Wellesley who had been sent to beat the Corsican upstart who had dared to make himself Emperor of France. Certainly Edgar heard Pa telling of his voyage to Portugal in 1811 with a spanking little fleet of merchant ships loaded with Galt, Allan and Ellis merchandise to dispose of at a fine profit to the campaigning English. Oh, yes, there had been a large profit. But what good was it if merchants had to worry about the Embargo Act and other inconsiderate prohibitions passed by the government?

Sometimes Edgar would go with Pa to the Port, at the Falls, to visit the Ellis and Allan warehouses or to watch the square-rigged ships winging home on their booming sails from all parts of the globe; and perhaps the view of another harbor would come to his mind, a view that his mother had set down, and which she left for him to treasure. He may also have recalled journeys on the James River with her and other actors and actresses. But now everything was different. Pa was like a king. Everybody greeted him. Everybody talked to him, hat in hand. Pa was a very important man.

The people Pa knew were important, too. Best of all, however, Edgar liked to visit the Mackenzies to see Rosalie, but more to play with John Mackenzie, to whom he looked up with the admiration of a boy for one a few years older.

Though time passed and John Allan did not trouble to take legal measures to adopt Edgar, he was known to friends and neighbors as Master Allan, and indeed no child of the Allans' own blood could have been more indulged. The best Nankin silk would be measured from the bolts in the store to make him his suits, and the finest velvet cut for his peaked hoods, weighted with a gold tassel at the point. With his delicate face dominated by the same large eyes as his mother's—eyes of a gray so deep that they seemed black—with his fair skin and his dark hair flowing over the shoulders, he looked, in the yellows and purples in which Mrs. Allan dressed him, like some doge's son escaped from a Renaissance canvas.

One wonders how such a child could have been given up without demur, almost with unconcern, by the Poe relatives. Had General Poe or any member of his family been in touch with the good Samaritans of Richmond who had taken in the orphans of David Poe? If so, the letters are lost. But one important communication exists, from David Poe's sister Eliza, then a girl of twenty, to Mrs. Allan.

Baltimore, Feb. 8th, 1813

Tis the Aunt of Edgar that addresses Mrs. Allen [sic] for the second time, impressed with the idea that A letter if received could not remain unacknowledged so long as from the month of July, she is induced to write again in order to inquire in the family's name as well as in her own name after the health of the Child of her Brother, as well as that of his adopted Parents. I cannot suppose my dear Mrs. Allen that A heart possessed of such original humanity as yours must without doubt be, could so long keep in suspence, the anxious inquiries made through the medium of my letter by the Grand Parents of the Orphan of an unfortunate son, surely ere this allowing that you did not wish to commence A correspondence with one who is utterly unknown to you had you received it. Mr. Allen would have written to my Father or Brother if it had been only to let them know how he was, but I am confident you never received it, for two reasons, the first is that not having the pleasure of knowing your Christian name I merely addressed it to Mrs. Allen of Richmond, the second is as near as I can recollect you were about the time I wrote to you at the springs where Mr. Douglas saw you, permit me my dear madam to thank you for your kindness to the little Edgar—he is truly the Child of fortune to be placed under the fostering care of the amiable Mr. and Mrs. Allen. Oh how few meet with such A lot—the Almighty Father of the Universe grant that he may never abuse the kindness he has received and *that* from those who were not bound by any ties except those that the feeling and humane heart dictates—I fear that I have too long intruded on your patience, will you if so have the goodness to forgive me—and dare I venture to flatter myself with the hope that this will be received with any degree of pleasure or that you will gratify me so much as to answer it—give my love to the dear little Edgar and tell him tis his Aunt Eliza who writes this to you. my mother and family desire to be affectionately remembered to Mr. Allen and yourself—Henry frequently speaks of his little brother and expresses A great desire to see him, tell him he sends his very best love to him and is greatly pleased to hear that he is so good and also so pretty A Boy as Mr. Douglass represented him to be—I feel as if I were wrighting to A sister and can scarcely even at the risk of your displeasure prevail on myself to lay aside my pen—with the hope of your indulgence in pardoning my temerity I remain my Dear Mrs. Allen yours

with the greatest respect
ELIZA POE [1]

It is a remarkably subtle letter for Eliza Poe to have written, implying a great deal more than it says. Delicately yet pointedly, Eliza taxes the Allans for not answering the letter she had written seven months earlier. She calls them Edgar's "adopted Parents" thereby making specific what Mr. Allan had not yet accomplished—that is, become Edgar's parent by due process of law. True, legal adoption was rare in the South outside the ties of blood; nevertheless, it was possible. Yet though by 1813 Edgar had been in the Allan household for two years and, according to tradition, had been baptized as Edgar Allan shortly after he entered the merchant's household, he was still an adopted son only by the grace of Mr. Allan and the devotion of a childless woman. Eliza made her point by the commas with which she separated Edgar's adoptive name from his own, in her address to "Mrs. Allen the kind benefactress of the infant Orphan Edgar, Allen, Poe." [2] She also qualified Edgar as "the Child of her Brother."

A question arises. Had Eliza Poe received help in composing the letter? The language is often high-flown and full of the flourishes of the stage dialogue of the day. She calls Edgar "the Orphan of an unfortunate son," which may well mean a child who had been deprived of his mother by death and whose father disastrous circumstances had placed beyond the possibility of supporting him. Finally Eliza declares: "Mr. Allen would have written to my Father or Brother." Who is this brother to whom she specifically alludes, if not David Poe? There had been four other sons in the family, one of whom, George, died in infancy while another, Samuel, had recently been lost at sea.[3] The other two, John and William, were still alive in 1813 and, since they never married, were presumably living with their par-

---

[1] *Ellis and Allan Papers,* Poe volume, Library of Congress.
[2] *Ibid.*
[3] See p. 66 for the reminiscences of John Howard Payne.

ents.[4] Had Eliza meant to refer to either of them, she would have singled him out by name. The fact that she simply mentioned her "Brother" would indicate the only one who would have had any direct interest in the orphan. She implies that this brother too was living at home—perhaps because of sickness or destitution, or both. In either case he, the father of Edgar, would be relieved to know that the motherless boy, the orphan, was well cared for, while the man who had once studied law would enjoy greater peace of mind if his son's adoption were made legal. This would explain both the direct appellation of "adopted parents" referring to the Allans and the veiled reminder that so far the adoption was really no adoption since they, the benefactors of the orphan Edgar, were not bound to him "by any ties except those that the feeling and humane heart dictates." That this brother, therefore, may have been David is also sustained by the fact that not once, after he disappeared from Mrs. Poe's life, had she been referred to as a widow, not even when the Richmond newspaper publicized her helpless state, to which widowhood would have lent an added pathos.

It is also strange that, considering the close friendship between the Allans and the Mackenzies, there should have been no mention of Rosalie in the letter. Such an omission would therefore confirm that the Brother was David, who had compelling reasons, whether or not he was justified, in ignoring the child of whose paternity he was not certain. In any case, though the hand of Eliza penned the letter, it was doubtless another's voice that dictated it.

Why had not Frances Allan answered Eliza Poe's first letter? Did she or her husband reply to the second, which Mr. Allan so carefully put away in his files? If Mrs. Allan failed of courtesy in the first instance it was surely through apprehension that the little boy, who by then had become dear to her, might be claimed by his relatives, and so silence was her best safeguard. As for the second letter, if its covert implications were pointed out to her by her husband, again silence would have been the safest answer.

Still, even in those days when good intentions could dispense with law, it is unlikely that one could "adopt" a child without the consent of the nearest of kin. It would appear that some exchange of letters did take place between Mr. Allan and General Poe. Edgar wrote of it years later, with manifest exaggeration of his grandfather's circumstances but, since he was addressing John Allan himself, with a closer adherence to the truth than was usual whenever he indulged in

[4] See Poe's letter to William Poe in Ostrom, *The Letters of Edgar Allan Poe*, p. 67.

autobiography. "It is well known to respectable individuals in Baltimore, and elsewhere, that my Grandfather (my natural protector at the time you interposed) was wealthy, and that I was his favorite grandchild— But the promises of adoption, and liberal education which you held forth to him in a letter which is now in possession of my family, induced him to resign all care of me into your hands. . . ." [5]

Those hands were large and capable. They could guide the progress of one of the most profitable enterprises in Richmond, and they could flutter over a flute, an instrument which, Mr. Allan carefully noted, cost him $21 at auction. They could pat the head of his little protégé or come down heavily, sometimes with a switch, on the place where punishment is traditionally administered. In his own estimation, as in the eyes of his neighbors, John Allan was a sterling, respectable, God-fearing, generous man who not only supported a whole clan of relatives and a covey of orphans in his native Scotland, but who had also taken into his home a motherless waif.

Virtue could do no more, and as far as John Allan was concerned it did not. Despite Eliza's letter, despite other correspondence that may have passed between Richmond and Baltimore, Edgar's status remained exactly what it was on the day that Frances Allan had taken him home. Since a wise caution had been John Allan's guide throughout his successful life in his dealings with facts and figures, he was exercising it now on a far riskier speculation. The object involved had a life and a will of its own. Moreover, Edgar's heredity was suspect. The father was unstable. He had abandoned a respected profession to dissipate his life upon the stage. Worse, he drank. As for the mother, while she had proved herself a good actress, as a woman she had been no better than most who followed her calling. He knew. There was that packet of letters she had left. Meanwhile Mr. Allan had put them safely away after reading them. They might prove a strong argument in his favor should his fears be realized. Only time could tell, and he gave it ample scope while performing his Duty—always with a capital letter—toward his small charge.

Frances Allan, on the other hand, more than made up for her husband's seeming coldness. An orphan herself, she knew the part that simple affection played in giving a child a sense of security. Consequently Edgar was closer to her than to Pa, who represented authority, power and justice, the last inflicted perhaps a little too often and too hard. But like all children Edgar had his way of puncturing the armor of his elders. One day, when he insisted on going out in the rain, Mr.

[5] *Valentine Letters.* Also Ostrom, p. 39.

Allan threatened him with a whipping. Edgar went out, but when he came back he handed Pa a bunch of freshly cut switches.

"What are they for?" asked Mr. Allan.

"To whip me with," said Edgar, who by now was inured to the punishment. This time, however, it all ended in an indulgent chuckle.

As Edgar was now old enough to learn his letters, he was sent in his best bib and tucker to a dame's school. From there he was soon graduated to Mr. William Ewing's academy for boys. One wonders whether during the year that Edgar spent at Mr. Ewing's institution he met Edwin Collier, for whose education Mr. Allan was also paying. If the honest merchant was ever struck by the incongruity of having an unacknowledged son of his in the same school with the boy he had ostensibly adopted he dispelled it quickly with a lift of his sardonic lips. Besides, he had many good works to his credit, enough to balance a peccadillo which many another Southerner would long since have put out of his mind.

As it was, he had subscribed a substantial amount for the building of the Monumental Church, completed in 1814, on the site of the old Richmond Theatre whose flames he had providentially escaped. He and his partner, Mr. Ellis, who had contributed twice as much, shared a pew in the church directly in front of the pulpit, within the line of fire of good Bishop Moore's thundering oratory.

Every Sunday the Allans, with Edgar between them, would drive to the amorphous edifice. A square, columned monument to the victims of the fire greeted one, its naïve figures amid the sculptured ruins, telling their woe in stone upon the crest. Beyond came the domed building with a portico and a round gallery crowning the roof. Then rose the bell tower, its conical turret topping the building like a foolscap of stone.

In the child Edgar the memory of his mother's association with the theater and its dramatic conflagration became linked, and he was always to maintain that she had perished in its blaze. It was a more fitting end, for the woman who had died so many noble deaths upon the stage, than her slow, painful flickering out in a sordid room. Beyond this abiding impression, Edgar's life revealed that neither his sessions at Sunday school, nor the piety of Mrs. Allan, nor the eloquence of Bishop Moore left any mark upon a mind whose heaven and hell were to belong to its own universe.

The long Sunday dinners always made up for the more serious part of the holy day. Since Mr. Allan kept a generous table and enjoyed sharing it, there were always guests to enliven it. Sometimes, after dessert, the little boy was set upon the board to recite, or to toast the company in diluted wine. These accomplishments in the child of actors had a double effect. While they delighted the company they reminded Mr. Allan of Edgar's origin and made him rely more than ever on the wisdom of trusting to time.

As for Edgar, except for Pa's disciplinary measures, his little world was untroubled. He expanded in the warmth of Ma's love. The friends of the Allans looked upon him as the son of the house and acted accordingly. Sometimes he would go visiting with Ma at the office of Mr. Dixon the printer, who had brought her up, and gape with a small boy's wonder at the complicated machinery of the printing press. Perhaps Mr. Dixon even indulged him by letting him try his hand at the type. Then there were also the visits of Ma's cousin, Mr. Edward Valentine, who loved a practical joke as much as any boy. How amusing to pull a chair from under someone about to sit down! Imagine the astonishment and the laughter! Edgar, unhappily, played the trick on one of Ma's most respectable and, as it happened, most rotund, callers. Pa took Edgar out of the room and the merriment was instantly quelled by the swishing of the familiar switches. A small incident but, in the world of a child, a significant one, certain to leave its impression. One did something to laugh and make others laugh, but one was made to smart for it. One laughed and the next moment one cried. Laughter and cruelty were always to color the quality of Poe's humor.

From the time Edgar had been taken into the Allan household he had had his Negro mammy, who treated the young master with the fond familiarity her position allowed. She would carry him off to the servants' quarters and, of a winter's evening, as he grew older, he would sit spellbound at her knee among the Negroes and listen, half in wonder, half in terror, to the rich lore which the transplanted race had accumulated from native memories and the New World. Suffering, hardships and death played their part in the tales and chants, as the narrators took turns telling what they had heard from the mouth of truth itself, or seen with their own eyes. The inborn genius of the Negro to dramatize lent reality to the most incredible tales and filled with "haunts" and ghouls the receptive young mind, already predisposed to belief by the evidence of his own experience. Had he not perhaps witnessed, in an age when childhood was not spared the grim realities, the lowering of the coffin into that gaping hole in St. John's burial ground? Certainly, as a small boy, he had a horror of everything connected with death; but the horror also held its own kind of fascination, renewed each time his mammy took him walking under the old trees of St. John's.

As a pet of Mr. Valentine's, Edgar sometimes went with him on pleasant excursions. Late one evening, as they were returning home, Mr. Valentine on his horse, with Edgar behind him clinging to his coattails, they reached a deserted stretch. Along the way, they rode past an abandoned cabin with a pale glimmer of gravestones rising nearby. Suddenly Edgar began to struggle frantically to get in front of Mr. Valentine. The boy's terror was too real for the man to laugh it away, so after helping him onto the saddle in front of him he asked why he was so frightened. "They will run after us and pull me off," said Edgar.

They were very real to the imaginative boy, and became almost palpable as he grew older. Nothing terrified him so much, he was to confess to his friend John Mackenzie, as imagining the feel of an icy hand upon his face in the dark, or to awaken suddenly and discover in the shadows an evil face peering into his own.

All these phantoms, however, were suddenly dispelled by the decision of Mr. Allan to take his family across the Atlantic on a venture which, consistent with his merchant's nature, combined business and pleasure.

CHAPTER IV

-»» · «€-

The Years in England

THE John Allan who was preparing to make the return journey to England was quite a different voyager from the fifteen-year-old lad who had crossed the ocean twenty years earlier. At thirty-five, he was a substantial man of business, a citizen of the United States since 1804, a respected member of society, the head of a household with a beautiful though too delicate wife, a delightful son now generally known as Master Allan, and a plump, pleasant sister-in-law who not only gave the merchant standing as a generous man but helped him to run his household with efficiency. In 1815 his firm had assets of over $220,000, enough for him to draw 335 pounds for his current needs. He expected to make an extended stay in England, for he added to his ready cash the proceeds from his household goods, sold at auction before his departure. Everything considered, in his own field and capacity he had not done badly. There are Napoleons of the market place as well as of the battlefield, and he was one of them.

The ship *Lothair,* lying at anchor for its passengers and their assorted goods and chattels, left the James on the momentous eve of an event which was to reverberate round the world. On the 17th of June, 1815, Napoleon, the hero of the daring Hundred Days to his admirers but the threat to world peace in the eyes of Europe, was holding his army on the heights facing Mont-Saint-Jean, where Wellington challenged with his forces. Between them lay the battlefield of Waterloo.

It was not until the *Lothair* reached Liverpool, on the 28th of July, that the voyagers learned the details of the battle. Mr. Allan was particularly interested. After all, Bonaparte—as he preferred to call him, thus democratically discrowning him—Bonaparte had stood in the way of his greater prosperity during the Peninsular Campaign. Conditions would be better the world over now that Europe could again breathe freely. "We got here yesterday at 5 P.M. . . ." he wrote his partner, Charles Ellis, in Richmond. "Frances and Nancey were

37

very sick but are now perfectly Hearty. Edgar was a little sick but soon recovered . . . Bonaparte is now at Torkay [*sic*] on the Bellerophen [*sic*]—Bordeaux has surrendered & France submitted to Louis except a few towns. . . ." [1]

For the captured Eagle on the *Bellerophon* nothing lay beyond the expanse of the South Atlantic but St. Helena, a rocky eyrie in the middle of it. For John Allan the opportunity for expansion in a country that had recovered its peace spread before him, unlimited. At least so he thought, while laying his plans for a London branch, to be called Allan and Ellis. He had told his wife that they would remain abroad only three years, but confidentially he admitted to his partner that it would take at least five. The expense of making an establishment, he argued, was too heavy for a shorter period.

For several years Mr. Allan's Scottish relations—a bevy of sisters, Mrs. Nancy Fowlds, Mrs. Elizabeth Miller, Mrs. Jane Johnston and Miss Mary Allan, as well as a horde of nephews and nieces—had been urging him to return to his native heath. One war or another had stood in the way of the visit. Now that the world was enjoying a breathing spell, it was at last possible. It was also more auspicious for the visitor. The poor orphan who had crossed the ocean with hardly a farthing in his pocket had now recrossed it with every evidence of success about him. Moreover, shimmering over him, a nimbus of future blessings, was the prospect of a tidy fortune from Uncle William Galt, who was considerably growing older every day.

Kilmarnock and Irvine, therefore, were in a dither of preparation for the American guests, from whom innumerable bounties had come through the years and whose immediate presence might prove even more rewarding. Probably it was this extended-hand policy that curtailed the visit of Mr. Allan to his sisters in Irvine, for in a very short time he had hurried his family to Kilmarnock. Certainly there could not have been time to send little Edgar to school in Irvine, as has been said, except on a visit with some cousin.

The Kilmarnock relatives too, it appears, suffered from the contagion of greed, and a sharp interchange of accusation and defense passed between the brother and his sisters after he had left the home grounds with his household. John Allan was not ungenerous when his humanitarian feelings prompted, but he resented being exploited—and accused of stinginess in the bargain. Distance healed the breach, however. The voluntary contributions to orphans and other needy members of the clan continued from a distance and John Allan had the peace of mind to go about his business.

[1] *Ellis and Allan Papers.*

From the seaport town of Greenock he wrote to Charles Ellis, to keep him posted on his progress. Tobacco seemed to be scarce at the time. "I flatter myself from the small quantity in London . . . that our sales will be profitable." He was concerned about France, however, and the lingering spirit of Bonaparte. France was far from being stabilized. "Louis is too lenient & too peaceable the French delight in War I believe they care but little who rules them provided that ruler indulges them in their Habit. . . . Provisions of every description are extremely low here and in this quarter they are in the midst of Harvest. . . ." [2]

While he was writing, on the 21st of September, 1815, Frances and Miss Nancy were in the room prompting him with messages for friends at home. Edgar, who would not be left out, urged: "Pa, say something for me. Say I was not afraid coming across the sea." [3]

For the child it had been a great adventure, that voyage of thirty-four days on that lone immensity of water whose uncertain mercies had roused terror in those older than himself. "Say I was not afraid . . ." His anxiety to have his courage known revealed the deep impression the sea had left upon his mind, where it would abide, to be transformed into works of beauty and terror. For the present it served a boy's proud boast, to be marveled at by Uncle Galt and Mr. Ellis and by his friend John Mackenzie. "Edgar's love to Rosa and Mrs. Mackenzie," Mr. Allan closed the letter, thus spanning the gulf between the foreign land and home.

As with the ocean, the strange, misty landscapes of Scotland, the quaint seaport of Irvine, the ruins of grim castles with their tragic lore and ghosts, the weirs and lakes—all these the young boy's memory stored away, like invisible seeds which would ultimately bear their harvest. Meanwhile Edgar, with the two women, followed Pa wherever business led, through Glasgow, through Edinburgh, whose Holyrood Castle still showed visitors the bloody stains of the unlucky Rizzio, who had dared to love Mary Stuart, through other storied cities and on to London. In the interim, during the summer weeks, they remained for a short time at "Flowerbanks," on the Cree Water, the handsome seat of William Galt. Pa must have felt relieved that, despite the presence of four orphans by the name of Galt, he was not made to thrust his hand into his pocketbook for their assistance.

London was a welcome change for Frances Allan after the ruder conditions in Scotland, whose climate had not agreed with her. She had a sore throat and, at Blake's Hotel, she had to be confined to her

[2] Ibid.
[3] Ibid.

room. "The rest of us are well but cursedly dissatisfied," Mr. Allan informed his partner.[4] Whatever it was that ailed Mrs. Allan, from then on she suffered from some recurrent illness, frequently alluded to in her husband's correspondence.

In the limited confines of hotel rooms and rented lodgings the Allans drew closer together. John Allan, who once envied Shakespeare what he had called his talent for writing, drew a warmhearted vignette of the family group, "by a snug fire in a nice little sitting parlor . . . with Frances and Nancy sewing and Edgar reading a little Story Book. . . . I have no acquaintances that call upon me and none whom I as yet call on." [5]

He complained that he had to pay six guineas a week for the furnished lodgings at 47 Southampton Row. He had taken them for six months, till he could find more suitable quarters and a "compting Room" for his business. Conditions, however, were far from prosperous in a country still feeling the aftereffects of a long war and, willynilly, the head of the new firm of Allan and Ellis had to bide his time. For the women the absence of their own hearth and friends deepened their homesickness. Even Edgar thought longingly of Richmond when a favorite playmate, Catherine Poitiaux, Ma's godchild, sent the message: "Give my love to Edgar and tell him I want to see him very much . . . tell him Josephine and all the children want to see him very much." [6]

Not long afterward Edgar had companions of his own age at the boarding school of the Misses Dubourg, to which Pa, over the tearful protestations of the women, had sent him, on the suggestion of his young clerk, at the now established firm with offices at Basinghall Street. George Dubourg was a brother of the schoolmistresses and therefore qualified to recommend them.

The school, in London's Chelsea district, occupied a modest turn-of-the-century house at 146 Sloane Street. The boys were provided with bed and board as well as instruction, religious teaching, and the devoted care of two maiden ladies. Master Allan's school accounting to midsummer, 1816, came to 12 pounds, 2 shillings. It was little enough, considering that, besides three months' maintenance and tuition, it included the pay of teachers and servants, a seat in church, medical and school expenses and the cost of his textbooks, as well as such incidental outlays as shoestrings and the repairing of linen. Fresnoy's *Geography,* Mavor's *Spelling* and the *Prayer Book* constituted

[4] *Ibid.*
[5] *Ibid.*
[6] *Ibid.*

the three pillars on which the Dubourg educational system was erected.

For Mrs. Allan the London apartment must have been dull enough without the presence of the lively boy; but there were the holidays when she could have him to herself. When the Allans had come to London the whole city, indeed all of Europe, was agitated over the question of the Elgin Marbles. For years, ever since Lord Elgin, the British ambassador at Constantinople, had brought them to London from Athens, the art world had been divided about them and for over a decade the glorious remains of the sculptures and friezes that had once adorned the Parthenon had been lying in a shed. In vain their champion, the painter Benjamin Haydon, fought for them and urged the government to buy them. In vain he enlisted the support of Goethe and Canova. Envy and self-interest stood in the way.

Then, after a struggle of thirteen years, came victory. The government bought the Marbles at half of what they had cost Lord Elgin and placed them in Montagu House, as the British Museum was then called. "And now came the last day of 1816," Haydon noted in his diary, "the year in which the Elgin Marbles were bought and which, therefore, should stand marked as an era in Art." [7]

That same year, on the 17th of October, General David Poe had died in Baltimore, in the 74th year of his age. The local newspaper described him as an early and decided friend of American liberty who promoted that cause during the Revolutionary War, and died as he had lived, a zealous Republican, regretted by an extensive circle of relatives and friends. His grave, however, was unmarked. The family was too poor to afford him such a post-mortem honor as a monument.

During 1816 and 1817 the Allans were living in Southampton Row—"West Side, seven doors South of Russell Square," the precise Mr. Allan specified—and therefore very near Montagu House and its treasures. Considering the stir which the Marbles had made, the Allans would scarcely have neglected visiting the museum with Edgar, who may there have caught his first glimpse of the classical Helen and those regions which were to enchant his imagination. Certainly the retentive memory which many years later could meticulously describe, in "Why the little Frenchman wears his Hand in a Sling," the second house which the Allans had occupied in Southampton Row would have held forever that first blaze of the glory that was Greece.

There were many sights and sounds in the London of those years to impress an alert lad: the endless crowds, the people intent upon themselves, unseeing—so different from the friendliness of Richmond. Occasionally violence would break out, as when the Prince's carriage

[7] B. Haydon, *Autobiography and Journals.*

was attacked by stones hurled by a desperate mob. On his visits home Edgar would hear talk of the distresses of a country which had been weakened by a war that had drenched Europe with blood. And Pa would tell of the thousands who were thrown out of employ or were working for wages that would hardly keep body and soul together.

That summer a more immediate worry affected the Allan family. Mrs. Allan's health, never too good in England, took a turn for the worse, and early in August Mr. Allan accompanied her to Cheltenham for the waters. As she gradually improved, he thought of his languishing business in London and decided to return to town, leaving his wife to enjoy by herself the pleasant resort life. Meanwhile Edgar, in the care of the Misses Dubourg, dutifully sent his childish notes to Ma, now that Pa, to whom he ordinarily wrote, was back in London.

With the opening of the new year an unwelcome reminder of past sins came to Mr. Allan, in a communication from Richmond. During his absence from home a Mr. William Ewing had been conscientiously imparting education to Edwin Collier. Now that nearly three years had elapsed, the schoolmaster felt that the submission of a bill would not be improper. What gave Mr. Allan umbrage, however, was not the legitimate request for money for his illegitimate son's education, but Mrs. Collier's attitude in the matter. "His mother informs me," wrote Mr. Ewing, "that she has frequently reminded your partner Mr. Ellis to mention Edwin's situation to you, but thinks that amid the hurry of important communications he has omitted the subject altogether. . . . You will confer a favor on me, and equally so on Mrs. Collier, by dropping a few lines to me through the medium of your firm, first opportunity, expressive of your concern for the tuition and education of the above child, as far as you may deem proper in regard to the future." [8]

It further emerged from the letter that Mr. Ellis had paid one of the bills. Worse, some teacher—Mr. Ewing assured Mr. Allan that it was not himself—had taken the improper step of actually warranting the firm for money due. After so much unpleasant business it was no salve to Mr. Allan's irritation to have solicitous inquiries made after the health of his "Lady Mrs. Allan and her Sister . . . and do not forget to mention me to their august attendant, Edgar." [9]

Mr. Allan's reply had none of his correspondent's jauntiness. It was curt and to the point. Mr. Ellis would give Mr. Ewing the sum still owing, but Mr. Allan would not pay any more of Edwin's expenses. He could not conceive who had the right to warrant the firm

[8] *Ellis and Allan Papers.*
[9] *Ibid.*

on his account. As for the august attendant, Edgar was a fine boy and Mr. Allan had no reason to complain of his progress. The heavy hand fell ruthlessly. Mr. Ewing, Mrs. Collier and the hopes of Edwin Collier were for the moment crushed.

Mr. Allan's laconic but, for him, generous praise of Edgar, following upon the dismissal of his obligations toward his natural son, had its significance in a temperament not overcharged with the tender emotions.

Before replying to Mr. Ewing, Mr. Allan had taken Edgar from the Misses Dubourg and entered him in the Manor House School at Stoke Newington, then a quiet, elm-shaded village on the outskirts of London. The change represented an advance for Edgar, both in status and in educational advantages. It was also a much more expensive school than the one he had attended. For Mr. Allan to make extra charges upon his pocketbook for Edgar also had its meaning: he now looked upon the boy as his son. By this time he could entertain no further hope of children from his wife who, in spite of her continual cures, still remained an invalid. Edgar had been under his roof for more than six years. The responsiveness and the expanding intelligence of the boy, who captivated even strangers, had penetrated his obdurate heart. Still, to the man disappointed in his wish for a legitimate heir the choice of Edgar was only a palliative. Even the adoption of Edwin Collier might have been preferable—at least Edwin was part his—but that would have been impossible since it meant confessing his infidelity to his wife. In any case that step was now out of the question, even if it had been considered, as his answer to Mr. Ewing made clear.

Meanwhile the recipient of Mr. Allan's paternal beneficence, the nine-year-old Edgar, all unaware of Pa's highhanded dealing with a debt of honor of a peculiar nature, was enjoying the benefits of a good English education.

Stoke Newington, a pleasant four-mile carriage drive northeast of Russell Square, had its roots deep in the past. The ancient road, first furrowed by Roman chariot wheels, had been made gracious through the years by the Englishman's love of trees—generations of venerable giants whose branches met overhead. They were the haunt of birds, among them the dark-plumaged ravens. Long afterward Poe was to recall: "That bird pursues me mentally, perpetually. . . . I hear its croak as I used to hear it at Stoke Newington, the flap of its wings in my ear." [10]

English history had also left its memorials in houses of the time of

[10] Frances A. Mathews, "Story of a Poem." Quoted in Phillips, *Edgar Allan Poe,* pp. 936-937.

Henry VIII. There was the palace of Earl Percy, who had had the misfortune of being named as one of Anne Boleyn's lovers and so, like her, lost his head on the block. Nearby rose the castle of Robert Dudley, Queen Elizabeth's favorite. Later periods also survived in the architecture, the Georgian and Queen Anne most predominantly.

Among these edifices, on a comparatively modern street, rose, or rather sat, the Manor House School, a two-story white building of various architectures. Ivy festooned the upper ledges of the ground floor windows and climbed up between the square-paned frames to the second floor. On either side of the steps leading to the entrance an enclosed parterre of box and other shrubbery was guarded by iron railings, themselves sentineled by square posts topped by large stone globes.

The house itself, which had grown by accretion as old houses have a way of doing, rambled toward a high brick wall in the rear which enclosed the playground. To discourage escapades from within or intrusion from without, the top of the wall bristled with fragments of broken glass embedded in mortar. At an angle of this formidable rampart was the massive studded gate, provided with jagged spikes as a double precaution. The flat roof had a singular adornment on either side, a pyramidal structure, no doubt the vaulted ceiling of the chamber below.

Within, the house sprawled, as irregular and unpredictable as a labyrinth, its rooms rising at different levels even on the same floor and reached by mysterious twists and turns. The schoolroom, long, low, narrow, with an oak ceiling and Gothic windows, was a havoc of time-blackened desks and benches—islands on which generations of boys had left, like castaways, their carved initials and other traces as evidence that, for a span of their lives, more or less against their will, they had been there. At one corner, a place of awe, rose the sanctum of the master, the Rev. Mr. John Bransby, who was also parson of the village church. In the other corners were the boxes, or enclosures, of the ushers. One box in particular held a special distinction in the eyes of the lads. In it had once sat Eugene Aram, executed for murder in 1759.

The story of the long-dead usher had fascinated generations of students and certainly it would not have escaped one who was to deal with the lower depths of the human psyche. Indeed, in both character and attainments Eugene Aram antedated both Roderick Usher in his culture and Auguste Dupin in the unusual power of ratiocination he revealed in defending himself of the charge of murder. Painstakingly, brilliantly, Aram sought to prove that the bones which had been uncovered were not necessarily those of the man whom he was accused of having murdered for profit some fifteen years earlier.

"Permit me, my lord, to observe a little upon the bones which have been discovered," Aram addressed the judge before whom he was tried. "It is said (which, perhaps, is saying very far) that these are the skeleton of a man. It is possible . . . but is there any certain known criterion which incontestably distinguishes the sex in human bones? . . . The place of their depositum, too, claims more attention than is commonly bestowed upon it for, of all the places in the world, none could have mentioned any one wherein there was greater certainty of finding human bones than a hermitage, except he should point out a churchyard; hermitages in time past, being not only places of religious retirement, but of burial too. . . . My lord, almost every place conceals such remains. . . . Here too is a human skull produced, which is fractured; but was this the cause, or was it the consequence of death? Was it owing to violence, or was it the effect of natural decay? If it was violence, was the violence before or after death?"

Despite his eloquence and his logic Aram was sentenced to death. "To die is natural and necessary. . . . But the manner of it is something which should, in my opinion, be decent and manly," he wrote before attempting suicide, when he left the verses:

> Come, pleasing rest! eternal slumbers, fall!
> Seal mine, that once must seal the eyes of all.
> Calm and composed my soul her journey takes;
> No guilt that troubles, and no heart that aches. . . .

The tradition of such a man, whose aura lingered in the Manor House, would have made a deeper impression upon the imagination of the Rev. Mr. Bransby's charges than he himself, a good but in no sense extraordinary man, could have exercised. At the time he was thirty-three years old, with a wife and an already large family whose pleasures he not unwillingly eschewed for the hunt. In fact, his pupils were always on the lookout for the mornings when he would be polishing his gun, which meant that he would be gone for the day.

One thing he had in common with the ill-fated usher. He was a sound classical scholar and a living encyclopedia of miscellaneous information, especially on the subject of botany. Whatever his other virtues, they made no deep impression upon Edgar, whose evocation of him in his reminiscent story, "William Wilson," was as inaccurate— no doubt for purposes of art—as that of the school itself was vivid. The Rev. Mr. Bransby, years later, suffered from a similar lapse of memory and could remember only that Master Allan was intelligent, wayward and willful, and that his parents spoiled him by giving him too much pocket money—an assertion which hardly jibes with Mr. Allan's Scottish prudence.

However, the careful merchant could not have grumbled at the little over twenty-three pounds per term that he paid for Edgar's schooling, for the single bed the boy slept in, for his textbooks and slates, and for the privilege of listening to the Rev. Mr. Bransby's sermons. This privilege the boys enjoyed twice during Sunday, first in the morning, when they were solemnly paraded to the one church in the village, and then again for the evening service. The lambs looked up at their reverend pastor and they were fed, for the modest fee of three shillings and sixpence for pew rent. The schooling itself, sound and thorough, with special emphasis on the classics, trained the young mind to discipline while awakening it to the moral values that form the backbone of character. It was at Stoke Newington that Edgar's consciousness first stirred to the eternal verities which, in one form or another, whether as allegories or as dramas of life, were to animate his writings. At any rate, it was the Manor House School which he chose as the background of "William Wilson," that drama of man and his conscience, so intensely personal despite its fictitious character that Poe even gave his double his birth date as well as many of his personal characteristics.

Mr. Allan was sufficiently pleased with Edgar's progress to write to Mr. Galt about it. The boy was growing wonderfully, he said, enjoyed a good reputation and gave proof that he was both able and willing to receive instruction. Business affairs, however, as well as the general health, of the family deteriorated steadily. The tobacco market had proved disappointing; a commercial venture with a London merchant had left Mr. Allan out of pocket. As for the London firm, its final crash came early in 1820, though Mr. Allan had heralded disaster for several months. Finally he swallowed his pride sufficiently to admit to the home office: "I have only about £100 here in the world, and I depend upon you." [11]

Mrs. Allan was glad to be returning home, though she had such an aversion to the sea that only the prospect of a reunion with her friends induced her to attempt the voyage. She had spent a great part of her English sojourn in health resorts in Dawlish and Tydemouth, in the lovely Devonshire country, from where she would keep her "dear hubby, her dear old man" informed of her progress and social activities. "I embrace every opportunity . . . for taking air and exercises. . . . I really think you have a great deal of Vanity to immagien you

[11] *Ellis and Allan Papers.*

are the cause of all my misery," she teased him. "I only wish my health would admit of my entering into all the gaieties of this place. I would soon let you see I could be as happy and contented without you as you appear to be in my absence as I hear of nothing but partyes at home and abroad but long may the Almighty grant my dear husband health and spirits to enjoy them. . . ." [12]

One wonders, on reading Frances Allan's correspondence, whether self-consciousness about her spelling and lack of style, rather than indifference, had kept her from answering Eliza Poe's inquiries about little Edgar.

Mr. Allan's health and spirits, despite his wife's good wishes, were not always of the best, but he was not one to complain of his physical disabilities. In March of 1820, however, he suffered his first serious attack of dropsy and, despite the precarious state of affairs at his office, he had to lie at home, afflicted by physical pain and financial anxieties. Worse, when he was able to return to his countinghouse, he found his position graver than he had anticipated, thanks to the activities of a light-fingered clerk. Discouraged and humiliated by his failure, he took Edgar out of school and wrote Mr. Ellis for cash to defray his voyage home.

Their last few months in England furnished the Allans, as well as the kingdom, with the denouement of the royal tragi-comedy which had been going on for several years. After the death of George III, in January, 1820, George Augustus, the dissolute fat Adonis of more than fifty, was preparing for his own coronation as George IV. Unexpectedly the solemnity was put off by his calling for a bill of divorcement against his wife, Queen Caroline, then living in Italy. When the Cabinet refused to act upon it, the King sent to both houses of Parliament a "green bag," purporting to contain evidence of Queen Caroline's adultery with her Italian chamberlain, and demanded her trial. Everyone talked of the "green bag." Would Queen Caroline try to prove her innocence? Or would she remain in Italy? To everyone's amazement, including the King's, she chartered a vessel after she had been refused passage on a royal ship, and sailed for England.

On June 8, 1820, John Allan wrote to Ellis from Liverpool, where, with his family, he was waiting to sail for home: "The arrival of the Queen produced an unexpected sensation. Few thought she would return, but the bold and courageous manner by which she effected it has induced a vast number to think her not guilty. She was received with immense acclamations and the populace displaced her horses, drew her past Carlton house. . . . The same day the King made a com-

[12] E. V. Valentine Collection.

munication to the House of Lords charging her with High Treason,
adultery. . . . The *Martha* . . . will not sail before Wednesday next
the 14th. . . ." [13]

The Allans were already across the Atlantic when all London was
enjoying the popular commentary on the royal scandal in the verses
of Leigh Hunt:

> "You swear—you swear"—"Oh Signor sì—"
> "That through a double door, eh,
> You've seen her *think* adulterously?"
> "Ver' true, Sir—Sì, Signore."

[13] *Ellis and Allan Papers.*

➔➤➤ • ⫷⫷⫶

Vision of Helen

CHARLES ELLIS was sweltering in his office when he had word that the Allans had landed in New York, after a voyage of five weeks. Richmond, that July, was particularly hot and Mr. Ellis was longing to join his wife, whom he had considerately sent to the mountains. "Mr. and Mrs. Allan are at last arrived in New York," he informed her on the 31st of the month, "and as soon as they get on, and settle down a little, I shall leave them the bag to hold and flee to the mountains." [1]

The travelers arrived home on the 2nd of August. The voyage along the coast of Norfolk, its waters crowded with gleaming sails and vivid hulls, held a welcoming excitement after the immense solitude of the ocean.

Since the old house on Tobacco Alley was still rented, the Allans went to live in Mr. Ellis' frame dwelling, facing a cool square and fronted by a row of lindens. Though Mr. Ellis longed to get away from the heat and the plaints of teething infants, whose discomforts he pityingly relayed to his wife, he had to play host to the Allans. "You would be surprised to see what health and color Mrs. A. has. . . . They are a little Englishised but it will soon wear off," he remarked.[2]

He may have been right about Mr. and Mrs. Allan's losing their English acquirement, but in Edgar's case he was reckoning with a remarkably keen intelligence and a memory that let nothing go. All his impressions of London, the tribes of clerks, with their pantaloons of black or brown, the individuals of dashing appearance, the peddlers with hawkeyes flashing, street beggars and pickpockets—all these Edgar stored away behind his broad, high brow. There too were etched the desolately beautiful landscapes of Scotland, the heaths and tarns, the storied crumbling castles with their ghosts. Stoke Newington, the misty-looking village with its deeply shadowed ave-

---

[1] *Ellis and Allan Papers.*
[2] *Ibid.*

nues, its Elizabethan castle and the nearer lore of a wicked and fascinating personality—all left their impressions, to be revived at the behest of a kindling imagination. Nor was the ocean with its terrible wonders ever forgotten.

The Allans had planned on only a brief stay at the Ellises' but it was not till the close of the year that they moved to a place of their own, a comfortable cottage facing Clay Street. Business had not prospered and Mr. Allan had not yet recouped his losses from the English venture. However, he did not neglect Edgar's education, so auspiciously begun in England.

The school of Mr. Joseph A. Clarke, to which Mr. Allan sent the twelve-year-old boy, could not compare with the Rev. Mr. Bransby's; but it also emphasized Greek and Latin and it had, moreover, the advantage of being much cheaper—less than eighteen dollars a quarter, including the texts of Horace and Cicero, pens, ink and paper. In view of the financial situation, even trifling items had to be considered, though comparatively Mr. Allan was still a prosperous man. He had changed since his return. He spoke little and often appeared worried. The London fiasco had also aggravated his innate regard for money. Mrs. Allan too was not the same. She soon lost the color which Mr. Ellis had admired and was now often ailing. Only Miss Nancy remained buxom and cheerful.

Fortunately the Mackenzies were not far away and with them Edgar had a second home. His five years in England and the broadening effect of travel had brought him closer to his friend John, who could no longer lord his seniority over such an intelligent, well-mannered young gentleman. Rosalie adored her handsome brother and showed it. She was a pretty blue-eyed girl with rosy cheeks and a ready laugh, but she had none of the striking qualities of Edgar, whose deep-gray irises exercised an instant fascination. Her face, on the contrary, seemed empty, without light. For the past year— she was now eleven—a change had been gradually coming over her, a progressive slowing down of her physical and mental powers. The Mackenzies noted it and were concerned. It was as if by some cruel spell Rosalie were being suspended in her growth halfway between childhood and youth, yet with neither the charm of the child nor the grace of maturity.

She was attending Miss Jane Mackenzie's school for girls, where she excelled in penmanship, if in little else. As she grew older her childish qualities became more noticeable, but she was by no means the moron that some biographers have made her. Indeed, it required a degree of shrewdness to have enabled her, toward the end of her life, to succeed in a field—obtaining money from others—in which her brother was to prove a notable failure.

Besides John Mackenzie and Rosalie, Edgar had Ebenezer, the son of the widowed Mrs. Burling, as a playfellow. They used to sit near each other in church and, even before the English voyage, Ebenezer had taught Edgar to swim. The somewhat older boy brought an element of excitement and adventure into their play, fostered by their sharing the magical life of the imagination when, by the dim firelight, they would relive in their reading the spellbinding saga of Robinson Crusoe. "Alas! the days of desolate islands are no more!" Edgar was to sigh, years later, after having dwelt in solitary islands of his own.

Still, the early years of adolescence in the graciously classical city of Richmond, which, moreover, offered boating on the James, swimming in the river creeks and colorful adventure along the docks and wharves, were rich in excitement for the growing lad, especially in congenial company. Of course there were the elegant parties which Ma and Pa gave for the entertainment of Edgar's young friends, when prim young girls in flounced dresses danced with miniature gentlemen or played charades for the enjoyment of their parents. But Edgar was so bored with the punctilious etiquette that he developed a chronic dislike for formal parties. He would rather have spent a day in the cotton fields than an hour at an Allan soirée. It was much more fun playing some practical joke, or swimming in the river with John Mackenzie, or setting fish traps in the company of waterfront boys known as River Rats, or making raids in the autumn on ripening orchards or turnip patches. "Many a time after the apple crop had been gathered in," John Mackenzie recalled, "we might have been seen, a half dozen of us, seated on a rail-fence like so many crows, munching turnips. We didn't object to raw sweet potatoes at times—anything that had the relish of being stolen." [3]

On Sundays the boys would have fish fries by the river or they would tramp through the woods for wild grapes and chinquapins. Mr. Allan, however, was not always in a mood to let him pass the holy day in that fashion; but the boy would slip out of the house, though he knew the ever-ready switch would be applied on his return. The accusation of ingratitude now began to appear in Mr. Allan's reproaches. At those times the long hooked nose and piercing eyes under the feathery brows gave Mr. Allan more than ever the look of a hawk about to swoop.

When Edgar was fourteen Mr. Allan sent him to the school kept

[3] Weiss, *The Home Life of Poe.*

by William Burke, an advance over that of Mr. Clarke. If the boy warranted it he would be given the best education Virginia afforded —a bright prospect since, in Charlottesville, Jefferson's dream of a university, built on the classical model and as fine as any in Europe, had been materializing in domes and pillars in a valley encircled by mountains. So far Edgar promised well, though he was beginning to mope too much, preferring his own company to making himself useful at Ellis and Allan's. Indeed, whenever he deigned to attend the store he preferred wasting his time scrawling verses to studying the price of tobacco or measuring out yards of calico. They were particularly Byronic verses, and Mr. Allan abhorred Byron. The influence, however, persisted in the fledgling chanticleer whose voice, because he strained too hard, cracked in falsetto and whose romantic anguish, because it was imaginary, became absurd. One day, to obtain an impartial opinion on Edgar's efforts, Mr. Allan took a batch of the boy's poems to Mr. Clarke, the schoolmaster. "His imaginative powers seemed to have precedence of all his other faculties," pronounced Mr. Clarke. "He gave proof of this in his juvenile compositions addressed to his young female friends." [4]

Cupid's messenger for these effusions was none other than Rosalie —Rosa, as the Allans called her. Delighted that she could be of service to Edgar, she would smuggle the poems into the virginal precincts of Miss Mackenzie's seminary and deliver them to the chosen damsel or, rather, damsels, for to the poet, in love with the idea of love, the fair recipient he addressed was purely accidental.

No one knows how long this assault on the virtuous ramparts had been going on. Several times, however, Miss Mackenzie, who had her suspicions, had seen Love's messenger bearing not only poetic tributes but also boxes of sweets purchased with Edgar's allowance or perhaps even appropriated from the store. Rosalie felt the smart of Miss Mackenzie's slipper on her tender flesh, but it was hardly likely that such vicarious punishment discouraged the amorous bard who, when inspiration failed, merely changed the names on his compositions to conform with the new flames.

Despite these distractions Edgar did not neglect his lessons. He had already acquired the habit of study, formed at Stoke Newington; he also possessed an acquisitive mind which delighted in the curiosities of life and literature, as well as in the solid staples. He could cap Latin verses with the scholar and show off his French in his unusual aptitude for languages. Yet, for all that, he was no pallid

[4] MS, Harvard College Library.

bookworm but a nimble athlete who could compete with the best in manly sports.

Perhaps he was spurred on to excel by some sense of inferiority which, consciously or not, he was made to feel. In those days the capital of Virginia prided itself on being the most aristocratic city in the South, with social distinctions marked to within a hairsbreadth. The Allans were among its most respected citizens and, considering their relation to Mr. Galt, among the richest. However, because of the publicity given to Elizabeth Poe's death, it was known that the boy taken into the Allan household was the son of an actress and therefore very low on the social scale which Mr. Allan had climbed to a considerable height, thanks to luck and to his ability. Children are notoriously conformist. Both at Mr. Clarke's and, now, at Mr. Burke's, it was no secret that Edgar Poe, the excellent student, the fine athlete, belonged by birth on a rung far below the one to which the kindness of the Allans had raised him. It was not a slip of the pen that made the masters address their bills to Mr. Allan for the instruction of Master Poe, whereas at Stoke Newington Edgar had been known as Master Allan. It was as if, with or without Mr. Allan's assent, the delicate inference was understood: that Edgar Poe was his son purely by the grace of his generous heart.

The adolescent is peculiarly sensitive and Edgar, by both nature and circumstances, was more vulnerable than most. His love of his mother turned to a gallant defense of her in the form of an inordinate desire to excel, as if to demonstrate that the son of an actress could, with little effort, best the proudest Virginia scion of them all. For some time one of his favorite tests, involving as much self-punishment as it demonstrated fortitude, had been to let some boy, far more powerful than himself, strike him full force in the chest. Stoically he would take the blow, though he confessed to a younger friend that he had a trick to break its force—by filling the lungs before the blow, and exhaling the air just before the impact. The admission redounded doubly to his credit, for while he stood the test to the admiration of the onlookers he had also the secret satisfaction of outwitting his opponent.

It may have been as much his desire to vindicate himself as to duplicate a Byronic feat that made him undertake a remarkable swimming exploit. While his friends were waiting expectantly in the flaming sun on Ludlam's Wharf, Edgar leapt into the James and swam the seven miles to Warwick. His schoolmates and playfellows, Robert Cabell, little Bob, the son of Judge Robert Stanard, and a curious crowd watched him make for the distant goal, while Mr. Burke followed him in a rowboat. For a while some of the boys kept up with Edgar by sprinting along the shore. Then he swam beyond their view till, proud and triumphant, he clambered up the banks of Warwick and from there trudged home. It would be curious to know Mr. Allan's reaction, but it is not recorded.

For some time the relations between Pa and Edgar had been suffering a critical change, partly because of mutual lack of understanding, partly because of the stresses inherent in adolescence. Ordinarily a growing boy is aided by an understanding father, who advises without seeming to do so and guides without tugging at the reins. Mr. Allan was accustomed only to command and in Edgar he had one of those recalcitrant personalities who early fix their gaze upon a goal which they cease to pursue only when they die.

By the age of fourteen, perhaps even earlier, Edgar had seen the glimmer of his constellation, and he knew it was not the Libra by which Mr. Allan measured the ups and downs of his, and other people's, success. As for Mr. Allan, he found it increasingly difficult to see in Edgar the heir he would have wished—a replica of himself, firm, granitic, a pillar of society to be pointed out in admiration, to be leaned upon if necessary. In Edgar, on the contrary, he found a reed and he could not conceal his disappointment and contempt.

During the conflicts that inevitably arose, Mrs. Allan played the part of the mediator, but the differences between the two were beyond the power of an invalid to heal. She could only comfort Edgar and seek to soften her husband who, in the end, considered himself the injured party, with everyone against him.

Edgar was thrown more and more upon himself. It was at this time, toward the middle of 1824, that he and his brother Henry began a desultory correspondence, with the knowledge of Mr. Allan. For the rest, he had his few friends, John Mackenzie, Robert Sully, whose father had long ago acted in the Virginia Company with Elizabeth Poe, and his young admirer, Bob Stanard, who had watched him perform his swimming feat. Edgar had also the understanding sympathy of Bob's mother, Mrs. Jane Stith Stanard.

She was one of those gentle, delicately sensitive women shaken to the soul by a breath that would not stir an aeolian harp, an intuitive nature that seized a thought before the word expressed it. She was a being so precariously balanced on the ledge of reality that the least emotional jolt threatened to throw her off.

One day Bob Stanard invited Edgar to his house and the lonely boy went willingly. First he admired Bob's various pets in the garden and then the two went indoors, where Mrs. Stanard was waiting for them. It was an instantaneous meeting of kindred spirits, Edgar's vague unhappiness reaching out for understanding while the young woman's sympathy—she was not quite thirty—responded with warmth to his unspoken need. He went to see her often after that, finding in her what his own mother would have given him had she lived. In a strange way Mrs. Stanard, judging by her portrait, resembled Mrs. Poe. She had the same enormous eyes and broad forehead, the same straight classical nose and delicately molded chin. She even wore a similar high-bodiced gown, its deep neckline revealing the throat and bosom. But, whereas Elizabeth Poe's face beamed with the archness of her smile, Mrs. Stanard's was clouded over by a melancholy that brooded in her eyes and set her lips to sorrow.

To Edgar she represented not only the mother he had lost but the ideal of romantic womanhood that he had encountered in his reading. He saw in her the purity and spirituality of a Beatrice, the beauty of a Helen, the sum of all the virtues that had inspired poets and made them immortal. More, she was what he felt himself to be, an alien transported from some holy land of the spirit to a world he could not call his own. In her he also found what he had longed for in vain at home, a receptive ear for his poetry and an understanding which could prune his excesses without destroying his growth. For Mr. Allan the boy's versifying was no more than an adolescent rash which time would cure. As for Frances Allan, it was an idiom foreign to her simple and insufficiently cultivated mind. She appreciated his efforts but they were beyond her comprehension.

For a year or more Edgar had been visiting the Stanard home when, one day, everything changed. Mrs. Stanard, they told him, was ill. He saw her once only after that. She was as beautiful as ever but the radiance had gone out of her face. She died insane on April 28, 1824. With her the only light in the lonely boy's life went out as well.

His grief was so intense that everyone remarked it. "I never saw in him . . . a sign of morbidness or melancholy," said John Mackenzie, "unless it was when Mrs. Stanard died, when he appeared for some time grieving and depressed." [5] It was also said that for many weeks Edgar would visit her grave at night. If the boy who was terrified of ghosts conquered his dread to this degree, his love had indeed been great. There is more plausibility, however, in Mrs. Clemm's

[5] Weiss, *op. cit.*

simple declaration: "Robert has often told me of his and Eddie's visits to her grave. . . ." [6]

Whether or not the fifteen-year-old Edgar mourned over the woman who had awakened him to his first ideal yet ardent love, the appalling reality of death now dug its ineradicable fibers into his psyche, already predisposed to such growth by the loss of his mother. The cruel severance of life by death and the unimaginable graveyard horrors of dissolution became the materials of his imagination, the palette and colors of his genius. But perhaps to spare the beings he loved the indignities of corruption, his dead were never really dead. By the power of his fancy he endowed them with a will to live which overpowered death itself, a sentiency beyond the extinction of the body, working like a vein of fire in the seemingly spent ember. One of his earliest poems, "Spirits of the Dead," written not long after Mrs. Stanard's death, exploited the theme:

> Thy soul shall find itself alone
> 'Mid dark thoughts of the grey tomb-stone;
> Not one, of all the crowd, to pry
> Into thine hour of secrecy.
>
> Be silent in that solitude
>   Which is not loneliness—for then
> The spirits of the dead, who stood
>   In life before thee, are again
> In death around thee, and their will
> Shall overshadow thee; be still.
>
> The night, though clear, shall frown,
> And the stars shall not look down
> From their high thrones in the Heaven
> With light like hope to mortals given,
> But their red orbs, without beam,
> To thy weariness shall seem
> As a burning and a fever
> Which would cling to thee for ever.
>
> Now are thoughts thou shalt not banish,
> Now are visions ne'er to vanish . . .

However, to the woman who gave him his first vision of ideal beauty, the Helen against whom he was to measure all perfection, he dedicated a monument which held nothing of death but was all glory and grandeur and light. He called it "To Helen."

[6] "Poe and Mrs. Whitman," by James A. Harrison. *Century Magazine*, January, 1909.

Helen, thy beauty is to me
   Like those Nicean barks of yore,
That gently, o'er a perfumed sea,
   The weary, wayworn wanderer bore
   To his own native shore.

On desperate seas long wont to roam,
   Thy hyacinth hair, thy classic face,
Thy Naiad airs have brought me home
   To the glory that was Greece
To the grandeur that was Rome.

Lo! In yon brilliant window-niche
   How statue-like I see thee stand,
   The agate lamp within thy hand!
Ah, Psyche, from the regions which
   Are Holy Land!

It was a monument lovingly sketched when Poe was only a boy and which he did not bring to perfection until the last decade of his life. But it does not alter the nobility of the design to know that the agate lamp which Helen held was at first a folded scroll, or that the brilliant window-niche had once been shadowy. Like the radiance suffusing the poem, the spirit of Helen was to pervade his life of the heart as it filled the life of his imagination.

CHAPTER VI

The Family Mystery

IN October of 1824 all of Richmond was seized with the fever that had been spreading from city to city for the honor of playing host to Marie Paul Joseph Roch Yves Gilbert Motier, Marquis de La Fayette, democratically known as General La Fayette. It was the General's third visit to America, his second as the nation's guest. The first time he had come on his own, in a ship freighted with the most revolutionary cargo that had ever crossed the Atlantic. With Baron de Kalb and eleven other officers, the nineteen-year-old La Fayette joined the embattled colonies to fight in the cause of freedom. He served as a Revolutionary soldier under Washington, received a ball in the leg at Brandywine, rose to the rank of major general at twenty, and witnessed the rout of Cornwallis. When he had revisited the Republic, it consisted of thirteen fledgling states—lean, draggled eaglets, exhausted from the struggle for independent life. He now found a powerful family of twenty-four prosperous entities, commanding a piece of the continent that stretched from the Atlantic border a thousand miles to the west. With the General came his son, George Washington La Fayette, and a scribulous secretary, Emile Levasseur. "The day of our arrival on Staten Island," wrote the faithful scribe, "a rainbow, one of whose limbs tinged Fort La Fayette with a thousand colors, appeared."

Indeed, wherever he went, as guest of the nation and of President Monroe, La Fayette's sky was overarched with rainbows. The humble and the great, from Atlantic fishermen to Brahmins of the highest caste, joined to do him honor by naming many things after him, among them a fish which till then had served the kitchen as plain goody, or oldwife. The fish, with its steep profile, looked remarkably like him.

To the blare of bands La Fayette passed through hundreds of triumphal arches from Albany to Kaskaskia and equally euphoniously named localities. Laurel wreaths were showered upon him, but he preferred to wear the cocked hat designed especially for him by Mr. Hurley of New York. His son George Washington ordered one like it, but when he offered to pay for it the patriotic hatmaker answered: "All the hats I could supply to the La Fayette family were paid for over forty years ago." His words were soon on every tongue and American males held their heads higher—in Hurley hats.

Everywhere the General was hailed by jubilant crowds. Veterans paraded before him in their faded uniforms, tattered banners fluttering aloft. Bells pealed, cannons roared. Mothers gave him their infants to hold. Little girls placed wreaths upon his peruke.

In Baltimore he was entertained in Washington's old army tent. Later he visited the President's grave. Levasseur noted: "He took his son and me by the hand and led us into the tomb. We knelt reverently near the coffin, which we respectfully saluted with our lips. Rising, we threw ourselves into the arms of La Fayette and mingled our tears with his."

The General made two other visits before leaving the city. The first was to the humble dwelling of Mrs. Poe, the widow of his old comrade-in-arms. Again tears flowed as he put his arms about the woman he remembered as an attractive young matron. "The last time I embraced you, madame," he sighed, "you were younger and more blooming."

Indeed, Mrs. Poe had little cause to look flourishing. She was old, ailing and poor, running her household on the irregular earnings of her sons and a small pension which the government had belatedly granted her. It was to the grave of General Poe that La Fayette paid his second visit. The modest burial mound in the First Presbyterian churchyard was still unmarked. On his knees, La Fayette kissed the sod above the doughty hero and, with tears in his eyes, exclaimed: "Here rests a noble heart!"

Before leaving Baltimore La Fayette was consoled by the gift of a ring containing strands of Washington's hair. At Charlottesville another present awaited the visitor—a rattlesnake with its fangs extracted, but still very sportive, to judge by its vigorous wrigglings. The rattler was really a delicate attention to the General's son, who had expressed a desire to own one. La Fayette himself, however, was the recipient of the biggest gift of all, voted to him by Congress: $200,000 in cash, and the grant of a township of public land in Florida.

It was at this glowing time that Richmond prepared to welcome the leader who had so ably helped to conduct the Virginia campaign in a perilous moment of history. Triumphal arches of evergreens, festooned with the national colors, rose at intervals in the line of approach. Richmond's fair virgins, fitted with new gowns, ample and vestal, practiced in them their poses as living statues. Schools and seminaries, Miss Mackenzie's among them, rang with solfeggi as the young ladies perfected their paeans of welcome. They too, like Mrs. Willard's damozels in Troy, were eager to chant:

> Columbia's daughters, lo! we bend
> And claim to call thee Father, Friend!

It fell to Richmond's youths to give the General's welcome a special and appropriate touch when they constituted themselves into a special guard of honor. Mr. Burke's academy, like the rest, forgot Cicero and Horace, forgot books and lessons, as the eager scholars tried on brave uniforms and practiced marching with other young gentlemen of the town. Edgar was in high excitement. From his brother Henry he may have heard of La Fayette's visit to his grandfather's grave. In any case, he had long known the significant part that General Poe had played in the Revolution.

It was with justifiable pride, therefore, that Edgar donned the uniform of the Richmond Junior Volunteers, or the Morgan Riflemen, and assumed a role of leadership in his rank of lieutenant. Throughout La Fayette's visit the young Volunteers, with sword at side and gun on shoulder—for they had been granted permission to draw them from the Armory—attended the General as his bodyguard. Even the Richmond vestals had to take second place before the dashing group of youths. But, like all joys, the happy days came to an end. La Fayette went on to other honors. The Richmond Junior Volunteers put off their uniforms and returned to the school bench. For a brief moment Edgar had shone in the aura of fame. He was always to long for it.

As for La Fayette, unless Edgar had made himself known to him as the grandson of General Poe, the youth would have been to him as anonymous as the rest. No intuition could have told the General that in the adolescent with the luminous eyes he was seeing a future poet. As it happened, before La Fayette left for France he was to have another encounter of whose significance he was to remain unaware.

Somehow, the township of Brooklyn had to wait until 1825 before it hit upon a suitable ceremony for the nation's guest to grace. It was the laying of a cornerstone for the Apprentices' Library—a humble task to offer the man who had officiated at the breaking of the ground for the Bunker Hill memorial. Yet the library, in its way, also was a monument to democracy.

That day Brooklyn's children were let off from school so that the General, when he descended from his barouche at the corner of Cranberry and Henry Streets, looked out upon a bank of well-scrubbed faces. The ceremonial trowel was already in the General's hand when someone noticed that the smallest children, in the front row, ran the danger of being pushed into the ditch by the eagerness of those behind them. The town dignitaries then stopped the proceedings to lift the youngsters, one by one, and carry them over to safety. La Fayette, with the rest, stooped to pick up a particularly sturdy lad of five or six. He was about to set him down when, tempted by his plump, shining cheeks, he kissed him, though there had been no poetic recitation to inspire his rapture. But the poetry was to come. Walt Whitman never forgot the thrill of having been held for an instant in the arms of greatness.[1]

In Richmond, meanwhile, after the brief flashing of the luminary and the reflected glory which all had enjoyed, life resumed its lusterless course. For Edgar it was an anticlimactic period of dissatisfaction and tension. Mr. Allan, after his reorganization of the firm earlier in the year, had more leisure on his hands and therefore greater opportunity to meddle in the affairs of others, particularly Edgar's, whose correspondence with Henry Poe he had been carefully supervising.

On the first day of November, 1824, Mr. Allan sat down to write a letter to Henry. He had just penned the salutation when he disgorged a torrent of complaint and abuse against Edgar. "I have just seen your letter of the 25th ult. to Edgar and am much afflicted, that he has not written you. He has little else to do; for me he does nothing and seems quite miserable, sulky and ill tempered to all the Family. . . . The boy possesses not a Spark of affection for us not a particle of gratitude for all my care and kindness towards him. I have given a much superior Education than ever I received myself. If Rosalie has to relie on any affection from him God in his mercy preserve her. . . . I feel proudly the difference between your principles & his & hence my desire to Stand as I ought to do in your Estimation. Had I done my duty as faithfully to my God as I have to Edgar, then had Death, come when he will, had no terrors for me. . . ."[2]

So far it was the splenetic outburst of a man who felt himself ill

[1] Frances Winwar, "Lafayette Returns," *University Review* (Summer, 1942), Kansas City.
[2] *Ellis and Allan Papers.*

rewarded for the beneficence he had lavished upon an ingrate. Still, one could question the wisdom of a man of forty-four pouring such a vial of wrath into the ear of a youth of eighteen, the brother of the maligned one at that. It may well be that Edgar, after the brief exhilaration of the La Fayette interlude, had returned to the brooding which everyone had remarked after Mrs. Stanard's death. It is also possible that the perceptive boy, now old enough to observe and interpret the behavior of his elders, had seen that something was rotten in the little Denmark of the Allan family. Moreover, gossip had no great distance to travel in the compact little capital. Like the cuttlefish, Mr. Allan may have been endeavoring to squirt a dark cloud to protect himself and at the same time blind the enemy he feared. Certainly there was as much desperation as malice in the venom he spewed out in the rest of the letter.

"But I must end this with a devout wish that God may yet bless him & you & that Success may crown all your endeavors & between you your poor Sister Rosalie may not suffer. At least She is half your Sister & God forbid my dear Henry that We should visit upon the living the Errors and frailties of the dead. . . ." [3]

Why the stress on Rosalie, mentioned with such pietistic consideration? Mr. Allan's pity, however, was not aroused by the girl's arrested development, which by this time was patent to all. What moved that sterling character was the conviction that Rosalie was only *half* Henry's sister—in other words, that she was illegitimate. By that accusation he sought perhaps to justify his own frailty, in case Edgar had discovered too much and might make a confidant of his brother.

Mr. Allan's letter makes the first open allusion to what has been known as the Poe family mystery. Yet like the Holy Roman Empire—"neither holy nor Roman nor an empire"—the Poe family arcanum was neither a secret nor a mystery. The tangible source, Mrs. David Poe's packet of letters, which Mr. Allan had long pondered, later fell to Edgar and, subsequently, to Mrs. Clemm, who always hinted at "dark family troubles that had worried Eddie." One of her first acts, after Poe's death, was to destroy these letters, believing that thus she would obliterate all record of these troubles.

Unfortunately, long before that, whatever secrets the packet contained had been revealed to other eyes. Indeed, Henry may already have known of the doubt that had been cast on Rosalie's legitimacy, for Mr. Allan's letter makes no revelation but boldly asserts: *At least she is half your sister.* In any case, whenever it was that Henry had made the discovery, the allegations in Mr. Allan's epistle were

[3] *Ibid.*

of too shocking a nature to keep to himself. What more natural than for Henry to share the painful knowledge with his brother, to whom, perhaps, it was no secret?

In 1827 the *Baltimore North American* which printed many of Henry Poe's effusions published a poem, "In a Pocketbook," preceded by the note: "In a pocket book I lately found three locks of hair, from which originated the following lines:

> My Father's—I will bless it yet—
> For thou hast given life to me;
> Tho' poor the boon—I'll ne'er forget
> The filial love I owe to thee.
>
> My Mother's too!—then let me press
> This gift of her I love so well—
> For I have had thy last caress,
> And heard thy long, thy last farewell.
>
> My Rosa's! pain doth dim my eye,
> When gazing on this pledge of thine—
> Thou wert a dream—a falsity—
> Alas!—'tis wrong to call thee mine!
>
> A Father! He hath loved indeed!
> A Mother! she hath blessed her son,—
> But Love is like the pois'ning weed
> That taints the air it lives upon."

It was signed with the initials W.H.P.—William Henry Poe.

There can be only one interpretation for these lines, the one which Thomas O. Mabbott and Hervey Allen originally gave, in *Poe's Brother:* that the Rosa of the poem was Rosalie, "a dream, a falsity" because she was not really the poet's sister. Hence he could not rightly call her his. Because of the initials they naturally attributed the poem to Henry. However, that same year Henry also published in the *North American* a number of selections from Edgar's recently printed *Tamerlane and Other Poems,* again signing them with his own initials. This fact and internal evidence in the poem itself point, rather, to Edgar as the author. First of all, Rosa was the name by which Edgar and the Allans knew Rosalie.[4] Then that lock of her hair, in the pocketbook, together with her father's and her mother's, would more likely have been found among the possessions of the Allans, who had kept for Mrs. Poe's orphans the few trifles which the young actress had left behind.

[4] See reference to her in Mr. Allan's letter, p. 39.

Again, though poetic license will permit a poet to transport himself wherever imagination dictates, it was Edgar and not Henry—then in Baltimore—who, in Richmond, had had his mother's long, last farewell. Moreover, both the meter and the rhyme scheme were those most frequently used by Edgar at the time of the writing, and are found in the opening quatrains of the poem "Tamerlane."

In the two closing lines of "In a Pocketbook" the poet reveals the bitterness of the knowledge he had acquired. It is a bitterness that makes him condemn love itself, the culprit evil. Its condemnation in such vehement terms becomes all the more significant after the apostrophe to his parents. "A Father! he hath loved indeed!" he cries, as if to draw a distinction between such love and the poisoning weed. Of his mother he can only say, "She hath blessed her son"—going from there to that other love "that taints the air it lives upon." Perhaps, as he wrote, the poet may not have been aware of the implications, but subliminal intentions will out.

If Henry and Edgar had such knowledge, how much did the Baltimore Poes know? Eliza's omission of any inquiry about Rosalie when she wrote to Mrs. Allan in 1813 is certainly open to the interpretation that Edgar's sister was no concern of the Poes. Neither then nor at any time did they manifest any interest in the girl. To them Rosalie might as well have been a stranger.

Stubbornly, through the years, doubt clung to the paternity of Rosalie. One authority unconvincingly tried to foist her upon Mr. Mackenzie; others contented themselves with inferences. Still others rejected the doubt halfheartedly in the pious observance of the dictum that only good should be said of the dead.

Still, the letters existed, read by Mr. Allan, who drew the obvious conclusion, preserved by Edgar and ultimately destroyed by Mrs. Clemm, who took the secret to the grave yet left the question behind her.

Edgar knew the letters' contents. He was never close to Rosalie and, as he grew older, felt ill at ease, if not overtly annoyed, by her too-demonstrative affection. Deep within, he sought to cancel the cause of his trouble by pretending he was younger than Rosalie, and in later life he would juggle his birth date with hers, as if by that expedient he could rid her of the taint of illegitimacy and himself of a gnawing doubt.

Why had Elizabeth Poe kept that obviously incriminating correspondence? Why was it not destroyed at her death? Why had Mr. Allan preserved it? And what made Edgar keep it and carry it with him on the many migrations of his agitated life? Obviously the letters had been worth keeping, for reasons of sentiment and, no doubt, for the importance of the correspondent. Moreover, that the letters existed at all implied that their writer was not of Mrs. Poe's immediate circle, or a member of her regular acting company. Also, he must have come within the orbit of her life during 1809 and 1810, to lend substance to the doubt surrounding Rosalie's birth. Furthermore, David Poe's behavior at that period has to be taken into consideration, since he was the one whom a sentimental attachment for another, on the part of his wife, would deeply affect.

The man could not have been either Fennell or Cooper, the two most renowned actors with whom Betty had been intermittently on the stage since 1807. They were neither young nor romantic. Moreover, she had then been in love with David, whose first son she had just borne. During 1807 and 1808 David Poe had appeared constantly on the boards, even in the smallest parts, in his ambition to perfect himself in the art. Though he drank convivially, he kept within the limits of sobriety.

Then, in the spring of 1809, came a noticeable change in him. His second son, Edgar, born in January, was a new source of responsibility in an existence dogged by insecurity. Now more than ever David felt the hazards of an actor's life. In desperation he went south to borrow money from a nephew. He was unsuccessful. On his return he found Boston in high excitement over the engagement of John Howard Payne. He noticed the exaltation of Betty as she played against so young and attractive a Romeo, so noble a Tancred, while he, David Poe, trailed along in insignificant roles. He now began drinking to excess. As Betty's star rose, his, on the contrary, sank lower and lower. He was a failure both as an actor and as a man.

Payne, at this time, was at the peak of his fame, the social lion wherever he went. Women swooned over him and men envied him. "Evidence . . . tends to show that Payne was not unlike the proverbial sailor, with his 'girl in every port,' " writes W. T. Hanson. "Certain it is that the number of the opposite sex with whom, at various times, he believed himself desperately in love could not be counted on the fingers of both hands." [5] Had Betty Poe been one of them? Only the letters could have told. Only the letters and the subsequent behavior of the individuals concerned.

Payne's Boston engagement, at any rate, saw the beginning of a friendship which was to bring within its sphere other members of the Poe family. "My early recollections of Baltimore," wrote Payne,

[5] W. T. Hanson, Jr., *The Early Life of John Howard Payne.*

"attach me to that city deeply, unalterably. What a society I recollect on my first visit there, in boyhood! . . . The survivors of the society of the time . . . will all remember a very eccentric and entertaining person there by the name of Sam Poe. He had a brother who, at one time, was on the stage. Sam was a sea captain but a better actor than his brother, though never on the stage himself. . . ." [6]

After his Boston performances Payne had played in Baltimore for twelve consecutive nights. The theater was filled to overflowing. He was the idol of the hour. While in that city it would have been natural for him to look up the Poes. At any rate, a friendship did exist with Samuel Poe. "He was lost, I understand, soon after I knew him," Payne recorded, "lost overboard on a voyage to the West Indies. . . ." [7] It is revealing that the one reference which Payne makes to David Poe is derogatory.

Then, in the spring of 1810, through March and April, Payne had again been acting with Elizabeth Poe, this time at the Park Theatre, where she had been playing since the previous September. They had four performances together, two of them in *Romeo and Juliet*. It was at this time that David Poe, who had not been seen on the boards for months, began drinking to excess. In July he vanished from Betty's life, though she was then pregnant.

After the season's closing performance that same July, Mrs. Poe was dropped from the Park Theatre roster while a stage cabal, headed by Cooper, compelled Payne to seek his fortunes elsewhere.

What link connected all these circumstances? Had David Poe deliberately left his wife out of jealousy and suspicion as to the paternity of the child she was bearing? F. W. Thomas, a reliable witness, speaking of David's disappearance, called it desertion, saying that he had been told by a lawyer intimate with the family that Edgar's father had deserted his mother in New York. Had Cooper dropped from his roster an actress he admired because he too may have entertained misgivings on moral grounds? It is certain that Mrs. Poe never played with Cooper again. At any rate, David Poe's disappearance at that particular time, combined with Elizabeth's pregnancy and cause for suspicion in the prevalent conception of stage morals, succeeded in building up a black cloud that has always overshadowed the Poe family. [8]

[6] Payne, "Random Scraps and Recollections from the Note Book of a Wanderer." *The Ladies' Companion*, August, 1837.

[7] *Ibid.*

[8] Certainly Rosalie did not look like Edgar or Henry, in feature or coloring. There is, however, a marked resemblance between her and Payne, judging by two likenesses showing them in their maturer years. The eminent portrait painter

When Henry Poe came to visit his brother in the summer of 1825, Mr. Allan's life had undergone a miraculous change, thanks to the considerate demise of his uncle, William Galt, who left him the bulk of his fortune while not neglecting his numerous kin. Mr. Galt had died in March. Not long after that the Allans installed themselves in the old house at Fourteenth Street and Tobacco Alley which Mr. Galt had also willed his favorite nephew. The old-fashioned building, however, did not suit the social ambitions of the now wealthy Allans, who yearned for a more aristocratic neighborhood. When the handsome house of the Andalusian flour merchant, Joseph Gallego, came up for auction after his decease, John Allan bid for it and got it for $14,950—a bargain, considering that Mr. Gallego had paid $4,000 more for it and had, moreover, beautified it with gardens, lawns, flower beds, grape arbors and fig trees dear to the heart of Mediterranean people.

Situated at Fifth and Main Streets, its double tier of columned porches along the right side, its gracious doorway and the tall, wide windows that let the sunlight into the high-ceilinged rooms of its two stories, told plainly that here was the impressive residence of a substantial citizen. Tall elms sentineled the entrance and a great sweep of garden descended beyond the lawns. In those days when views were in fashion, the Allan house afforded one of the finest, the Valley of the James, stretching out for miles.

The house, originally built for the United States marshal, David Meade Randolph, had been designed for entertaining. A large, octagonal dining room led to the front room directly across the hall. Up above was an even larger octagon, a vast ballroom, whose lusters had lighted many an elegant occasion. There were, besides, a guest room and three or four other bedrooms and alcoves. As the master of the house, Mr. Allan appropriated the front chamber on the second floor, over the entrance, commanding the comings and goings along the drive.

Oddly enough, in an edifice with such an abundance of space, Edgar was allotted a small room on the second floor, in the northeast corner, just off the turn of the stairs. But he had the panorama of the James, with its calm islets along the frothing rapids and a view of the sky and the stars at night. Ma saw to it that it was comfortably

---

Gerald Brockhurst, when shown the pictures of Payne and Rosalie, without knowing who they were, declared: "Allowing for the difference in their age when the likenesses were made, there is a distinct resemblance in the setting of the eyes, in the spring of the nose and its length, and also, discounting the man's beard, in the chin line."

furnished and that there was a shelf for Edgar's *Don Quixote* and *Joe Miller,* his Milton and Byron, his Scott and his Coleridge and whatever odds and ends of books he had been able to appropriate from the Ellis and Allan shelves. Such imported periodicals as the *Edinburgh Review* and *Blackwood's,* as well as the *London Critical Review* and the *Ladies' Magazine* the Allans kept, as in other fine Richmond houses, in an appropriately massive bookcase, topped with some bust, like that of Pallas, which the Allans had brought from England. Mr. Allan contributed an item to Edgar's room, a brass desk set consisting of an inkwell and a sandcaster, which had been given to him or which he had bought in 1813. At any rate, his name and the date were on it. The set had its appropriate place on Edgar's writing table, where, besides providing him with ink, it served as a reminder of what shining glory one might attain if, like Mr. Allan, one worked hard enough.

It was to the new house that Henry Poe, in a nautical uniform, came to visit his brother. He was taller than Edgar, though slight, like him, with a pleasant countenance that was both spiritual and sensual. His service, either in the merchant marine or in some branch of the navy, had given him the opportunity to see the world, during voyages that often kept him from home for months. It also allowed the unstable and too-precocious youth the license to indulge his propensity to drink and women, both of which also found sublimation in poetical outpourings.

To Henry his brother's lot, in contrast to his own, must have seemed like something out of a fairy tale. There was no Empire furniture decorated with ormolu in Grandmother Poe's house. There were no marble busts by Canova, no rich draperies and deep carpets, no paintings; there was no beautiful agate lamp at the head of the landing. After the death of General Poe the situation of the Baltimore Poes had become so grave, what with Grandmother Poe's paralytic stroke and the drowning of Samuel Poe, that the helpless old woman had to abandon her home and go to live with her daughter Maria, who had married a widower, William Clemm, in 1817. There, at least, Maria's good management made the widow's small pension stretch to the limit. There too, when on land, Henry made his home.

To the youth who had had to make his own way in the world so early in life, Edgar was indeed the child of fortune that Eliza Poe had called him. What a luxurious dwelling, what wealth, and what elegance of wardrobe in Edgar's closet! One may be sure that Mr. Allan took the opportunity to point out in the presence of Henry the many advantages enjoyed by the sulky and ill-tempered boy, who possessed not a spark of affection or gratitude for his benefactors.

Did the two brothers talk of Mr. Allan's letter, complaining so bitterly about Edgar? Did they go to the Mackenzies to visit Rosalie? Did Henry, who was probably seeing his sister, a plump, awkward girl of fourteen, for the first time, surreptitiously scan her face with its large nose and blue eyes, and compare it with Edgar's and his finely cut features and deep-gray, almost black, irises? Still, even if the brothers did trouble themselves with thoughts of past unhappiness and future sorrow, they were both young and both poets. It was far better to scan the heavens through the telescope on the veranda of the Allan house, and conjecture on what the stars held for them.

Part Two

CHAPTER VII

-》》》 • 《《《-

First Love

ONE day the two brothers, accompanied by Edgar's friend Ebenezer Burling, went to call on Miss Royster, at her house on Fifth Street, opposite the Allans'. The Roysters had long known both partners of the Ellis and Allan firm, in John Allan's case sufficiently well for Mr. Royster to have lent him money during a difficult period, late in 1810. Their friendly relations had continued through the years, though it was not until the favorable change in the Allan fortunes that Edgar began to visit the young lady of the house. He had become aware of Elmira after his grief over the death of Mrs. Stanard had subsided but while the poetic melancholy for the lost Helen still lingered, making the grieving heart especially vulnerable.

Sarah Elmira Royster was about Edgar's age. She was not beautiful but she had a graceful figure and a wistful face framed in glossy black hair, parted in the middle. Her eyes, large and grave, possessed that hint of sadness which always appealed to Edgar. The mouth was sensual but finely curved. She was at that stage when the body was beginning to shape itself into womanliness, though the face was still a child's, with a child's wonder.

The romantic boy fell in love with her, another Byron with his Mary Chaworth. Elmira returned his love with all the innocence of her sixteen years. He began to call on her. Sometimes he would take her out for a walk, leading her to a place that had long been dear to him, the lovely old garden across from the house of Charles Ellis. It was within its walled enclosure, in the shade of its lindens, amid clouds of fragrance from roses and honeysuckle, that he first dreamed of love and poetry and fame. It was here that he began to speak to Elmira of his future and of his ambitions.

Since, after the inheritance the Allans had risen in prestige, the Roysters did not discourage the visits of their "son," an excellent catch, whom many a matron of Richmond would have been happy to capture for her daughter. Moreover, even before their good for-

73

tune, the Allans had moved in the best Richmond circles, which included the Stanards and Chief Justice Marshall, Judge Cabell and Dr. Brockenbrough. As for the lad himself, he was an accomplished young gentleman in his behavior, reserved, soft-spoken and with impeccable manners. Still, to those who knew—and who did not, in that close society?—there remained the stigma of Poe's actor parents, a stigma, however, which could be overlooked if one considered the wealth he might someday inherit.

So Edgar, happy in his Elmira, was often in her parlor, confiding his dreams, or singing with her some sentimental ditty of the period, while she primly accompanied their voices on the piano. Sometimes he brought Mr. Allan's flute, which he had learned to play, and entertained her with a simple melody. Most of the time they would simply sit and hold hands, letting their young hearts speak for them. Edgar, who was skillful with the crayon, delighted to sketch her. One of these portraits shows a childlike face gazing out thoughtfully on the world. Under its draperies the budding young body is awkwardly outlined, yet a delicate sensibility still glows in the drawing.

"He was a beautiful boy," Elmira remembered the Edgar of those days. "Not very talkative. When he did talk though he was pleasant but his general manner was sad. . . ." [1]

Edgar had cause for sadness. Turmoil reigned in the Allan family despite affluent circumstances. If the sins of Mr. Allan had not yet caught up with him, rumor had, penetrating even the massive portals of his new house. Just how much Frances Allan learned one cannot know, but it was enough to bring her unhappiness and to make the walls echo with recrimination. Under the circumstances the presence of a sixteen-year-old of more than ordinary awareness was hardly desirable to the man who only recently had closed his hypocritical letter to Henry Poe by commending him to God, adding: "Rely on him my brave and excellent boy who is ready to save to the uttermost." It may be he was hoping that divine salvation would also include a sinful hypocrite.

Meanwhile, since March, 1825, Edgar had ceased attending Mr. Burke's school. He had reached the age when young men were expected to decide on their future career, and that career Mr. Allan took for granted would be the honorable one which he himself had so lucratively pursued. Toward that end he had seen to it that Edgar made himself useful at the store, measuring out yard goods, filling out orders and sometimes even delivering them. But, though Edgar himself was harnessed, his mind enjoyed its freedom to dream its

[1] Valentine Collection.

dreams beyond the computation of profit and loss. It was also at leisure to brood upon the wrongs inflicted upon the dreamer who already thought of himself as a poet. Sometimes, as he sat idle before the clutter of bills and orders on the counting table, he would scribble whatever occurred to his fancy. "Poetry. By Edgar A. Poe—" he wrote on a sheet covered with a reckoning in Mr. Allan's bold hand-writing. Below, in an almost microscopic hand, Edgar added:

> Last night with many cares by—toils opress'd [*sic*]
> Weary . . . I laid me on a couch to rest—[2]

Whether he had been interrupted that day in November, 1824, or whether inspiration failed, he left the couplet suspended. As poetry it gave little indication of future greatness, though it uncannily fore-shadowed the mood of the first two lines of "The Raven," even to the occurrence of the word "weary." As an expression of Edgar's state of mind it told much. The period coincided with that of Mr. Allan's letter to Henry. The two facts together—Edgar's couplet and Mr. Allan's diatribe against him—were not only warnings but actual confirmation of the tempests between them. Edgar was no longer a child. Mr. Allan found him inconvenient to have around, especially when he saw that in the domestic camp Edgar was aligned against him. Under the circumstances his wisest move would be to send him packing, but that move would have to be made in consonance with his claim that so far he had done his duty toward Edgar more faithfully than toward God.

He was therefore as much affronted as shocked when Edgar would not hear of dedicating himself to the cashbox. There were scenes and altercations when the hard-hitting merchant hurled accusations of ingratitude at his stubborn opponent's head, while demanding how Edgar expected to earn his bread which, so far, had been provided by him, John Allan. Had he not already given him, who lived by the grace of his charity, a much superior education than he had re-ceived himself? What did the ingrate intend to do?

Perhaps like the autobiographical Thingum Bob, in his satire of a later day, Edgar answered: "Father, pardon me. . . . It is my firm intention to cut the shop. I would be an editor—I would be a poet. . . . Pardon me and aid me to be great. . . . I will repay you by making you the father of a genius. . . ."[3]

It may be Edgar also pointed out that such education as he had had, though superior to Mr. Allan's, was not sufficient to equip him

[2] *Ellis and Allan Papers.*
[3] "The Literary Life of Thingum Bob, Esq."

for a career. Perhaps, however, even without such argument, Mr. Allan may have been troubled by public opinion, which assuredly would expect such a prominent citizen, especially in his present affluence, to give his son the utmost advantages.

As it happened, thanks to Jefferson's talent for materializing his dreams, Edgar would not have to go far away. In March of that very year of 1825, the University of Virginia had opened the doors of higher learning to its first students.

Though not the Oxford of the New World which Jefferson had envisioned, the ranks of classical buildings about a rectangular lawn, dominated by the Rotunda, had a natural setting which many a European university, hemmed in by the accretion of centuries, might have envied. The town of Charlottesville itself, founded on part of the Castle Hill estate of Washington's friend Thomas Walker, had the beautiful Rivanna flowing through it and, for a battlement, the irregular and constantly changing setting of the Blue Ridge and the Ragged Mountains.

The Rotunda, modeled on Rome's Pantheon, was a symbol of aspiration made concrete in stone, although of the half hundred students whose names were inscribed in the matriculation records that first semester, few indeed knew of either Pantheons or symbols. However, it was enough for its farseeing originator—whose tireless hand, besides writing requests for contributions, had also drawn up the architectural plans—that at last, through nautilus stages of building statelier mansions from a modest beginning in 1817, the University of Virginia was a visible fact, glowing from marble façade and mighty dome. To the man nearing his eighty-third year, it had the weightiness of a monument. Thus, when he assessed his claims to be remembered, he chose for his epitaph: "Here was buried Thomas Jefferson, author of the Declaration of American Independence, of the Statute of Virginia for religious freedom, and Father of the University of Virginia."

Greater than the physical aspects of the university were the animating ideas that would give it significance. Founding his system on the European seats of learning, Jefferson abolished the formal class with its compulsory attendance. He made military drill and chapel worship optional, and dispensed with discipline in his faith that young gentlemen, placed upon their honor, would live up to their title and respect the code. The better to break the barrier between student and authority, he would often invite a few of the young men to Sunday dinner at Monticello, and he encouraged the professors to follow his example.

Unfortunately the young gentlemen, though from eminent and

worthy families, were, in matters of behavior, as wild as the untilled acres which surrounded the architectural discipline of the university buildings—with the difference that it was far simpler to tame wild nature into lawns and gardens than to make such scholars as Jefferson dreamed of out of the unruly material placed under the guidance of his staff of imported professors. Most of them had been culled from Oxford and Cambridge. Professor George Blaettermann alone had been born in Germany. There was also an American, George Tucker, whom the aged charmer had lured from the halls of Congress to become chairman of the faculty and adorn the podium of Moral Philosophy. Perhaps Tucker's was the hardest task of all, for he had to take disciplinary measures in an institution that frowned upon discipline and inculcate moral philosophy in minds that had small notion of either morals or philosophy. The others, competent in their particular fields, represented the best instructors available at the time; but, accustomed as they were to the academic tradition of Europe, with its almost ritualistic procedures, they often found themselves unable to cope with the results of Jefferson's innovations.

The noble experiment was in its second year when, for various reasons, Mr. Allan thought it expedient to send Edgar to the University of Virginia. For the purpose, he first engaged a tutor to prepare the boy for matriculation. Dutifully Edgar studied his lessons while managing to spend part of his time with Ma, who looked upon his impending departure as a mournful necessity. For the lonely woman it would mean parting from a being she cherished, whose love had sustained her in the trying times which had fallen upon the household, despite Mr. Galt's shower of gold. Her husband's dropsy had grown worse. He now had to lean upon a stout stick which, whenever his temper exploded, he would brandish like a lance, at the risk of losing his balance. "Old Swell-foot," unsympathetic townsfolk called him.

During these trying times Elmira's parlor, or the linden-shaded garden where they would walk hand in hand, became Edgar's refuge. Their hearts beat joyfully at the thought of their marrying and living happily ever after, as the fairy tales promised, and to make that happiness come true they pledged themselves to each other. "I was about fifteen or sixteen when . . . I engaged myself to him," Elmira remembered.[4]

When the time came for Edgar to leave for Charlottesville, in the middle of February, 1826, it was not Mr. Allan but his invalid wife who sat beside the youth in the carriage that Mr. Galt had left her in

[4] Valentine Collection.

his will. The old Negro coachman, James Hill, noticed that as they sat, clasping each other's hand during the journey, Mrs. Allan and the young master looked very sad.

Both had their reasons. For Mrs. Allan it meant being more alone than ever in that grand house, more divided than ever from the husband she now knew to be unfaithful and whose autocratic nature brooked no contradiction. For her the departure of Edgar put an end to the only comfort she had in her empty life. Edgar's sadness sprang from his having to leave Elmira, and perhaps more from his associations with the city which he had known as home. In Richmond his mother had enjoyed her final triumphs. There her body lay, in that grave near the wall in the old burial ground. There he had caught his first glimpse of ideal beauty, grieved over his first loss and thrilled to the stirrings of his poetic imagination. In Richmond he had parted from Rosalie and, earlier, said good-by to Henry, about to embark as a midshipman for South America. Somehow Edgar's memories were a series of good-bys, some already made final by death.

Before taking leave of Mrs. Allan, Edgar drew the coachman aside to give him a letter and a small package for Miss Royster. The packet held a parting gift, a purse in mother-of-pearl. There were embraces and tears as he parted from Ma and friendly good-bys with Jim Hill. The carriage then disappeared in the distance and with it the moneyed ease it had denoted. As his portion of that wealth Edgar had with him $110, supplied by Mr. Allan to defray his immediate expenses at the university, which amounted to $150.

It was on St. Valentine's Day, sacred to lovers but not to scholars, that Edgar's name and vital statistics were recorded in the matriculation book. In the uncanny way of cold facts in revealing what is not stated, the simple notations told much. The new student, one of a record 177, was called *Poe;* his *guardian* was John Allen (*sic*); his place of residence, Richmond. A gulf of nearly ten years lay between Master Edgar *Allan* of the Stoke Newington Manor House School and the Edgar A. *Poe* of the University of Virginia. A still wider chasm divided the grave-faced youth and the man who had once allowed him to use his name. Now that, for this first time, Edgar was left to face life alone, it was with the understanding that he was to do so not as Allan but as Poe.

For some time, since Edgar's adolescent awareness of the facts of life, the situation at home had been building up to a crisis because of the growing resentment in Mr. Allan at finding himself silently, and at the same time overtly, accused for his sins. In his own estimation he was no worse than most men and a great deal better than many, yet he was made to feel guilty. By an illogical though human reversal, he began to believe that he was the injured party. Accordingly, he resented Edgar's loyalty to Mrs. Allan and her no less faithful defense of Edgar in his occasional flouting or paternal authority. As, with time, the family alignment became more precisely defined, Mr. Allan began to see himself on the losing side—because of this stranger whom he had taken into his house in a moment of weakness, to please his childless wife.

He was virile, despite his ailment, and if his wife's health continued declining as it had been doing, there might be another Mrs. Allan someday, by whom he would have legitimate offspring. As for Edgar, Mr. Allan had assumed a responsibility and he was willing to fulfill it; but he was doing it out of duty, which is punctilious, rather than out of love, which is generous. Being what he was, John Allan saw to it that love never infringed upon duty. Clearly, his duty was to give the boy an adequate preparation for his start in life. It was as much as the best of fathers grant the sons of their own flesh and blood. Edgar could expect no more.

Edgar did expect more, however. But it was in the sphere of sympathy and understanding, to which the good merchant was an alien by the limitations of his nature. Though not an evil man—indeed, except for his sins of the flesh which, in his situation, the whole male population of Richmond would have condoned—he was a model of rectitude, though of that rectitude which would sooner break than bend. He knew what was right and what was wrong to the least shading of their white or black, but in practice he chose to ignore the variations.

He therefore felt duty bound to clarify his position with regard to Edgar, when letters began arriving from Charlottesville to Elmira in Richmond. Mr. Allan and Mr. Royster were friends and neighbors. Both occupied a respectable position in the community. What more desirable than an alliance between the son of the one and the daughter of the other, particularly when the young people had already plighted their troth? Unfortunately matters did not stand between Mr. Allan and his son as Mr. Royster and, no doubt, the rest of Richmond had been led to believe. The upright merchant, therefore, thought it his duty to illuminate him. Mr. Royster reacted as any father of an idolized daughter would when he learned that the apparent heir of the Allan house was unlikely to be an heir at all. Without disturbing Elmira's dream by a word, the Roysters simply intercepted Edgar's letters to her and saw to it that hers never reached him. To make doubly sure that Elmira would not pine away, Mr. Royster introduced another

Romeo upon the scene—Mr. A. Barrett Shelton, wellborn, mature and, most important, rich.

In a day when parental authority was law, the young girl submitted, even if she was left a prey to doubt and sorrow. How could Edgar have forgotten her so soon? Not a word from him. Not even the least reply to her letters. Wounded at the thought that she could have meant so little to him, encouraged in her mistaken belief by her parents, who missed no opportunity to extol the rich Mr. Shelton, Elmira little by little resigned herself to the new courtship. She was nearing seventeen, a ripe age as Southern marriage went.

Edgar, meanwhile, was attuning himself to university life, which in its pristine days held many a discord. He registered for two courses in the term closing December 15, 1826: Professor Blaettermann's classes in French, Italian and Spanish, and Professor Long's in Ancient Languages and Literatures. He lodged briefly in a chamber on the west side of the lawn and then moved to Number 13, West Range, which he occupied by himself. The room, on ground level, was simple, spacious, with a fireplace in which he could burn whatever he found unworthy in the pages he was now covering, and a door that opened upon the country, with its backdrop of the Ragged Mountains. The single window looked out unaesthetically upon the woodpile of Conway's boardinghouse.

Within, the walls and ceiling of the room were smooth and inviting. With the help of an illustrated volume of Byron's works Edgar soon converted his lodging into a poet's shrine by copying the steel engravings in charcoal upon every available inch of space. If, among the pictures was one of Mary Chaworth playing the tinkling spinet for the lovelorn poet, what memories it must have brought of Elmira, whose letters had suddenly, unaccountably ceased. What could have happened? Was she ill? Had the Roysters left town? But that would not have kept Elmira from writing. Had she—the thought was torture—had she, like Mary Chaworth, fallen in love with another? There seemed to be a conspiracy of silence about Elmira in the correspondence from home.

Despite his anxiety and the torment of his imaginings, Edgar managed to be included among the top four students in the Senior Latin Class and the best eight in Senior French. In Professor Blaettermann's course in Italian Literature he distinguished himself to the point of eliciting praise for a verse translation from Tasso. "Das is gud," interjected the young German as he scanned the lines with lifted finger, amazed at having found one responsive voice in the wilderness. Like

Blaettermann, Professor Long too had reason to be pleased with Edgar's progress in the classics.

Under Jefferson's system the school curriculum gave the students a long full day in which to work or idle. Shortly after sunrise, William Wertenbaker, the librarian and official alarm clock, would go knocking at the doors to rouse the young men, some of whom had barely gone to bed. Classes began immediately after breakfast. Since Edgar's courses started at seven and ended at nine, he had the rest of the day to spend as he pleased. Reading was one of his pleasures. The endlessly fascinating Byron, now more than ever adored for having died so fittingly at Missolonghi, was still the poet idol of the day, and although the university library excluded him, Number 13 West Range thrilled to the low, well-modulated voice of its occupant reading of Childe Harold and the Isles of Greece to a handful of youths who were as much impressed by the inspired face of the reader as by the poetry.

His own poems Edgar kept for the most part to himself and a few privileged intimates. He was more generous, if also more reckless, with his attempts in prose. One evening he was reading an original story of a certain Gaffy while his friends sat listening by the fire, now and then quaffing their hot apple toddy. The story was long, the name of the hero unromantic. Partly in fun they began criticizing the tale and the hero when, with an impulsive gesture, Edgar flung the manuscript into the fire. In a moment it was turned to ashes, but the name "Gaffy" Poe with which he was christened that evening clung to him for a long time.

In his reading he meandered mostly through the regions of his choice. There was the much frowned-upon Shelley, whose atheistical reputation had outlived his premature death. There too was Keats, his lyre broken but his music still echoing. Above them towered the giants, Coleridge and Wordsworth. Of the two it was Coleridge whom Edgar read with deeper interest and emulous zeal, especially the disquisitions on poetry. Above them both, however, Edgar, sharing the myopia of his age, placed Byron's friend, the popular Tom Moore, with his graceful lyrics and his Oriental poetic romances. Another Thomas, the Scottish Campbell, Poe devoured for his melancholy ballads and haunting refrains.

On the ponderous, scholarly side was Charles Rollin's *Histoire Ancienne* wherein Edgar delved into Greece and Rome, his Holy Land of the spirit, the dictionary coming to his aid whenever French failed him. In that language he also attempted Voltaire, though what he read by that saturnine genius has left little discernible trace in his work. Italian and Spanish were not neglected, nor did Edgar fail to make use of Nicholas Dufief's aid to the study of language in its English translation, *Nature Displayed in her Mode of Teaching Language to Man.* The descriptive subtitle could not but have appealed to the intellectually acquisitive youth of quick perceptions and phenomenal memory, especially in its offer of an infallible method of acquiring a language "in the shortest time possible, deduced from the analysis of the human mind and consequently suited to every capacity." The words had the sort of ring to allure a curious intellect which preferred interest and diversity to depth.

As far as Edgar's scholarship was concerned, neither the professors nor Mr. Allan had cause to complain. At any rate, Pa seemed pleased with his progress and in May sent him a uniform coat, six yards of striped cloth for pantaloons—probably from the Ellis and Allan stock —and four pairs of socks. After all, whether as son or ward of John Allan, the boy must make a good appearance.

However, while showing so much concern for the outward man, Mr. Allan kept Edgar on such short financial rations that the youth was soon crying famine. Life at the university consisted of much more than studying and attending classes. A whole colony of merchants, each with his special ware or service to dispense, had sprung up about Charlottesville, and it was to the little courthouse town, with its few hundred residents, that the university's gilded youth resorted to release energy which their studies scarcely tapped. Many of them made no pretense whatever of their true purpose, in which learning played little part. They had merely shifted their locale, no doubt on family insistence, but their mode of life remained unaltered. One arrived with his tandem of blooded horses, his personal servant and his dogs. Another brought his case of dueling pistols. All carried with them their large or petty vices and a common eagerness to indulge them.

Quarrels and violence were thus the order of the day in a community to which none other than Professor Blaettermann set a shocking example by cowhiding his screaming wife in public. As for fights between men, brutality prevailed and everything was permitted—gouging, biting, every foul means of winning a victory. "I saw the whole affair," Edgar wrote home of one such fray between two fellow students. "It took place before my door—Wickliffe was much the stronger but not content with that—after getting the other completely in his power, he began to bite— I saw the arm afterwards—and it was really a serious matter— It was bitten from the shoulder to the elbow—and it is likely that pieces of flesh as large as my hand will be obliged to be cut out. . . ." [5]

Previously, that same Wickliffe had been one of a group suspended for grave infractions which had caused the Grand Jury to meet. Immediately the students, especially those whose names were on the sheriff's list, took to the woods, carrying bedding and provisions with them. There were some fifty on the list, but as only one was expelled the moral victory seemed slight indeed. Fighting, gambling and drinking went on as before, despite the dormitory supervisors upon whose beneficial influence Jefferson had relied. But since these hotelkeepers, as they were called, consisted of gentlemen in reduced circumstances, they willingly closed an eye to what was going on, when they did not actively participate. Gambling, according to the tenets of the day, was a gentleman's sport, and the young bloods indulged in it freely.

Death, however, spared Jefferson the worst of the students' exploits, if also the Fourth of July celebrations of 1826. On that same day another grand old man, John Adams, left the world. For two months the faculty and students wore mourning on the left arm, but the tenor of their days remained unchanged.

Edgar had entered into his new life unprepared both financially and psychologically for what was expected of him. Within a week he wrote Mr. Allan for money, only to be answered by a letter full of abuse. When Pa finally sent the balance of what was owed the university, Edgar had exactly one dollar left over for himself. If Mr. Allan had intended telling Edgar that henceforth he was washing his hands of him he could not have done it more explicitly. But since Edgar was already at the university, he had to go on. As it was, the report spread that he was heir to a large fortune. Not only was he expected to live up to that reputation but, in the code of honor that admitted no infraction, he had to do so like a gentleman, that is, with utter disregard for cash. In vain he wrote Pa to send money for his books, for his expenses. To the first request Mr. Allan responded by sending superfluities from the shelves of the store—a two-volume *Cambridge Mathematics* and *Gil Blas*—books for which Edgar had no earthly use. As for the expenses, Mr. Allan felt that he had contributed enough and refused to pay a cent more than he thought necessary. Unfortunately, between Mr. Allan's estimate of the necessity and the actual need there was a gulf wide enough to ruin a life. Edgar had no choice but to borrow.

"Books must be had, if I intended to remain at the institution," he explained after the fact "—and they were bought accordingly *upon*

[5] *Valentine Letters*. Ostrom, *The Letters of Edgar Allan Poe*, p. 6.

credit. In this manner debts were accumulated and money borrowed of Jews in Charlottesville at extravagant interest. . . . It was then that I became dissolute, for how could it be otherwise? I could associate with no students except those who were in a similar situation with myself—altho, from different causes— They from drunkenness, and extravagance—I, because it was my crime to have no one on Earth who cared for me, or loved me. . . ." [6]

When Mr. Allan finally sent him aid, a mere hundred dollars for debts of honor and necessity which had mounted to four figures, it was too late. In his extremity Edgar had even tried to borrow from James Galt, who, from scruples of conscience, refused him the loan. "I then became desperate and gambled—until I finally involved myself irretrievably," Edgar confessed in the same letter. It did not soothe Mr. Allan's feelings to be told with manly directness: "It was wholly and entirely your own mistaken parsimony that caused all the difficulties in which I was involved. . . ." [7]

In that statement Edgar told no less than the truth. Because of Mr. Allan's niggardliness Poe had started out in debt at the university, where everything had its price, from his washing which the Negro women collected every Monday, to the sticks of wood for the fire in his hearth. He began getting what he needed on credit, a credit which the shopkeepers were glad to extend on the prospects of his rumored inheritance. At last the amount became like the proverbial snowball, gaining size with its momentum. Then, in a panic, Edgar began to gamble, hoping that luck would be on his side. But even so early unmerciful disaster followed fast and followed faster till he was inextricably deep in debt.

The night before Edgar left for Richmond for the Christmas holidays, William Wertenbaker, the librarian, walked with him to West Range. It was cold in Number 13, and the fire had died out. Impulsively Edgar took a small table, broke it up, flung the pieces upon the hearth and, with the help of some tallow candles, rekindled the fire. Talking sadly to Wertenbaker all the while about his unpaid bills and his gaming debts, he kept feeding the flames with other fragments of broken furniture. He owed about two thousand dollars, he said—a debt of honor which he was honor bound to pay.

There was a curious if unconscious finality in his burning up of his possessions, as if he felt a premonition that he would nevermore return. In a corner his small, studded, ironbound leather trunk was al-

[6] *Ibid.* Ostrom, pp. 40-41.
[7] Ostrom, p. 41.

ready packed with his clothes, his books and the manuscripts of his poems. He left nothing behind that might imply his return.

The following morning, with a group of other students, he took the Charlottesville coach. They were going home. He was going to Richmond, where he had good reason to dread Mr. Allan's wrath.

CHAPTER VIII

→≫ · ≪←

Arrival and Departure

AS IT happened, Edgar had had a foretaste of that wrath during a brief visit which Mr. Allan, with less concern for his dropsy than for his pocketbook, had made to Charlottesville several months earlier, when Edgar's unpaid bills had begun arriving, an unwelcome flock, to roost upon his rooftree. Whatever occurred at Number 13 during that explosive meeting had not chastened Edgar sufficiently, however, to keep him from incurring other debts, this time with Samuel Leitch, Jr., a merchant tailor in Charlottesville. The Christmas holidays were coming, Edgar had reasoned. He would be going home, where at last he would see again the unresponsive Elmira and find out the explanation for her silence. He must look his best to regain her love if absence had made her heart less fond. Besides, one always had new clothes for Christmas. Therefore he had spared no expense, as Mr. Leitch's bill revealed in its matter-of-fact listing, which mentioned among other luxuries a generous yardage of Super Blue Cloth, Bombazette, padding, staying; a set of the best Gilt Buttons; a pair of Drab Pantaloons and trimmings, and other finery. Edgar purchased, besides, a fine London hat and a velvet vest, to go with the elegant suit which Mr. Leitch confected for him.

Edgar arrived in Richmond on the day before Christmas. Not without trepidation, he ran up the front path between the elms and up the familiar steps into the house. Ma welcomed him with joy. Mr. Allan too had kind words for him. He had even given approval for a surprise Christmas Eve party to which Ma invited Edgar's Richmond friends. For Mr. Allan there was comfort in the fact that his expenditures at the university had not been a total loss. Edgar, he was glad to admit, had stood his final examinations with great credit to himself. Now one must wait and see.

After the first greetings and embraces Edgar was impatient to dash across the way to see Elmira. It was only to have the door shut in his face, after someone's voice informed him that she was not at home—

that Miss Royster had left Richmond. Eventually Edgar was to know the whole story, perhaps through Ma and Miss Nancy, the servants, or his friends in that close community. At any rate, that lover of sad mementos was to keep almost to the end of his days an illustration which symbolized for him his lost Elmira. It showed a white-clad maiden with streaming black hair, bowed over in grief, her face buried in a handkerchief, while at the foot of her settee a "fatal letter," discovered too late, tells the story of the deception of which she and her lover had been the victims.

To Edgar the news of Elmira's engagement to Mr. Shelton came as a brutal shock, but by that time Elmira had learned to live with the prospect of becoming the wife of a well-to-do gentleman who had demonstrated his regard by his unfailing attentions. She married him at seventeen—willingly, for even in the South, in those days, no young girl could have been forced into an undesired marriage.

To the disappointed, lovelorn youth, whose suffering his poetic sensibilities tended to aggravate, the loss of Elmira meant personal humiliation as well. Another man had been preferred to him, another to whom, willingly or not, Elmira had been given—had given herself, after all their vows. His pride, always vulnerable, was as cruelly wounded as his heart. But he had that balm which could assuage all wounds, that weapon which could wreak vengeance: his imagination which, at his command, became all things.

He had already exercised it in the poems which he had brought back with him from the university. He would exercise it now, as the proud, ambitious, all-conquering Tamerlane who won a world as a footstool for the woman he loved. After all, he, Edgar Poe, had ambitions as great as ever swelled the breastplate of the mighty conqueror, though his own were in other realms. Penniless, living on the charity of John Allan, he had that within him which could lift him far above the moneygrubbing merchant, above Mr. Royster, who did not think him, Edgar Poe, good enough for his daughter.

Toward Elmira, however, he felt nothing but love. She, like him, had been a sacrifice to family ambition. Yet he could not drive out of his mind their hours together at the piano, their walks in the rose-bowered garden which their love had turned to a place of enchantment. He could not forget the vows they had exchanged, the future they had planned, in the euphoria of an emotion which they had scarcely understood. Perhaps even now Elmira still loved him as he loved her. Nevertheless, in the humiliation of his rejection, something had died in him, revivifying with its death that pride which the unhappy vicissitudes of his young life had nurtured in him. He told his story, therefore, in the words of the dying conqueror, with all his aspirations and ambitions.

> My passions, from that hapless hour,
>   Usurp'd a tyranny which men
> Have deem'd, since I have reach'd to power,
>   My innate nature—be it so:
>   But, father, there liv'd one who, then—
> Then—in my boyhood—when their fire
>   Burn'd with a still intenser glow,
> (For passion must, with youth, expire)
>   E'en *then* who knew this iron heart
>   In woman's weakness had a part.
>
>   .   .   .   .
>
> We grew in age—and love—together,
>   Roaming the forest, and the wild;
> My breast her shield in wintry weather—
>   And, when the friendly sunshine smil'd,
> And she would mark the opening skies,
> *I* saw no Heaven—but in her eyes.
>
>   .   .   .   .
>
> I was ambitious—have you known
>   The passion, father? You have not:
> A cottager, I mark'd a throne
> Of half the world as all my own . . .

That throne Tamerlane-Poe, for purposes of art, succeeded in achieving, if only in the realm of his imagination. Then evil fate struck.

> I reach'd my home—my home no more
>   For all had flown who made it so.
> I pass'd from out its mossy door
>   And, tho' my tread was soft and low,
> A voice came from the threshold stone
> Of one whom I had earlier known—
>   O, I defy thee, Hell, to show
>   On beds of fire that burn below,
>   A humbler heart—a deeper woe.

How early Edgar arrived at such emotional purgation through poetry it is difficult to determine. He may have begun his long poem at the university in the anguish of his fears at Elmira's inexplicable silence, or he may have been impelled to it by the shock of certain knowledge. He had finished it, however, by the early summer of 1827.

Among his books there had long been a copy of Nicholas Rowe's drama, *Tamerlane,* probably once owned by his grandmother, Mrs. Arnold, and subsequently by his mother, for on the flyleaf appeared the autograph, dimly traced in pencil: Elizabeth Arnold. Moreover, among the actors listed—the edition was dated 1714—was a Mr. Arnold. The association of his mother and remoter Arnolds with the acting of the play, would have been enough to stir Edgar to read it. Then there was also that greater tragedy, Christopher Marlowe's *Tamburlaine the Great,* which Edgar could not have overlooked in some volume of the Elizabethan dramatists, either at the university library or among the stock of Ellis and Allan—for Mr. Allan had expressed admiration for at least one great Elizabethan.

In his state of humiliation and rebellion Edgar naturally sought revenge to salve his spirit. He obtained it in a sphere where those who persecuted him could not touch him—that of poetry. There Poe-Tamerlane conquered, till he could find no more worlds for his dominion.

> When Hope, the eagle that tower'd, could see
> No cliff beyond him in the sky,
> His pinions were bent droopingly—
> And homeward turn'd his soften'd eye.

Alas, home revealed itself no home to him in the world of reality, no place of refuge from bills and warrants. Its walls served only to confine him with Mr. Allan and his ill-concealed desire to have him, Edgar, out of the way. How else could Edgar interpret his reproaches, even in front of the servants, that he was eating the bread of idleness? He had often helped at Ellis and Allan's. He would have been willing to take his place behind the counter again, while waiting to return to the university. But Edgar soon realized that his days there were over. Not only did Mr. Allan refuse to pay his debts of honor, the only condition under which Edgar could have gone back to Charlottesville without losing caste, but he also lumped together with them Edgar's legitimate expenses.

Twice George W. Spotswood, Edgar's hotelkeeper, had written to Mr. Allan for payment, only to be ignored. At last, exasperated, he wrote again: "I presume that when you sent Mr. Poe to the University of Virginia you felt yourself bound to pay all his necessary expenses. . . . Mr. Poe did not board with me but as I had hired a first rate servant who cost me a high price—I consider him under greater obligations to pay for the service of my servant." [1]

[1] *Ellis and Allan Papers.*

Mr. Spotswood, like all the other creditors, pleaded in vain. Mr. Allan had no intention of mitigating a situation which, deftly handled, might succeed in relieving him of a burden that had become irksome.

Mrs. Allan as usual tried to heal the breach between the two incompatible individuals. She could do nothing, in her weakened state, but comfort Edgar and perhaps slip him a little pocket money. She doubtless pleaded with her husband to soften his heart, and it may have been at such a moment that, unwittingly, Edgar had overheard Mr. Allan say that he had no affection for him. The hurt to Edgar was keen enough for him to confront Mr. Allan with what he had overheard—"when you little thought I was listening and therefore must have said it in earnest." [2]

The smoldering antipathy between the two foreboded an explosion. It occurred on March 19, 1827, when, after hearing Mr. Allan order him out of the house once too often, Edgar impulsively left home. Little more than a week later Mr. Allan, in a letter full of financial details to one of his sisters, added almost blithely, after a comment on his wife's failure to improve: "I'm thinking Edgar has gone to Sea to seek his fortunes." [3] Not a word of the part he himself had played toward compelling Edgar to seek those fortunes, whether on sea or land. How subtle also that "I'm thinking," implying the uncertainty of a fond father at the impulsiveness of an inconsiderate son.

Edgar had had no choice but to leave home. While accusing him of eating the bread of idleness Mr. Allan had done nothing to help him earn that bread. Indeed, a letter of Edgar's, applying for employment with a Philadelphia company with which Mr. Allan had dealings, only added fuel to his fire when it was referred back to him. How dare Edgar humiliate him before his business associates? It was a deed to be expected of a "black-heart" who knew neither affection nor gratitude.

Again recriminations poured out in long, repetitive tirades that served no purpose but to set nerves and tempers on edge. The gambling debts, always the gambling debts, and then the drinking— Yes, he, John Allan, had heard all about it—his *son,* drunk, disgracing the untarnished respectability which he, Allan, had always maintained. Here Edgar, who knew what that respectability was really worth, may have spoken out at last with more plainness than tact. As the injurious truths struck home, Allan's ire became rage. "Get out of here!" One

[2] *Valentine Letters.* Ostrom, p. 7.
[3] *Ellis and Allan Papers.*

can hear him roar the words, as he waved his stick in the air. "Leave my house and find out what it means to starve!"

A final tirade—and a quivering, impulsive eighteen-year-old tore out of the house. Where could he go? He was no longer welcome at the Roysters'. His pride would not let him seek out any of the Allan relatives. He went therefore to the Court House Tavern. There, after he had composed himself sufficiently, he wrote Mr. Allan a long letter justifying himself for leaving home.

"Sir," he addressed the man he had called Pa. "After . . . what passed between us this morning, I can hardly think you will be surprised at the contents of this letter. My determination is at length taken—to leave your house and indeavor [sic] to find some place in the wide world, where I will be treated—not as *you* have treated me. . . . Since I have been able to think on any subject, my thoughts have aspired, and they have been taught by *you* to aspire, to eminence in public life." Such ambitions could not be achieved without a college education, but in a capricious moment Mr. Allan had blasted his hope. "I request that you will send me my trunk containing my clothes & books—and if you still have the least affection for me, as the last call I shall make on your bounty to prevent the fulfillment of the Prediction you this morning expressed, send me as much money as will defray the expences [sic] of my passage to some of the Northern cities & then support me for one month by which time I shall be enabled to place myself in some situation where I may not only obtain a livelihood, but lay by a sum which one day or another will support me at the University— Send me I entreat you some money immediately. . . . If you fail to comply with my request—I tremble for the consequence. . . ." [4]

If John Allan was gratified by the allusion to the high aspirations he had inculcated in Edgar, his mood changed quickly at the suggestion that he dip his hand into his moneybags. He took up his pen and, attuning himself to his sanctimonious style, charged Edgar once more with ingratitude. Unless his heart was made of marble, Poe would have to admit that he had given him, Mr. Allan, much cause to fear for his future. How could worthy ambition be achieved if Edgar insisted on wasting his time on such trash as *Don Quixote* and *Gil Blas*? If he reprimanded Edgar, it was only to correct his faults. Here the man who set store by his sense of humor could not resist taunting the youth who, while defiantly breaking all ties, asked for money or—he trembled for the consequences. He, Allan, had done all he could for the rebel. As for Edgar's accusations, Allan would not condescend to

[4] *Valentine Letters*. Ostrom, pp. 7-8.

defend himself, as the world would reply for him. With that he sealed his epistle, self-righteously congratulating himself on not sending either trunk or money.

Desperate, Edgar wrote again the following day, modifying the salutation to "Dear Sir," and charitably assuming that his foster father had not received his earlier request. "I am in the greatest necessity," he was forced to admit, "not having tasted food since Yesterday morning. I have no where to sleep at night, but roam about the streets— I beseech you as you wish not your prediction about me to be fulfilled . . . to lend if you will not give me as much money as will defray the expense of my passage to Boston ($12) and a little to support me until I shall be enabled to engage in some business. . . . Give my love to all at home," he closed, adding, "I have not one cent in the world to provide any food." [5]

Yet even to this cry Mr. Allan remained deaf. Indulging his sinister humor, he contented himself with adding an "s" to Poe's signature and the comment: "Pretty Letter."

Somehow Edgar managed to obtain the cash to leave Richmond, probably through Mrs. Allan and the Negro servant, Dabney Dandridge, who later told of carrying packages from the house on Main Street to his young master. Mrs. Allan was desolate at the turn events had taken, but she was powerless to bring about a reconciliation. Edgar was too proud to seek it and Mr. Allan did not desire it.

A few days after Edgar had left home, a letter arrived for him from a youth, Edward G. Crump, from whom he had borrowed money. "I should be glad if you would write to me even as a friend," Edward assured Edgar. "There can certainly be no harm in your avowing candidly that you have no money if you have none but you can say when you can pay me if you cannot now. . . ." [6]

Edgar never received the letter. Methodically, Mr. Allan made upon it the sardonic notation: "Edw G. Crump Mar 25, 1827 to E.A Poe, alias Henri le Rennet." One can almost see the curl of amusement about the harsh mouth as he penned the alias under which the desperate youth was trying to make a new beginning—or had Poe given himself this new name to throw the hounds with the warrants off his scent?

The name itself had a meaning for Edgar if, perhaps, for no one else. Always fond of puns—they abound in his work—he created for himself a symbol by which to guide his new life: Henri le Rennét— Henry the Reborn. He could have spelled it more conventionally,

[5] *Ibid.* Ostrom, pp. 8-9.
[6] *Ellis and Allan Papers.*

René, but that would have been too obvious. He chose, instead, a form that was wholly unacceptable in French but which satisfied his private needs. In a sense the change of name also signified an earnest desire in the youth to escape those tendencies in Edgar Poe which had brought him to the present pass.

When he started out from Richmond he was not alone. Ebenezer Burling, his old friend from Memorial Church days and a merry companion on many an escapade, had joined him on the new one. Though Ebenezer came of a good family, the Allans had frowned upon the friendship. The boy had a wild streak. He also liked to frequent the taverns from which, more often than not, he emerged with an unsteady gait. It was probably through Ebenezer, who had his own kind of credit at such establishments, that Edgar had not been wholly on the streets.

Whatever the plan the two concocted together, they got as far as Norfolk. There, whether Burling had started out drunk, sobered up and thought of the alarm to his family or whether he was simply carrying out Edgar's scheme, he left le Rennét to forge his new life alone and himself returned to Richmond. The stories he spread had such a tinge of romance that they could have come only from the hero himself. Edgar had sailed away to Europe where, like Lord Byron, he was going to fight side by side with the Greeks in their struggle for freedom. From there he would make his way through Europe, then to St. Petersburg. Edgar would show them all of what adventurous stuff he was made.

Reality, alas, was unromantic enough. While even Mr. Allan had been taken in sufficiently by the stories to believe that Edgar had gone to sea, the adventurer was working his way to Boston on a coal barge.[7] His mother, according to her own words, had found her best friends there. Perhaps the city of his birth would befriend him also. Somewhere among the few possessions that old Dab had smuggled out of the house for him were the manuscripts of his poems. The best justification that he had not misspent his life lay in those neatly written pages. Boston was New England's literary center. He would try, if not to storm it, at least to make some small dent in it.

The trees of the Common and the gardens of the tidy New England houses were showing their first green, that day in mid-April when, after renewing his childhood vision of the Harbor, Edgar, alone, poor yet hopeful and ambitious, trudged the streets of Boston in search of work and shelter. What success he had in either venture could not have been spectacular for, six weeks after his arrival, Edgar, aban-

[7] Woodberry, *The Life of Edgar Allan Poe*, Vol. I, p. 67.

doning his symbolic pseudonym, changed it to a more conventional Edgar A. Perry. This time it was neither secret symbolism nor fear of the warrant server that prompted the change, but the foreignness of le Rennét, with its hint of aristocracy, which would have raised quizzical eyebrows when, on the 26th of May, 1827, the slender youth with the refined lineaments enlisted as a private in the United States Army. What brought him to the decision was less patriotic fervor than a compromise with Mammon, all too niggardly in his opportunities for the erstwhile le Rennét.

According to Thomas H. Ellis, Edgar had been for a time on the Boston stage, a plausible profession for the son of actors to attempt, particularly since he had distinguished himself at school in declamation. But opportunities were either wanting or he failed to make an impression.

In the vital information he gave the War Department, Edgar A. Perry described himself as twenty-two years old, a native of Boston, five feet, eight inches in height, with gray eyes, brown hair and a fair complexion. He gave his occupation as clerk. The only questions Poe answered accurately were those pertaining to his birthplace and his physical appearance about which, in any case, he could not have lied. For some reason the erstwhile Reborn had suffered an incarnation into a man four years older, with a commonplace name and a modest position. The romantic had become the average man who must by all means fit into the normal pattern the Army required.

All unsuspecting that in Edgar A. Perry lay hidden a poet whose chief concern at the moment was to see his work in print, the army issued him his uniform and the raw recruit was sent to Fort Independence at Boston Harbor, to join Battery H of the First Artillery. Even with his change of name and other efforts at conformity, Edgar stood out as the one white merle among the blackbirds. Soon after his preliminary training he was transferred to the Quartermaster's Office.

Meanwhile, in his Boston wanderings, he had made the acquaintance of a youth of his own age, Calvin F. S. Thomas, who had recently acquired a printing shop on Washington Street. "Tamerlane" had grown into a poem of some four hundred lines. Poe had, besides, a number of shorter lyrical pieces. The fonts in the shop were new and inviting. Calvin Thomas was willing to put them to use. Thus, in midsummer of 1827, *Tamerlane and Other Poems* saw the light of print, if not exactly of publication.

It was a small book, little more than a pamphlet, wrapped in a buff cover and containing some forty pages. The title, in large letters, appeared on the face, together with other matter, and was enclosed in a decorative scroll. The author chose to remain anonymous and simply indicated that the work was "By a Bostonian." Perhaps as an apology *pro vita sua* he cited on the cover the lines of Cowper:

> Young heads are giddy, and young hearts are warm,
> And make mistakes for manhood to reform.

They might speak to a flinty heart in Richmond, if the poems themselves meant nothing, or remained unread.

Either Poe took a dismal view of the public that would be interested in his work or his finances did not permit a larger printing, for the first edition consisted of less than fifty books. At that, the bulk remained upon his hands, except for the few copies he sent out to the press. The little volume received mention in several magazines and, in 1829, was listed in Samuel Kettell's *Specimens of American Poetry* —all of which offered too meager a diet to a friendless poet hungering for recognition. *Tamerlane,* at any rate, was out and paid for, not by Mr. Allan, but, extraordinarily enough, by Uncle Sam who, since the latter part of May, had been providing Edgar's salary. Not in his wildest dreams of fame would Edgar have imagined that in 1919 a copy of his 1827 *Tamerlane and Other Poems* would fetch $11,600 at an Anderson Gallery sale.

Like all young poets not yet sure of themselves, the Bostonian had to explain himself in a preface. The greater part of the poems, he said, were written when the author had not completed his fourteenth year. They were not intended for publication. "Why they are now published concerns no one but himself."

In part, that concern was indeed personal. Whether in the tale of Tamerlane, which dealt so little with the historical character that he could have been any proud, ambitious man—Poe, aggrandized, as he had seen himself—or in the short poems, it is the personality of the writer that comes through, at times with disturbing clarity. Also, despite the sometimes limping measure, the forced rhyme and the flaws of style which Poe found is necessary to correct and correct again, he emerges as a poet, his wings not yet fledged but giving promise of lofty flight.

As a man he portrays himself proud, beauty-loving, independent, and unwilling to compromise with the "rabble-men" among whom

> Lion ambition is chained down—
> And crouches to a keeper's hand . . .

For him what Shelley called Intellectual Beauty becomes integrity of soul, and beauty itself a secret delight to be brooded upon until, transformed by the quality of his imagination, it finds its place in that visionary world that was his true home. In "Dreams," he gave a glimpse of that world.

> 'Twas once—and *only* once—and the wild hour
> From my remembrance shall not pass—some power
> Or spell had bound me—'Twas the chilly wind
> Came o'er me in the night, and left behind
> Its image on my spirit—or the moon
> Shone on my slumbers in her lofty noon
> Too coldly—or the stars—howe'er it was
> That dream was as that night-wind—let it pass.
>
> I have been happy—tho' but in a dream.
> I have been happy—and I love the theme.
> Dreams! in their vivid colouring of life,
> As in that fleeting, shadowy, misty strife
> Of semblance with reality, which brings
> To the delirious eye, more lonely things
> Of Paradise and Love—and all our own!
> Than young Hope in her sunniest hour hath known.[8]

Beauty and terror had to mingle to stir his soul to the ultimate thrill—beauty and terror and death. He played upon the theme in "The Lake."

> In youth's spring it was my lot
> To haunt of the wide world a spot
> The which I could not love the less;
> So lovely was the loneliness
> Of a wild lake, with black rock bound,
> And the tall pines that tower'd around.
> But when the night had thrown her pall
> Upon that spot—as upon all,
>
> .   .   .   .
>
> My infant spirit would awake
> To the terror of the lone lake.
> Yet the terror was not fright—
> But a tremulous delight,
> And a feeling undefin'd,
> Springing from a darken'd mind.
> Death was in that poison'd wave
> And in its gulf a fitting grave

[8] Version from Morgan Library manuscript.

> For him who thence could solace bring
> To his dark imagining;
> Whose wild'ring thought could even make
> An Eden of that dim lake.

Even without Poe's assurance that the poem had been written in his boyhood, its awkwardness of style and metre betrays the tyro. What is revealing in these lines is the confession that the youth had very early discovered his haunted realm.

To the real world that had inflicted its own wounds, to one who had betrayed a vow, he addressed an elegiac set of verses called simply "To ——":

> I saw thee on thy bridal day—
>   When a burning blush came o'er thee,
> Though happiness around thee lay,
>   The world all love before thee:
>
> And in thine eye a kindling light
>   (Whatever it might be)
> Was all on Earth my aching sight
>   Of Loveliness could see.

Oddly enough, at about the same time that year, the *Minerva* printed a poem by Henry Poe, on the theme of broken vows, called also "To ——." It closed:

> Farewell! thy face is clouded now,
>   But soon a thousand smiles will flutter
> Around thy lips, and that proud brow
> Shall wear away the plighted vow
>   Thy lying lips now softly utter.

Did Henry's verses also refer to Elmira's marriage or was he lamenting a hurt of his own? The two brothers had been keeping up their correspondence since Henry's return to Baltimore from his last voyage. Each had his troubles—struggles with poverty, illness—which were confided to the other. It was therefore natural that Edgar should have written to Henry of the broken engagement, of his running away from Richmond to seek his own fortunes. It was exactly the romantic situation to appeal to a youth with literary ambitions. Combining Edgar's broken romance with what he, Henry Poe, had seen of life, and borrowing style and manner from the popular romances of the day, Henry produced the story *The Pirate,* which was published in the Baltimore *North American,* the weekly paper for which he was writing. As a brotherly gesture Henry also printed excerpts from Edgar's little volume—under his own initials.

Evidently the broken romance still had unexploited possibilities, for in 1827 it inspired Henry's colleague on the *North American,* Lambert A. Wilmer. Mere prose would not do in treating so melancholy a Byronic hero, so hapless a damsel, so throbbing a love story. Wilmer retold it all in verse. He called the poem *Merlin,* transferred the locale to the Hudson to avoid sticking too close to reality, but kept the heroine's name, Elmira. It may have given Edgar a taste of the fame for which he hungered to find himself twice celebrated—in prose and in verse—in the *North American.* Not even Byron and Mary Chaworth had received such attention.

CHAPTER IX

Poet in Uniform

AS the New England winter drew closer, with its rigors, a Southerner in Battery H of the First Artillery who accidentally had been born a Bostonian, welcomed the orders which transferred the company to warmer climes. With his group Edgar A. Perry boarded the brig *Waltham* in Boston Harbor on the 8th of November, 1827, and ten days later found himself at Fort Moultrie, Sullivan's Island, Charleston Harbor, on the level coasts of South Carolina.

The walls of the old fortress, near the back channel, rose protectively, a symbol of strength for the cluster of rickety buildings that had sprung up nearby, disputing the scant soil with the bristly palmetto. The island itself, a three-mile spine of sea sand a quarter of a mile wide at its thickest, stretched like a sea serpent with Fort Moultrie, its head, on the western end. The long body, green from an undergrowth of sweet myrtle, was protected from the assaults of the sea by a hard line of beach. One might easily have imagined it, with its thick vegetation and sense of remoteness, as the hiding place of pirates in the days of the buccaneers. Indeed, something of that lore hung about the place, an added attraction for at least one member of Battery H, who had already discovered for himself the hidden haunts of the marsh hen and heron in the solitary explorations which his hours of leisure allowed. The closest approach to civilization, Charleston itself, its harbor bristling with masts from all over the world, was not accessible without inconvenience, but Edgar found amusement there with the rest in the camaraderie of youth. Apparently he had no close friends, though he was on cordial terms with Colonel William Drayton.

More than human companionship, however, what Edgar sought after the infantry drill, the exercises at the guns and the clerical hours in the Quartermaster's Office, was the privacy to indulge his love of reading and, most of all, his faculty for transforming reality into the more vivid realities of his imaginings. Everything he saw etched itself upon his mind—the shape, the green-and-gold coloring of a beetle, the restless fluttering of sand butterflies, the melancholy drapery of Spanish moss festooning oak and cypress, the height of the tulip tree with its peculiarly smooth trunk which, in age, grew a gnarled and uneven bark; the bristly palmetto, its dry fronds rattling in the wind, amid the eerie calls and whirrings of nocturnal creatures. The plash and motion of the sea made themselves part of that memory, as did the mystery of the stars, silent and inaccessible, in their unfathomable heavens. Visions, impressions, fertilized his creative fancy and, in absorbed quiet, he gave them form.

It was the heavenly bodies, often observed at home through the telescope and now, in the almost communicable nearness of the low-hanging heavens, breathing their secret to his soul, that stirred him again to poetry. He was writing shorter pieces, with more conscious lyricism and greater care for form, among them a sonnet inveighing against science and revealing both his new manner and his revolt from reality.

> Science! true daughter of Old Time thou art!
>   Who alterest all things with thy peering eyes.
> Why preyest thou thus upon the poet's heart;
>   Vulture, whose wings are dull realities?
> How should he love thee? or how deem thee wise,
>   Who wouldst not leave him in his wandering
> To seek for treasure in the jewelled skies,
>   Albeit he soared with an undaunted wing?
> Hast thou not dragged Diana from her car?
>   And driven the Hamadryad from the wood
> To seek a shelter in some happier star?
>   Hast thou not torn the Naiad from her flood,
> The Elfin from the green grass, and from me
>   The summer dream beneath the tamarind tree?

Though Science had torn him metaphorically from his equally metaphorical tamarind tree, the poet in uniform was at the time deep in his wandering through the jewelled skies; and if his treasure could not be weighed in the diamond cutter's balance, it had value above and beyond such computation. He was writing a symbolic poem, longer than "Tamerlane" and bolder in concept, against the background of the starry universe itself. "Al Aaraaf," he called it, after the Arabic for the medium between heaven and hell, a sort of purgatory but without punishment of any kind.

Using the poet's prerogative, he transferred Al Aaraaf to the star which the Danish astronomer, Tycho Brahe, discovered in Cassiopeia in 1572 and which, conveniently for Edgar's purposes, suddenly appeared and disappeared. To Al Aaraaf, accordingly, went those who after death chose to make it their dwelling. They did not enjoy immortality, as one would expect, but there elected to live a second life of high excitement, to sink at last into oblivion. "I have imagined that some would not be pleased . . . with an immortality even of bliss," commented the young philosopher.[1]

Meanwhile, during the hours that Edgar's leisure allowed, he transferred himself to the realm where he felt at home, the land which held

> Oh, nothing of the dross of ours—
> Yet all the beauty—all the flowers
> That list our Love, and deck our bowers . . .

The poem embodied the first of the grandiose ideas that were to fill Poe's mind, ideas that often were no more than merely apprehended, only to fade in nebulous speculation, but which at times he materialized into hybrid forms, part from the Science which he decried, and part from his imagination. The combination afforded a clue to the duality of his psyche. In "Al Aaraaf" it was Beauty that he set out to sing—Beauty, the visible manifestation of the divine and man's surest safeguard against sin. He personified it in the girl, Nesace, the reigning spirit of the burning star.

> 'Twas a sweet time for Nesace—for there
> Her world lay lolling on the golden air,
> Near four bright suns—a temporary rest—
> An oasis in desert of the blest.
> Away—away—'mid seas of rays that roll
> Empyrean splendour o'er th' unchained soul—
> The soul that scarce (the billows are so dense)
> Can struggle to its destin'd eminence . . .

It was a vision of glory scarcely consonant with the diurnal scene of barracks and offices. To the youth it afforded the essential atmosphere of his being where, removed from reality, he basked in ideal Beauty, amid the music of the spheres and of his own song. It was growing in technique and lyricism, that song, through which he interspersed enraptured roulades:

> Arise! from your dreaming
>   In violet bowers,
> To duty beseeming
>   These star-litten hours—

[1] Ostrom, *The Letters of Edgar Allan Poe,* pp. 17-18.

>And shake from your tresses
>   Encumber'd with dew
>The breath of those kisses
>   That cumber them too—
>(O! how, without you, Love!
>   Could angels be blest?)
>Those kisses of true Love
>   That lull'd ye to rest!

While Poe dreamed of tresses encumbered with dew, the stalwart young blades of Company H found their pleasures, or bought them, in the discreetly lighted Charleston houses which dispensed them despite the frowning dignity of the colonial mansions. Not that Artificer Perry—he had been raised in rank—was not as good a sport as the rest when it came to taking a glass or rolling the dice or playing a game of seven-up. But the other manly pastimes were not for him. The wound of his lost Elmira was still too raw, the vision of the departed Helen too holy to be desecrated. Besides, he knew himself to be different from other men. "In the strange anomaly of my existence," he was to write in one of the most percipient of his many self-portraits, "feelings with me *had never been of the heart,* and my passions *always were* of the mind." [2] (The italics are his.) Long before that, however, he had made another and more revealing admission in the lyric which he had first called "Preface" and later "Romance," written at Fort Moultrie or perhaps at Fortress Monroe, Virginia, whither the garrison had removed in December, 1828:

>I could not love except where Death
>Was mingling his with Beauty's breath—
>Or Hymen, Time, and Destiny
>Were stalking between her and me.

This declaration startled the reader of the 1831 edition of his poems, as it still does anyone who comes upon it. He later realized the implications of this sinister confession, for he suppressed it in future issues. The lines may have meant no more than the ruefulness of one whom Death had robbed of his beloved: in childhood, his mother; in adolescence, the sympathetic woman who had awakened him to poetry. Still, the lines have an inescapeable explicitness in that *I could not love.* Very early in his awareness the association of love and death had taken root. It was as much part of him as his brain that could create visions of beauty and also imagine horrors which, from boyhood, had made him start up in the night in terror.

---

[2] "Berenice," Griswold edition, 1853, Vol. I, p. 441.

Meanwhile "Al Aaraaf" had reached completion. Poe knew it was a better work than "Tamerlane," with fewer echoes and a greater consciousness of what, beyond the content, converted verse to poetry. He was also writing more personal lyrics wherein, like Shelley and Keats and other young poets before him, he gave expression to world-weariness and a sense of failure, before he had experienced them.

> The happiest day—the happiest hour
> My seared and blighted heart hath known,
> The highest hope of pride and power,
> I feel hath flown. . . .
>
> But were that hope of pride and power
> Now offered with the pain
> Ev'n *then* I felt—that brightest hour
> I would not live again. . . .[3]

Such verses were no better and no worse than those of his brother Henry, but the unique quality of Edgar's imagination was now beginning to emerge. None but Poe, in his clime and in his day, could have written the lines in "Romance" which he was earnestly to declare, "have never been surpassed." [4]

> Of late, eternal Condor years
> So shake the very Heaven on high
> With tumult as they thunder by,
> I have no time for idle cares
> Through gazing on the unquiet sky.
> And when an hour with calmer wings
> Its down upon my spirit flings—
> That little time with lyre and rhyme
> To while away—forbidden things!
> My heart would feel to be a crime
> Unless it trembled with the strings.

On the first day of January, 1829, Edgar obtained his promotion to regimental sergeant major. As a noncommissioned officer he could rise no higher, but that did not trouble him as he had no ambition for a career in the army. He knew that his field in life was quite a different one, but because of the terms of his enlistment, he still had more than three years to serve out of the required five. Before the garrison sailed from Fort Moultrie he had already considered his circumstances and discussed them with his company commander,

[3] "The Happiest Day."
[4] Letter to John Neal, Dec. 29, 1809. Ostrom, p. 35.

Lieutenant J. Howard, to whom he revealed his incognito and the reasons for his leaving home. Lieutenant Howard took an interest in him and sought the counsel of other officers. Sergeant Major Perry could be discharged, they agreed, but he must first be reconciled with his foster father.

Swallowing his pride, Edgar had then written to Mr. Allan and, on receiving no answer, further explained his situation to him. Meanwhile John Allan had communicated with an intermediary, Mr. John O. Lay, to whom he complacently expressed the opinion that Edgar had better remain as he was, until the termination of his enlistment. Agitated by that threat to his emancipation, Edgar wrote to Mr. Allan once more and, though he addressed him with frigid formality, propitiated his good graces by showing unusual solicitude for his health. Then he went to the point.

"Lieut Howard . . ." he wrote, "promised me my discharge solely upon a re-conciliation with yourself— In vain I told him that your wishes for me . . . were, and have always been those of a father & that you were ready to forgive even the worst offences— He insisted upon my writing you. . . . He has always been kind to me, and, in many respects, reminds me forcibly of yourself—" On the tail of this blandishment, he recapitulated his position. "The period of an Enlistment is five years—the prime of my life would be wasted—I shall be driven to more decided measures if you refuse to assist me." As if ashamed of the moral threat, he added: "You need not fear for my future prosperity. . . . I feel that within me which will make me fulfil your highest wishes. . . ." [5]

Such optimistic auguries carried little weight with the practical Scotsman who had been enjoying peace in his household and had no intention of disrupting it. Experience had taught him that, whenever unpleasantness threatened, the best policy was to do nothing. Accordingly, he ignored this letter also. Poe wrote again, on the 22nd of December, 1829. "All that is necessary to obtain my discharge from the army was your consent in a letter to Lieut J. Howard . . . this being all that I asked at your hands, I was hurt at your declining to answer. . . ." After all, he, Edgar Poe, was no mongrel waif, as Mr. Allan would see. "Lieut Howard has given me an introduction to Col: James House. . . . He spoke kindly to me, told me he was personally acquainted with my Grandfather Gen Poe . . . & reassured me of my immediate discharge upon your consent. It must have been a matter of regret to me, that when those who were strangers took such deep interest in my welfare, you who called me

[5] *Valentine Letters.* Ostrom, p. 10.

your son should refuse me even the common civility of answering
a letter." If it was Mr. Allan's wish to forget that he had ever been
his son, he was too proud to remind him again. "I only beg you
to remember that you yourself relished the cause of my leaving your
family—Ambition. If it has not taken the channel you wished it, it
is not the less certain of its object. Richmond & the U. States were
too narrow a sphere," he said grandly, "and the world shall be my
theatre." [6]

It was the sort of comment calculated to make Mr. Allan's nostrils
quiver. The world—well, let him have it, provided he kept out of
Richmond. Let him go back to St. Petersburg from where he had
headed his letters to Mrs. Allan, but let him not trouble his hearth
again. In vain Edgar pleaded in the pathetic disorder of conflicting
emotions, as he now swaggered, now abjectly submitted. "My father
do not throw me aside as *degraded*. I will be an honor to your name.
. . . If you determine to abandon me—here I take my farewell. . . .
Neglected—I will be doubly ambitious, & the world shall hear of the
son whom you have thought unworthy of your notice." [7] Time has
not handed down the wry comment, if any, of the man who is remembered solely for his accidental association with the youth he
was so anxious to shake off.

Not long after writing this letter, Edgar was taken to the Fortress
Monroe hospital with a fever. His nerves, stretched to the breaking
point, had given him warning. On his recovery, seeing that Mr. Allan
still ignored him, he wrote to his boyhood friend, John Mackenzie,
begging him to see his foster father and plead his case in person.

It was no longer discharge from the army that he sought, but the
opportunity of obtaining a cadet's appointment at the Military Academy of West Point. With the advantage of his present station in the
army and his having passed through the practical artillery training,
his cadetship, he computed with rosy optimism, would be run through
in six months. Undeterred by Mr. Allan's silence, Edgar, on the heels
of John Mackenzie's good offices, repeated the facts in still another
letter to "Dear Sir" on February 4, 1829. "I made the request to
obtain a cadet's appointment . . ." he wrote, "partly because in
making the request you would at once see to what direction my
'future views & expectations' were inclined." [8]

The likelihood of Edgar's presence being removed from the close
proximity of Richmond to the protective distance of New York

[6] *Ibid.* Ostrom, pp. 12-13.
[7] Ostrom, p. 12.
[8] *Valentine Letters.* Ostrom, p. 13.

worked the miracle where nothing else had availed. Perhaps too, Mrs. Allan, now on her deathbed, had added her pleas to those of the youth whom she, at least, had loved as a son. Surely she must have seen those letters with their reiterated: "Let me know how my Ma preserves her health. . . . Give my love to Ma. . . . My dearest love to Ma. . . ." However it was, perhaps because he knew he was fulfilling his wife's wishes for the last time, John Allan wrote to Colonel House, applying for a brief leave of absence for Edgar.

The application came too late. On the morning of Saturday, February 28, 1829, while Edgar was answering the roll call at Fortress Monroe, Frances Allan obeyed the ultimate summons. To the last she had pleaded with her husband to soften his heart toward Edgar, while she listened for the impetuous opening of the front door and the sound of familiar steps, unheard for so long. When she knew that Death would arrive before Edgar, she had her husband promise not to bury her until Edgar had looked upon her face for the last time. It was a promise that Mr. Allan could not keep, for Edgar was not to reach Richmond until March 3, the night of Mrs. Allan's burial.

"If she had not have died while I was away there would have been nothing for me to regret," Edgar wrote Mr. Allan at a time when plain speaking was medicine to both their souls. *"Your* love I never valued—but she I believed loved me as her own child." [9]

In her he had lost another of the women between whom and himself Time, Destiny, and Death had stalked.

At Shockoe cemetery, beside the grave whose funeral flowers still had the colors of life, he realized the magnitude of his loss and was prostrate with grief, aggravated by that other tombstone nearby, covering what corruption had left of the lovely Helen. But death was not the end, he had affirmed again and again, for, though unseen, the departed still hovered about one. He had given expression to that belief in "Visit of the Dead" in the *Tamerlane* volume:

> The spirits of the dead, who stood
> In life before thee, are again
> In death around thee, and their will
> Shall then o'ershadow thee—be still . . .

Mr. Allan took cognizance of Edgar's presence enough to wish to exhibit him with the proper decorum under the circumstances. He therefore ordered for him from Mr. Ellis a suit of black clothes, a

[9] *Ibid.* Ostrom, p. 41.

hat and a pair of gloves. He may even have given the impecunious young soldier a little pocket money to defray his expenses. At any rate, for several days Edgar stayed in the Allan house and their common grief wrought so benevolently that "dear Sir" again became "my dear Pa." From Fortress Monroe Edgar wrote him: "I have had a fearful warning & have hardly ever known before what distress was. . . . In the morning of my departure I went to your room to tell you good-bye—but, as you were asleep, I would not disturb you." [10]

If not peace, a temporary truce was established between the two men. What mattered most to Edgar, however, was that at last he had obtained Pa's consent to his discharge from the army—on the understanding that he go to West Point. For Edgar, entering the Military Academy was not a goal but an expedient toward ultimately attaining the freedom to pursue his true purpose. It was necessary for him to compromise, on Mr. Allan's terms, and he did. As for Mr. Allan himself, the new freedom he had obtained by his wife's death opened up for him greener fields, in which he had not scrupled to dally even during her lifetime. He was still young enough to marry again after the proper period of mourning. Under the circumstances, the farther away he kept Edgar the better for himself.

Colonel James House, therefore, was called upon to send the necessary request to the general commanding the E. Department, U.S.A., New York. Considering the official nature of the document, the biographical information on Edgar A. Perry compounded so much fiction with fact that it would have sorted well with the literary efforts of brother Henry and Lambert Wilmer.

"The said Perry," read Colonel House's letter of March 30, 1829, "is one of a family of orphans whose unfortunate parents were the victims of the conflagration of the Richmond theatre, in 1809. The subject of this letter was taken under the protection of Mr. Allen [sic] a gentleman of wealth and respectability, of the city, who, as I understand, adopted his protégé as his son and heir; with the intention of giving him a liberal education, he had placed him at the University of Virginia from which, after considerable progress in his studies, in a moment of youthful indiscretion he absconded—and was not heard from by his patron for several years; in the mean time he became reduced to the necessity of enlisting into the service. . . . Since the arrival of his company at this place, he has made his situation known to his Patron . . . who reinstates him into his family and

[10] Ibid. Ostrom, p. 15.

favor—and who in a letter I have received from him requests that his son may be discharged on procuring a substitute. . . ." [11]

Judging by the contents, the document resulted from a triple collaboration. Colonel House's contribution consisted of his putting together the facts provided him by Edgar and Mr. Allan, in applying for the discharge. Mr. Allan's lay in a letter wherein, while making his request, he explained the estrangement from his son, whom he had reinstated into his favor. Considering the provocations of the scapegrace who "absconded" from the university, Mr. Allan cuts a creditable figure. Certainly such a misstatement could not have come from Edgar, who knew the plain truth: that only Mr. Allan's refusal to pay even his legitimate debts had kept him from returning to Charlottesville and, to a great extent, had reduced him to the necessity of enlisting into the service, as Colonel House put it, with more realism than tact.

Edgar's contribution to the misinformation, however, also had its share of conscious error. The family of orphans, in its inclusiveness, confounded the particular in the general. There might have been three, there might have been a half dozen. By having both parents perish in the Richmond conflagration, the family ghosts were laid. By placing the fire in 1809 instead of 1811, when it occurred, Rosalie, with her doubtful parentage, was left in the realm of the unborn.

Before Sergeant Major Perry could be discharged the required substitute had to be procured, One was found, a Sergeant Samuel Graves. Unfortunately, at the time that Graves turned up neither Colonel House nor Lieutenant Howard was present to make the negotiation. Ordinarily, the bounty for a new recruit who offered himself as a substitute was $12, the amount which Edgar had specified to Mr. Allan. Graves, however, was a sergeant and his price was $75 which, needless to say, Edgar did not possess; for though relations between him and Pa were more cordial than they had been, the purse strings, unlike those of the heart, were not allowed to relax. Poe, therefore, obtained his freedom by giving Sergeant Graves $25 in cash, and a note for the remaining $50.

Edgar was discharged on the 15th of April. However, he did not leave Fortress Monroe until about a week later, when he set out for Richmond, morally fortified by three letters of recommendation from his superior officers. The better to assure Edgar's appointment at the Military Academy, Mr. Allan pulled a few strings and obtained other laudatory documents, among them a letter from Andrew Stevenson, the Speaker of the House.

[11] Original letter in War Department Records.

On setting out for Washington Edgar carried, among other papers, an introduction to the Hon. John H. Eaton, Secretary of War, from none other than Pa himself. When he decided to write that letter Mr. Allan must surely have done so from an earnest desire to further Edgar's cause. It turned out to be almost a recapitulation of the facts incorporated in the letter of Colonel House, with a dose of self-commendation added. "He left me in consequence of some gambling debts at the University . . . because (I presume) I refused to sanction a rule . . . making debts of honor of all indiscretions. I have much pleasure in asserting that he stood his examinations . . . with great credit to himself. . . . Frankly, Sir, do I declare that he is no relation to me whatever; that I have many whom I have taken an active interest to promote theirs; with no other feeling than that, every man is my care, if he be in distress. For myself I ask nothing, but I do request your kindness to aid this youth in the promotion of his future prospects. . . ." [12]

No allusion here of any adoption of Edgar as his son and heir. On the contrary, Mr. Allan affirmed that Edgar was no relation to him whatever—merely one of those on whom he bestowed his charity out of the goodness of his heart. Among the many did he include his son, Edwin Collier? As for Edgar, the letter would have told him with cruel explicitness that despite the years he had spent under Mr. Allan's roof he had made no dent in that marble heart. The son and heir was no more to him than an impersonal "this youth."

[12] Dated May 6, 1829. Quoted by Hervey Allen; also by Quinn.

CHAPTER X

⇥⇥⇥ · ⇤⇤⇤

Baltimore and "Al Aaraaf"

THE Washington trip, despite the frigidity of Mr. Allan's send-off, proved successful. Not only did Edgar impress the Secretary of War favorably, but he also secured a recommendation to West Point from Judge John J. Barber. The appointment to the Military Academy now seemed assured. Heartened by the augury, Mr. Allan sent Edgar $100 for his expenses, though not without cautioning him to be careful of how he spent it.

Edgar was in Baltimore on the 20th of May, 1829, when he received the draft, and he hastened to thank "Dear Pa" for it. Before this, however, warned by some instinct that his foothold in the Richmond mansion was becoming increasingly precarious, he had decided to look up his relatives. "I have succeeded in finding Grandmother & my relations," he wrote, "but the fact of my Grandfather's having been Quater [*sic*] . . . Master General of the whole U.S. Army during the Revolutionary War is clearly established—but its being a well known fact at Washington, obviates the necessity of obtaining the certificates you mentioned." [1]

There, let Mr. Allan digest those facts. The orphan he had taken into his home had an ancestry to be proud of. After all, not even Mr. Allan could boast of a grandfather who had been in a position of trust which embraced the *whole* U.S. Army. Other information he had somewhere acquired worried him a little for its possible consequences on the expected appointment. "Since I have been in Baltimore I have learnt something concerning my descent which would have, I am afraid, no very favourable effect if known to the *War* Dept: viz: that I am the grandson of General Benedict Arnold." [2]

Of course there was no ground for his believing such an absurdity, but notoriety, as well as fame, has its thrills.

Beyond the mention of his grandmother, the General's widow,

[1] *Valentine Letters*. Ostrom, p. 16.
[2] *Ibid*. Ostrom, p. 22.

Edgar said nothing of the rest of his relations. As it happened, Mrs. David Poe, helpless from paralysis, was living with her thirty-nine-year-old daughter, Mrs. Maria Clemm, whose husband had died in 1826, leaving her with a son of eleven, Henry, and a little girl of seven who already gave promise of unusual beauty. In their early meetings the usual confidences were exchanged between the relatives, to bridge the chasm of their past and, perhaps, among other things Mrs. Clemm told Edgar the curious fact of how her little daughter had been baptized with the name Virginia on the day that her two-year-old sister, also called Virginia, had been buried.

With Grandmother Poe and Mrs. Clemm also lived Edgar's brother, Henry, back from his voyages. He was employed in the law offices of Mr. Henry Didier, who, long ago, had pored over Blackstone with David Poe. For the sake of the old friendship with the father Mr. Didier had befriended the son who, indeed, was in need of help. Henry's health, broken by his unrestrained life as much as by tuberculosis, was further damaged by drink. His ambition for literary fame and the foreknowledge that his span of life was limited only intensified his recklessness. It was a dismal picture of poverty and privation that Edgar painted, not long after his proud boast about Quartermaster General Poe. "My grandmother is extremely poor and ill. My aunt Maria if possible still worse and Henry entirely given up to drink & unable to help himself, much less me. . . ." [3]

The only certain income contributed to that household derived indirectly from Grandfather Poe beyond the grave, in the annual pension which the state government allowed his widow in compensation for the thousands of dollars—Poe set the figure at $40,000—which General Poe had advanced to the state of Maryland.[4] Mrs. Clemm supplied what she could with her needle, supplemented by her thrifty management which stretched both food and money to the limit. Her son Henry, too, in those days when necessity sent children out to work, brought in his small pittance as a stone-cutter's apprentice. The obverse of the medal of Grandfather Poe's past glory was, to say the least, depressing.

Under the circumstances Edgar could not have been a steady lodger at Mrs. Clemm's, where, in any case, his position as guest would have seemed anomalous, considering his connection with Mr. Allan, of whose wealth his brother Henry had been witness. The alternative could only have been a cheap hotel, if possible in a shared room.

[3] *Ibid.* Ostrom, p. 29.
[4] *Ibid.* Ostrom, p. 92.

That was exactly the situation in which he found himself in June, 1829, while waiting to ascertain the fate of his application at West Point and, more anxiously, of the poems which he had submitted for publication to the Philadelphia firm of Carey, Lea and Carey. To economize on the cash which, after many requests, he received in driblets from Mr. Allan, he had taken a room at Beltzhoover's hotel, with a cousin of his, Edward Mosher. Like most of his good intentions, it misfired.

One night, while Edgar was sleeping, Mr. Mosher relieved him of all his money—"About $46, of which I recovered $10 by searching his pockets the ensuing night when he acknowledged the theft—I have been endeavouring in vain to obtain the balance from him—he says he has not got it & begs me not to expose him—& for his wife's sake I will not." [5] So Edgar wrote in extenuation of his new demands on Pa, who was becoming increasingly irked by this prolonged drain upon his pocketbook. That West Point matter was taking much too long and his patience, never stoical, was being sorely tried.

Here too Edgar sought to placate him. His hopes, however, rested in the manuscript of "Al Aaraaf" which, with other poems, he had submitted in May to Isaac Lea for, as he put it, his tenderest consideration. His letter, a medley of erudition and brashness with a quotation from the Spanish and a mystico-astronomical explanation of "Al Aaraaf," revealed the earnest poet and the insecure youth, the latter endeavoring, through affected sophistication, to sell the former. Of one thing he was certain. "If the poem is published, succeed or not, I am 'irrevocably a poet,' . . . I should add a circumstance," he appended on a humbler note, "which, tho' no justification of a failure, is yet a boast in success—the poem is by a minor & truly written under extraordinary disadvantages. . . . I cannot refrain from adding that Mr. Wirt's voice is in my favor. . . ." [6]

Following the pattern of the tyro, diffident of success, he sought to attain it by clinging to the coattails of one who had achieved it. William Wirt was not a poet but he enjoyed a certain fame for a biography of Patrick Henry and his *Letters of a British Spy*. He had also served as a U.S. attorney general, a post which he had held with distinction until his recent retirement in Baltimore. While Edgar had been looking up his relatives there he had also renewed his acquaintance with Mr. Wirt, who treated him with greater consideration than is usual between the arrived and the aspiring.

The good man actually took the time to read "Al Aaraaf." The

[5] *Ibid.* Ostrom, p. 22.
[6] *Ibid.* Ostrom, p. 19.

poem, which would have been caviar even to a sophisticated literary taste, left him in a state of bewilderment for which he tactfully blamed himself. "The truth is, that having never written poetry myself, nor read much poetry for many years, I consider myself as by no means a competent judge. . . . It will, I know, please modern readers—the notes contain a good deal of curious and useful information. . . ." [7] He considerately suggested others to whom Edgar might go for advice, among them Robert Walsh, editor of the *American Quarterly Review*. Edgar called upon him, hopeful of a personal introduction to the publishers, Carey, Lea and Carey. Mr. Walsh, unfortunately, had left town. Undeterred, Poe availed himself of the editor's name.

Though Isaac Lea was impressed by the prestige of Wirt and Walsh, as well as by Poe's letter and the profound unintelligibility of "Al Aaraaf," he, like all publishers, had to consider his cashbox. Poetry, unless it were Lord Byron's or Tom Moore's—preferably in a pirated edition—never paid. Edgar Poe might be a genius but Carey, Lea and Carey could not afford the luxury of discovering him. If the young man could insure the firm against loss, then, perhaps, something could be arranged.

Following this slim thread of hope Edgar approached the source from which financial aid could flow. He had no illusions about Mr. Allan's opinions about poetry, for Pa had expressed them often enough. Still, Edgar took his chances, again availing himself of the backing of Mr. Wirt and Mr. Walsh, as he hoped, not in vain. "At my time of life," he opened his attack, "there is much in being *before the eyes of the world*—if once noticed I could easily cut a path to reputation." It was very difficult to get a poem published, he explained. "If Mssrs [*sic*] Carey, Lea & Carey, should decline publishing (as I have no reason to think they will not—they have invariably declined it with all our American poets) that is upon their *own risk* the request I have to make is this—that you will give me a letter to Messrs Carey, Lea & Carey saying that if in publishing the poem . . . they shall incur any *loss*—you will make it good to them." [8] The cost, he went on to explain, would be $100 at the utmost, supposing that not a single copy were sold. "I would remark, in conclusion," he propitiated the stern deity, "that I have long given up *Byron* as a model—for which, I think, I deserve some credit." [9]

[7] MS in Boston Public Library. First published by T. O. Mabbott.
[8] *Valentine Letters.* Ostrom, p. 20.
[9] *Ibid.* Ostrom, p. 20.

Mr. Allan's response was withering to all hopes. "Replied to Monday 8th June 1829 strongly censuring his conduct & refusing all aid," he noted on the last page of Poe's letter. He had sent Edgar $100 only three weeks earlier. The new request pledging him to the same amount, following so close upon that recent tug on his purse strings, was too much.

Edgar was all contrition in his reply of June 25, and hinted at returning home. "In whatever errors I may have been led into, I would beg you to judge me impartially & to believe that I have acted from the single motive of trying to do something for myself." He gagged in swallowing his pride; still, he did not give up. "I hope you will give me a favourable answer concerning my poem tho' I will strictly abide by your decision." [10]

Out of patience, Mr. Allan adopted his strategy of silence, in the salubrious comfort of Lower Byrd, his country estate of six thousand acres on the James, some fifty miles from Richmond. It was only part of his inheritance from William Galt. It may be that consideration of his own luck and a twinge of conscience wrought upon him sufficiently to let him send Edgar a little money, though not without the taunt that men of genius ought not to apply to his aid. Edgar's anxiety to return home he left without comment. Time enough to discourage it if the subject came up again.

June passed. July was drawing to an end. In the suffocating atmosphere of Baltimore, between the discomfort of cheap lodgings and the crowded warren of Grandmother Poe's house, Edgar longed for the breath of the luxury he had once enjoyed. Mr. Allan could not have been more rudely explicit: "I am not particularly anxious to see you." [11]

"I could not help thinking that [the words] amounted to a prohibition to return," Edgar replied, with remarkable restraint. He knew now, as he had not known before, that he was not wanted. His pride flamed. "If I had any means of support until I could obtain the appointment, I would not trouble you again—I am conscious of having offended you formerly—greatly—but I thought *that had been forgiven*. At least you told me so. . . ." [12] It was a flare-up instantly extinguished by his need. The fate of his "Al Aaraaf" depended upon Pa's good will. "As regards the poem . . . I can publish it upon the

[10] *Ibid.* Ostrom, p. 22.
[11] *Ibid.* Ostrom, p. 26.
[12] *Ibid.* Ostrom, p. 26.

terms you mentioned—but will have no more to do with it without your entire approbation. . . ." [13]

That approbation never came. Salving his pride with a polite lie—that he had made a better disposition of the poem elsewhere—Poe recalled his manuscript from the publishers. "As I am unacquainted with the method of proceeding in offering my piece for acceptance (having been sometime absent from this country) would you, Gentlemen, have the kindness to set me in the right way . . ." he requested, with disarming naïveté.[14] He was referring to the periodicals whose possibilities he was thinking of exploring. As for absence from the country, it was no more than the fib with which he sought, then and later, to cover up his period of service in the army.

With his poems on his hands again and, despite his assertion, with no disposition for them whatsoever, he began sending them to magazine editors. Some passages of "Al Aaraaf" had already appeared in the *Baltimore Gazette,* on the 18th of May, 1829. He now looked beyond Baltimore, to New England, where he hoped to find the audience he sought. The entrée, oddly enough, did not come from any literary connection, but from his own relatives.

Not far from Grandmother Poe and Mrs. Clemm lived Poe's uncle, Henry Herring, who had married Mrs. Clemm's younger sister, Eliza. She had died at the age of thirty, but the widower looked after his family comfortably, through a thriving lumber business. Poe was often at the Herring house, not only because of his attractive young cousin, Eliza, but for the literary atmosphere of the place. Both Henry Herring and Edgar's uncle George Poe, had belonged to the "Tusculum," an intellectual club whose magazine was edited by none other than John Neal, now owner of the *Yankee and Boston Literary Gazette.*

John Neal had risen to power in the world of letters. Besides the poems and novels he had published, he had the cachet of four years among New England's famous writers from whom he had acquired not a little of his force and manner. Starting out of Portland, Maine, John Neal set himself up as editor. Within a few years he had established himself as a pundit of criticism. To him, not without fear and trembling, but also with hope, Poe sent his poem "Fairy-land," which he now called "Heaven."

It was a lilting lyric, singing through a fantastic landscape of dim vales and shadowy floods, and moons that wax and wane—again—again—again.

[13] Ostrom, p. 26.
[14] *Ibid.,* p. 27.

And they put out the star-light
With the breath of their pale faces
About twelve by the moon-dial,
One more filmy than the rest

.   .   .   .   .   .

Comes down—still down—and down
With its centre on the crown
Of a mountain's eminence,
While its wide circumference
In easy drapery falls
Over hamlets, over halls . . .

.   .   .   .   .   .

Over spirits on the wing—
Over every drowsy thing—
And buries them up quite
In a labyrinth of light—
And then, how deep!—O, deep!
Is the passion of their sleep.
In the morning they arise
And their moony covering
Is soaring in the skies,
With the tempest as they toss,
Like——almost anything—
Or a yellow Albatross.
They use that moon no more
For the same end as before—
Videlicet, a tent—
Which I think extravagant:
Its atomies, however,
Into a shower dissever,
Of which those butterflies,
Of Earth, which seek the skies,
And so come down again,
(Never-contented things!)
Have brought a specimen
Upon their quivering wings.

In its lightness and whimsicality it is so unlike any other lyric of Poe's as to be unidentifiable as his except for the eeriness of the fantasy and the variation in the music that make one catch one's breath as much with delight as surprise. For once, too, the humor is deft and graceful. One can almost hear Poe reciting the dancing lines to Mrs. Clemm, his chief listener, and the laughter of the delighted Virginia, who would have caught the melody, if not the meaning, of the song.

John Neal saw the poetry in it, and it was a very happy youth who read in the September, 1829, issue of the *Yankee and Boston Literary Gazette:* "If E.A.P. of Baltimore—whose lines about 'Heaven' though he professes to regard them as altogether superior to anything in the whole range of American poetry, save two or three trifles referred to, are, though nonsense, rather exquisite nonsense—would but do himself justice [he] might make a beautiful and perhaps a magnificent poem. There is a good deal here to justify such a hope. . . . He should have signed it Bah! We have no room for others."

Besides forestalling W. S. Gilbert's "Nonsense, perhaps, but oh, what precious nonsense," by more than half a century, John Neal proved himself a prophet. To Edgar, who had almost been made to feel by Mr. Allan that writing poetry was a crime, the words of encouragement—in print, too!—came as the one hopeful ray in an existence of uncertainty and waiting. From Richmond Pa was rumbling impatiently at the failure of the promised appointment to materialize. Edgar had assured him that the Minister of War had given him strong hopes for September, yet it was October and West Point remained as much of a mirage as ever. Almost, Mr. Allan blamed Edgar for the inconsiderateness of Washington in not relieving him of his charge—or was Edgar merely temporizing to get more money out of him?

In reality the youth was performing miracles in stretching the doles from home. Thanks to Mrs. Clemm, however, he could always be assured of at least shelter amid the poverty and sickness of that household. Despite his struggle, Edgar had to keep reassuring Pa that all would go well. If the appointment did not come soon or if he, Edgar, would have to wait until June of the following year, "I would not desire you to allow as much as that ($4) per week because by engaging for a longer period at a cheap boarding house I can do with much less—say even 10 or even 8$ pr month—any thing with which you think it possible to exist." [15]

How often, through his life, was he to struggle with the smallest figures in the losing endeavor of achieving the maximum of results! In the same letter he requested Pa to send him his trunk which contained some books and letters—"& if you think I may ask so much perhaps you will put in it for me some few clothes as I am nearly without." That trunk was to follow him like a doppelgänger to the end of his life.

In his dismal situation it was a relief for him at last to write a letter that did not beg or propitiate, a letter into which he could pour

[15] *Valentine Letters.* Ostrom, p. 30.

out his aspirations in the hope of being understood. For the first
time someone—and that person John Neal—had given him a word
of hope. "I am young," Edgar wrote him "—not yet twenty—*am
a poet*—if deep worship of all beauty can make me *one*—and wish
to be so in the common meaning of the word. I would give the
world to embody one half the ideas afloat in my imagination (by the
way, do you remember, or did you ever read the exclamation of
Shelley about Shakespeare, 'What a number of ideas must have been
afloat before such an author could arise!'). . . . I am and have been
from my childhood, an idler. It cannot therefore be said that

> I left a calling for this idle trade
> A duty broke—a father disobeyed—

for I have no father—nor mother. I am about to publish a volume
of 'Poems' the greater part written before I was fifteen. . . ." [16]
    He could not have given a better self-portrait—this lover of
beauty, this dedicated poet, this child without father or mother, who
was to remain eternally hungering for love and protection.
    Not one to let the iron cool where his poetry was concerned, Poe
struck with fervor, using John Neal's praise to good advantage. Even
Mr. Allan became sufficiently interested in the poems to want to read
them. "I would have sent you the M.S. of my Poems long ago for
your approval," Edgar replied, "but since I have collected them they
have been continually in the hands of some person or another. . . ." [17]
The Baltimore firm of Hatch and Dunning now had them. Unlike
the rest, they decided to take the risk of publishing them. Their
terms were generous. They would print the book and give the author
250 copies. Edgar let Pa know about it immediately. Here was
added proof that others, besides himself, considered him a poet.
    It was the proudest moment of his life. Yet in the letter in which
he had written of his good fortune he was compelled to beg Mr.
Allan for further aid. A poet must eat, like any other mortal; his
shoes wear out and can stand so much mending and no more. At
the time he had been awaiting an answer from Hatch and Dunning
his suit was threadbare. He lacked the barest necessities. He owed
his landlady for his lodging—and he had not had any money since
August. (It was now November.) The $80 he received barely cov-
ered his debts. "If I purchase a piece of linen of which I am much
in want," he wrote Pa, "I shall have none left for pocket money—&
if you could get me a piece or a ½ piece at Mr. Galt's and send it

[16] *Yankee and Boston Literary Gazette,* December, 1829.
[17] *Valentine Letters.* Ostrom, p. 31.

to me by the boat, I could get it made up gratis by my Aunt Maria—" [18] Mr. Allan, meanwhile, had gone to the springs, to recruit his health and spirits.

Poe forgot his poverty in the exaltation of "Al Aaraaf" in print and of the notice which John Neal gave the book in his magazine, that December. Not only did Mr. Neal publish excerpts from the poem, but he also printed the letter in which Poe had defined his poetic credo. "He is entirely a stranger to us," Mr. Neal told his readers, "but with all their faults, if the remainder of 'Al Aaraaf' and 'Tamerlane' are as good as . . . the extracts here given . . . he will deserve to stand high—very high—in the estimation of the shining brotherhood."

Perhaps, as Poe read these words, his own pronouncement on Neal in a letter to Carey, Lea and Carey, came to plague his conscience. "Mr. John Neal . . . who now & then hitting, thro' sheer impudence, upon a correct judgment in matters of authorship, is most unenviably ridiculous whenever he touches the fine arts. . . ." [19]

How correct was Neal's estimate of Poe? That he had his reservations Neal showed in the rest of his introduction. "Whether he *will* do so, however, must depend, not so much upon his worth now in mere poetry, as upon his worth hereafter in something yet loftier and more generous—we allude to the stronger properties of the mind, to the magnanimous determination that enables a youth to endure the present . . . in the unwavering belief, that in the future he will find his reward." That unwavering belief Poe had long held, else he would have submitted to Mr. Allan's efforts to shape him after his own image. The reward the future mercifully concealed.

That December of 1829, when *Al Aaraaf, Tamerlane and Minor Poems* appeared, was in no way different from any other December except to the poet. Pa had softened to the extent of giving him permission to return to Richmond. What, if anything, Mr. Allan perceived in the little volume beyond its format and its unpronounceable title, he kept to himself. The "Sonnet—to Science," which opened it, he probably found intelligible, though as a man of progress he may have reprehended the sentiment. As for the title poem—even with Poe's learned notes (in four languages) which Mr. Wirt had commended for their useful information—it was a mystery known only to the poet.

For that matter, a mystery it remained, its allegory as tormenting as that gemmy flower whose dew

[18] *Ibid.* Ostrom, p. 34.
[19] *Ibid.* Ostrom, p. 27.

Deliriously sweet, was dropp'd from Heaven
And fell in gardens of the unforgiven
In Trebizond—and on a sunny flower
So like its own above that, to this hour,
It still remaineth, torturing the bee
With madness, and unwonted reverie . . .

Much unwonted reverie has gone into it on the part of scholars, but the meaning remains elusive. "Al Aaraaf" was Poe's first serious expression of his worship of Beauty. He was not to enunciate his ideas on the link between poetry and beauty until later, but he had already put into practice his conviction that the first element of poetry was the thirst for beauty. "Beauty is the sole legitimate province of the poem. . . . That pleasure which is at once the most intense, the most elevating, the most pure, is, I believe, found in the contemplation of the beautiful. When, indeed, men speak of Beauty, they mean, precisely, not a quality . . . but an effect—they refer, in short, just to that intense and pure elevation of *soul*—*not* of intellect, or of heart . . . which is experienced in consequence of contemplating 'the beautiful.' "[20]

That beauty he personified in Nesace, the guiding Beatrice of that "oasis in desert of the blest" which he had imagined into being. No Piccarda Donati nor Empress Constance people Nesace's realm, but personified flowers—Sephalica, Nyctanthes, Nelumbo and Clytia, pondering between many a sun—

And thy most lovely purple perfume, Zante!
Isola d'oro!— Fior di Levante!

These words were to reappear in his sonnet "To Zante." Oddly enough, the Italian phrases derive from Chateaubriand's *Itinéraire de Paris à Jérusalem: "Je souscris à ses noms d'Isola d'oro, de Fior di Levante."* However, they suit the paradisaic mood of "Al Aaraaf" 's opening and add their own music, though at the expense of *fior,* which Poe split into a dissyllable for his purposes.[21] As for the star's affording a world for the departed spirits, there is Dante's line: *Dice che l'alma alla sua stella riede*—He says the soul returneth to its star.[22] Poe knew his Dante, and there were witnesses enough to prove that he could quote many passages of the *Divina Commedia* by heart.

Other influences from his omnivorous reading also found their way into the mystic region of Al Aaraaf: the Oriental color and

[20] "The Philosophy of Composition."
[21] See G. Tusiani, *Sonettisti Americani,* pp. 28-29.
[22] *Paradiso,* Canto IV.

imagery of the Koran, which he was said to have had at his finger's
ends, and the romantically heightened pseudo-Eastern atmosphere
of *Lalla Rookh*. Yet, though the ingredients came from all parts of
the world, the resulting confection was entirely Poe's own. No one
else could have written:

> Quiet we call
> "Silence"—which is the merest word of all.
> All Nature speaks, and ev'n ideal things
> Flap shadowy sounds from visionary wings—
> But ah! not so when, thus, in realms on high
> The eternal voice of God is passing by,
> And the red winds are withering in the sky . . .

Then, for magic of sound and fancy, there is the invocation to
Ligeia, personifying the music of nature:

> Ligeia! Ligeia!
> My beautiful one!
> Whose harshest idea
> Will to melody run,
> O! is it thy will
> On the breezes to toss?
> Or capriciously still
> Like the lone Albatross,
> Incumbent on night
> (As she on the air)
> To keep watch with delight
> On the harmony there?

The poem, in whose second part the characters, Ianthe and Angelo,
figure almost as wraiths in the overwhelming immensity, evolves in
a series of descriptive moods, whether spoken by the two or painted
by the poet. All one knows of the shades is that they loved, and
because of that love

> They fell: for Heaven to them no hope imparts
> Who hear not for the beating of their hearts.

What is the ultimate meaning? Poe himself probably sought none,
for to him an instructive poem was anathema. He offered his visions
of ultramundane beauty; he created his moods, and his mission of
poetry was done.

The notes that generously supplement the work are revealing, but
more of the man than of the poet. "I have often thought I could
distinctly hear the sound of darkness as it stole over the horizon,"
he confesses in one. The sorrow experienced in the realm of Al

Aaraaf, he explains in another, "is that sorrow which the living love to cherish for the dead, and which, in some minds, resembles the delirium of opium."

Had Poe already become initiated to the use of opium, to write so authoritatively? Henry Poe had been taking the drug as a palliative for the disease that was slowly sapping his life. More likely, Poe may have derived his knowledge from his brother and from his own curious reading.

On the subject much has been made of Baudelaire's attribution of the drug's influence upon Poe's style. "Inanimate Nature, so called, partakes of the nature of living beings and, like them, thrills with a supernatural and galvanic thrill. Space is deepened by opium; opium imparts a magical sense to all its colors and makes all sounds vibrate with a more meaningful sonority." [23] Others have pointed out Poe's frequent attribution of the properties of one sense to another as a further indication of the use of the drug. Yet both the feeling of unfathomable space, the heightening of nature's attributes in color and sound, and the dovetailing of sense perceptions already exist in the young Poe. The descriptions of Nesace's celestial regions overwhelm with their vastness, sound and color, and Poe himself stressed his conscious transference of sense attributes by particularly commending to Neal's attention the verses wherein ideal things "Flap shadowy sounds from visionary wings." The source lay in Poe's imagination and not necessarily in a drug to which at the time he may, or may not, have been initiated.

In the everyday world Poe, before leaving for Richmond, undertook to sell a Negro slave for Mrs. Clemm. It was, of all unlikely tasks, among the most unlikely for a poet. But Poe, discounting the accident of his birth in Boston, was a Southerner and had accepted without question the environment in which he had grown up. Slavery was part of it, and so were class distinctions. As Mrs. Clemm brushed and repaired his outworn suit, he felt not the less a patrician, if not by birth, certainly by the ideas afloat in his imagination. Some of them he had embodied in the slim octavo, bound in crimson sprinkled with gold, copies of which he was taking with him to Richmond, as proof that complete strangers had had enough faith in him to risk money on his success. That, more than anything the book contained, would speak for him to Mr. Allan.

[23] Preface to *Histoires Extraordinaires*, 1856. Trans. of passage by F. W.

CHAPTER XI

Israfel

THE return of the prodigal was quite different from his earlier departure. He arrived in Richmond threadbare, to be sure, but with the nimbus that publicity imparted. Not only John Neal but other editors were becoming aware of him and, though not to the degree that the poet would have desired, still gratifyingly. If only critics had not felt obliged to take back with one hand what they gave with the other! "The author, who appears to be very young, is evidently a fine genius," Mrs. Sarah Hale, famous for "Mary Had a Little Lamb," told the readers of her *Ladies' Magazine,* that January of 1830. Then she dimmed the praise by adding, "but he wants judgment, experience, tact." Still, she was reminded of Shelley by sections of his long poems. That, for the moment, was glory enough. Edgar had less reason to be pleased with the Baltimore *Minerva* which often gave space to Henry's poems. Though John H. Hewitt, the editor, praised "Tamerlane" and quoted extensively from the shorter poems, he dealt cavalierly with "Al Aaraaf."

Still, the prestige of a published volume had its effect. Pa ordered a number of necessary items for Edgar—gloves, wool hose, and a fine London hat. If there was no mention of a new suit in Mr. Allan's meticulous bookkeeping, it was not because he wished to exhibit the prodigal in all his shabbiness as a salutary lesson. When the impulsive youth had quit home he had left behind a wardrobe worthy of Beau Brummel.

The old house with its marble busts and ormolu-accented furniture, with its air of comfort and its pleasant lawns, the beaming servants welcoming back Master Edgar, played upon his susceptible emotions. All this, as well as the love of Ma and Pa, had once been his. Then had come the change, partly through his fault but also through Mr. Allan's incapacity to bend. Still, the old affection might reawaken. Was he not obeying Pa in the West Point matter? Had he not shown that he had not wasted his time? That he had begun to make good the promise that "the world shall hear of the son whom you have thought unworthy of your notice"? It was only the limited world of Richmond which he was now impressing by the power of his name in print. Yet others, like Mrs. Hale and many whom he would never know, might even then be reading his poems, indeed, might be admiring his favorite lines on the Condor wings and shadowy sounds.

Pa, however, had powerful reasons for wishing Edgar more than ever out of the way. A Mrs. Elizabeth Wills, in Richmond, claimed to be pregnant by him, the respected Mr. Allan. The thought, while reassuring him again of his vigor, troubled him for the scandal that might ensue if his paternity were known. In any case he had no wish to run the danger of Edgar's finding out. The West Point expectation had been dragging on long enough. Mr. Allan now took matters into his own hands. Through Senator Powhatan Ellis, Thomas Ellis' brother, he managed to set the wheels of bureaucracy spinning and, to his great satisfaction, the appointment at last materialized in March, 1830. Poe would not be due at West Point until June, but the prospect of ultimate relief helped to make the burden of Edgar's presence bearable.

Meanwhile the published poet, renewing old friendships about town, was splurging all the colors of his imagination to cover with romantic luster his period of service in the army. His brother Henry's experiences furnished him excellent local color which, heightened by his own inventiveness, out-Byroned Byron. Edgar had traveled all over the world, voyaged across oceans and continents, enjoyed dangerous adventures in Paris, in St. Petersburg. His stay-at-home friends listened open-mouthed and then went off to repeat the narrative. Through the uncanny workings of fiction, oft repeated, the tales eventually reached Russia itself and were solemnly included as fact in Russian encyclopedias.

Suddenly, while Edgar was enjoying his imaginary triumphs, reality came knocking at the door. Sergeant "Bully" Graves, his old army substitute, was writing him to demand the return of certain loans which he and a certain Downey had made him. According to Graves, Downey had already applied to Mr. Allan but had been turned away. Unfortunately, though Edgar, to all outward appearances, was again the son of the house, he was as usual kept on skimpy financial rations. To offset his inability to repay the loan he passed off the matter brashly in his reply, adding an incautious fillip that was to ruin his chances forever with Mr. Allan.

"As to what you say about Downey Mr. A very evidently misunderstood me and I wish you to understand that I never sent any

money by Downey whatsoever—Mr. A is not very often sober—
which accounts for it. . . . I have tried to get the money for you
from Mr. A a dozen times—but he always shuffles me off. . . ." [1]

On that 3rd of May, 1830, before Edgar had sat down to write
to Graves, he had had a violent quarrel with Mr. Allan. With two
such antipathetic temperaments, the least provocation brought on a
storm. Feelings flared up, bitter words fell like hail. One can hear
Mr. Allan's inevitable allusions to Poe's actor parents and—a bolt
that never missed its mark—the taunts relating to Rosalie's birth.
Edgar then countered with accusations reflecting on Mr. Allan's
morals, on his sobriety. "As for Sergeant Graves—I did write him
that letter," Edgar admitted when confronted by Mr. Allan with
the charge. "As to the truth of its contents, I leave it to God, and
to your own conscience. . . . The time in which I wrote it was within
a half hour after you had embittered every feeling of my heart against
you by your abuse of my *family,* and myself, under your own
roof—and at a time when you knew that my heart was almost
breaking. . . ." [2]

No doubt Mr. Allan had been indulging in the bottle. Long before
his wife's death he had sought elsewhere what she could not give
him. The fruit of his latest liaison was expected shortly and he was
understandably ill at ease. He was so relieved when his uncomfortable
charge set out for Baltimore that he accompanied him to the steamboat. As they parted Edgar had a premonition that their farewell
was final.

Edgar went directly to Mrs. Clemm's house, which, by now, had
become home. There he was sure of the affection for which he hungered and of admiration given unreservedly, if also uncritically. For
Mrs. Clemm Eddie, as she called him, could do no wrong. For him
Muddie, Virginia's baby-name for her mother, was becoming more
and more the substitute for the parent he had so early lost.

He was not long in Baltimore, for, late in June, he was taking his
entrance examinations at West Point, prior to his pledging his oath
on the 1st of July. At about the same time, in Richmond, Mrs. Wills
was presenting Mr. Allan with twin sons. Such double proof of his
virility reached Mr. Allan at his Lower Byrd plantation, where he
was spending the summer months, varying them agreeably with visits
to his friends, the John Mayos, at their Belleville estate.

As chance would have it, the Mayos were at the time enjoying
the company of Mrs. Mayo's niece, Louisa Gabriella Patterson, a

[1] *Valentine Letters.* Ostrom, p. 36.
[2] *Ibid.* Ostrom, pp. 41-42.

maiden-lady of thirty. She was not beautiful but neither was she unhandsome, despite the heaviness of her features. Her mouth was well shaped and firm; her keen eyes were intelligent, and there was a certain wholesomeness about her vigorous figure. Moreover, Miss Patterson had the advantage of being well connected. Besides the Mayos, she counted among her relatives Mrs. Catherine Livingston, of Livingston Manor.

Although of an age when maiden-ladies were left to wither on their maiden stalk, Miss Patterson still possessed much to captivate a mature widower. Evidently Mr. Allan overcame with a whirlwind courtship whatever coy resistance the lady put up, for before summer's end they had set their wedding date for the 5th of October.

If it was Mr. Allan's wealth that attracted Miss Patterson, there was indeed plenty—enough to offset the disadvantages of his dropsy and the twenty years' difference in their ages. From a certain point of view what appeared to be disabilities might turn out advantages in the end. Miss Patterson showed remarkable tolerance on another matter, the peccadillo that had materialized as twins, which the honest Scotsman confessed to her. As no secrets now stood in the way of their union, they went to New York, where, in the house of the bride's parents and with a circle of Galts, Ellises and other wellwishers about them, the marriage was celebrated.

Edgar was not among the guests. In fact he had no knowledge of the event until he learned of it indirectly through Richmond friends who were visiting the Point. "I was greatly in hopes that you would have come on to W. Point while you were in New York," he wrote "Dear Sir" on the 6th of November, 1830, "and was very much disappointed when I heard you had gone on home without letting me hear from you. I have a very excellent standing in my class—in the first section in every thing and have great hopes of doing well. . . . I have seen Gen. Scott here since I came, and he was very polite and attentive—I am very much pleased with Colonel Thayer, and indeed with every thing at the Institution. . . ." He made no mention of the marriage, but toward the close of the letter he added, "Please give my respects to Mrs. A and to Mr and Mrs Jas Galt and Miss V. . . . I was indeed very much in hopes that the beauty of the river would have tempted yourself and Mr and Mrs Jas Galt to have paid us a visit." [3]

The formal address in itself indicated strained relations. Since July he had had no word from Mr. Allan. Edgar was grieved and hurt, and very much concerned. There he was, at the Academy, living at

[3] *Ibid.* Ostrom, pp. 38-39.

28 South Barracks, with two other cadets to share the confined quarters and austere simplicity, the drills and endless routine of military discipline and no privacy for the poetry that was his true vocation. He found himself in his predicament out of obedience to Mr. Allan's wishes, among youths far younger than himself, a man of twenty-two. Though he had given his age as nineteen for the record, the beardless boys were quite aware of the disparity and jokingly insisted that the superannuated Poe "had procured a Cadet's appointment for his son, and the boy having died, the father had substituted himself in his place." [4]

His dreams of future greatness were not sufficient to make him bear without resentment the time wasted in the eternal changing of uniforms, winding of sashes and polishing of buttons, thanks to Lieutenant Joseph Locke, the overseer of South Barracks, whom he had known as a martinet at Fortress Monroe. Worse, the man had a spiteful way of ferreting out information and going to the authorities with it. Poe had his revenge by lampooning him in verses which the other cadets gleefully repeated:

> John Locke was a notable name;
>   Joe Locke is a greater: in short,
> The former was well known to fame,
>   But the latter's well known "to report."

For the sake of the freedom which he was planning to obtain as soon as possible, Edgar was willing to mark time. Mr. Allan, meanwhile, was not only ungenerous with his letters, but he also kept his purse strings obstinately tight. Except for the four blankets which the Academy required each cadet to provide, Mr. Allan had given Edgar little else. However, at West Point, as at Charlottesville, there were places where impecunious young gentlemen could barter one commodity for another. Such a place, a general store combined with a liquor shop, was kept by Old Benny Haven—out of bounds, but accessible. One by one Edgar's blankets had exchanged the warmth of fine carded wool for the comfort of the brandy bottle, shared with his roommate, Cadet T. H. Gibson, and a few others. Then, his mind stimulated by the liquor and his troubles temporarily forgotten, he would hold forth on the subjects closest to his true interest.

"Campbell is a plagiarist," he declared one evening, after picking up a volume of Campbell's poems and contemptuously flinging it aside. His startled companions turned to him for elucidation. Taking up the book again, he opened it at a certain page and continued:

[4] *Harper's New Monthly Magazine,* November, 1867.

"There is a line more often quoted than any other passage of his: 'Like angel visits few and far between,' and he stole it bodily from Blair's *Grave*. Not satisfied with the theft he has spoiled it in the effort to disguise it. Blair wrote, 'Like angel visits *short* and far between.' Campbell's 'few and far between' is mere tautology." [5]

The youths were of course impressed by such learning, which dared also to be so iconoclastic. It was no wonder that he early established a reputation for genius. According to Cadet Gibson, poems and squibs of local interest were daily issued from Number 28 and went the rounds of the classes. Nevertheless, in spite of Poe's reputation and the excellence of his class standing, both the professors and the cadets had set him down, as the saying was, for a "January Colt."

None knew it better than Edgar himself. The news of Mr. Allan's marriage and the utter disregard he had shown for his, Edgar's, needs further confirmed him in the disaffection for a cadet's life and the career that would follow. He knew now that he had little to expect from his adopted father in Virginia who was very rich, as he had described Pa to David Hale, his fellow cadet, whose mother had praised his poems in her magazine. Edgar also fed the gullible youth his usual adaptation of Henry's adventures, adding this time that he, Edgar, had been graduated from an English college—thus conferring upon himself a degree which he had failed to obtain in Charlottesville and which he would endeavor to eschew at the Academy.

Threatened in all his expectations by the marriage which would, doubtless provide Mr. Allan with heirs of his own blood, Edgar knew that he had little to hope for in the future. However, at this juncture it was not the former Miss Patterson and her hypothetical children who threatened his prospects, but his incautious statement about Mr. Allan's not being very often sober.

The accusation had wounded the newly married pillar of society. It was only natural that he should impart to his bride the cause of his agitation, and to show her the offending letter. Whether Mr. Allan distorted the facts to plead his case or whether Louisa Allan misinterpreted them for reasons of her own, Edgar was made to appear in a damaging light in her account of him, years later, to Thomas Ellis.

"Mr. Poe," she wrote, "had not lived under Mr. Allan's roof for two years before my marriage. . . . His letters were very scarce and dated from St. Petersburg, Russia, although he had enlisted in the army. . . . After he became tired of army life, he wrote to his benefactor, expressing a desire to have a substitute if the money could be sent to him. Mr. Allan sent it, Poe spent it; and after the substitute was tired

[5] *Ibid.*

out, waiting and getting letters and excuses, he . . . enclosed one of Poe's letters to Mr. Allan, which was too black to be credited. . . . Mr. Allan sent the money to the man, and banished Poe from his affections. . . ." [6]

The only unimpeachable statement was the last. From the moment John Allan had read Edgar's letter he determined to cut him out of his life. It was no sudden decision, however. Even before Frances Allan's death he had almost succeeded on several occasions in shaking off the unwanted burden. At last, in this act of blackest ingratitude, as he interpreted it, John Allan found the perfect pretext to free himself forever and wrote to Edgar in no uncertain terms that he wished no longer to be troubled by any further communication from him.

"As to your injunction . . . rest assured, Sir, that I will most religiously observe it," Edgar replied on the 3rd of January, 1831. But first he poured out all his grievances. Did he, as an infant, solicit Mr. Allan's charity and protection? At the time Mr. Allan interposed, his Grandfather Poe was wealthy and would have taken him, his favorite grandchild, into his family. "But the promise of adoption, and liberal education . . . induced him to resign all care of me into your hands. Under such circumstances, can it be said that I have no *right* to expect anything at your hands?" All the humiliations he had suffered from lack of money at the university came pouring out in a flood. "After nearly 2 years conduct with which no fault could be found—in the army, as a common soldier—I *earned,* myself, by the most humiliating privations—a Cadet's warrant which you could have obtained at any time for asking. . . . You sent me to W. Point like a beggar." Then came the bolt. "The same difficulties are threatening me as before . . . and I must resign."

Since John Allan was casting him off, there was no need for further pretense. Poe knew the hardships to which he would be exposed, alone and unfriended. He was willing to chance them all for the freedom to indulge his true career. "I have no more to say—except that my future life (which thank God will not endure long) must be passed in indigence and sickness. . . ." [7]

One thing alone he asked of Allan, that, as his nominal guardian, he would send him written permission to resign. Even if Mr. Allan refused this last request, it would be useless, for Edgar could leave the Point without permission—except that his guardian's refusal would deprive him of the little pay which would be due him as mileage.

[6] *Richmond Standard,* April 22, 1880.
[7] *Valentine Letters.* Ostrom, pp. 41-42.

John Allan ignored that pathetic plea. He had firmly shut the door on Poe and he refused to open it the least crack for fear of having him put his foot into his house again. Let Edgar neglect his duties at West Point, as he threatened. Let him be dismissed. The man who had complacently declared, "Every man is my care, if he be in distress," made an exception of the youth whom all Richmond looked upon as his son. Instead of answering Edgar, he noted on his letter: "I . . . did not from its conclusion deem it necessary to reply. . . . I do not think the boy has one good quality. He may do or act as he pleases. . . . His letter is the most barefaced onesided statement."

Edgar was as good as his word in the reckless desperation into which he was thrown by Mr. Allan's indifference. When, after waiting for days, he had no word from Richmond, he began systematically to neglect his duties. On the 28th of January, 1831 a court-martial convened at the Academy to try a number of students, among them Cadet Poe. The charges against him were gross neglect of duty for absenting himself from parades and roll calls and other academical functions and for disobedience of orders. Cadet E. A. Poe was found guilty on all the charges and specifications and the court decreed that he be dismissed the service of the United States, the decree to be effective on the 6th of March, 1831.

Poe did not wait until then. He had business in New York, business more important to him than anything else that life could offer. He was having a new edition of his works published, with a preface and a number of new poems, some of them written at the Academy. He had shown the manuscript to Colonel Sylvanus Thayer, who had been sympathetic to him from the first. Although the Colonel did not know one metre from another, he saw nothing in the poems to disapprove, and since the cadets were willing to help one of their fellows toward fame by contributing cash, he permitted them to subscribe toward the volume. The transfer of money occurred painlessly, the subscribing cadets being docked seventy-five cents of their pay in return for a copy of the book when it appeared. With the publication costs thus assured, Edgar arranged the negotiations with Elam Bliss, a New York publisher.

On the 19th of February, therefore, with the faithful doppelgänger trunk packed with his few belongings, Edgar, in what odds and ends of clothing he had been able to assemble, and with his West Point greatcoat covering a multitude of shabbiness, descended toward the wharf for the boat that was to take him to New York. It was a raw, bitter day. He had been sick and his ear ached. Because of Mr. Allan's refusal to send the required permission, Poe had been deprived of the $30.35 that would have been his mileage money. Also, thanks to Mr. Allan's miserliness, Edgar's Cadet's pay of $16 a month had been applied toward what he owed the Academy.

It was a miserable, suffering piece of humanity that, on leaving the ferry, lost itself in the indifference of New York. The only person Poe knew in the city was Elam Bliss, who had gone to West Point to arrange for the publication of the poems, but Edgar's pride would have forbade his presenting himself to him in that condition.

One can only surmise from what wretched hole and from what depths of despair Edgar, in bitter humiliation, wrote for help, on the 21st of February, to the man who was largely responsible for his situation.

"It will however be the last time that I trouble any human being . . ." he traced in a shaky hand. "I now make an appeal not to your affection because I have lost that but to your sense of justice— I wrote to you for permission to resign. . . . I, as I told you, neglected my duty when I found it impossible to attend to it, and the consequences were inevitable—dismissal. . . . The whole academy have interested themselves in my behalf because my only crime was being *sick*. . . . I refer you to Col Thayer to the public records, for my standing and reputation for talent . . . if you had granted me permission to resign—all might have been avoided. I have not strength nor energy left to write half what I feel. . . . You one day or other will *felll* [*sic*] how you have treated me. . . . I have caught a most violent cold and am confined to my bed—I have no money—no friends— I have written to my brother—but he cannot help me . . . besides a most violent cold on my lungs my *ear* discharges blood and matter continually and my headache is distracting. . . . Please send me a little money—quickly—and forget what I said about you—God bless you." In a postscript he added, "Do not say a word to my sister. I shall send to the P.O. every day." [8]

He sent to the post office in vain. The cry for help which would have wrung the last coin from a beggar left John Allan unmoved, except indeed to praise a stern God for the salutary lesson taught a disobedient youth.

Somehow, perhaps through the kindness of Mr. Bliss or from whatever odd jobs he might have obtained, Poe managed to survive while waiting for the publication of his book. In March, however, the difficulties of earning a living once again loomed forbiddingly—or was it heroic fervor that made him apply to Colonel Thayer, with an astounding request? He intended, he said, to leave for Paris at the first

[8] *Ibid.* Ostrom, pp. 43-44.

opportunity to obtain an appointment in the Polish Army, if possible, through the influence of the Marquis de La Fayette. Any assistance that might lie in the power of Colonel Thayer, like a certificate of standing in his class, a letter to a friend in Paris, or to the Marquis himself, would be appreciated. However, the Byronic offer fell flat before the stare of common sense. He had as little success from his application for an editorial position with the *Baltimore Gazette*. His thoughts, evidently, were now turning toward the city that offered the only hearth at which he was certain of welcome.

At last, in April, 1831, Elam Bliss brought out *Poems*, by Edgar A. Poe—Second Edition, as the title page specified. His debt to West Point Edgar discharged with the words: "To the U.S. Corps of Cadets this volume is respectfully dedicated."

Never had so rarefied a gift been made to such unsophisticated recipients. By an odd coincidence, just as the U.S. Army had indirectly paid for *Tamerlane*, future generals financed the new volume.

Unlike the earlier poems, there was nothing tentative in this latest work. Poe took it seriously and expected the world to take it on his terms—those of a dedicated artist. He had given the best of himself. Perhaps a few would appreciate his offering. That he was uncertain of his reception he revealed in his motto, "Tout le monde a raison"— Everybody is right or, in other words, everybody is entitled to his own opinion. As for himself, he knew the merit of his work. For the elucidation of the reader, however, he offered a prefatory letter, expounding his theory of what a poem should be. "A poem, in my opinion, is opposed to a work of science for having, for its *immediate* object, pleasure, not truth: to romance, for having for its object an *indefinite* instead of a *definite* pleasure, being a poem only so far as this object is attained. . . ."

It was the first enunciation of his poetic principle, to be expounded in the future in other essays. However, either through willful omission or by an oversight, the youth who had so recently excoriated Campbell for plagiarizing Blair, omitted quotation marks from a lengthy passage lifted bodily out of Coleridge's *Biographia Literaria*.[9]

The worth of the volume, however, lay not so much in any prose exposition as in the handful of new poems which, if Poe had written nothing else, would have assured America of an original genius. No native poet, so far, had been capable of the classical purity of "To Helen," here published for the first time, or of such allegorical evocations as that of "The Doomed City," later "The City in the Sea," where Poe's ultramundane vision saw:

[9] Mr. Joseph Wood Krutch was the first to make the discovery.

No rays from the holy heaven come down
On the long night-time of that town;
But light from out the lurid sea
Streams up the turrets silently—
Gleams up the pinnacles far and free—
Up domes—up spires—up kingly halls—
Up fanes—up Babylon-like walls—
Up shadowy long-forgotten bowers
Of sculptured ivy and stone flowers—
Up many and many a marvellous shrine
Whose wreathèd friezes intertwine
The viol, the violet, and the vine.
Resignedly beneath the sky
The melancholy waters lie.
So blend the turrets and shadows there
That all seem pendulous in air,
While from a proud tower in the town
Death looks gigantically down.

Music as well as imagery contributed to the total effect, making of such a line as "The viol, the violet, and the vine" so complete a harmony of sense and sound that, seventeen years later, in England, it was to inspire a new school of poetry in the young Pre-Raphaelites.

"The Valley Nis"—Sin, inverted—another allegorical landscape of the soul, also dealt with evil, but with a Dantesque vision, as in the Fifth Canto of the *Inferno,* where the souls are eternally whirled about. Poe wrote:

Now each visitor shall confess
The sad valley's restlessness.
Nothing there is motionless—

Another, perhaps the most personal of the poems, embodied in form and content Poe the man, but even more, the poet. Perhaps originally inspired by the lines of Béranger,

Son cœur est un luth suspendu;
Sitôt qu'on le touche, il résonne . . .

Poe made the thought his own by adapting it to his purpose:

In Heaven a spirit doth dwell
    "Whose heart strings are a lute";
None sing so wildly well
As the angel Israfel,
And the giddy stars (so legends tell),
Ceasing their hymns, attend the spell
    Of his voice, all mute.

.   .   .   .

And they say (the starry choir
    And the other listening things)
That Israfeli's fire
Is owing to that lyre
    By which he sits and sings—
The trembling living wire
Of those unusual strings.

.   .   .   .   .   .

If I could dwell
Where Israfel
    Hath dwelt, and he where I,
He might not sing so wildly well
    A mortal melody,
While a bolder note than this might swell
    From my lyre within the sky.

Meanwhile the poet who challenged Israfel had no roof that he could call his own nor sufficient clothes and food for his body.

→≫ • ≪←

CHAPTER XII

"Come Rest in This Bosom"

AGAIN, as before in his need, Edgar took his trunk and carpetbag to Mrs. Clemm's. Baltimore, though not so large a city as New York, was steadily gaining in importance. Its port, crowded with sails and clippers whose figureheads broke the waters of two oceans, had also several lines of side-wheel steamers which linked it with modern progress. Recently it had forestalled its rivals, New York and Philadelphia, with that newfangled mode of locomotion, the Baltimore and Ohio Railroad. Though its first cars were drawn by equine power, the "iron horse" would soon be chugging and tooting and clattering along on steam. What drew Edgar, more than the progress of science, was Baltimore's publishing business. Besides its newspapers, the thriving metropolis had a number of periodicals and a group of contributors that kept the publications from inanition. Here, where Henry had a number of literary connections, Edgar hoped to find employment.

The sad little household, located by the Baltimore City Directory in Mechanic's Row, Wilk Street, was, if anything, more depressing than ever. Grandmother Poe was fast sinking into doddering senility. Sadder still was Henry, only twenty-four, yet, as everyone could see, not long for this world. No one gave his malady a name but the symptoms were recognizable in that slow decline and that spitting of blood that would ultimately consume him. More often now, and for longer periods, Henry had to take to his bed, where, in the attic which Edgar had come to share, the two would indulge their dreams of fame.

Occasionally, on Henry's good days, the brothers would go calling on some flame of Henry's or renew an acquaintance which might lead to some salaried employment for Edgar, as work for Henry was now out of the question. He was confirmed in his drinking habits, which, at least, gave him temporary forgetfulness and the illusion of health. Laughing and unaware, Diddie, as the nine-year-old Virginia was called, brought with her childhood gaiety the only spark of brightness to that house.

How they existed was a miracle whose secret Mrs. Clemm alone knew. In poverty's shifts and devices to make a meal for three serve six, she was past master from long practice. Her housekeeping made every doorknob and candlestick sparkle and, with the summer coming on, the minutest plot of soil, every flower pot, was coaxed to yield its tribute to brighten the parlor.

Mrs. Clemm herself was a pillar of strength. Tall, sturdy, with a massive yet handsome face whose pale eyes seemed to have faded through secret weeping, whose lips had set from habit to a smile of resignation, she was the matriarch of that family whose members, from the youngest, Virginia, to the oldest, Grandmother Poe, spanned four generations. In her sober dress, always spotless, with her white widow's cap framing her face in its starched folds, Mrs. Clemm looked like some lay nun about her duties, as she went the rounds with her wicker basket to provide for her dependents. The passer-by would have thought she was out marketing, and in a sense she was, though as she stopped by, at her Poe or Herring relatives' or at her good neighbors' doorsteps, the coin she gave was a grateful look or a gentle "Thank you." Grandmother Poe's annual pension was still the staple income—and she was seventy-five years old.

Edgar's quest for employment proved futile. Early in May, 1831, he had written to William Gwynn, of the *Baltimore Gazette,* for the post which he understood had been left vacant by his cousin, Neilson, son of Jacob Poe. Mr. Gwynn did not deign to answer, still nursing a smart administered by Edgar, who prefaced his request by making apologies for foolish conduct upon a former occasion—no doubt a blistering reproof to the editor for not having shown sufficient appreciation of "Al Aaraaf." Poe then applied to another acquaintance, Dr. Nathan C. Brooks, for the post of usher at the boys' school which Dr. Brooks had recently established. The young lads of Reisterstown, Maryland, however, were not destined, like the washerwomen of Charlottesville, to tell their grandchildren that they had once known Poe.

Though not on a salary, Edgar was nonetheless working—in prose now, giving form to the promptings of a bizarre imagination. The periodicals accepted tales and stories. Sometimes they even paid for them. In the intervals of nursing his dying brother Edgar would forget reality by letting his fancy roam from Baltimore to France, to Jerusalem, to Hungary. In no mood for laughter in the near presence of death, he would still, like a boy challenging the terrifying dark, seek to mock the mystery that appalled him. So he wrote of the Duc de L'Omelette who, on finding himself in the other world, does not at first believe it. "I took thee, just now, from a rose-wood coffin inlaid with ivory," Baal-Zebub assures him. "Thou wast curiously scented, and labelled as per invoice. Belial sent thee—my inspector of Cemeteries. The pantaloons, which thou sayest were made by Bourdon, are an excellent pair of linen drawers, and thy *robe-de-chambre* is a shroud of no scanty dimensions." [1]

The story resolved itself in a jest. A wry jest was also the theme of "A Tale of Jerusalem," wherein two Jews lower a basket of tribute to the Romans below and haul up, instead of the fattened firstlings of the flock they had expected—a pig. Yet at the time that Poe had been writing these dubious divertissements, he had also conceived "Metzengerstein," a powerful tale of Gothic horror based on the doctrine of metempsychosis. In this case the vengeful spirit of a horse on a tapestry transfers itself to the body of another, for retributive justice.

Essentially it is a moral tale of sin and its wages in death. But the atmosphere of grandeur surrounding the inner evil of a soul is so suggestively evoked that it is as much an active part of the tale as the character of Metzengerstein, or the steed that rode him into the flames of the hell which he himself had created. The close had the impact of an apocalyptic vision. "The fury of the tempest immediately died away, and a dead calm suddenly succeeded. A white flame still enveloped the building like a shroud, and, streaming far away into the quiet atmosphere, shot forth a glare of preternatural light; while a cloud of smoke settled heavily over the battlements in the distinct colossal figure of—*a horse*." [2]

In vain scholars have pointed out the presence of a horse in a tapestry in Disraeli's *Vivian Grey,* which Poe is known to have read. Everything in the natural world is, and has been, and every creative artist has helped himself to the bounty surrounding him. The test of genius lies in the use he makes of it. The one flaw in "Metzengerstein" derives from Poe's habit of supporting, with learned quotation in a plurality of languages, his not always well-assimilated knowledge— here in an excerpt from "an acute and intelligent Parisian" who makes no fewer than five mistakes in a single sentence. Evidently Poe had reading knowledge of French and Italian but was not sufficiently versed in either language to write it with authority.

That summer of 1831 the *Philadelphia Saturday Courier* announced a prize of $100 for the best story submitted. Poe sent five tales, among them "Metzengerstein." The prize, however, went to a now-forgotten genteel female, Delia S. Bacon, for "Love's Martyr." Poe

---

[1] "The Duc de L'Omelette."
[2] "Metzengerstein."

enjoyed only the pleasure of seeing his stories in print in the 1832 issues of the magazine.

Meanwhile, on the 2nd of August, 1831, Henry Poe's name, misspelled, had appeared in print in the Baltimore papers. He had died the previous night, and friends and acquaintances were invited to attend his funeral, at nine that morning, from the dwelling of Mrs. Clemm. He was twenty-four, the age of his mother on her death from the same disease. There was no "rose-wood" coffin for him, only the plain casket which the family could afford—not without hardship to the living. To the crude reality of poverty Henry's death meant one less mouth to feed, one less invalid to tend, a little more room in the crowded house, one misery spared to the living. He had had a small talent and he had done what he could with it. For him the epitaph that David Gray, the poet of the *Luggie,* wrote for himself, on dying, years later, at the same age and of the same ill, would have been appropriate:

> 'Twas not a life,
> 'Twas but a piece of childhood thrown away.

Henry's death also meant the sundering of the closest tie Edgar had with his own flesh and blood. The youth had been reckless of his health and life, but he had possessed the creative spark which, more than birth, made the two brothers kin. Rosalie alone remained. Now, at twenty-one, she was what she had been at twelve, what she would always be—an unpredictable, arrested being and an embarrassment to her brother. The only relative who valued and loved him, to whom he could go with his few joys and his many disappointments, was Mrs. Clemm, whose ample bosom had room for that tormented head, whose ampler heart took him in, never to abandon him in life or in death.

Poe's other Baltimore kin, the Herrings and the Neilson Poes, looked with mistrust on the youth who had once been their envy as the spoiled darling of the rich Allans. His present castoff state could only argue for some flaw in his character. Surely the virtuous gentleman who had written such a letter to Henry Poe about Edgar had not ventured on it without unpardonable provocation. Mr. Herring, therefore, frowned upon Edgar's visits to his adolescent daughter Elizabeth and on that poetry writing of his, which turned female heads, none too steady to begin with. The prosperous lumber merchant had other plans for his daughter.

Neilson Poe's censorious attitude had more to do with the impropriety of a grown man's allowing himself to be coddled by his aunt and who wasted his time scribbling when he should have been employed at some remunerative work. He himself, Edgar's junior by eight months, was already a respected and responsible citizen, married to Josephine Emily Clemm, a half sister of little Virginia's. Neilson also foresaw trouble in the presence of a male of over twenty-one— even though he was a blood kin—in a household of women, now that Henry Poe was dead and Henry Clemm had run off to sea. Virginia was a very pretty child and it would not be long before she became an even prettier girl. The Neilson Poes, watching from the wings, disapproved of the evolving complications.

It may be that Henry's death or the indefinable sorrow latent in the human situation moved Edgar, after many months, to write to Mr. Allan. He was by himself, he explained, thinking of old times and old friends until his heart was full. "When I think of the long twenty one years that I have called you father, and you have called me son, I could cry like a child to think that it should all end like this. You know me too well to think me interested—if so: why have I rejected your thousand offers of love and kindness? . . . When I look back upon the past and think of every thing—of how much you tried to do for me—of your forbearance and your generosity, in spite of the most flagrant ingratitude on my part, I can not help thinking myself the greatest fool in existence. . . . But I am fully—truly conscious that all these better feelings have *come too late*. . . . I have nothing more to say—and *this time,* no favor to ask. . . . May God bless you— Will you not write one word to me?" [3]

It was the outpouring of a heart and soul surcharged with feeling, during one of those moments when a man stands face to face with his conscience—a William Wilson of the story Poe was yet to write, facing his accusing double. Being a man and an honest one, Edgar admitted his faults. Being a poet, he was so carried away by his emotions that he overdramatized his guilt.

In any case, the strong man who, like the forbidding crag, still had a crevice where frail things may grow, responded to this outburst of sentiment. Despite the differences which had embittered them against each other, there had been the early years when the pretty boy was exhibited at dinner parties to toast the guests and amuse them with recitations. Then had come the long English period, perhaps the closest in the family relationship, when Edgar had been known as Master Allan.

Memory softened the stern heart. Mr. Allan answered the letter and also sent a little material help. Unhappily for Edgar, not long after receiving this unexpected bounty he was forced by ill luck to apply for

[3] *Valentine Letters.* Oct. 16, 1831, p. 46.

more. Two years earlier he had incurred a debt, as much on his brother Henry's account as on his own, a debt which, as he said, he never expected to have to pay. Now, suddenly, he was arrested and would face imprisonment unless he procured the money. He had made every exertion to obtain it, but in vain. Now, on the 18th of November, 1831, he wrote to his "Dear Pa" explaining his situation. He would rather have done anything on earth than apply to him again after his late kindness. "If you will only send me this one time $80, by Wednesday next, I will never forget . . . your generosity.—if you refuse God only knows what I shall do, & all my hopes & prospects are ruined for ever. . . ." [4]

If Edgar had been arrested for debt, he was not overstating his case, for the laws of Baltimore imposed jail sentences for sums of even a fraction of that amount. Indeed, the city jails were jammed with debtors unable to meet their obligations. Edgar's letter cried out its urgency in every sentence, but Wednesday passed, and another Wednesday followed, and not a word—not to mention a bank draft—came from Mr. Allan. On the 5th of December Mrs. Clemm added her plea to Edgar's. The poor boy had no one else to turn to, she wrote Mr. Allan. Edgar had been very kind to her and was in debt to no one except for that amount. She herself had been able to raise $20 toward the payment, but that would not be enough.

The two let ten more days pass in anxious waiting. When no relief came, Edgar, goaded and distraught beyond endurance, pleaded again in terms that must have cost him agonies of self-abasement. "I know that I have no longer any hopes of being again received into your favour, but, for the sake of Christ, do not let me perish for a sum of money which you would never miss. . . . You are enjoying yourself in all the blessings that wealth & happiness can bestow, and I am suffering every extremity of want and misery. . . . I know you have never turned a beggar from your door, and I apply to you in that light, I *beg* you for a little aid. . . . If you wish me to humble myself before you I am humble. . . ." [5]

Unknown to the desperate suppliant, Mr. Allan, not so hardhearted as he seemed, had been working on the matter in his own way. He had reason to be generous. Among the blessings which happiness could bestow he had received, the previous September, an heir of his own blood, whose lusty voice was probably penetrating his sanctum as he pondered what to do about the youth who, two decades earlier, had given him the illusion of paternity.

[4] *Ibid.* Ostrom, p. 47.
[5] *Ibid.* Dec. 15, 1831. Ostrom, p. 48.

To the man who kept every scrap of paper he ever received, and who was constantly and obsessively poring over, and annotating, Edgar's communications, every word was fraught with meaning. On reading the letter of November 18, with the request for $80, he may have confronted it with another, written exactly two years earlier, in which Edgar had thanked him for that sum sent him. His suspicious mind may have associated the two and drawn a conclusion detrimental to Edgar.[6]

However, the reiterated plea, with its augmenting despair, and Mrs. Clemm's substantiation of Edgar's straits, made him take action. "Wrote on the 7th Decr. 1831 to John Walsh," he noted on Edgar's letter, "to procure his liberation & to give him $20 besides to keep him out of further difficulties. . . ." Whether deliberately or from some unexplained desire to make Edgar suffer from his present misfortune, he did not post the letter until the 12th of January, 1832. "Then I put it in the office myself," he recorded.

To the harassed family on Wilk Street the intervention of Mr. Walsh came as an angelic visitation, especially if, with Edgar's ransom, the emissary brought "$20 besides." The Christmas holidays, in poverty, had contrasted sadly with the cheer and plenty of the Richmond mansion, the parties of young people in Edgar's honor, the gifts, the New Year's calls. Something of these and earlier days Edgar had recalled to Mr. Allan in a final plea, before the advent of Mr. Walsh. "For the sake of what once was dear to you, for the sake of the love you bore me when I sat upon your knee and called you father do not forsake me. . . ."[7]

Happily he did not know that the $20 brought by Mr. Allan's emissary marked the last subsidy he was to receive from Richmond. As a stern believer in the rights of the blood Mr. Allan now had closer demands upon his fortune. He was getting on in years. His disease was incapacitating him more and more, so that he was now often inactive in his easy chair. Such indications of mortality turned his practical mind toward the distribution of his worldly goods. He began pondering his final will.

The new year brought its imponderable events to the individual as to the world. In England the passing of the Reform Bill shared the public press with the nefarious doings of Burke and Hare, who made

[6] The coincidence is pointed out by Ostrom in his notes, Vol. I, p. 38. As for Poe's arrest, Professor Quinn's researches, through Mr. Louis H. Dileman and Dr. J. Hall Pleasants of Baltimore, who examined the contemporary jail records, produced no evidence of Poe's having been arrested or imprisoned. Quinn, p. 190.

[7] *Valentine Letters.* Ostrom, p. 49.

a profitable business of providing fresh corpses for the dissecting table of Dr. Knox by the simple expedient of killing their victims. In France, hope of restoring the Empire died with Napoleon's son, once King of Rome. Death also claimed Germany's Goethe, Scotland's Walter Scott, France's Cuvier and Maryland's ninety-six-year-old Charles Carroll, the last surviving signer of the Declaration of Independence. Italy and Greece were carrying on their struggles for independence. In Washington Andrew Jackson's domestic policy brought him in conflict with the United States Bank of Philadelphia for failing to establish a sound new form of currency, and "wildcat" became a new word in the language to denote banking institutions which issued worthless paper money and created financial panic. In New York summer brought an epidemic of Asiatic cholera that spread with appalling consequences to Albany, Rochester and other cities. In their anguish over the sick and dying, the usually demonstrative New Yorkers made little fuss over their new toy, the first horse-drawn streetcars.

In Baltimore Edgar Allan Poe fell in love.

Mary Devereaux was a pretty young woman whose chief assets were an alluring chevelure of reddish-blonde curls and a bright disposition. She lived with her parents on Essex Street, but the rows of buildings were so arranged that the back of Mrs. Clemm's house faced the courtyard and rear windows of the Devereaux dwelling.[8]

One day, when Edgar chanced to look out from his attic study, his gaze was drawn by the bright hair of a girl sitting at the window of the house across the courtyard. Soon they began a Pyramus and Thisbe exchange of signals which emboldened the young gallant to send Virginia for a lock of the shimmering hair—a bold request, in those days, indicative of serious intentions, to judge by the calfish awkwardness and trepidation with which a more mature lover asked the same favor, fourteen years later, of the poetess who was to become Mrs. Browning. It revealed Edgar as strangely headlong and impulsive.

After the exchange of signals, notes passed back and forth between the lover and his lass, the messenger being little Virginia, till the two reached the conventional understanding which allowed Edgar to visit Mary in her parlor. Again, as during his boyhood courtship of Elmira, the tender interviews were accompanied by music, and often he would beg Mary to sing him his favorite song, Tom Moore's

[8] The chief source of the Poe-Devereaux episode is Augustus Van Cleef's "Poe's Mary" in *Harper's New Monthly Magazine*, March, 1889, written as told to him by Mary Devereaux.

"Come Rest in This Bosom," while the family listened from a discreet distance in another part of the house. The words floated upon the air, creating their effect upon the youth.

> Thou hast call'd me thy Angel in moments of bliss
> And thy Angel I'll be, 'mid the horrors of this,—
> Through the furnace, unshrinking, thy steps to pursue,
> And shield thee, and save thee,—or perish there too!

"The intensity of their expression is not surpassed by anything in Byron," Poe wrote of the verses. "There are two of the lines in which a sentiment is conveyed that embodies the *all in all* of the divine passion of Love. . . ." [9]

This sentiment spoke directly to the heart of the insecure youth who needed, and was ever to need, a woman's comfort and protection against some secret to which he alluded in himself. In fact, whether to borrow a romantic aura or merely to be noticed, Poe had begun to shroud himself in a metaphorical cloak. Part of it was the pose of the "poet accursed," as the French were to name a generation of bards largely derived from Poe's influence. Most of it Poe genuinely believed to be a fate to which he was doomed.

"He was not well balanced; he had too much brain. He scoffed at everything sacred and never went to church," the ingenuous Mary sought to sound the unfathomable. "If he had had religion to guide him, he would have been a better man. . . ." [10] Perhaps—if by religion Mary meant the churchgoing to which Edgar had been exposed as a boy. Unfortunately the Protestant Episcopalian teachings of the Allans' church had lost out to the worship of beauty which, as Psyche, Poe had long since enshrined in a niche of his own Holy Land. Another dark secret of the Poe family was also hinted at by Mary: "Mrs. Clemm also spoke vaguely of some family mystery, of some disgrace." [11]

Such confidences on the part of Edgar and his aunt betoken more than an "understanding" between the young people, who considered themselves virtually engaged. They would go out walking in the evening to the outskirts of Baltimore and sit together on the hill slopes. "He was passionate in his love. . . . When he loved, he loved desperately," Mary recalled. [12]

Although also tender and affectionate, Edgar had a stormy temper

[9] In "The Poetic Principle."
[10] Van Cleef, *op. cit.*
[11] *Ibid.*
[12] *Ibid.*

and was very jealous. To tease him, one evening, when a friend of her brother's was calling, she sang at the young man's request Edgar's favorite song. As she was accompanying herself at the piano and the interloper turned the leaves, Edgar paced up and down like Othello, one hand behind his back, while he bit the nails of the other. Suddenly, in a passion, he snatched up the music and flung it to the floor. The lovers' quarrel that followed was soon patched up, but another, which succeeded it some nights later, had unanticipated consequences.

As usual, Mary had been waiting for him to call, but the night wore on and Eddie did not appear. At ten o'clock her mother advised her to go to bed, but as Mary had been crying from disappointment, she remained as she was with her head on her arms on the sill of the parlor window, shaded by the half-open shutters. When Eddie finally made his appearance, Mary could tell at once that something was wrong. She opened the door and went out. As it was a moonlight night she asked him to sit on the stoop, as often before.

He explained that he had met some cadets from West Point, old friends of his, who invited him to join their party at Barnum's Hotel, where they all had supper and champagne. He had got away as soon as he could. Mary knew his reaction to even a glass of wine and that night he had had more than one, as she soon found out. From her account Edgar made advances of a far more passionate nature than Mary could grant without the protection of a wedding ring. When he grew too insistent she jumped past him, off the stoop, ran around through the alley way to the back door and ran into her mother's room.

"Mary! Mary! What's the matter?" cried Mrs. Devereaux.

The girl had scarcely opened her mouth when Edgar came dashing into the room after her. "Go upstairs!" Mrs. Devereaux told her daughter, who was already on her way up, in her agitation. Edgar turned toward Mrs. Devereaux. "I want to talk to your daughter," he said imperiously. "If you don't tell her to come downstairs I will go after her. I have a right to," he added.

Mrs. Devereaux was a stalwart woman and not easily cowed. "You have no right to! You cannot go upstairs," she said.

"I have a right," Edgar insisted. "She is my wife now in the sight of Heaven!"

Somehow Mrs. Devereaux prevailed upon him to go home and to bed.

After such a scene the too-impetuous lover was forbidden the house and little Virginia was sent trotting back home with the letter she carried unwanted and unopened. Poe persisted. Mary finally yielded and read the missive, which addressed her formally, accused her of being heartless and unforgiving, and indulged in satire at her expense. Soon the Poe-Devereaux fracas became a family affair. Mary's mother showed the letter to the grandmother, who in turn handed it over to Mary's Uncle James, a man of fifty, who kept ,a store. Uncle James, called upon to defend pure maidenhood, wrote a severe letter to Edgar.

The poet was affronted as well as incensed. He did something so completely out of character that it is scarcely believable—unless, as on the night he had alarmed Mary, he was again intoxicated. At any rate, one afternoon he bought a cowhide. Edgar then sought out Uncle James at his store and proceeded to administer justice as he saw fit. The man's sons and his wife, in seeking to restrain the unmanageable youth, tore his frock coat at the back from the skirts to the collar. Unmindful of his appearance, Edgar, his honor satisfied, put the cowhide up his sleeve and strode through the streets to the Devereaux house, where he demanded to see Mary's father.

At the commotion—for Edgar had picked up a retinue of boys on the way—Mary came downstairs. Edgar pulled out Uncle James' letter and told them all what he had done. Then, flinging the cowhide at Mary's feet, he said: "There! I make you a present of that!"

After so public a scandal the Devereaux family moved to Philadelphia, but the relations between the Devereaux women and Mrs. Clemm remained friendly. Mrs. Clemm no doubt imputed the unpleasant scene to the fact that her Eddie had been "sick, not himself," the terms she used, with perhaps more insight than she knew, for the effects of drink upon him.

According to Dr. J. W. Robertson, in a painstaking study of Poe and alcohol, the poet was indeed sick, and of a sickness which in his own day had not yet been named. "Dipsomania necessarily is an alcoholic inheritance. It is characterized by periodical seizures in which the subject, because of changed personality, is temporarily irresponsible, and cannot, at all times, be held accountable for his behavior or his acts. . . . There are periods of both elation and depression. . . . Often visionary schemes are undertaken without corresponding capacity to understand their real difficulties. . . ." [13] Most of the characteristics Poe already showed. The others, his alternating periods of elation and depression and his penchant for grandiose schemes, were shortly to manifest themselves.

[13] J. W. Robertson, *Edgar A. Poe*, pp. 4, 93.

For the present alcohol had lost him the one woman toward whom he felt for the first, and perhaps the only, time, the full-blooded passion of a male. Between the Mary Devereaux episode and the loves that were to follow intervened the imponderables of his personality.

CHAPTER XIII

-》》》 • 《《《-

Disinherited

MEANWHILE, in the late spring of 1832, Mr. Allan had been blessed with another son whom he called William Galt in gratitude to the man who had made him rich. The advent of a second heir and his awareness of not having many more years to live, decided him to make his long deferred will. He had sinned, but he was honest. In the document which he set out to write, and which he began "In the name of God," he kept nothing from his Deity or from his conscience. Its composition was not the matter of an hour or of a day. He produced a carefully thought-out testament in which he remembered not only his wife, his sons and relations, but also the fruits of his indiscretions, these last referred to with suspicion tinged with humor. "I desire that my executors shall out of my estate provide . . . a good English education for two boys sons of Mrs. Elizabeth Wills which she says are mine. I do not know their names. . . ." [1]

Name after name, of sisters, cousins, nephews, of Miss Valentine, who had remained a part of his household, of Galts, Johnstons, Fowlds, filled the pages. But nowhere was there any mention of Edgar, the equivalent of whose English education he so thoughtfully provided for the illegitimate sons he was not quite certain were his. Like Poe, Edwin Collier had also been excluded. A sin of such long standing had canceled itself out—unless death had already done Mr. Allan that favor.

By an ironic twist, it was to prevent what had already happened that Edgar, hearing rumors of the will, decided to visit Richmond. He had not been there for two years nor had he heard from Mr. Allan since the providential arrival of Mr. Walsh. Poe had first gone to the Mackenzies', as much for friendship's sake as to be brought abreast of the news. What feelings he experienced on walking along

[1] From copy of Will. Allen, Appendix, pp. 694-695.

147

the familiar path, between the sentinel trees, and up the steps of the Allan house—for many years his home—his heart alone knew.

According to the Mackenzie tradition, based on Edgar's account, the moment Old Dabney opened the door the young master told him to take his carpetbag up to his room. The old Negro, glad yet embarrassed to see him, informed him that there was no longer such a room, as Mrs. Allan had converted it to a guest chamber. Edgar scarcely had time to control his anger when Mrs. Allan came into the parlor. As Poe had not announced his visit, she had no idea of who he was and therefore, understandably, resented his presence in her house and, even more, his interference in her affairs, for he lost no time in expressing his hurt at the changes. Something, too, about the authoritarian manners of the lady—so different from his gentle Ma's—and the added evidence that his was a lost cause, filtering down from the upstairs nursery in the squalling of William Galt Allan, made him lose his temper. Harsh words flew back and forth, Edgar's accusing the fertile matron of having married for money, and Mrs. Allan rejoining scornfully that he had no right to be there as he was nothing but an object of her husband's charity. Bitter words, but true—of a truth that had certainly come out of the lion's mouth.

Alarmed by Edgar's manner, Mrs. Allan sent one of the servants to summon her husband from his office and also rudely indicated that she would welcome Edgar's departure from her house. Remembering that it had been his home long before she had come to it, Edgar stubbornly clung to his chair in the parlor. Why did not Miss Nancy come down to speak for him? Surely she must have heard his voice. As it happened, Miss Valentine had gone out, so that he was deprived of her intercession—that is, provided she had been inclined to give it.

Then, suddenly, along the walk of the side entrance, Edgar heard the well-known thumping of Old Swell-Foot's cane. The memory of boyhood chastisements, of Pa's terrible temper, flooded his mind, warning him that this was hardly the atmosphere for a conciliatory meeting, especially with injured virtue standing there, waiting for her defender. Prudently Edgar dashed out by the front door, leaving Mrs. Allan to give, unchallenged, her version of the story.

Poe never got to see Mr. Allan during his stay in Richmond, and only once again did he communicate with him. This was on the 12th of April, 1833, and then to repeat once more the, by then, threadbare lament of his being without friends, without means, and absolutely perishing for want of aid. "And yet I am not idle—nor addicted to any vice—nor have I committed any offence against society which would render me deserving of so hard a fate. For God's sake pity me, and save me from destruction." [2]

For John Allan it was merely another case of the boy who had cried "Wolf" too often. He ignored Edgar's letter, finding silence, as usual, the most expedient answer. He had his two infant sons to cheer his old age and extend his memory on earth. In the meantime he was poring over his will, making changes and adding codicils.

Some six weeks before receiving Edgar's last letter Mr. Allan had heard of the death of one of Mrs. Wills' twin sons. "There is therefore only one to provide for," commented the testator, with a hint of satisfaction.[3] That providential occurrence left $4,000 more for the estate—a sum which would have meant fortune, independence, and freedom from harrowing worry to a struggling poet, and purchased many necessities for the house at No. 203 North Amity Street, to which Mrs. Clemm now moved her few possessions and her little family.

It was a small, narrow, two-story brick edifice with a double chimney and a large dormer window perched in the middle of the steep roof. If the poet appropriated the customary garret, he was at least assured of light. The household still held Grandmother Poe, now a helpless wraith of seventy-seven. Though the frailest of them all, she still provided the one solid prop on which the family leaned, for while she breathed there would always be that pension from the government. Henry Clemm was seldom at home and could not be counted upon for aid. Mrs. Clemm, therefore, plied her needle and taught Virginia, who helped with the simpler sewing. The eleven-year-old girl was maturing early, and her graceful form already suggested the grace of the woman she was to be. She adored her cousin Eddie and showed it with unrestrained endearments and childish romps.

The change of locale did not improve the financial situation and it was a hard autumn and a still harder winter that faced the family. Yet Poe had been working more intensely than ever. After the publication of his tales in the *Philadelphia Saturday Courier* he thought of trying his luck with other magazines and had been writing one story after another, each touched with his wild fancy and written in a chiseled prose that had no parallel in contemporary American style, plagued as it was by plangent, sentimental nonsense that had been dubbed the "Laura Matilda school."

That July of 1833 the weekly Baltimore *Saturday Visiter* an-

[2] *Valentine Letters.* Ostrom, p. 50.
[3] Allen, p. 695.

nounced a contest, offering a prize of $50 for the winning short story and $25 for a poem. The magazine had already published some verses of Poe's, "Serenade," in April of that year; but, except for the stories in the *Philadelphia Courier,* he had had no success in getting them accepted, although he had been sending them out—once, at least, to the editors of the *New England Magazine,* with the post-script, "I am poor." [4]

When he learned of the contest, he already had a number of tales on hand. Heartened by the *Saturday Visiter's* assurance that its editors were desirous of encouraging literature by serving their public with the best, Poe saw to it that they had plenty of his own to choose from, and sent six of his stories, exquisitely traced in Roman char-acters and bound together in a small volume entitled *Tales of the Folio Club.* For the poetry competition he submitted "The Coliseum," a rhythmic evocation of ruin and grandeur in blank verse.

Edgar's heart had so often sickened from hope deferred that he could not have been sanguine of the results of this latest wooing of luck. Meanwhile the manuscripts piled up in the offices of the pub-lishers, to be considered by the judges, John P. Kennedy, a noted member of the Baltimore bar and author of a recently published novel, *Swallow Barn;* John H. B. Latrobe and James H. Miller. As Southerners who liked their ease, they decided to turn their manu-script reading into a pleasant meeting and, furnishing themselves with old wine and good cigars, they gathered, one afternoon, in the back porch of Mr. Latrobe's house on Mulberry Street. Beside the round table rested a capacious wastebasket for rejected manuscripts.

Since Mr. Latrobe was both the host and the youngest judge, he had the task of opening the packages and reading the manuscripts. Many of the entries they turned down at once as of the Laura Matilda school. Others they flung into the basket after the first few paragraphs. It almost looked as if they would find nothing worthy of the prize when Mr. Latrobe came upon a booklet which had almost been overlooked. While Mr. Kennedy and Dr. Miller were refilling their glasses and lighting their cigars to obviate the boredom of the reading, Mr. Latrobe perused the *Tales of the Folio Club* in silence. "It seems as if at last we have a prospect of awarding the prize," he said after a while.

At first the two laughed incredulously, but when Mr. Latrobe began reading aloud, going on from one story to another, they lis-tened, absorbed, and only interrupted him to exclaim: "Excellent! Capital!" Edgar A. Poe seemed to have everything—genius, style,

[4] Ostrom, p. 53.

originality and a flawless logic and imagination combined in a rare consistency. The lawyer judges were particularly impressed by the writer's analysis of complicated facts and his unraveling of circumstantial evidence. Assuredly the man deserved the prize. But which story should they choose? "MS. Found in a Bottle" and "A Descent into the Maelström" for a time held the balance. After much discussion, "MS. Found in a Bottle" won.

Mr. Latrobe then went on to the poetry which, on the whole, was of better quality than the prose, though of no rare merit. The tedium, however, was allayed by the wine and enshrouded in fragrant tobacco. One poem, "Song of the Winds," by a certain Henry Wilton was set aside for consideration, so also was "The Coliseum," by Poe. His lines had sweep and power and the same evocativeness that invested his stories. They had also a rhythmic pulse that vitalized the scene of fallen grandeur:

> Here, where a hero fell, a column falls!
> Here, where the mimic eagle glared in gold,
> A midnight vigil holds the swarthy bat!
> Here, where the dames of Rome their gilded hair
> Waved to the wind, now wave the reed and thistle!
> Here, where on golden throne the monarch lolled,
> Glides, spectre-like, unto his marble home,
> Lit by the wan light of the hornèd moon
> The swift and silent lizard of the stones! . . .

The judges were inclined to award the poetry prize to Poe also, but they finally decided in favor of Henry Wilton, who turned out to be the editor of the *Visiter,* John H. Hewitt, writing under a pseudonym.

Meanwhile, between hope and despair, Poe waited for the weeks to pass. At last, on the 12th of October, 1833, the Baltimore *Saturday Visiter* published the judges' letter, with their decision. More gratifying than even the prize money to the penniless Edgar was the praise which those gentlemen gave to his stories. "It would scarcely be doing justice to the author of this collection to say the tale we have chosen is the best of the six offered by him. . . . These tales are distinguished by a wild, vigorous and poetical imagination, a rich style, a fertile invention, and varied and curious learning."

Poe's imagination was indeed all that they said, but it also had qualities entirely his own which could be defined only as Poesque, and were to remain Poesque despite more than a century of assiduous imitation at home and in the literatures of Europe, particularly of France. Compounded as it was of the otherworldly perceptions of his psyche, colored by his fancy and rendered credible by his analytical mind, it gave a new dimension to matter, while extending the limits of the intangible, which, by Poe's magic, attained body and form. His qualities had been evident as early as "Metzengerstein." He applied them with greater mastery to his prize story of the huge, mysterious ship, wandering in a sea "where the ship itself will grow in bulk like the living body of a seaman."

Told in the first person, this story of a shipwreck in the archipelago of the Sunda Islands has the immediacy of participation, yet all the awe of a living nightmare. The narrator, tossed about in a frail bark in a stupendous storm, is suddenly warned by his companion of new danger threatening in the gigantic waves.

"We were at the bottom of one of these abysses. . . . As he spoke, I became aware of a dull, sullen glare of red light which streamed down the sides of the vast chasm where we lay, and threw a fitful brilliance upon our deck. Casting my eyes upwards, I beheld a spectacle which froze the current of my blood. At a terrific height directly above us, and upon the very verge of the precipitous descent, hovered a gigantic ship. . . . Although upreared upon the summit of a wave more than a hundred times her own altitude, her apparent size still exceeded that of any ship of the line or East Indiaman in existence."

In detail he described her dingy black hull, her single row of cannon, the battle lanterns swinging to and fro upon her rigging. "But what mainly inspired us with horror and astonishment, was that she bore up under a press of sail in the very teeth of that supernatural sea, and of that ungovernable hurricane. . . . For a moment of intense terror she paused upon the giddy pinnacle as if in contemplation of her own sublimity, then trembled and tottered, and—came down."

Here the inanimate, as in many of Poe's later works, becomes animate. Matter is endowed with volition. In the face of such unearthly power the position of man in the universal scheme is reversed. Anything can then happen, and it does, to the complete conviction of the reader, yet without loss of that sense of mystery on which Poe relied for his effects, which, paradoxically, he obtained by lucid rationalization. Though the terrifying ship crashes down upon the bark, the narrator is saved. "Our own vessel was at length . . . sinking with her head to the sea. The shock of the descending mass struck her, consequently, in that portion of her frame which was already under water, and the inevitable result was to hurl me, with irresistible violence, upon the rigging of the stranger." [5]

[5] Note an almost identical rescue in the recent *Andrea Doria-Stockholm* collision.

Frances Valentine Allan
Poe's Foster Mother
Painting by Thomas Sully

*(Valentine Museum,
Richmond, Virginia)*

John Allan
Poe's Foster Father

*(Maryland Historical
Society)*

Edgar Allan Poe
Crayon portrait by Flavius J. Fisher
(Valentine Museum, Richmond, Virginia)

Frances Osgood
Painting by Samuel S. Osgood
(*The New-York Historical Society*)

Sarah Helen Whitman
From a portrait by C. J. Thompson

R. W. Griswold
Painting by Samuel S. Osgood
(*The New-York Historical Society*)

Edgar Allan Poe
Painting by Samuel S. Osgood
(*The New-York Historical Society*)

That rescue in itself would have made a story. For Poe it was merely the point of departure for a series of weird encounters with the strange denizens of that floating world. Were they flesh and blood, these awe-inspiring ancient men, whose knees trembled with infirmity, whose gray hairs streamed in the tempest, whose souls were enshrouded in impenetrable meditations? Was he, the narrator, recording his adventures to enclose in a bottle, the only substantial thing among the phantom men of a phantom ship? "Their eyes have an eager and uneasy meaning; and when their figures [6] fall across my path in the wild glare of the battle-lanterns, I feel as I have never felt before, although I . . . have imbibed the shadows of fallen columns at Balbec, and Tadmor, and Persepolis, until my very soul has become a ruin. . . ." The stupendous close, sounding with the howling and shrieking of the tornado amid the ramparts of ice towering away into the sky, foreshadows the final scene of *The Narrative of Arthur Gordon Pym*.

In "MS. Found in a Bottle" Poe brought to perfection his technique of the short story, already applied with effect in "Metzengerstein." His style, like the brushwork of the artist, had become recognizably his own. Besides a command of language scarcely to be found in the publications of the day, he already had a mastery of those subtle rhythms that set the pulse-beat of the emotion he sought to arouse. His nuances he achieved as much through his style as through the workings of his prismatic imagination. Thus early he had found his form, in both poetry and prose. Henceforth he had only to develop it to a perfection worthy of the ideas seething in his mind.

Observing the protocol of those unsophisticated days, the happy prize winner set out on his round of visits to thank the judges. He found a friend and guide in John Pendleton Kennedy, who needed no second sight to discover the gnawing poverty in the neatly dressed, though shabby youth with the erect, almost military bearing. Poe was wearing a black frock coat buttoned to the throat, a black stock, with other articles of attire that had seen better days. Mr. Latrobe, whom he visited next, remarked: "The award in Mr. Poe's favor was not inopportune. Gentleman was written all over him . . . and although he came to return thanks . . . there was nothing obsequious in what he said or did. . . . The expression of his face was grave, almost sad, except when he became engaged in conversation." [7] Dr. James Miller's impressions were not recorded.

---

[6] The word appears as "fingers" perhaps through an error, in the Griswold edition, and has thus been perpetuated.

[7] Sara S. Rice, *A Memorial Volume*, 1877.

Poe also met his fellow prizewinner, John Hill Hewitt, whom he had reason to remember unpleasantly from some scathing remarks on "Tamerlane," whose metre he qualified as "a pile of brick bats." In the gladness of their joint honors they now became friends, despite bygones and present rivalry. Poe, however, would explain, to anyone who cared to know, that his own "Coliseum" had won the poetry prize as well—which was true—but that it had been given to Hewitt's poem because he, Poe, had already captured the larger award.

With Mr. Kennedy's encouragement Poe now tried to interest his old friends, Carey, Lea and Carey, in the publication of *Tales of the Folio Club*. Nothing came of the attempt. All that he obtained, besides the prize money and the ephemeral glory of his triumph, was an additional $15 from Miss Leslie, who edited a popular annual, for a story which she never published.

It was therefore not surprising that when the fragrance of his laurels faded Poe began looking about for some steady, remunerative work. An attempt at teaching school came to naught, though here too Mr. Kennedy did his best to help. Again, after the all too brief respite, the same miserable situation prevailed in the little house on Amity Street.

Virginia, meanwhile, did not go to school, but her education was not being neglected. Mrs. Clemm, who had been a schoolteacher at different times, had not overlooked her daughter. Edgar, too, from the beginning, had undertaken to teach the little girl, and when he was not writing the two, in the intimate relationship of cousins, bent over their books together, as he imparted the rudiments of French and combined teaching with a tender and deepening affection. Elizabeth Herring, the other cousin who had attracted Poe, and to whom he inscribed a copy of *Al Aaraaf,* was soon to be married. It would not be long before Virginia, too, would find a husband, for, with her deep violet eyes, her dreamy lids fringed with long lashes, and her fine features, she was already remarkable.

If Mr. Allan ever heard of Edgar's prize he gave no sign. To his peculiar mind, concerned more with price than with value, what were $50 against his own fortune, which Edgar estimated at $750,-000? Moreover, he was concerned with his approaching end. Nothing had availed to arrest the progress of his disease, neither visits to the Springs, with a domestic retinue that would have done honor to an Eastern potentate, nor the solicitude of his doctor and his wife. He was unable to lie down. Night and day he now rested in his armchair and only occasionally got up to stumble across the room. He had continued working at his office while his strength lasted. Finally, in December of that year, he avowed his defeat and, summoning his old partner, Charles Ellis, set his affairs in order.

Some intimation of the approaching end reached Edgar and Mrs. Clemm. Influenced by legends of deathbed remorse and changes of heart, aunt and nephew, reviewing the past in their ever-present necessity, discussed a final attempt at reconciliation on the part of Edgar. A letter would be futile as Mr. Allan had not written to him for nearly three years. A visit to Richmond would be best.

Sometime in February, 1834, Edgar, with the memory of his previous disastrous assault on the bulwarks of wealth and respectability still fresh, found himself once again before the door of the Richmond mansion. He rang the bell. As chance would have it, Mrs. Allan was at that moment passing through the hall and opened the door herself. Without preamble Edgar asked to see Mr. Allan. In vain the startled woman explained that her husband was too ill to see him, that the doctors had expressly forbidden the sick man's room to anyone but the nurses. Edgar would not be put off. Thrusting her aside, he flew up the stairs and made his way to Pa's old bedroom over the lawn, Mrs. Allan hastening after him.

The old man, much wasted but for his swollen legs, was propped up with pillows in his armchair, his cane within reach. At the sudden commotion he looked up from the paper he was reading. At first he could not believe that sudden materialization at the door and gaped, incredulous; but when Edgar stepped into the room the old man instantly seized his cane, shook it violently in the air, and threatened to strike him if he came closer.

The two stared at each other. In those seconds of confrontation the whole drama of their relationship focused into a symbolic tableau: the moneyed, practical man stricken by death, yet still powerful, menacing the enemy, the visionary who, clinging to his hope of realizing his vision, risked all—comfort, wealth and the power it conferred—rather than compromise.

"Get out! Get out!" the old man shouted.

They never saw each other again.

Despite the doctor's prohibitions, one visitor called upon Mr. Allan unannounced, at the conventional hour of eleven o'clock, on the morning of March 27, 1834. Mrs. Allan had been summoned upstairs by the cries of one of the children. Looking in also upon her husband, sitting in his invalid's chair, she saw that he was not moving. Then she noted that his jaw had dropped. Her screams brought the servants. It was too late. Death had come before them.

Part Three

CHAPTER XIV

→》》 · 《《←

Poe and the Artificial Paradise

IF, after learning of Mr. Allan's death, Poe still hoped that the reading of the will would have held some mention of the boy who had sat upon that stern man's knee and called him father, he was disappointed. Yet even if he had been remembered, the strong-willed, unsentimental Mrs. Allan would have barred him as she did the few who had been included outside the strictly limited family relationship. Although the testator had appointed her as executrix, she promptly repudiated the will and, at the Circuit Superior Court of Law held for Henrico County in Richmond, renounced the executorship and declared that she would not accept the provision of any part of it. The Wills child and his mother could fend for themselves; so also could the Collier boy and others who had no legitimate rights, though Allan blood flowed in their veins. With the two sons and the posthumous daughter she bore her husband, she lived bountily provided for in the Richmond establishment, at the Byrd plantation, or wherever she chose to dwell. Her tough stock survived for nearly fifty years after Mr. Allan's demise. Not so the sons on whom the heir-conscious merchant had counted to perpetuate his name. Despite his care to force the hand of fate, in the end he lost.

With the last thread of his tenuous hope now snapped, Edgar was thrown completely upon his own resources. He had never let his pen lie idle, but he now wrote as never before—stories chiefly, as they were more likely to sell. However, he was also proving his talent on a drama in blank verse, *Politian*.[1] Although its characters, Politian, Castiglione, Di Broglio, Baldazzar, Alessandra and the ill-fated heroine, Lalage, had leapt out of the world of his curious reading, the plot itself, based on an actual murder in Kentucky, in 1825, had been magnetizing money out readers' pockets for nearly a decade in such popular accounts as *The Kentucky Tragedy* and *Beauchamp's Con-*

---

[1] See *An Unfinished Tragedy by Edgar A. Poe . . . now first edited with notes and a commentary,* by Thomas Ollive Mabbott (Richmond, 1923).

fession. At the very time that Poe was writing his drama, another poet, Thomas Holley Chivers, who was later to become his friend, was busily scratching away at his *Conrad and Eudora,* on the identical theme. The scribulous Chivers, however, beat Poe by four acts, as Poe abandoned his tragedy after eleven scenes.

It was the first time that Poe had used reality for the purposes of art, though in the transposal it was to suffer an extraordinary change, and not only geographically. In life, a certain Colonel Solomon P. Sharp had seduced a spinster, Ann Cook, who bore her shame in silence and retirement. A few years later a young lawyer, Jereboam O. Beauchamp met her, fell in love with her and offered marriage. Miss Cook, for her own good reasons, refused, but on his persisting she confessed the cause of her reluctance. "I will marry you," she said, "but you must first kill Sharp."

Beauchamp challenged the villain to a duel, but Sharp had no wish to risk his life. Frustrated of her vengeance, Miss Cook married Beauchamp but threatened to kill her seducer herself. This her chivalrous husband would not allow. One November night Beauchamp roused Sharp out of his bed and, when he came to the door, stabbed him through the heart. Beauchamp was arrested, tried, and sentenced to hang. During the period of waiting his wife, who had been cleared of complicity, was allowed to share his cell.

Their *solitude à deux* aroused some latent literary urge. Mr. Beauchamp wrote his *Confession* while Mrs. Beauchamp tuned her lyre to *Poetical Pieces.* Shortly before Beauchamp's execution the two tried to commit suicide. Mrs. Beauchamp died of her wounds, but her husband survived, to meet his doom on July 7, 1826. They were buried in the same grave. The sod had scarcely turned green over them when Gervis S. Hammond brought out the *Confession* of the departed, together with Mrs. Beauchamp's verses. And so the profitable flood began.

In Poe's drama, that strangely named Englishman, Politian, Earl of Leicester, who visits his friend Castiglione in what may be Renaissance Rome, is both Beauchamp and one of the many self-portraits of the poet:

> A man quite young
> In years, but grey in fame. I have not seen him,
> But Rumour speaks of him as of a prodigy
> Preëminent in arts and arms, and wealth,
> And high descent. . . .
> No branch, they say, of all philosophy
> So deep abstruse he has not mastered it. . . .

> They speak of him
> As of one who entered madly into life,
> Drinking the cup of pleasure to the dregs.
> Ridiculous! . . .
> He is a dreamer, and a man shut out
> From common passions.

The attributes of wealth and high descent existed only in Poe's imagination; such fancies were the blessings which art allowed. The rest of the characterization embodied the contrary reports of rumor and fact.

When Politian arrives upon the scene the heroine Lalage (Miss Cook), the Duke Di Broglio's ward, has already been seduced by his son, Castiglione, who is about to marry Alessandra, a noble lady. Lalage, in despair, broods revenge, and when that valuable prop of costume drama, the Monk, arrives to dissuade her, she pushes aside his Crucifix, draws her cross-handled dagger and, raising it aloft, cries:

> Behold the cross wherewith a vow like mine
> Is written in Heaven!

In a moonlit garden Politian, who had already fallen in love with Lalage's voice, singing a sad ballad, declares his passion. At first the lady demurs, despite his protestations:

> Sweet Lalage, *I love thee—love thee—love thee* . . .
> .   .   .   .
> Not mother, with her first-born on her knee,
> Thrills with intenser love than I for thee.

Again, through his creative unconscious, Poe revealed himself. The ultimate intensity of love that he could offer was that of a mother for her child. Passion did not exist for him. Whenever it appeared in his works it was, more than anything, a fervor of the mind.

The enamored Politian, like Beauchamp, swears to avenge Lalage's honor, though not without qualms of conscience. In the solitude of the Coliseum he indulges in a soliloquy—the poem which Poe had already written on the ruined amphitheater. In the midst of it Lalage seeks him out, to remind the laggard that, while he temporizes, the villain is at the very steps of the altar with his new flame. Politian thereupon rushes forth, presumably to redeem her honor with his dagger.

If *Politian* proves anything, it is that drama was not Poe's forte, in spite of a few effective moments. "The Coliseum" still remains its best poetical section. Poe eventually removed it, together with the major part of the play, leaving only five scenes for publication.

The drama of life was meanwhile going on, with the usual stresses and strains in the struggle of making a living, in Poe's case by spinning out his imagination in the intricacies of his tales. There were hours when his garret study was as haunted as the vast chambers and moldering halls of the palaces he described in the world of his creations, out of space, out of time. Building his fancies about some beautiful, doomed Morella or Berenice, he related the experience in his own person, describing himself, his emotions, his ambitions and desires. In everything he wrote, if he was not the protagonist, his personality in any case pervaded the tale. Most frequently the focal point was the narrator himself, upon whose consciousness events and characters impinged, striking the somber fires of his genius. Even when the idea of a tale was borrowed, as "The Assignation," from E. T. A. Hoffmann, and "Morella," from Henry Glassford Bell's "The Dead Daughter," [2] it emerged as his own creation for the strictly Poesque qualities which he transmitted to it.

Happily for Poe in his stringent need, he was able to publish his stories through the untiring offices of Mr. Kennedy, who succeeded in interesting Thomas Willis White, a Richmond printer, in his protégé's work. Mr. White's *Southern Literary Messenger,* started in 1834, was only seven months old but it showed signs of thriving. Unique among Southern periodicals of the time, it showed its independence by being selective and by daring to venture on the unconventional. At that, its readers could scarcely have been prepared for the tale of monomania and horror which appeared in the issue of March, 1835, and bore the euphonious name of "Berenice."

With what tranquil meditation on the misery of human life it began. How graciously the reader was introduced to the hero, Egaeus, scion of an ancient line who lived, immersed in books and strange lore, in the gloom of his hereditary halls. From the outset he confessed: "The realities of the world affected me as visions . . . while the wild ideas of the land of dreams became, in turn, not the material of my every-day existence, but in very deed that existence utterly and solely in itself."

The words were the words of Egaeus but the portrait was that of Poe, as he indicated by the approximation of Egaeus to Edgar. In the same manner, with an irony that struck brutally home, he called himself Oinos—Wine—in the awesome vision of plague and death, the parable, "Shadow," a transmutation into his personal art, of the cholera plague of 1832. The stirring effect of the voice, in the

[2] In the *Edinburgh Literary Journal,* January, 1831.

parable, crying out, "I am SHADOW, and my dwelling is near the Catacombs of Ptolemais," had actually derived from a dream which Poe had had during the epidemic. In it a great black bird flew into his room and filled him with horror by saying, "I am the spirit of the Cholera and you are the cause of me." [3]

Certainly death engrossed his imagination during this time, and even the nostalgic stanzas, which he interpolated in "The Visionary," among the most musical of his rare love poems, have yet a sense of irremediable loss, later acknowledged by the title he gave them, "To One in Paradise."

> Thou wast that all to me, love,
>   For which my soul did pine—
> A green isle in the sea, love,
>   A fountain and a shrine,
> All wreathed with fairy fruits and flowers
>   And all the flowers were mine.
>
> .   .   .   .
>
> For, alas! alas! with me
>   The light of Life is o'er!
> "No more—no more—no more—"
>   (Such language holds the solemn sea
>   To the sands upon the shore)
> Shall bloom the thunder-blasted tree
>   Or the stricken eagle soar!
>
> And all my days are trances,
>   And all my nightly dreams
> Are where thy dark eye glances,
>   And where thy footstep gleams—
> In what ethereal dances,
>   By what eternal streams.

Death also hung, a menacing shadow, in the tale of Berenice and Egaeus. "Berenice and I were cousins, and we grew up together in my paternal halls. Yet differently we grew—I, ill of health and buried in gloom—she, agile, graceful, and overflowing with energy; her's the ramble on the hill-side—mine the studies in the cloister; I, living within my own heart, and addicted, body and soul, to the most intense and painful meditation—she roaming carelessly through life, with no thought of the shadows in her path. . . . Oh, gorgeous and fantastic beauty! . . . And then—then all is mystery and terror, and

[3] J. R. Thompson, in *Philadelphia Evening Bulletin,* Jan. 19, 1909.

a tale which should not be told. Disease—a fatal disease, fell like the simoon upon her frame; and, while I gazed upon her, the spirit of change swept over her. . . ."

Thereupon followed a tale of obsessive mania, culminating in a necrophilic act, told with such force as still to rouse a shudder. Mr. White, indeed, demurred at the horror, but Poe defended it, oddly enough, for journalistic reasons, at the same time giving an analysis of his art. "The history of all Magazines," he wrote, "shows plainly that those which have attained celebrity were indebted for it to articles *similar in nature—to Berenice*. . . . You ask me in what does this nature consist? In the ludicrous heightened into the grotesque: the fearful coloured into the horrible: the witty exaggerated into the burlesque: the singular wrought out into the strange and mystical. . . . To be appreciated you must be *read,* and these things are invariably sought after with avidity. . . . The effect—if any—will be estimated better by the circulation of the Magazine than by any comment upon its content." [4]

However, "Berenice" is more significant for what it reveals of Poe himself and of his life at that time. Like Egaeus, he had been in ill-health and buried in gloom, not in Egaeus' domain of Arnheim but in the house on Amity Street, where, in the privacy of his study, he had learned to cushion reality with the drug whose uses had earlier been revealed to him through his brother Henry. Yet despite overwhelming evidence of opium-taking, both in Poe's life and in his works, pious biographers have not only blinked at the admission but have often blinded themselves to the fact.

First of all, opium, also known as morphine or salt of opium, as well as laudanum or wine of opium, was procurable in Poe's day without prescription. At that very time, in England, Elizabeth Barrett, with the sanction of her doctors, had slowly become addicted to the drug. Indeed, in 1833, at Sidmouth, she dreamed as weird and psychologically revealing an opium dream as any that Poe had ever transferred to paper. The lengthy poem, "A True Dream," which Miss Barrett wrote about it, was significantly never published in her lifetime.

In it she described herself unsealing a vial, from which smoke came wreathing out, assuming different shapes: a fair young child who kissed her with lips hard and cold as stone, sucking away her breath; and then three serpents, twining amid noisome poison slime.

[4] Ostrom, pp. 58-59.

Anon outspake my wildered heart
    As I saw the serpents train—
"I have called up three existences
    I cannot quench again. . . ."

Outspake that pitying brother of mine—
    "Now nay, my sister, nay,
I will pour on them oil of vitriol,
    And burn their lives away. . . ."

I saw the drops of torture fall;
    I heard the shrieking rise,
While the serpents writhed in agony
    Beneath my dreaming eyes.

And while they shrieked, and while they writhed,
    And inward and outward wound,
They waxed larger, and their wail
    Assumed a human sound. . . ." [5]

Wilkie Collins, a boy of eleven in 1835, was also, in his maturity, to induce those artificial paradises of opium which were so often hells. He, too, had his phantoms, some of which found their habitat in his works, while others pursued him in life. One of his familiars was a green woman with fangs for teeth, who would lie in wait for him at the bend of the stairs when he went up to bed, and wish him good night by biting a piece out of his shoulder.[6]

Poe's visions, sublimated into his works, from now on revealed the unmistakable characteristics of the opium dream. As such they were recognized in Poe's day by Dr. John Carter, later by that connoisseur of the drug, Charles Baudelaire, and admitted with reluctant yet admirable candor by the poet's biographer, George F. Woodberry, who concluded his findings: "No candid mind can exclude the suggestion . . . of its share in the morbid side of Poe's life." [7]

Poe himself made no secret of his intimate familiarity with the drug. Indeed, he would have derived a certain thrill from the knowledge that his chosen master, Coleridge, had been addicted to it since early adolescence. In Poe's day, moreover, when it could be obtained without difficulty in its various forms, and when its dangers were not

[5] *New Poems by Robert and Elizabeth Barrett Browning.* Ed. Sir Frederick G. Kenyon.

[6] See Nuel Pharr Davis, *The Life of Wilkie Collins.*

[7] Woodberry, *The Life of Edgar Allan Poe,* Vol. I, p. 303.

widely known, it had not yet acquired its ill-fame. Still, Poe was scrupulously discreet in his use of it, and it was only in unguarded moments that his secret slipped out. His cousin, the former Miss Herring, declared that "she had often seen him decline to take even one glass of wine . . . but that for the most part, his periods of excess were occasioned by a free use of opium. . . . During these attacks he was kept entirely quiet and they (Mrs. Clemm and Virginia) did all possible to conceal his faults and failures." [8]

As even the best-guarded secrets will out, Poe obtained his catharsis through his fiction, wherein the allusion to opium, sometimes voiced with the directness of confession, comes openly to the surface. "I had become a bounden slave in the trammels of opium, and my labors and my orders had taken a coloring from my dreams," declares the lover in "Ligeia." In "The Fall of the House of Usher" the narrator is plunged into "an utter depression of soul which I can compare to no earthly sensation more properly than to the afterdream of the reveller upon opium—the bitter lapse into every-day life—the hideous dropping off of the veils." He then describes Usher's voice, which "varied rapidly from a tremulous indecision . . . to that abrupt, weighty, unhurried, and hollow-sounding enunciation—that leaden, self-balanced and perfectly modulated guttural utterance, which may be observed in . . . the irreclaimable eater of opium during the periods of his most intense excitement." Later still, in "The Oval Portrait," Poe reveals a specialist's knowledge of the subject.

"At length I bethought me of a little packet of opium which lay with my tobacco in my hookah-case," says the protagonist, "for at Constantinople I had acquired the habit of smoking the weed with the drug. I sought and found the narcotic. But when about to cut off a portion I felt the necessity of hesitation. In smoking it was a matter of little importance how much was employed. Usually I half-filled the bowl of the hookah with opium and tobacco cut and mingled, half and half. Sometimes when I had used the whole of this mixture I experienced no very peculiar effects; at other times I would not have smoked the pipe more than two-thirds out, when symptoms of mental derangement, which were even alarming, warned me to desist. But the effect proceeded with an easy gradation which deprived the indulgence of all danger. Here, however, the case was different. I had never swallowed opium before. Laudanum and morphine I had occasionally used. . . . But the solid drug I had never seen employed. . . . I resolved to proceed by degrees. I would take a very small dose in the first instance. Should this prove impotent

8 Woodberry, *op. cit.,* Vol. II, p. 428.

I would repeat it; and so on, until I should find an abatement of the fever, or obtain that sleep which was so pressingly requisite. . . ."

The passage, of inordinate length for the briefness of the tale, was published in full in April, 1842, when the story appeared in *Graham's Magazine,* as "Life in Death." It was suppressed in subsequent publication. The omission was not without significance.

CHAPTER XV

->>> • <<<-

The Marriage

POE'S correspondence with Mr. White through the spring and summer of 1835 and the stir created by the short stories and articles which Poe submitted to the magazine convinced the publisher that he would be useful on his staff. Why he took so long in making up his mind might be explained by rumors of Poe's irregular habits and of some mysterious illness from which, Poe assured him, he had recovered, though his doctor had told him that nothing but a sea voyage would have saved him. At any rate, late in June, Mr. White broached the subject. "Nothing would give me greater pleasure," Poe replied. "I have been desirous, for some time past, of paying a visit to Richmond . . . and if, by any chance, you hear of a situation likely to suit me, I would gladly accept it, were the salary even the meanest trifle. . . . What you say . . . in relation to the supervision of proof-sheets, gives me reason to hope that you might possibly find something for me in your office. . . ." [1]

Such eagerness to accept so unimportant a task and at the merest trifle of a salary clearly betrayed the writer's need. So also did his subsequent painstaking calculation of the payment due him for the columns taken up by his "Hans Pfaall"—thirty-four, to do justice to his tongue-in-cheek, highly imaginative account of the good Dutchman's balloon trip to the moon. Poe's letter, dated July 20, 1835, was written thirteen days after an event which had cut off the only steady income of the family: the death of the government's pensioner, Mrs. David Poe, at the age of seventy-nine. It was a serious loss, the demise of that small, inert being who had needed so little and provided so much—$240 a year!

For Mrs. Clemm the impending departure of Edgar for Richmond was of greater concern than the death of her mother, for now he remained the sole potential support of the family. The dangers of his being alone in the city where he had childhood friends, some of them

[1] Ostrom, p. 63.

168

marriageable young ladies, were patent. The menace to the Amity Street household grew more threatening as the time of departure approached. Mrs. Clemm, who had guided her raft to safety by skillful maneuvering, was not going to let it founder now. Edgar was twenty-seven, Virginia nearly thirteen, an age not too young for marriage, according to Southern standards. Though small, she was graceful and well proportioned. Moreover, since the Mary Devereaux episode, Edgar seemed to have ignored all other women.

However, his interest in Virginia, at first no more than cousinly, had heightened as she grew older. The childhood features had molded themselves to delicacy and beauty. The lustrous eyes flashed in laughter, yet softened with tenderness for her cousin Eddie. Her lips, pouting like those of a child, nevertheless had a sensuality which, together with her heavy-lidded gaze, proclaimed her a woman. That is, until she laughed, or talked with the suggestion of a lisp which she never outgrew. Her forehead it was, however, that most appealed to Poe—the forehead high, pale and singularly placid which, with others of her attributes, Poe had given to the cousin whom Egaeus loved. But unlike Berenice, unlike the profoundly learned Morella for whom she also posed, Virginia had only girlhood fancies and the simple concerns of everyday life behind that lofty brow. In the contrast of her beauty and her ingenuousness, which she retained through life, she incorporated for Poe the ideal which he had borrowed from Francis Bacon: "There is no excellent beauty that hath not some strangeness in the proportion." Characteristically Poe misquoted it in "Ligeia": "There is no exquisite beauty without some strangeness in the proportion."

Poe's attraction to his young cousin had not escaped Mrs. Clemm, nor, for that matter, the Neilson Poes, who were perturbed by it. Yet that the attraction might have gone beyond Edgar's delight in youth and beauty had not at first occurred to anyone but Mrs. Clemm, and then only as a reason for keeping the breadwinner in the family. However, by the time Edgar left for Richmond toward the middle of August, a violent upheaval of his emotions had occurred, brought on by his sudden awakening and aided by Mrs. Clemm's enlightenment. At any rate, during his weeks at the *Southern Literary Messenger* he was in an acute state of alternate excitation and depression.

The cause of his trouble lay in a communication of Mrs. Clemm's. The Neilson Poes, she wrote, concerned over the situation at Amity Street and strongly disapproving the engagement of Virginia to Edgar at such an early age, offered to take her into their own house until she was old enough to know her own mind.

For a woman who knew Edgar's instability, it was rash of Mrs. Clemm to impart such information, especially at a time when so much depended upon his peace of mind. Still, she may have been prompted by her anxiety to keep her family together.

The news threw Poe into such a state of despair that he became incoherent. Hysteria as well as anguish cry out in the emotionally unrestrained letter of August 29, 1835, whose shaky writing and misspelled words imply the presence of the treacherous comforter he sought in times of stress. He was blinded with tears, he said. He had no wish to live another hour. "I love, *you know* I love Virginia passionately devotedly. I cannot express in words the fervent devotion I feel towards my dear little cousin—my own darling. . . . Oh think for me for I am incapable of thinking. All my thoughts are occupied with the supposition that both you & she will prefer to go with N. Poe; I do sincerely believe that your *comforts* will for the present be secured—I cannot speak as regards your peace—your happiness. You have both tender hearts—and you will always have the reflection that my agony is more than I can bear—that you have driven me to the grave—for love like mine can never be gotten over. It is useless to disguise the truth that when Virginia goes with N. P. that I shall never behold her again—that is absolutely sure. Pity me, my dear Aunty, pity me. I have no one now to fly to. . . . It is useless to expect advice forom [*sic*] me—what can I say?— Can I, in honour & in truth say—Virginia! do not go! . . . I had procured a sweet little house in a retired situation. . . . I have been dreaming every day & night since of the rapture I should feel in having my only fieids [*sic*]—all I love on Earth with me there. . . . But the dream is over. Oh God have mercy on me. What have I *to live for?* Among strangers with *not one soul to love me.* . . . The tone of your letter wounds me to the soul— Oh Aunty, Aunty you loved me once—how can you be so cruel now? You speak of Virginia acquiring accomplishments, and entering into society—you speak . . . in so worldly a tone. . . . Adieu my dear Aunty. *I cannot* advise you. Ask Virginia. Leave it to her. Let me have, under her own hand, a letter, bidding me *good bye*—forever—and I may die—my heart will break—but I will say no more." He added a message for Virginia. "My love, my own sweetest Sissy, my darling little wifey, think well before you break the heart of your cousin. Eddy." [2]

Between the lines details emerge which bear interpreting. Granted that the Neilson Poes had made the offer to care for Virginia—there

---

[2] *Ibid.*, pp. 69-71. First published by Quinn, *Edgar Allan Poe Letters and Documents in the Enoch Pratt Library.* Edited by A. H. Quinn and R. H. Hart.

is only Mrs. Clemm's assertion for it—why had the ordinarily considerate woman been in such haste to impart it to one whose stability was shaken by the least emotion? Edgar had taken on his duties at the *Messenger* on a trial basis, since Mr. White wrote to a correspondent that Mr. Poe was tarrying with him a month. It was therefore important that he prove himself, particularly since Mr. White had already been forewarned about him by kindly busybodies. What pressure had been brought to bear upon Mrs. Clemm to compel her to disturb Edgar's peace of mind at such a time?

It was nothing less than poverty, with its threat to her hearth. Grandmother Poe was gone. There was no news of her son, who was still at sea. She alone could not earn enough for herself and Virginia. Edgar was their sole hope. The only way to secure him was by binding him to Virginia, whom he, the passionless man, had now, in his panic, convinced himself of loving passionately.

On Poe's part panic also derived from a similar source. The orphan, whom misfortune had twice deprived of a mother and a home, found his security once again threatened. Where could he go if Mrs. Clemm and Virginia left him? What place could he, the homeless, call home? How many reminders Richmond held of what his life might have been! Every morning, after leaving the boardinghouse of Mrs. Poore, he had to pass the old store of Ellis and Allan, on Main and Fifteenth Streets, before he clambered up the outside stairs to his office at the *Southern Literary Messenger,* right next door. Little had changed, though Mr. Allan was dead. The same rich smells of tobacco and spices hung upon the air. Familiar faces passed by; remembered sounds ticked back the past in his memory. If Ma had not died, if Mr. Allan had not married again, or if only the old man had been less unforgiving. But the volumes for review cluttered his table, at the office. Piles of letters had to be answered. The empty columns of the *Messenger* were waiting to be filled with articles and criticisms and the fancies spun out by his imagination.

There were still many in Richmond who desired his company, and Mr. White himself, a robust gentleman who enjoyed his table and his liquor, often invited his young editor to dine. Afterward, his daughter, a wide-eyed virgin with an effective voice, would recite from Shakespeare or discuss literary matters with the erudite and romantic-looking young man.

One day Poe was invited to a party at one of the fashionable Richmond mansions. Mrs. Shelton—Elmira—was to be among the guests. Quietly and unremarked, Poe went upstairs to the drawing room which commanded the comings and goings of the graciously curved double staircase and, standing within the embrasure of a window opposite the entrance, watched the guests as they arrived. At last he saw her, ascending the stairs alone and stopping at the landing to remove her wraps. She was about to enter the drawing room when Poe's burning eyes arrested her. For a moment the two were linked by that stare which held all their past, their love, their parting. Then another presence following close upon Elmira's footsteps abruptly awakened them to reality. Mr. Shelton lost no time. Wrapping his wife's cloak about her, he hurried her out of the house.

Despite Edgar's involvement with Virginia, this glimpse of a happiness that might have been moved him deeply. Still, he was worried because a fortnight had passed since he had written to Mrs. Clemm and she had not yet answered. His depression, aggravated by his loneliness, built up into hysteria. Almost in a panic he wrote to Mr. Kennedy: "Through your influence Mr. White has been induced to employ me . . . at a salary of $520 per annum . . . but alas! it appears that nothing can now give me pleasure. . . . Excuse me, my dear Sir, if in this letter you find much incoherency. My feelings at this moment are pitiable indeed. I am suffering under a depression of spirits such as I have never felt before. I have struggled in vain against the influence of this melancholy. . . . Console me—for you can. But let it be quickly—or it will be too late . . . oh pity me! . . . Write me then, and quickly. Urge me to do what is right. . . . Fail not— as you value your peace of mind hereafter." [3]

The faithful friend found himself at a loss on how to advise him. Those blue devils that had invaded Poe were part of his youth and temperament, and he should try to exorcise them. "Rise early, live generously, and make cheerful acquaintances," he advised Israfel, going on to a solution that surely sent a shudder through those heartstrings that were a lute: "Can't you write some farces after the manner of the French Vaudevilles?—if you can—(and I think you can)—you may turn them to excellent account by selling them to the managers in New York. . . ." [4]

Mr. Kennedy's advice fell on deaf ears, for on the 21st of September Mr. White wrote to Lucian Minor: "Poe has flew [sic] the track already. His habits are not good. He is in addition a victim of melancholy. I should not be at all astonished to hear that he had been guilty of suicide." [5]

Poe had indeed "flew the track"—in the direction of Baltimore.

[3] *Ibid.,* p. 73.
[4] Griswold Collection, Boston Public Library.
[5] See D. K. Jackson, *Poe and the Southern Literary Messenger.*

Mrs. Clemm had won. On the 22nd of September, 1835, the day after Mr. White's letter, Poe, just returned from Richmond, went to the Superior Court of Baltimore, 8th Judicial Circuit, and took out a license "to CELEBRATE THE RITES OF MARRIAGE between a certain Edgar A. Poe and Virginia E. Clemm of Baltimore County." [6]

According to Mrs. Clemm's testimony, a clandestine ceremony was performed by the Rev. Mr. John Johns at Old Christ Church but, except for the intention, in the issuing of the license, no record of such a marriage has come to light.

Poe remained in Baltimore for the rest of the month. By the 8th of October he was back at his post on the *Messenger,* though not without fatherly warning from Mr. White, who believed in being explicit about their future relations. "That you are sincere in all your promises, I firmly believe," he wrote to Poe on the 29th of September. "But, Edgar, when you once tread these streets, I have my fears that your resolve would fall through,—and that you would again sip the juice, even till it stole away your senses. . . . No man is safe who drinks before breakfast!" . . .[7]

Whatever Poe's provocations to seek forgetfulness, whether the pain of ancient memories or his own personal devils, this time he had insurance against temptation in the presence of his aunt and Virginia. According to a letter of Mrs. Clemm's to William Poe, a newly discovered and most helpful first cousin, she and Virginia had accompanied Edward to Richmond.

The emergence of William Poe had come about through a complimentary letter he had sent to Edgar from Augusta, where he lived. Were they by any chance related? he inquired. Edgar lost no time in answering his admiring and well-to-do correspondent. Indeed they were related, Poe assured him, tracing the family line and indulging his usual free fantasy, whereby his mother appeared as an English lady and Mr. Clemm, his aunt's husband, as a gentleman of high standing and some property. But, alas, Mr. Clemm "died about nine years ago without any property whatever, leaving his widow desolate and unprotected. . . . I sincerely pray God that the words which I am writing may be the means of inducing you to unite with your brothers and . . . friends, to send her the *immediate* relief which it is *utterly* out of my power to give to her just now. . . ." [8]

William Poe was quick to respond, especially when Mrs. Clemm,

[6] Text of license reproduced in Allen, *Israfel,* Appendix V.
[7] Griswold Collection, Boston Public Library.
[8] Ostrom, p. 68.

an experienced suppliant on her own account, took pen in hand.[9] Helpful amounts came winging in from Augusta, Georgia, to the boardinghouse of Mrs. James Yarrington, where Edgar had now esconced himself, Mrs. Clemm and Virginia, at $9 a week for their board and the privilege of overlooking Capitol Square. One wonders how the three managed to live in one room, large though it was.

By January of 1836 Poe was earning $800 a year. In the mood for making new resolutions, Edgar and Mrs. Clemm, with nothing on hand, hit upon a scheme to better their situation: Mrs. Clemm would open a boardinghouse. Mindful of the source from which occasional blessings had been flowing, Edgar approached a rich cousin of William Poe's, inviting him to finance Mrs. Clemm's proposed establishment. "Many of the widows of our first people are engaged in it, and find it profitable," Poe defended the respectability of the enterprise. The openhanded William Poe could be counted upon to advance $100. He, Poe, would endeavor to match the amount. "If then you would so far aid her in her design as to loan her, Yourself 100, she will have sufficient to commence with. . . ." [10] George Poe, a banker in Mobile, with a sound sense of the value of hard cash, could detect the present need between the lines and sent a check. The boardinghouse scheme, however, faded out into the realm of the unaccomplished.

In the meantime Poe had been building up the prestige of the *Messenger* by securing the contributions of well-known authors and, more significantly, by endeavoring to raise the level of letters both by example and by criticism. Though Mr. White would not openly give him credit for it, Poe had the complete editorial management of the magazine while he, the owner, concentrated on the business side of it. Soon the amazing increase in circulation justified Mr. White's re-employment of his young editor.

Meanwhile Poe was becoming known throughout the country, though not to the entire satisfaction of some of his contemporaries, whose works for a change received genuine, if at times rough, criticism, instead of the polite reciprocal praises which ordinarily passed for reviews. In the adolescence of American letters the tacit urge, in creative writing as in criticism, was either didactic or ameliorative, with emphasis on the excellence of the home product. To Poe, acquainted from adolescence with foreign literatures and criticism, par-

---

[9] See her letter, written soon after her husband's death, seeking financial help from a judicial functionary. *Maryland Historical Magazine* (Baltimore), Vol. IV, 1911.

[10] Letter of Jan. 12, 1836. Ostrom, p. 80.

ticularly the work of the great English arbiters and powerful contemporary reviewers in *Blackwood's* and the *Quarterly,* the world of letters was one and therefore he abhorred local distinctions. A book was good or bad on its own merits, whether written by a Londoner or a Bostonian. On that basis alone it should be judged. Moreover, it was neither the message nor the moral value of a work that gave it merit, but its intrinsic worth as art, Poe maintained, uttering heresy in a society where spiritual and moral improvement was everywhere sought for, like the jewel in the toad's head.

Critics, as a rule, were well-known individuals for whom reviewing an occasional book was merely a side line to teaching, serving on the bench or practicing law. For them the value of a book as literature was secondary to its worth as a moral guide. However, to one who, like Poe, sought aesthetic rather than ethical values in a creative work, the traditional principle was anathema. Therefore, whenever the decoratively bound poetical works of a covey of literary ladies, including Mrs. Lydia H. Sigourney, one of the most prolific in moral volumes, challenged his critical pen, he did them full justice—in his way. Of course anguished plaints re-echoed from the dovecotes and ruffled feathers flew. To Mrs. Sigourney's protests against his treatment of her *Zinzendorff, and Other Poems,* Poe sent a soothing letter. The friends who had convinced her that his review was unfavorable had entirely misconceived the spirit of his criticism, he assured her. Let her read again the concluding sentences of the critique. She would, he hoped, still allow him to send her the *Messenger?* She would indeed, cooed the forgiving lady.

The men whose works he attacked were not so easily appeased. Though on the whole Poe was justified in his charge of inanity, subservience to British literary dictation, logrolling and other unethical practices to push a worthless book, he made himself many enemies. He also numbered admirers in the thousands—but they were less powerful.

Spurred on by his success he published his satirical skit, "Lionizing," on the making of literary reputations by the art of puffery. All one needed were quotations, especially from England. "Wonderful genius!" said the Quarterly. "Superb physiologist!" said the Westminster. "Clever fellow," said the Foreign. "Fine writer!" said the Edinburgh. . . . "Who can he be?" said Mrs. Bas-Bleu. "What can he be?" said big Miss Bas-Bleu. "Where can he be?" said little Miss Bas-Bleu.[11]

The public read the *Messenger,* laughed and subscribed. Poe treated

[11] See "Lionizing."

his readers to scenes from *Politian,* to samples of the volume he planned to publish someday, *Tales of the Grotesque and Arabesque*— named eruditely from the curious designs which, Cellini said, were found in the ancient grottos of Rome. Neither Roman grotto nor Gothic horror, however, produced his works, which sprang from the inmost chamber of his imagination. More than ever now the themes dealt with death; with the struggle to preserve identity even after dissolution; with the mysterious, the wonderful and the terrible in the human psyche. Poe was aware of the source. "I maintain that terror is not of Germany, but of the soul—that I have deduced this terror only from its legitimate sources. . . ." [12]

Yet while he was conceiving or writing some of his most characteristic tales he was living as normal a life as he was ever to enjoy. He had employment, which took him to his office every weekday; he had a home at Mrs. Yarrington's with his aunt and his cousin, whom he was about to marry.

Passers-by who saw Virginia, in the late spring of 1836, on her visits to Rosalie at Miss Jane Mackenzie's school, would have been shocked to learn that the gay child, swinging or skipping rope with the rest of the pupils, was soon to figure in a marriage bond, dated May 16 of that year, in the Court of Hustings for the city of Richmond. "This day," read the last paragraph of the document, "Thomas W. Cleland, above named, made oath before me, as deputy Clerk . . . that Virginia E. Clemm is of the full age of twenty-four years. . . ." [13]

According to statistics, Virginia was still three months short of her fourteenth birthday and looked younger. Mr. Cleland, a boarder at Mrs. Yarrington's and a friend of Poe's, was either affected with blindness or obligingly closed his eyes and committed perjury for friendship's sake.

No time was allowed to elapse between the issuing of the bond and the marriage, performed that same afternoon in Mrs. Yarrington's parlor, with its stuffed birds and other boardinghouse art. If the Rev. Mr. Amasa Converse, a Presbyterian minister and editor of the *Southern Religious Telegraph,* saw any discrepancy between the little girl in a grown-up traveling dress, hat and veil, and the dark-haired, somber man of twenty-seven, whose gravity made him look older than his years, he did not allow it to interfere with the ceremony, though later he admitted that the bride *did* seem to be rather young. However, since the large, dignified woman who was the bride's mother con-

---

[12] From the preface to *Tales of the Grotesque and Arabesque.*
[13] From facsimile of the original marriage bond.

sented freely to the wedding, he saw no reason to demur. Many a girl, as young or younger, had been married in his day, in Richmond.

The wedding guests were not many—Mr. White and his daughter Eliza, men from the *Messenger* staff, some of Mrs. Yarrington's friends and the lady of the house herself, who had earlier that day helped Mrs. Clemm to bake the wedding cake. Neither the Mackenzies nor Rosalie figured among those present. The Mackenzies had shown their sentiments too plainly on that strange, involved relationship and they, like others in Richmond, laid the blame on Mrs. Clemm for permitting, if not engineering, the marriage. Judge Stanard, however, and Edgar's old playmate, Robert, were among the first to call.

CHAPTER XVI

-»»» • «««-

Sojourn in New York

BRIDE and groom spent their two-week honeymoon in Petersburg, Virginia, where Poe had several literary acquaintances. For the first time Edgar and Virginia were free of the mothering presence of Mrs. Clemm. They were feted at parties and entertained at dinner. Yet beyond the excitement of the holiday and the exhilaration of her brief independence, marriage could have meant little to the child who, unlike other brides of her age, remained a child, and was to remain virginal for several years, if not to the end.

The authority is none other than Edgar himself, quoted in a letter of Amos Bardwell Heywood, the brother of Annie Richmond, who was to have such emotional ascendancy over the poet toward the end of his life. Poe was visiting the Richmonds, after a lecture in Lowell, and, in a reminiscent mood, talked about his life. "He . . . went to live with an aunt who had a beautiful daughter named Virginia," Mr. Heywood reports. "A great intimacy sprang up between them and they came to look upon each other as brother and sister. Notice that was the kind of affection—a brotherly and sisterly affection and nothing more or less. . . . He married her at the early age of 13. . . . Although he loved her with an undivided heart he could not think of her as his wife, as any other than his sister, and indeed he did not for two years assume the position of a husband, still occupying his own chamber by himself. . . . He spoke of his wife in the most eloquent and touching manner, the tears running down his cheeks in torrents. Spoke of her as beautiful beyond description, as lovely beyond conception. . . ." [1]

Heywood, a schoolmaster of twenty-four, wrote his letter incorporating Poe's conversation on October 2, 1848, when every detail was still fresh in his mind. Whatever the value of Poe's reminiscences, they

---

[1] Frederick W. Coburn, "Poe as seen by the brother of 'Annie,'" *New England Quarterly,* September, 1943.

nevertheless help to throw light upon his otherwise inexplicab
havior on his return to Richmond after the honeymoon.

For a time bride and groom continued to live with Mrs. Cle
their one room at Mrs. Yarrington's, Poe going to the *Messenger* with
reawakened zeal on the promise of the augmented salary which he
was to receive in November. As the problem of making ends meet
still persisted, he and Mrs. Clemm set their minds to work. Grandmother Poe was dead, it is true, but had her claim on the government died with her? General Poe had left other heirs, especially Mrs.
Clemm. Accordingly, a few days after returning from his honeymoon,
Poe wrote to a certain James H. Causten, who was tangentially connected with the French spoliation claims in Washington, related the
tale of General David Poe's contribution of some $40,000 to the
government, and presented his case. "It appears to me (and to some
others to whom I have mentioned the subject) that my aunt, Mrs.
Maria Clemm (who now resides with me in Richmond, I having
married her daughter) has a claim against the U.S. to a large amount
which might be carried to a successful issue if properly managed. . . ." [2]

The vision of thousands of dollars showering down upon their need
from a grateful government beguiled the dreams of Poe during the
period of expectancy, only to fade away in unsuccess. Thus, in his very
real and by now chronic impecuniosity, Poe was obliged to apply to
his old friend Mr. Kennedy for the loan of $100, explaining the rea-
son for his straits in a rigmarole which, if it did not make Kennedy
smile, surely caused him to shake his head at the impracticability of
poets. Mr. White, it seemed, had bought a new house with the view
of renting it to Mrs. Clemm and boarding himself and his family with
her. Since the arrangement appeared advantageous, Poe set out at
once to buy furniture on credit. "But upon examination of the
premises purchased, it appears that the house will barely be large
enough for one family," Poe lamented, too late, "and the scheme is
laid aside, leaving me now in debt . . . without the means of discharging it on which I had depended. . . . Our Messenger is thriving
beyond all expectation and I myself have every prospect of success. . . .
I presume you have heard of my marriage," he added laconically.[3]

The furniture had not been bought in vain. Mrs. Clemm eventually
rented a cheap tenement on Seventh Street, let out rooms and kept
a boarder or two, supplementing the income with dressmaking. Seldom, however, was Poe to be found at home after his hours at the
Messenger office. A change had been observable in him since his

[2] Ostrom, p. 92.
[3] *Ibid.*, pp. 95-96.

marriage, mentioned so cursorily to Kennedy. His growing reputation, both as an original genius and as a redoubtable critic, had opened many doors to him in Richmond, while his romantic appearance unlocked feminine hearts. As an old gentleman of that city put it, "Poe is one of the kind whom men envy and calumniate and women adore"—a definition which held both commendation and indictment.

The reason for both lay in Poe's ambiguous personality, never more clearly revealed than in the stories "Eleonora" and "Morella." While revolving about one of his favorite themes, the death of a beautiful woman, they give idealized portrayals of Virginia and of their own relationship, at the same time allowing glimpses into his complex personality. "I come of a race noted for vigor of fancy and ardor of passion," he begins without preamble in "Eleonora." "Men have called me mad; but the question is not yet settled, whether madness is or is not the loftiest intelligence—whether much that is glorious—whether all that is profound—does not spring from disease of thought—from *moods* of mind exalted at the expense of the general intellect. They who dream by day are cognizant of many things which escape those who dream only by night."

It was Poe, trying to make a virtue of the insanity which he suspected and was always to dread in himself.[4] The story, however, is an account, rather, an allegory, of the perfect love which he believed that he and Virginia experienced for each other. "She whom I loved in youth . . . was the sole daughter of the only sister of my mother long departed," he wrote, altering fact to suit his wishful desire for a closer link with the mother he adored, rather than with the father whom he scarcely remembered. "It was one evening at the close of the third lustrum of her life . . . that we sat, locked in each other's embrace, beneath the serpent-like trees, and looked down within the waters of the River of Silence at our images therein. We spoke no words during the rest of that sweet day. . . . We had drawn the god Eros from the wave. . . . The passions which had for centuries distinguished our race, came thronging with the fancies for which they had been equally noted, and together breathed a delirious bliss over the Valley of the Many-Colored Grass. A change fell upon all things. Strange, brilliant flowers, star-shaped, burst out upon the trees. . . . The tints of the green carpet deepened; and, when one by one, the white daisies shrank away, there sprang up in place of them, ten by ten of the ruby asphodel. And life arose in our paths. . . ."

They loved, purely and simply, for "she was a maiden artless and

[4] According to Mrs. Shew, who nursed both Poe and Virginia toward the end, Dr. Valentine Mott declared that Poe had a brain lesion.

innocent as the brief life she had led among the flowers. No gui[
guised the fervor of love which animated her heart." But one da[
had seen that the finger of Death was upon her bosom." It w[
death, however, that grieved her but the thought that he would someday love another. "And then and there I threw myself . . . at the feet
of Eleonora and offered up a vow, to herself and to Heaven, that I
would never bind myself in marriage to any daughter of earth. . . ."
With the death of Eleonora, "the star-shaped flowers shrank into the
stems of the trees . . . and one by one the ruby-red asphodels withered
away; and there sprang up in place of them . . . eye-like violets, that
writhed uneasily and were ever encumbered with dew. . . ." The
promise was forgotten. He married another. "And once—but once
again in the silence of the night, there came through my lattice the
soft sighs which had forsaken me. . . ."

Stripped of allegory the story tells of the dawning awareness of love
in two cousins who had been brought up together, of their happiness
in the Valley of the Many-Colored Grass—suggested to Poe by the
many-hued landscape of the James' bordering vales and woodlands—
and of the promise of fidelity exacted by the girl. That promise, no
mere poetic invention, was to recur in the future. It is noteworthy that
in the story the girl, not the youth, is described as full of the "fervor
of love."

In "Morella," a tale in a similar mood, though essentially an invention on the theme of the persistence of identity after death, the narrator begins: "With a feeling of deep yet most singular affection I
regarded my friend Morella. Thrown by accident into her society many
years ago, my soul, from our first meeting, burned with fires it had
never before known; but the fires were not of Eros, and bitter and tormenting to my spirit was the gradual conviction that I could in no manner define their unusual meaning, or regulate their vague intensity. Yet
we met; and fate bound us together at the altar; and I never spoke of
passion, nor thought of love. . . ."

The fires were not of Eros, he admitted. Were they solely of the
imagination, or for some fulfillment beyond that of love and passion?
Like Eleonora, Morella is the active participant in the relationship.
"She . . . attaching herself to me alone, rendered me happy." It is the
same with Ligeia, the heroine in the story which Poe preferred above
all others for possessing the highest quality of imagination. "Of all the
women whom I have ever known," says the protagonist, "she, the out-
wardly calm, the ever-placid Ligeia, was the most violently a prey to
the tumultuous vultures of stern passion." She loved him, loved him
so absorbingly that, even beyond death, in one of the most macabre

struggles ever penned, she took possession in her own person of the body of the second wife.

In these writings, as elsewhere, there is much self-revelation. He himself once stated: "The supposition that the book of an author is a thing apart from the author's self is, I think, ill founded. . . . What poet, in especial, but must feel at least the better portion of himself more fairly represented in even his commonest sonnet than in the most elaborate and most intimate personalities?" He left, besides, a penciled note on one of his manuscripts: "All that I have here expressed was actually present to me. Remember the mental condition which gave rise to Ligeia. . . ." [5]

Whatever the cause—whether sublimation through creativity or whether Poe suffered from some organic flaw—there was an inhibiting factor in his relations with women. It is patent in his life and revealed in his works. Studies have been made and theories propounded on physical and psychic complexities in Edgar Allan Poe. They range from Joseph Wood Krutch's persuasive study, that Poe may have been impotent, to Princess Marie Bonaparte's psychoanalytical exegesis, that because of the death of his mother in his impressionable childhood, Poe was a potential sado-necrophilist who, cognizant of his terrible urges, stopped short of the sexual act in his relations with women. She also found in him "a strong constitutional bisexuality. This was what caused Poe, in his extreme deference to the fiats of morality, so markedly to avoid the Mother—and Woman—and to end his literary career in the cosmic, homosexual phantasy known as *Eureka*." [6]

Certainly, at this date, speculation is futile. One knows, however, that in at least one instance Poe's wooing of Mary Devereaux, the intensity of his sexual approach frightened her away. Yet one also knows that for the first two years of his marriage he did not assert his rights as a husband—whether from consideration for Virginia's youth, from the repressions inculcated by the Allan upbringing, or from some physical or psychic incapacity, it is impossible to ascertain.

Yet shortly after his marriage Poe scandalized Richmond by his neglect of his wife and his flagrant attention to other women. His behavior so outraged respectability that more than once Mrs. Mackenzie took it upon herself to remonstrate with him. She wasted her breath. For days Poe would put up at some hotel or boardinghouse. In vain Mrs. Clemm waited for the salary which he would ordinarily transfer from his pocket to her capacious hand. In vain Virginia sat up hopefully for "Buddy" to come home. When, at last, he would return, it

[5] See Helen Whitman, *Edgar Poe and his Critics*.
[6] Marie Bonaparte, *Life and Works of Edgar Allan Poe*, pp. 635-636.

was to go to bed, "sick." With this excuse Mrs. Clemm would then report at the *Messenger* office, where the work had piled up unattended, while Mr. White would shake his head over his editor, so talented and so irresponsible.

Poe's drinking indicated emotional disturbance. His pursuit of other women, after his marriage, was doubtless an aftereffect of that disturbance. He, the almost morbidly pure, was endeavoring to clear himself of the suspicion of some sexual anomaly and in his anxiety was overplaying his role. Such behavior, however, only served to prejudice his reputation, already undermined by his drinking. Others besides the Mackenzies disapproved of the disparate marriage and blamed Mrs. Clemm for countenancing it, if not for bringing it about.

In their circles they talked of his flirtation with Eliza White; of his encounter with Elmira; of the love poem by a certain "Sylvio," in the *Messenger,* obviously addressed by Poe to his boyhood love. They pitied the "child-bride" whom they still had occasion to see, playing as lightheartedly as ever, among Miss Jane Mackenzie's pupils. One day Virginia had been visiting Rosalie when Edgar came to call for her. On seeing him Virginia ran to him with such abandon that Mrs. Mackenzie's propriety was shocked. All this was strange, very strange. Not only those who knew the Poe-Clemm household, but even the shopkeepers, found much to ponder when they discovered that the little girl marketing beside her tall, masculine mother was "Mrs. Poe."

For Edgar, however, when not moved by his inner compulsion to put up a front before the world, the home which Mrs. Clemm made for him was his refuge from reality—that reality in which he felt a stranger. There, at least, he was adored and made much of by two women for whom he was the center of existence—their provider, the cherished adopted son of the one, the husband and brother of the other, in a complex sentimental incestuousness which it pleased him to introduce into his imaginative writings again and again. That married cousinship was to Edgar what the relation with his half sister Augusta had been to Byron—a flouting of convention. With the two women, the strong mother and the sylphlike girl whose strange beauty, which made others uneasy, exalted him to weird flights, he felt secure and beloved. With them there was no need of pretense. They knew who he was and what he was. They forgave him his weaknesses and admired him for his genius without knowing exactly in what that genius consisted. Mrs. Clemm would listen patiently while he discussed his ideas or read to her some strange fantasy. Whenever she could not follow him in his flights she had the wisdom to approve of them. Anyway, those figures of his creativeness materialized into compensation in cash which in turn provided the family its daily bread. At home he was king; he felt at ease and, at times, even happy.

In the world, in which genius, if not misunderstood, is looked upon with suspicion, he felt compelled to make himself noticed. He had begun drawing attention as a youth with his swimming feat, between which and Byron's, he had recently assured Mr. White, there was no comparison. "Any swimmer 'in the falls' in my days, would have swum the Hellespont, and thought nothing of the matter. . . ." [7] He had continued to draw attention to himself by his rebellious life, and now by the originality of his writings and his fearless hard-hitting literary criticism.

Toward the ladies, however, Mrs. Hemans, Caroline Norton and the flaming Letitia Landon, he had the chivalry of the Southern gentleman, and where he could not honestly praise the song he chanted the virtues of womanhood itself. "Yes!" he once affirmed in the *Messenger,* "while it is the fashion to sneer at the purity of woman's heart, and while a pack of literary debauchees are libelling our mothers and our sisters unopposed, from the ranks of that insulted sex have risen up defenders of its innocence. . . . Hear in what eloquent numbers Mrs. Norton vindicates her sex . . . God bless her who has written this."

Yet, though occasionally influenced by sentimentality, he could detect and praise a masterpiece, as in his review of Alessandro Manzoni's *I Promessi Sposi,* in what was probably the first English translation of the Italian novel, already established as a world classic though it had appeared in 1827. Poe also praised Longfellow's *Georgia Scenes* and was quick to recognize the mainspring of Hawthorne's creativeness in *Twice-Told Tales* which he called "the product of a truly imaginative intellect, restrained, and in some measure repressed, by fastidiousness of taste, by constitutional melancholy."

Mediocrity, on the other hand, roused his spleen and he seemed to dip his pen in it. Of course the men whose works he slashed and "used up" let out howls of protest, but their clamor only made his name better known and increased the subscription list. On the whole, Mr. White had every reason to be pleased with the success of his magazine.

Yet, by the end of 1836, Mr. White had had enough of his editor. Highly as he thought of Poe's talents, he confided to Lucian Minor two days after Christmas (which Poe probably had overcelebrated, with the usual fateful results), he, White, would be compelled to give him notice in a week or so. Three months earlier he had dismissed him, but had been prevailed upon to take him back on condition that

[7] Ostrom, p. 57.

he stop drinking. Poe, unhappily, had not kept his promise. "Added to all this, I am cramped by him in the exercise of my own judgment," White complained. "It is true that I neither have his sagacity, nor his learning—but I do believe I know a handspike from a saw. . . ."[8] It is not difficult to visualize in Mr. White's complaint the imperious young editor withering with a look the literary pretensions of the illiterate, vulgar, although well-meaning man, as Poe once described him.

Poe was not averse to leaving the magazine which he had built up from an obscure sheet to a periodical of national circulation. Yet, while Mr. White had grown wealthy on its returns, Poe had received a comparatively minuscule salary and that intangible asset, a reputation. In the *Messenger* of January 3, 1837, he informed his readers: "Mr. Poe's attention being called in another direction, he will decline, with the present number, the Editorial duties of the 'Messenger.' His critical notices for this month end with Professor Anthon's Cicero. . . . With the best wishes to the *Magazine,* and to its few foes as well as to its many friends, he is now desirous of bidding all parties a peaceable farewell."

As for himself, he had made friends and foes in inverse ratio while gaining notoriety as a formidable critic. His seemingly impersonal note, however, concealed shrewd calculation. Professor Charles Anthon, of Columbia College, held valuable publishing connections in New York, where his influence lent weight to his pronouncements. It had not been without forethought that Poe had selected the professor's *Cicero* for a highly laudatory review, considering his intended move to New York, which had been agreed upon with Mrs. Clemm. Anyone reading his carefully balanced sentences of exposition and praise would scarcely have associated the critic with the man who, in the same magazine, had damned Mattson's *Paul Ulrich* with such virulence that one could not help pitying the victim. "The book is despicable in every respect. Such are the works which bring daily discredit upon our national literature. We have no right to complain of being laughed at abroad when so villainous a compound . . . of incongruous folly, plagiarism, immorality, inanity and bombast, can command at any moment both a puff and a publisher."

That he himself had not been able to obtain a publisher—Harper & Brothers had declined to print his tales—without doubt colored his resentment of inferior work glorying in both print and praise. However, the January, 1837, number of the *Messenger* in which his valedictory had appeared, also contained, besides his sonnet "Zante" and

[8] J. S. Wilson, in *Century Magazine,* Vol. LXXXV.

"Ballad," the opening section of the longest tale he had so far undertaken, *The Narrative of Arthur Gordon Pym.* It would be book
length. Perhaps it would interest the Harpers, whose publications he
had generously praised.

Since Poe's reputation had preceded him, especially in his merci-
less flaying of Theodore S. Fay's *Norman Leslie,* the literary find of
an earlier season in New York, the climate he encountered on his
arrival with Mrs. Clemm and Virginia was of the coolest, especially
among the Knickerbocker literati, who had extended themselves in
laudation of their discovery. As was often the case, Poe's harshness
toward *Norman Leslie* had not been entirely unmotivated. His vulnerable temperament seldom forgave a slight, and never forgot one.
In 1831 Poe had presented a copy of his *Poems* to Mr. Fay, then one
of the editors of the *New York Mirror,* in the hope of having it reviewed. A notice did eventually appear, but it was brief and, when
not taxing the poems with unintelligibility, damned them with very
faint praise indeed. If, as Poe believed, Fay had written the review,
he had suffered for it in Poe's exacerbated vindictiveness of *two* eyes
for an eye.

He knew there was no hope for him on the *Mirror,* which had already attacked him in an article wherein the accusation he was so
fond of hurling boomeranged against himself. The New York *Quarterly Review,* however, with whose editor Poe had been in correspondence, offered prospects. Indeed, Dr. Hawks had written in a
manner to whet Poe's cutting edge: "I wish you to fall in with your
broad-axe amidst this miserable literary trash that surrounds us. I
believe you have the will, and I know you will have the ability." [9]

Whatever little nest egg Mrs. Clemm had brought to New York,
early in 1837, was hardly enough to provide food and a temporary
roof over their heads, in a shabby boardinghouse at Sixth Avenue
and Waverly Place. For Edgar, who had all the virtues and prejudices
of the Southern gentleman, along with the pride of Lucifer, the Astor
House would have made a better setting. Indeed, but for unmerciful
disaster—in circumstance and, even more, within himself—such elegance might have been his. At twenty-eight, he had a considerable
body of work behind him. Besides his books of poetry, he had written enough stories for two full volumes, if only he could succeed in
getting them printed. Moreover, thanks to his articles, the *Messenger*
had spread his fame both as a critic and as a writer of imagination.
New York, with its many publishing houses and a population of

[9] Gill, p. 83.

three hundred thousand, would surely provide him with a livelihood and an audience.

Unfortunately the city, like the rest of the United States, was then in the grip of one of the worst financial crises that the country had ever experienced. As bank after bank suspended its operations, the government found that its paper issue had disastrously increased. Moreover, Andrew Jackson's attacks against the Bank of the United States had shaken public confidence so that it had to suspend all specie payments. As a result, during the worst of the panic in New York, the failures in the market amounted to more than $100,000,000 in one fortnight alone. Prices on flour, fuel and other necessities doubled and quadrupled. In the once-opulent metropolis people were dying of starvation.

Poe found his hopes of conquering literary New York dimming day by day. After a single, ponderous criticism of J. T. Stephens' *Incidents of Travel in Egypt,* in which he aired knowledge of Hebrew which he did not possess, and otherwise exposed himself in his worst pedantic vein, he did nothing more for the *Quarterly Review.* Mrs. Clemm's china teapot was empty, and the family had to live.

Leaving Waverly Place, they moved to a small, two-story frame building at 113⅓ Carmine Street, with a steep, shingled roof and iron railings at the front steps. They took along with them a fellow boarder from their previous residence, William Gowans, a thriving bookseller whose shop, on Broadway, was frequented by the literary coterie of New York. On him, and possibly a few other boarders, Mrs. Clemm depended for the support of the family.

Mr. Gowans was enchanted with the household and in later years waxed rhetorical about it. "For eight months, or more, 'one house contained us and one table fed.'" He found Poe one of the most courteous, gentlemanly and intelligent companions he had ever met, and swore he had never seen him the least affected by liquor. "He had an extra inducement to be a good man as well as a good husband, for he had a wife of matchless beauty . . . her eye could match that of any houri, and her face defy the genius of a Canova to imitate; a temper and disposition of surpassing sweetness; besides, she seemed as much devoted to him and his every interest as a young mother is to her first born. . . ." [10] Evidently the mother-son relationship in love, which Poe had extolled in *Politian,* existed in life between him and Virginia.

Others besides Mr. Gowans noted the attachment of the young couple who, in the evening, would stroll hand in hand among the

[10] William Gowans, *Catalogue of American Books,* No. 28, 1870.

tombs in St. John's Green, nearby, in melancholy enjoyment. At times, when Virginia was not well, she would sit at one of the upper windows and watch him as he paced up and down in his peculiar way, with one hand behind his back, rubbing his thumb and forefinger together.

With no paid literary work to count on, despite his ceaseless visits to the various magazine and newspaper offices, Poe turned to his imaginative tales and also finished *The Narrative of Arthur Gordon Pym*. The Harpers, while refusing to publish his stories, had imparted to him their experience—that American readers had a decided preference for works in which a single connected narrative occupied the whole volume. Poe now had the very thing to offer them. In June of 1837 the Harpers accepted *Arthur Gordon Pym* but delayed publication until the following year. That same June the *American Monthly* included in its pages one of Poe's explorations into the night of the human mind, "Von Jung, the Mystific."

The adventures of Arthur Gordon Pym, however, though set in the fearful theater of Poe's imagination, had their origin, as he himself indicated, in Benjamin Morrell's *Narrative of Four Voyages to the South Seas and the Pacific,* which the Harpers had published in 1832, and in the address which the advocate of polar exploration, Jeremiah N. Reynolds, made before the House of Representatives in 1836, followed by his appointment as the head of the expedition—"a station which we know him to be exceedingly qualified to fill," as Poe had commented in the *Messenger*.

Reynolds, whom Poe may have met, fascinated him as only the armchair traveler can be fascinated by living experiences. His own adventures, the voyages to foreign lands, the sojourn in Russia, may have fooled some of his listeners but he had known the tales for what they were. Reynolds, however, had actually lived his experiences, and a book of his, an account of his voyages on the frigate *Potomac,* had come out in 1835, also under the Harper imprint.

Such books were popular and Poe, as well as the publishers, had hopes for *Pym*. Indeed, the better to capture the gullible public the fictitious adventures were presented as actual happenings, doubtless at the suggestion of the author, who loved nothing better than a hoax, in his contempt for the intelligence of his fellows as well as in his need to fortify himself against his insecurity.

Accordingly, the title page specified Arthur Gordon Pym as of Nantucket and described his adventures as "comprising the details of a mutiny and atrocious butchery on board the American brig Grampus on her way to the South Seas, in the month of June, 1827. With

an account of the recapture of the vessel by the survivors; their shipwreck and subsequent horrible suffering from famine etc. . . . and the
massacre of her crew among a group of islands in the Eighty-Fourth
Parallel of Southern Latitude; together with the incredible adventures
and discoveries still farther South to which that distressing calamity
gave rise."

The introductory note, signed "A. G. Pym," lent further support to
the ruse, when Pym circumstantially declared: "Among the gentlemen in Virginia who expressed the greatest interest in my statement,
more particularly in regard to that portion of it which related to the
Antarctic Ocean, was Mr. Poe, late editor of the *Southern Literary
Messenger*. . . . He strongly advised me, among others, to prepare at
once a full account of what I have seen and undergone. . . ." The
request, from such a source, could not be ignored. Arthur Gordon
Pym wrote his story.

And what a story. With the matter-of-factness of a clerk setting
down his accounts, Mr. Pym, after a deceptively realistic beginning,
unveils hells of torture and suffering, of cannibalism and insanity,
which have few parallels in literature or life, but for the horrors of
Buchenwald and Belsen, that will forever indict man's inhumanity to
man, as exemplified in our own century. Pym (Poe) is like another
visitor to Hell. But, whereas the Florentine attenuated the grimmest
tortures with his compassion, it is absent in Poe's narrative, as if the
spectator enjoyed horror for horror's sake, or created it to satisfy
some compelling need. Everything is relayed with dispassionate precision and then suddenly made vivid by a striking detail, as in the
discovery, by the shipwrecked men, of the oncoming brig on which
they placed their hope of salvation.

"No person was seen upon her decks until she arrived within
about a quarter of a mile of us. We then saw three seamen. . . . Two
of them were lying on some old sails near the forecastle, and the
third, who appeared to be looking at us with great curiosity, was
leaning over the starboard bow. . . . This last was a stout and tall man,
with a very dark skin. He seemed by his manner to be encouraging
us to have patience, nodding to us in a cheerful although rather odd
way, and smiling constantly, so as to display a set of the most brilliantly white teeth. . . . The brig came on slowly. . . . Of a sudden,
and all at once, there came wafted over the ocean from the strange
vessel . . . a smell, a stench, such as the whole world has no name
for. . . . We saw the tall stout figure still leaning on the bulwark . . .
but his face was now turned from us. . . . His arms were extended
over the rail, and the palms of his hands fell outward. . . . On his

back, from which a portion of his shirt had been torn, leaving it bare, there sat a huge sea-gull busily gorging itself with the horrible flesh. . . . As the brig moved farther round us so as to bring us close in view, the bird, with much apparent difficulty, drew out its crimsoned head, and, after eyeing us for a moment as if stupefied, rose lazily from the body upon which it had been feasting, and, flying directly above our deck, hovered there a while with a portion of clotted and liver-like substance in its beak. The horrid morsel dropped at length with a sullen splash immediately at the feet of Parker. May God forgive me, but now, for the first time, there flashed through my mind a thought, a thought which I will not mention. . . ."

Such a passage went further than even the most sensational fiction had a right to go, and there were many more like it. Perhaps for the natural revulsion these horrors aroused, the book fell short of the success which both the publishers and the author had anticipated, for sales lagged, even though, according to Mr. Gowans, who knew his business, Harper & Brothers had the means of distributing a whole edition in a week.

The narrative, however, had such verisimilitude that both the reviewer in *Burton's Gentleman's Magazine* and several critics in England, where *Pym* went into a second edition, treated the account as fact. The success of his hoax afforded Poe the only triumph he could enjoy. At home the returns from the sales were meager, while abroad they were nonexistent for lack of proper copyright laws to protect literary property from land pirates.

Despite its piled-up horrors and gruesome details, the narrative closed on a note of mysterious grandeur, akin to "Siope—A Fable," the only other tale besides "Von Jung" which Poe was able to publish while in New York. As Pym's frail boat is rushing onward, "Many gigantic and pallidly white birds flew continuously now from beyond the veil, and their scream was the eternal *Tekeli-li*. . . . And now we rushed into the embraces of the cataract, where a chasm threw itself open to receive us. But there arose in our pathway a shrouded human figure, very far larger in its proportions than any dweller among men. And the hue of the skin of the figure was of the perfect whiteness of snow."

In another generation, in France, Jules Verne found inspiration in those lines for his own *Sphinx des Glaces,* which is at once a sequel to Poe's narrative and a solution of Pym's mysterious end. At the close the magnetic Sphinx of the Snows, which had the power to attract anything made of steel, lay revealed and there, clinging to its side, was the frozen body of Pym, his gun with its metal barrel still strapped to his shoulder.

CHAPTER XVII

→≫ • ≪←

The Haunted Palace

THOUGH Philadelphia, by 1838, had lost some of its supremacy as a metropolis, it was nevertheless only second to New York, whose population it was close to matching. As a literary center it could still hold its own, what with a number of thriving publishing houses, a group of solidly established periodicals, like the *Saturday Evening Post* and the more recent *Burton's Gentleman's Magazine,* whose critic had fallen for Poe's hoax by reviewing *Arthur Gordon Pym* as actual adventure. There were, besides, numerous satellites about the larger planets, offering altogether a more promising outlook for Poe who, disillusioned by the coldness of New York, had come, late in August, to try what he hoped would be a happier fortune. Philadelphia had already proved friendly to him. One of its magazines, the *Casket,* had given him his first taste of literary fame, at a time when the ex-West Point Cadet needed encouragement, by reprinting his sonnet "To Science" from his 1829 volume. It was in Philadelphia, too, that he had published his first short story and received helpful advice from Carey, Lea and Carey. Certainly he could hope that the city of brotherly love would give some of it to a struggling poet.

At that time Philadelphia, like many other cities, was being tossed by the wave of intolerance that had been sweeping the country over the question of abolition. In vain Wendell Phillips and other anti-slavery advocates mounted the lecture platform to gain sympathizers for their cause. Not long since, a proslavery mob in Alton, Illinois, had murdered the editor of the abolitionist newspaper, the Rev. E. P. Lovejoy, and destroyed the printing press. In Philadelphia itself, that summer of 1838, a similar mob had burned down the office of the *Pennsylvania Freeman.* Lost in the howling crowd, John Greenleaf Whittier, a dedicated humanitarian of liberal convictions, with the power to express them in prose and verse, saw his strongest weapon against intolerance go up in smoke.

Unlike Whittier or, for that matter, Emerson, Poe took little interest in public affairs, in fact, in the world of humanity about him. While at the *Messenger,* books on questions which agitated the country had come to him. He had reviewed them, but they had been merely part of his daily work. On the question of slavery, however, he did express himself—to defend the institution for the reciprocal benefits which slave and master obtained from each other: loyalty on the part of the one, care and responsibility on the part of the other. The Bostonian who had been brought up as a Southerner had, in spite of himself, imbibed the convictions of the slaveholding family which had controlled his most impressible years. As the Virginian that he always described himself—just as he, the theist, would qualify himself as Episcopalian because as a boy he had sat in the pew of a church of that denomination—he reacted consistently. But these responses had nothing to do with the essential Poe, or with the world in which he had his true habitation. There, in the realm of his imagination, he was, like the spider in its web, the center and creator of all that intricate beauty about him, spun out of himself, owing to himself alone its fabric and design. There, removed from the reality which he despised for its capacity to do him harm, protected by the warmth and love of the only two beings he trusted, he was himself, and lord of his universe.

Reality, nevertheless, impinged upon his consciousness and sometimes even claimed attention in his writings—not in the tales which were the product of his true genius but in satire and humor. Just as in "Lionizing" he had satirized the practice of puffery, in "The System of Doctor Tarr and Professor Fether," he cast doubt upon the sanity of the sane, while in "Some words with a Mummy," one of his final expressions, he questioned so-called progress through the device of having a revived Egyptian mummy, Count Allamistakeo, express his opinions.

Evidently nothing of which contemporary America boasted was matter for pride, neither the Bowling-Green Fountain in New York nor the Capitol at Washington, "adorned with no less than four and twenty columns, five feet in diameter. . . . I then mentioned our steel," the narrator went on, "but the foreigner—Allamistakeo—elevated his nose. . . . We then spoke of the great beauty of Democracy, and were at much trouble in impressing the Count with a due sense of the advantages we enjoyed in living where there was suffrage *ad libitum,* and no king. . . . When we had done, he said that, a great while ago, there had occurred something of a very similar sort. Thirteen Egyptian provinces determined all at once to be free, and to set a magnificent example to the rest of mankind. They assembled their wise men, and concocted the most ingenious constitution it is possible to conceive. For a while they managed remarkably well; only their habit of bragging was prodigious. The thing ended, however, in the consolidation of the thirteen states, with some fifteen or twenty others, in the most odious and insupportable despotism that was ever heard of upon the face of the Earth. I asked what was the name of the usurping tyrant. As well as the Count could recollect, it was *Mob*."

Here Poe the misanthrope spoke out, as well as the Virginia gentleman who had no high regard for the wisdom of the collective mind, especially in matters of the common good. In a sense, too, he was blaming that same Mob, concerted society, for the injustices done him, the artist, by its failure to award him the pre-eminence he felt he deserved, not to mention an adequate living. Most of all, in that scorn of the mob was the explicit declaration of his superiority to it and, beyond it, to the rest of humanity. It was an alarming symptom which, in more objective moments, he felt called upon to defend as, once, in a letter to James Russell Lowell: "I am *not* ambitious— except negatively. I, now and then feel stirred up to excel a fool, merely because I hate to let a fool imagine that he may excel me. . . ." [1]

The truth of the matter was that for him the fool, multiplied, represented the rest of mankind, for which he had neither love nor fellow feeling. Whenever he dealt directly with his contemporaries, as in his reviews, he was more generous with the loud damns than with the faint praise because of the power, even if it sprang from fear, which that severity procured him. Not that his harshness was unjustified toward the general run of mediocrity which, since the days of printing, has come pouring out of the presses. But he broke at the wheel not only the butterfly but the mosquito, whose own irritating nature foredoomed it to early extinction.

The same ruthless scorn appeared in those sketches which ostensibly had their being in the real world, as distinct from the realm of Poe's loftiest imaginings. Thus, in such skits as "Loss of Breath," "How to Write a Blackwood Article" and similar cruel, macabre burlesques, he indulged in a sadistic humor which repels, as mocking laughter would repel in the presence of death. Yet the horrors in themselves—the sensations of a man on being hanged; a decapitation by the revolving hand of a steeple clock—are less awful than the graveyard imaginings of "The Fall of the House of Usher," the insane fixation of the hero in "Berenice," or the appalling obsession of the

[1] Ostrom, p. 256.

narrator in "The Tell-Tale Heart," perhaps because both hanging and decapitation may fall within the experience of unhappy man, in the world he inhabits. The horrors of the imaginative tales, on the other hand, though presented in circumstantial detail and convincing realism, are so far removed from normal experience that, while one shudders with that "new thrill" which Poe introduced into fiction, one also recognizes his art. In such recognition reality bows before imagination and the reader turns with relief to the daylight streaming through the window, or to the lamp which illuminates Poe's terrible pages.

As the necessity of earning a living threw Poe into the alien everyday world, he reasserted his vision of himself with greater force in his imaginative writings. As Roderick Usher—from what depth of the subconscious had he summoned up the name of the Ushers who had befriended his mother?—he could describe himself in his study, with his pale complexion, "an eye large, liquid, and luminous beyond comparison; lips somewhat thin and very pallid, but of a surpassingly beautiful curve . . . a finely moulded chin, speaking in its want of prominence, a want of moral energy . . . these features, with an inordinate expansion above the regions of the temple, made up altogether a countenance not easily to be forgotten." It was a portrait painted to the life, which was to recur in one phase or another in his finest tales.

With that personal beauty there was always a canker of some psychic abnormality which Poe also recognized in himself, both in its benign and in its evil forms, which became transmuted into his works. "I regard these visions, even as they arise," he wrote of "Ligeia," the result of one such mental condition, "with an awe which, in some measure, moderates and tranquillizes the ecstasy. I regard them through a conviction that this ecstasy, in itself, is of a character supernal to nature—is a glimpse of the spirit's inner world." [2]

That inner world, however, was as often a dispenser of nightmare as of beauty, both of which mingle in "Ligeia," as in his most characteristic works. In one of his earliest poems, "Romance," he showed his awareness of that combination, in the "painted paroquet" that taught him to lisp his earliest word, and in the "eternal Condor years" shaking the very heavens with their tumult. His inner life had always been one of conflict, with his mind as the battleground and, off somewhere in its darkest recesses, the shadow of insanity which might someday manifest itself.

[2] Gill, pp. 89-90.

In Philadelphia he sought to exorcise that shadow by bringing it
into the open, in a superlative expression of his obsessed genius, the
poem "The Haunted Palace." By that title, he explained to Rufus
Griswold in a letter, he meant a mind haunted by phantoms—a
disordered brain. The allegory, as baroque in conception as it is pure
in form, is, in its precision of detail, almost as frightening as the
microscopic carving with which the lonely prisoner seeks to stave
off insanity.

Conceiving the head as a palace, the dominion of Thought, Poe
traces its downfall in six cumulative stanzas:

> .   .   .   .
>
> Banners yellow, glorious, golden,
>   On its roof did float and flow,
> (This—all this—was in the olden
>   Time long ago,) . . .
>
> .   .   .   .
>
> Wanderers in that happy valley,
>   Through two luminous windows, saw
> Spirits moving musically,
>   To a lute's well-tunèd law,
> Round about a throne where, sitting
>   (Porphyrogene!)
> In state his glory well-befitting,
>   The ruler of that realm was seen.
>
> And all with pearl and ruby glowing
>   Was the fair palace door,
> Through which came flowing, flowing, flowing
>   And sparkling evermore,
> A troop of echoes, whose sweet duty
>   Was but to sing,
> In voices of surpassing beauty,
>   The wit and wisdom of their king.
>
> But evil things, in robes of sorrow,
>   Assailed the monarch's high estate.
> (Ah, let us mourn!—for never morrow
>   Shall dawn upon him desolate!)
>
> .   .   .   .
>
> And travellers, now, within that valley,
>   Through the red-litten windows see
> Vast forms, that move fantastically
>   To a discordant melody,

> While, like a ghastly rapid river,
>   Through the pale door
> A hideous throng rush out forever
>   And laugh—but smile no more.

As in a medieval morality play, each feature of that noble edifice passes in review: the golden hair, the banners yellow; the eyes, in the luminous windows which, with the coming of evil, glow luridly; the teeth and lips, in the fair palace door, through which under the dominion of Thought music flows—till vast forms, moving fantastically to discordant sounds, take possession of the monarch's realm. Then, through the pale door a hideous throng rush out "and laugh—but smile no more."

Now, more than a century after its publication, the poem still has the power to affect one profoundly, as much by its new musical nuances as by the fantastic quality of the conception. Poe was proud of it, so proud that when, in November, 1839, Longfellow's "The Beleaguered City" appeared in the *Southern Literary Messenger,* he immediately set up a cry of plagiarism, certain that the New England poet had been influenced by his poem which the *American Museum* had published, without a title, in April of that year. There is a slight similarity in the two works, but to one ridden like Poe by his fixation it was enough to justify his suspicions. From that moment Longfellow became fixed in his mind as a plagiarist, an opinion which he was to air *ad nauseam* whenever he had the power and the space in which to do so.

Even though Philadelphia was to prove the closest to a peaceful haven that Poe ever had, he still carried with him the phantoms of his private universe, of which Death was the sovereign majesty. Poe had sought to exorcise his dread of insanity in a poem. By that same magic, in "The Conqueror Worm," he endeavored to deal with Death. Here the allegory is actually performed, as

> An angel throng, bewinged, bedight
>   In veils, and drowned in tears,
> Sit in a theatre, to see
>   A play of hopes and fears,
> While the orchestra breathes fitfully
>   The music of the spheres . . .

The mimes mutter and mumble, enacting their parts, flying hither and thither like puppets at the bidding of vast formless things, chasing a Phantom that is never attained, round a circle that always leads to the self-same spot—

And much of Madness, and more of Sin
    And Horror the soul of the plot.

But see, amid the mimic rout
    A crawling shape intrude!
A blood-red thing that writhes from out
    The scenic solitude!
It writhes!—it writhes!—with mortal pangs
    The mimes become its food,
And the angels sob at vermin fangs
    In human gore imbued.

Out—out are the lights—out all!
    And over each quivering form,
The curtain, a funeral pall,
    Comes down with the rush of a storm,
While the angels, all pallid and wan,
    Uprising, unveiling, affirm
That the play is the tragedy, "Man,"
    And its hero, the Conqueror Worm.

Himself one of the helpless mimes, Poe nonetheless took the edge off Death's triumph by acknowledging his own foreordained place in the cruel play. By externalizing his fears he was able to live with them.

His lesser, though equally real, nightmares he treated in much the same way. "He disliked the dark and was rarely out at night when I knew him," recalled George R. Graham, who knew Poe well. "On one occasion he said to me, 'I believe that demons take advantage of the night to mislead the unwary—although you know,' he added, 'I don't believe in them.' " [3] Though Graham knew that Poe enjoyed mystifying his listeners, he was also aware of the poet's inner life whose activities he revealed in his works.

At that time, however, Poe's existence, at least on the surface, was as normal as it was ever to be. After temporary lodgings in various boardinghouses, he had moved to a small wooden lean-to of three rooms built against a brick building on Arch Street. From there, after other removals, dictated by his finances and his family's needs, he went on to Coates Street, near Fairmount Park, to a house that had the pleasant advantage of a garden.

For all that Philadelphia was one of the oldest centers of letters— indeed, more than a century earlier it had lured the Bostonian, Benjamin Franklin, to found his press there, leaving the *Saturday Eve-*

[3] Graham in letter to Gill. Quoted in Gill.

ning Post as the monument of his success—Poe found it difficult to earn a living. Yet, besides Franklin's *Post,* Philadelphia published a number of magazines with a wide circulation, like *Godey's Lady's Book* with which Poe was already acquainted, *Burton's Gentleman's Magazine, Graham's Casket* and several others.

After endeavoring in vain for months to find regular employment with one of the periodicals, Poe turned to whatever offered. Of all unlikely projects for the author of "The Fall of the House of Usher," it was the writing of a textbook on shells, *The Conchologist's First Book: or A System of Testaceous Malacology,* to be used in the schools. When it was ready, Poe took out a copyright in his name and the book was issued in April, 1839, by the Philadelphia firm of Haswell, Barrington and Haswell. "The animals, according to Cuvier, are given with the shells," the title page said of the illustrations which indeed beautifully reproduced the subjects among the reeds and sedges of their natural habitat. "A great number of new species added," the description continued, "and the whole brought up, as accurately as possible, to the present condition of the science."

Unfortunately, among the lavish information there appeared not the least reference to Captain Thomas Brown's *The Conchologist's Text Book,* published in Glasgow several years earlier, and from which Poe had derived his expertise in the matter of testaceous malacology by means of that skillful paraphrasing of another's original which, whenever he had the least suspicion of it in a literary work, made him shout: "Plagiarism." He did, however, give full credit for particular contributions to Cuvier, who could not have cared anyway, since he had been dead for seven years. Poe also admitted his indebtedness to Professor Thomas Wyatt, whose *Conchology,* brought out in an expensive edition by Harpers the previous year, Poe had incorporated, again in paraphrase, but with the author's consent.

The part played by Professor Wyatt appears somewhat disingenuous. Because of its high price the book in its original format had not sold well. Since Harpers refused to reissue it in a cheap edition, Wyatt, loath to lose a deserved reward for his efforts, paid Poe, who badly needed the money, for his labors and the use of his name. Beyond the $50 Poe received, he had little satisfaction from his hack work. Worse, he soon found himself at the receiving end of the accusation he was so ready to make against others. To his young admirer, George W. Eveleth, he later sought to explain away the onus which, deservedly or not, had fallen upon him because of the ill-augured work. *"All* School-books are necessarily made in a similar way. The very title-page acknowledges that the animals are given 'according to Cuvier.' The charge is infamous. . . ." [4] He made no mention, however, of that undoubting Thomas whom he had so generously pilfered.

As it was, Poe had extenuation enough for undertaking the task, which, by its very nature, could have given him no pleasure except that of assuring money for his family. Virginia's health had begun to fail and, though the doctor gave no name to the ailment, he advised air and sunlight, which had prompted the move to the Coates Street house. Money, as always, was hard to come by. Although Edgar had published "Ligeia," "The Haunted Palace" and a number of light sketches in the *American Museum,* which his Baltimore friends, Nathan C. Brooks and Dr. Joseph E. Snodgrass, had newly established, the rewards were negligible. "Ligeia" brought him only $10, at the rate of some 80 cents a page; the rest, being slighter, netted him less. But even those frail straws failed him when the magazine went under after a few months. His free-lance journalism, a review of N. P. Willis' *Tortesa* and fleeting articles in ephemeral publications which, in the prolonged depression, died almost as soon as they were born, netted him next to nothing. In his pressing straits, Poe wrote to William E. Burton, asking for employment in the *Gentleman's Magazine.*

Mr. Burton, a hearty English comedian with a large, mobile face that served him well in the old broad farce in which he excelled, was not content to conquer one muse but he must also woo another. Fancying himself a littérateur as well as an actor-manager and playwright, he had recently produced a successful play, *Ellen Wareham,* in which he combined his talents. Earlier, in 1837, despite the financial panic, he had intrepidly founded his magazine.

Since it issued from Philadelphia, he decked the *Gentleman's* title page with a head of Franklin, a scroll, a book and a sprig of laurel; to justify its name he also printed a quotation from De Vere, describing a gentleman as not a man of high or low rank, but as one whose distinction is of the mind. A keen businessman who derived inspiration from the Exchange opposite his offices, he was quick to see Poe's value to his magazine. Losing no time, he offered Poe $10 a week for two hours' editorial work a day. Poe would then have leisure for anything else he chose, "supposing that you did not exercise your talents in behalf of any publications interfering with the prospect of the G.M. I shall dine at home today at 3. If you will cut your mutton

[4] Ostrom, p. 343.

with me, good," he closed in the tone of Micawber, whom he used to portray to the least gesture on the stage.[5]

Poe did not wait to be asked twice for that pleasant occupation. Over the mutton the two came to an agreement and with the July, 1839, number of the *Gentleman's Magazine* Poe's name appeared jointly with Burton's as editor.

[5] Letter in Griswold Collection, Boston Public Library.

CHAPTER XVIII

->>> • <<<-

The Grand Project

ALTHOUGH Poe was glad to be editing Burton's magazine, which gave him a hearing as well as an income, he had been nurturing the ambition of having a literary vehicle of his own, unhampered by boundaries of any sort and regarding the world as the true province of the author. In it would be expressed honest and fearless opinion on public matters, while the literary reviews would be guided by the purest rules of Art. For the present he could only dream while putting his ideals into practice in another man's paper. His more urgent ambition was to see a collection of his stories in print. For that purpose he assembled a prospective volume to be called *Tales of the Grotesque and Arabesque.*

Meanwhile the exponent of honest and fearless opinion indulged his honesty and fearlessness in critiques which, as usual, applied chastisement much more often than praise. In a review of James F. Cooper's *History of the United States Navy* he was unusually generous, only to turn with uplifted rod to Cooper's latest novels, which had nothing to do with the case. They were so silly and so badly done, Poe said, that they had led the public "to suspect even a radical taint in the intellect, an absolute and irreparable mental leprosy." [1] More than once Mr. Burton must have had his digestion spoiled by dread of libel suits brought on by his rash, if fearless, editor.

Poe soon became a noted figure in the well-scrubbed streets of the city of brotherly love. Neighbors near the house with the large garden would see him passing by their windows, enveloped in the long Spanish cloak which had become the fashion. Although he was not an habitué of the literary salons, he soon had a number of acquaintances and a few friends, for he did not readily admit anyone into his intimacy. Among them was Lambert A. Wilmer of Baltimore days. He, too, like Edgar, had shifted about from place to place in the insecure life that journalism enforced. A few years earlier

[1] *Gentleman's Magazine,* July, 1839.

Wilmer had left Baltimore, lured like Edgar by the promises of Philadelphia, and without a penny in his pocket had made the journey on foot all the way.

One of his first acts of friendship was to publish Poe's grotesque, "The Devil in the Belfry," in one of the magazines with which he was connected. The story was one of Poe's ostensibly humorous efforts which, with their attempt at dialect—Dutch-English, this time—and their farfetched puns, *Vondervotteimittiss*—I wonder what time it is—are among his most irritating attempts at laughter. Another of these skits, "The Man that was Used Up," Edgar published in *Burton's Gentleman's Magazine.*

The subject for hilarity in this instance was one Brevet-Brigadier General John A. B. C. Smith, a fine-looking, impressive fellow who had fought against the Kickapoos, so called. Early one morning the narrator calls upon the general before he is dressed and the Negro servant leads him to his master's bedroom. "I looked about, of course, for the occupant, but did not immediately perceive him. There was a large and exceedingly odd-looking bundle of something which lay close by my feet on the floor, and as I was not in the best humor in the world, I gave it a kick out of the way. 'Hem! ahem! rather civil that, I should say,' said the bundle, in one of the smallest, and altogether the funniest little voices, between a squeak and a whistle. . . ." The bundle was the general, to whom the Negro handed the artificial legs, arms, bosom, eyes and everything else that made him the handsome man which the world saw. This execrable piece of cruel buffoonery was meant to throw the reader into gales of mirth.

Passing from such humor to "The Fall of the House of Usher," which also appeared in *Burton's Magazine* at about the same time, is like going from the chamber of horrors in a wax museum to the light of day, even though the subject is, if anything, more horrifying. The one, however, echoes to the grim laughter of the madhouse; the other is transformed to terrible beauty by the imagination of genius. Between the two crouched the unfathomable enigma of Poe's personality.

A month later, in *Burton's* for October, 1839, Poe republished from Miss Leslie's annual, *The Gift,* one of his greatest stories, "William Wilson," second only to "The Fall of the House of Usher" and perhaps a pendant to it through the link of the poem, "The Haunted Palace," which Poe had introduced into the earlier tale. Both stories deal with moral disintegration, in Roderick Usher through latent insanity, in William Wilson through a sense of predestination toward evil. Like Usher and most of Poe's heroes, William Wilson descends from a long line distinguished for imaginative and easily excitable temperaments. In William Wilson these qualities reach their extreme.

The story, unlike most of Poe's fiction, is not set in the vague semi-Gothic décor of his imaginative tales but in a recognizable landscape, the England of his boyhood at Stoke Newington. Indeed, except for the latitude allowed the creative imagination, Mr. Bransby's school is recognizably depicted. But there all touch with reality ends, for essentially "William Wilson" is what Poe, in his loathing of didacticism, would have abhorred: a moral tale, built round the concept of the dual nature of man, with Poe himself projected in its central figure.

As with most creative works, which seldom spring full grown from their originator's mind, "William Wilson" had an honorable ancestry, from the earliest allegory of the struggle of good and evil in the human soul to its treatment in William Godwin's powerful novel, *Caleb Williams,* which had stirred the English-speaking world in 1794. In it man and his conscience are embodied in the guilty Falkland and in Caleb Williams, the sharer of his secret. Poe was well acquainted with Godwin's work and often referred to it. However, he need have sought no further than in his own dual nature for his theme, for William Wilson and his double are no more than Poe's imaginative recognition of the conflict in the theater of man's psyche —the clash between the moral conscience and the instinct-driven, unprincipled ego.

In his tale he externalized the conflict through William Wilson and his double, that other William Wilson, of exactly the same age, who resembled him like a twin and who invariably appeared at crucial moments in his evil career, to admonish him, always in a whisper. But William Wilson pursued his sinister pleasures undeterred, till the end came, at a masquerade in the palace of the Neapolitan Duke Di Broglio, when William Wilson ran his sword through his alter ego.

"A large mirror—so at first it seemed to me in my confusion— now stood where none had been perceptible before; and as I stepped up to it in extremity of terror, mine own image, but with features all pale and dabbled in blood, advanced to meet me. . . . Thus it appeared, I say, but was not. It was my antagonist—it was Wilson, who then stood before me in the agonies of his dissolution. . . . Not a thread of all his raiment—not a line in all the marked and singular lineaments of his face which was not, even in the most absolute identity, *mine own!* It was Wilson; but he spoke no longer in a whisper, and I could have fancied that I myself was speaking while he said: *'You have conquered and I yield. Yet, henceforth art thou*

*dead—dead to the World, to Heaven and to Hope! In me didst thou
exist—and, in my death, see by this image, which is thine own, how
utterly thou hast murdered thyself."*

But William Wilson was not dead, for he lived with the characteristics of Roderick Usher in Oscar Wilde's Dorian Gray, after an
earlier rebirth as des Esseintes in Huysman's *À Rebours*. Indeed, the
very core of *Dorian Gray*—the theme of the sins of Dorian etching
themselves in the features of his portrait, is contained in the final
words of Wilson's double: "See by this image, which is thine own,
how utterly thou hast murdered thyself."

Poe's externalizing of his internal conflicts may have made him
see himself more clearly. At any rate, Mrs. Clemm was called upon
less often to plead that Poe was "sick." As it was, he had to keep
sober for his editorial work and for his own compositions. For even
if, as Baudelaire was to maintain, Poe's drinking acted both as a
stimulus to his imagination and as a mnemonic device, to enable him
to recapture his visions, he still had to have a clear head to write with
his incomparable lucidity. Moreover, even if, indeed, "the poet had
learned to drink as a conscientious author exercises himself by filling
up notebooks," [2] Poe would have had to be in a constant state of
inebriation, to judge by the body of his work.

Late in December of 1839, Poe at last realized one of his dearest
ambitions, the publication of twenty-five of his stories, *Tales of the
Grotesque and Arabesque*. The Philadelphia firm of Lea and Blanchard brought them out in two handsome volumes. The *New York
Mirror* was quick and generous with its praise, featured on the front
page, in the first column. Mentioning particularly "William Wilson,"
"The Fall of the House of Usher" and "Morella," the critic, L. F.
Tasistro, granted him a high place among imaginative writers. "For
there is a fine poetic feeling, much brightness of fancy, an excellent
taste, a ready eye for the picturesque, much quickness of observation,
and great truth of sentiment and character in all these works. . . ."
The rest was calculated to make Poe's heart bound with pleasure.
"There is scarcely one of the tales . . . in which we do not find the
development of great intellectual capacity with a power for vivid
description, an opulence of imagination, a fecundity of invention,
and a command over the elegances of diction which have seldom
been displayed even by writers who have acquired the greatest distinction in the republic of letters. It would be, indeed, no easy matter
to find another artist with ability equal to this writer for discussing

---

[2] Baudelaire, in introduction to 1856 edition of *Histoires Extraordinaires*.

the good and evil—the passions, dilemmas and affectations . . . the virtue and vice by which mankind are by turns affected. . . ." [3]

Mr. Tasistro had seen what the stories contained in imagination and originality, as well as in distinction of style and awareness of the inner conflicts of man. He was still too close to the phenomenon to distinguish Poe's universality, which transcended all borders and was eventually to make him known to the world.

If one is to believe Poe, too often prone to invent praise when reality failed him, none other than Isaac D'Israeli, author of *Curiosities of Literature,* had lauded him even before Mr. Tasistro. America itself, however, let the volumes languish in the publishers' warehouse. In any case, Poe would have realized nothing from the sales, for even if the edition had sold out the profits would have gone to Lea and Blanchard. He had to be content with a number of copies for his own use and the pleasure of seeing his work in print.

Meanwhile his relations with Burton had not been running smoothly. Poe grew restless and dissatisfied. At bottom it was again the understandable discontent of a superior intellect unequally yoked with mediocrity, which had, moreover, the advantage of power on its side. Once more Poe found himself doing the major part of the work, building up the standards and the circulation of the magazine, and receiving from it all a salary hardly commensurate with his contribution. As early as the 21st of September, 1839, he had written to Philip P. Cooke, a Virginia poet whom he admired: "I send the 'Gentleman's Magazine.' . . . Do not think of subscribing. The criticisms are not worth your notice. Of course I pay no attention to them—for there are two of us. . . . Therefore for the present I remain upon my oars—merely penning an occasional paragraph. . . . As soon as Fate allows I will have a Magazine of my own—and will endeavor to kick up a dust. . . ." [4]

Soon the idea of his own magazine became a fixation, but he did not neglect his duties. The critiques and articles flowed from his pen, and with the January, 1840, number of *Burton's,* he began an adventure serial, *"The Journal of Julius Rodman,* being an Account of the First Passage across the Rocky Mountains of North America," based more or less on the expeditions of Lewis and Clarke, and perhaps suggested by a book which had come out early in 1839—John K. Townsend's *Narrative of a Journey Across the Rocky Mountains to the Columbia River.* Moreover, the previous year Poe had reviewed at great length Washington Irving's *Astoria,* an account of the fur

[3] *New York Mirror,* Dec. 28, 1839.
[4] Ostrom, pp. 118-119.

trade in the Northwest. All contributed in some measure to Poe's new narrative, which had its share of his peculiar thrills, though it could not compare with *Arthur Gordon Pym* in interest or imaginative flight. Poe himself may not have been displeased when, in June of 1840, he put an end both to the *Journal of Julius Rodman* and to his connection with *Burton's Magazine*. That same month the *Philadelphia Saturday Courier,* in its issue of the 13th, told the world that Mr. Poe would be launching his own periodical, *The Penn Magazine,* in January of 1841. The grand project, long dreamed about, promised at last to materialize. Its title, with its pun on Penn and Pen, was typically Poe-like.

Judging by the parting letter of Poe to Burton, on the 1st of June, 1840, their relations had long since reached the breaking point. "Your attempts to bully me," Poe wrote, "excite in my mind scarcely any other sentiment than mirth. When you address me again preserve if you can, the dignity of a gentleman. If by accident you have taken it into your head that I am to be insulted with impunity I can only assume that you are an ass. . . . You first 'enforced,' as you say, a deduction of salary: giving me to understand thereby that you thought of parting company— You next spoke disrespectfully of me behind my back—this is an habitual thing—to those whom you supposed your friends, and who punctually retailed me, as a matter of course, every ill-natured word you uttered. . . ." [5]

The final reason, however, was that Burton had advertised the *Gentleman's Magazine* for sale without notifying him about it. For that matter, Poe had been going about soliciting interest in his own *Penn,* unbeknown to his employer. It was not altogether ingenuously that he went on to explain: "Had I not firmly believed in your design to give up your Journal, with a view of attending to the Theatre, I should never have dreamed of attempting one of my own. . . . What have I done at which you have any right to take offense? . . ." [6]

Poe's plan for his own magazine was doubtless one of Burton's grievances, but it was Poe's drinking of which he had openly complained. If one is to believe Poe's first biographer, Griswold, Burton had gone on a tour leaving the conduct of the magazine to Poe. On his return Burton found that not only had his printers not received a line of copy, but that Poe had obtained transcripts of the subscription lists for his own *Penn.* That evening he found Poe "at one of his accustomed haunts," as Griswold put it.

"Mr. Poe, I am astonished," Burton upbraided him. "Give me my

[5] *Ibid.,* pp. 131-132.
[6] *Ibid.,* p. 132.

manuscripts so that I can attend to the duties you have so shamefully neglected, and when you are sober, we will settle."

"Who are you to presume to address me in this manner?" Poe countered. "Burton, I am the editor of the Penn Magazine—and you are *a fool*." [7]

The inference was that Poe was drunk, a condition of which Burton had complained before. He made the mistake of voicing his displeasure to Dr. Snodgrass, who lost no time in retailing his information to Poe, who threatened to sue and obtain damages.

"You are a physician," Poe exculpated himself with Snodgrass, "and I presume no physician can have difficulty in detecting the *drunkard* at a glance. You are, moreover, a literary man, well read in morals. You will never be brought to believe that I could write what I daily write, *as* I write it, were I as this villain would induce those who know me not, to believe. In fine, I pledge you, before God, the solemn word of a gentleman, that I am temperate even to rigor. . . ." [8]

Strangely enough, despite the days Mrs. Clemm had had to go to Mr. Burton pleading that "dear Eddie" was sick, despite the times the neighbors had seen him come unsteadily home, Poe was writing nothing less than the truth. He knew his condition as well as any doctor and far better than most of his contemporaries, and no authority has stated his case better than he did in that same letter to Dr. Snodgrass. "I never was in the *habit* of intoxication. . . . But, for a brief period, while I resided in Richmond, and edited the *Messenger,* I certainly did give way, at long intervals, to the temptation held out on all sides by the spirit of Southern conviviality. My sensitive temperament could not stand an excitement which was an everyday matter to my companions. . . . For some days after each excess I was invariably confined to bed. . . ." [9] He was physically and psychically intolerant of alcohol, which acted upon him like a poison. To the dispassionate observer, however, who saw only the symptoms and not the disease, Poe's condition could only signify drunkenness.

Despite his uncordial parting from Poe, the genial Burton still had a fatherly interest in the young man who had so competently built up his magazine that, when he sold it, the new buyer paid him $3,500 without demur. "There is one thing more," Burton said to George Rex Graham, as they were sealing their bargain, "I want you to take care of my young editor."

[7] Griswold, *Memoir,* Vol. I. *Works of Edgar Allan Poe,* p. xxxiii.
[8] Ostrom, p. 156.
[9] *Ibid.*

The new owner, at twenty-seven, was even younger than his editor and offered an eloquent example of the American ideal of the self-made man. As a boy, after his father, a Philadelphia merchant, had lost his fortune, Graham had put himself through school by learning the trade of a cabinetmaker. He then studied law and was admitted to the bar at the age of twenty-five. At the same time he was dabbling in journalism and finally joined the editorial staff of the *Saturday Evening Post.* Before long he had bought himself Atkinson's *Philadelphia Casket,* a magazine of genteel literature designed for ladies. He now merged the *Casket* and the *Gentleman's Magazine* and renamed the two *Graham's Magazine,* starting out with a subscription list of 5,000.

For Poe, acceptance of the editorial post meant defeat. He had counted on launching his own *Penn* but, with no financial backing nor sufficient subscribers, he had for the present to set aside his plan. Nevertheless, he continued to send out letters, generally written on the back of the prospectus which promised, among other inducements, an honest and fearless opinion on all subjects. "It will endeavour to support the general interests of the republic of letters, without reference to particular regions; regarding the world at large as the true audience of the author."

In that early, self-assertive epoch of literary cliques and regional jealousies, such a world outlook was daringly revolutionary. On the literary and aesthetic side, the *Penn* offered works "from the highest and purest sources . . . and pictorial embellishments . . . by the leading artists of the country." For all this, which would fill two 500-page volumes a year, the subscription was only $5 per annum, payable in advance. Still the subscribers were slow to entice, and Poe's discouragement led as usual to physical collapse, which kept him in bed for the first two weeks of the new year.

On the 17th of January, 1841, he was nonetheless writing to Dr. Snodgrass, who had inquired about the prospects of the *Penn:* "They are *glorious*—notwithstanding the world of difficulties under which I labored and labor . . . I must now do or die—I mean in a literary sense." [10]

In order *not* to die he had to compromise, though never at the expense of his integrity as an artist. To the December, 1840, issue of *Graham's,* he had contributed one of his finest psychological studies, "The Man of the Crowd." The story contained no overt violence, no horror of the usual variety. Instead, the drama enacted itself in the deepest reaches of the crazed mind of a man whom some mysterious

[10] *Ibid.,* pp. 151-152.

compulsion drove to mingle and wander in the crowd which, in an endless current, carried him hither and yon, without his ever attaining peace or finding the thing he sought. He was a sort of Wandering Jew, confined to a narrower circle, therefore more concentrated in the sin, guilt or crime which persecuted him without remedy.

Here it is not the Man of the Crowd who is telling his story. His course, his moods, his actions are relayed by the observer, who had first remarked him from the large bow window of a coffeehouse in London. The man was old. His face was fiend-like in its evil. His clothes were ragged, but in the glare of a street lamp one could see that his linen, although dirty, was of a beautiful texture. "Through a rent in a closely-buttoned and evidently second-handed *roquelaire* which enveloped him, I caught a glimpse both of a diamond and of a dagger." Symbolically, despite outward poverty, the man was rich and possessed of the capacity to do evil.

From street to thronged square the observer followed him, noting his terror when he found himself alone and gasping as if for breath until he could throw himself once again amid the crowd. All night long, till dawn, all of next day, the observer pursued him. "As the shades of the second evening came on, I grew wearied unto death, and, stopping fully in front of the wanderer, gazed at him steadfastly in the face. He noticed me not but resumed his solemn walk. . . ."

For suggestion of corroding evil and the self-inflicted hell of conscience, "The Man of the Crowd" is a more powerful story than "William Wilson," even though the drama is not externalized. Edgar had drawn the theme from the profoundest springs of his personality. Six years after John Allan's death he, the victim of the old man's avarice and cold blooded calculation, had "gazed at him steadfastly in the face" and meted out punishment through the immortality of his works, in which Mr. Allan had never believed.

It was another of Poe's stories, however, in *Graham's* for April, 1841, that introduced a new and brilliant facet of his many-sided genius: his power of ratiocination, as he called it. He had already given some examples of it, particularly in "Maelzel's Chess Player," wherein he had exposed the mechanism of the famous chess automaton which the Bavarian, J. N. Maelzel, had been exhibiting all over the world. Now, by using the same methodical exposition and logical analysis, Poe set about solving a baffling crime in "The Murders in the Rue Morgue," at the same time creating a novel literary figure and a new form of fiction, the modern detective story.

The shift from the fantastic tale to that of ratiocination had not been made from mere literary caprice, else Poe would have laid his story of the murderous orang-utan in the setting of his fantastic world. Instead, he set it in Paris, though in a nonexistent Rue Morgue, and surrounded it with the characters and details of everyday life. Moreover, he made sure from the outset of the story that the reader should be truly impressed with *the mental features discussed as the analytical, the faculty of resolution and the calculating power*. To their praise and exposition Poe devoted four long paragraphs before he began the narrative which introduced his famous incarnation of these powers, his detective, Monsieur C. Auguste Dupin.

M. Dupin was related to his other heroes only by his being a young gentleman "of an excellent, indeed of an illustrious family, (who) by a variety of untoward events, had been reduced to such poverty that the energy of his character succumbed beneath it." Again, he was Poe's alter ego, this time of the deep thinker and ratiocinator who could solve riddles and expose frauds—but who, as Edgar Allan Poe, was ridden, deep within, by the terror of becoming insane and therefore had to prove his sanity by the ingenuity of his reasoning faculties.

The story, the atrocious murder of a mother and her spinster daughter in a miserable quarter of Paris, was such as might have been cried out in the Paris streets by the news hawkers of the day. All the circumstances were baffling—from the location of the bodies, the animal violence of the murders, the apartment locked from the inside, and other puzzling circumstances, among them a seeming lack of motive.

By the device of reporting the testimony of some dozen individuals the lives and characters of the victims were established, but in the conflicting accounts of what the various witnesses thought they had seen or heard the mystery only deepened so that it appeared almost insoluble.

"The Parisian police, so much extolled for *acumen,* are cunning but no more," Poe's amateur sleuth pronounced. "They make a vast parade of measures. . . . By undue profundity we perplex and enfeeble thought. . . . We will go and see the premises with our own eyes."

In the clarity of Dupin's insight, all the details that had escaped the foolish police fell into place. These were no simple murders. Either a madman had perpetrated them, some raving maniac, or— Yes, Dupin had been right in his deductions from the evidence he had uncovered. An item in a newspaper convinced him that he had found the culprit as he read that, on the morning of the murders, a large tawny orang-utan had been caught in the Bois de Boulogne.

"The Murders in the Rue Morgue" created a sensation not only for its novelty but for the amazing ingenuity of its telling. Scholars have sought to trace influences for the invention of Dupin by citing *Unpublished Passages in the Life of Vidocq, the French Minister of Police,* which ran serially in *Burton's Magazine* in the autumn of 1838 and which Poe must have read, for, in the character of Dupin, he had something to say about the gentleman. As for the nature of the murderer, W. E. Waller suggested that Poe may have seen an extract from the *Shrewsbury Chronicle* for July, 1834.[11] It reported that some traveling showmen had brought to town a ribbed-faced baboon, which they had taught to commit robberies by climbing up great heights, as in the case of Poe's orang-utan. One night a Shrewsbury woman discovered the baboon in her bedroom and when she made an outcry it attacked her so fiercely that her husband was glad to let it escape out of the window. Still, thousands of readers had seen the article, but it was Poe who, if he read it, detected in it the material for his art.

He made the most of the situation in the account of the brute violence of the near-human orang-utan and its helpless victims, a situation that gave added stimulus to an imagination which drew its deepest inspiration from dead or dying women, from animated corpses, from appalling cruelties, and from physical and moral torment. One cannot but wonder at the strange absorption of a creative mind that, oblivious of the two adoring women—mother and daughter—in the same house with him, could write in their proximity: "The apartment was in the wildest disorder. . . . On a chair lay a razor, besmeared with blood. On the hearth were two or three long and thick tresses of grey human hair, also dabbled in blood, and seeming to have been pulled out by the roots. . . . Of Madame L'Espanaye no traces were to be seen; but an unusual quantity of soot being observed in the fire-place, a search was made in the chimney and (horrible to relate!) the corpse of the daughter, head downward, was dragged therefrom. . . . The body was quite warm. . . . Upon the face were many severe scratches, and, upon the throat, dark bruises and deep indentations of finger nails. . . . After a thorough investigation . . . the party made its way into a small paved yard . . . where lay the corpse of the old lady, with her throat so entirely cut that, upon an attempt to raise her, the head fell off. The body, as well as the head, was fearfully mutilated. . . ." Freud could have made much of that situation in exploring Poe's latent impulses.

By a curious circumstance this story, a few years later, brought

[11] See *Notes and Queries* (London, May 17, 1894).

about an amusing wrangle between two Paris journals and revealed that in the matter of piracy French journalism was as adept as the American, before the advent of proper copyright laws.

"The other day," reported the *Entr'-Acte* of October 20, 1846, "an important paper was accusing M. Old-Nick (the writer, M. Forgues) of stealing an orang-utan. This interesting animal was browsing in the pages of *La Quotidienne* when M. Old-Nick saw it, found it to his liking and appropriated it. No doubt our confrère needed a groom. It is a well-known fact that for a long time the English have been . . . training orang-utans in the art of carrying letters on a vermeil tray. . . . It would seem, still according to the same paper, that after stealing the orang-utan from *La Quotidienne*, M. Old-Nick surrendered it to *Le Commerce* as something of his own. I know that M. Old-Nick is a very clever and very honorable youth, and rich enough on his own account not to have to appropriate other people's orang-utans. . . . I must say that I had read his story in *Le Commerce;* it had great charm of wit and style. . . . *La Quotidienne* had also published it in three feuilletons. The orang-utan of *Le Commerce* had only nine columns. Therefore it must have been of a different order of literary quadrumane. Not at all! It was the very same; only it belonged neither to *La Quotidienne* nor to *Le Commerce*. M. Old-Nick had borrowed it from an American novelist whom he is now inventing in the *Revue des Deux Mondes*. This novelist is called Poë: and I say nothing to the contrary. . . . While waiting for the truth to come out we are compelled to admit that this Poë is a very clever and entertaining fellow when arranged by M. Old-Nick." [12]

[12] Translated from the French by F. W.

CHAPTER XIX

→›› • ‹‹←

The Warning

JUST as *Burton's Magazine* had prospered under Poe's editorship, *Graham's* soon experienced a gratifying rise in circulation. What with his stories and poems, Poe's name was being noted at home and, to believe him, also in literary circles abroad where, according to him, none other than the redoubtable John Wilson—"Christopher North" of *Blackwood's*—had entered into an engagement with him to furnish material for his Edinburgh periodical. Since Poe closed the letter imparting this information to Dr. Snodgrass with the caution: "Keep this secret, if you please, for the present," the secrecy may have been imposed by the fact that such a desideratum had occurred only in Poe's imagination. However, in that same letter Poe added: "My forthcoming Tales are promised a very commendatory Review in that journal from the pen of Prof. Wilson." [1] Such a review, whether by Wilson or by another pen, did appear, though not until November, 1847, when the critic particularly remarked "The Man of the Crowd."

For the moment Poe was not harassed by money worries. He was making $800 a year at *Graham's,* exclusive of payments for short stories or poems of his which appeared among the literary contributions. Mrs. Clemm began buying little luxuries for the house and Virginia was promised a harp, on which to accompany herself when she sang in her clear, sweet though small voice. She was also offered a fawn by a Virginia gentleman for her garden, but Poe could think of no mode of conveyance for the little animal. "Some friend from Petersburg may be about to pay us a visit," wrote he, hopefully, to Mr. Hiram Haines. "In the meantime accept our best acknowledgments, precisely as if the little fellow were already nibbling the grass before our windows. . . ." [2]

If neither friend nor fawn arrived from Petersburg, Poe had acquaintances enough in Philadelphia, for through *Graham's* he came in

[1] Ostrom, p. 116.
[2] *Ibid.,* p. 129.

contact with the city's extensive publishing world—the writers, intellectuals and artists who would come into his office. There he met the Englishman, John Sartain, publisher and illustrator, whose fine engravings were always in demand. There too Poe renewed the link with the past in the painter, Thomas Sully, whose nephew Robert had been Edgar's schoolmate in Richmond and whose father, Matthew Sully, had trod the boards of the Virginia Company at the same time with Elizabeth Poe. That alone would have endeared Thomas Sully to her son.

Then, in the early spring of 1841, Poe met the man who was destined to play in his life the role of a malefic "William Wilson." The Rev. Dr. Rufus Wilmot Griswold, a Baptist minister and a littérateur, looked young for his dignified title and therefore ambushed his twenty-six years behind a fringe of beard. He wore his hair long and parted in the middle over a broad intellectual brow, whose loftiness he would unconsciously indicate by his habit of sitting with an elbow on a table, his folded hand against his cheek and the outstretched forefinger on his temple. His eyes, large and thoughtful, were arched by fine brows. His nose was straight, though perhaps overlong and with too sensual a spread of nostril. The well-cut mouth was lifted by a smile which, however, did not soften its severity. He was a noticeable man and his whole expression denoted that he knew it.

He was born in the thriving, central Vermont town of Rutland, some twenty miles from Poultney, where Horace Greeley as a boy, had first tasted printer's ink in the local paper. Griswold's parents were farmers, which, in those days of vast acreages embracing valleys and mountains, would indicate that they were well-to-do. At any rate they could afford to give their son a good education, which he further enriched by his encyclopedic memory, his travels abroad, and an inveterate ambition to get ahead of his fellows. Unfortunately, though tormented by the urge to create, he had neither genius nor originality, so that beyond serving on various newspapers and periodicals in Boston and New York, he had done nothing of distinction. The sermons and pious songs which he had succeeded in publishing had certainly not entitled him to any measure of fame.

Being a shrewd judge of men, as well as of himself, Griswold relinquished wooing the muses on his own account and decided, rather, to prey upon the vanity of his fellows by bringing out a *Biographical Annual*. This first opus concerned itself with eminent persons recently deceased and comprised a pious coronal of tributes with vital—rather, mortal—statistics. It proved so popular that the gratified doctor quickly followed it with a still more rewarding tome, *Gems from*

American Female Poets, each singing dove receiving her meed of praise in the introductory notices. The public bought and asked for more. It was only a step from this to the most lucrative flattery of all—an anthology embracing the whole poetic scene.

It was while collecting material for his *Poets and Poetry of America* that Griswold, according to his own statement, met Poe, in the spring of 1841. "He called at my hotel, and not finding me at home, left two letters of introduction. The next morning I visited him and we had a long conversation about literature and literary men. . . ." [3]

The *two* letters of introduction would indicate eagerness on Poe's part to make the acquaintance of the already notable anthologist. They met early in May. By the 29th of the month Poe was sending him a number of poems to include in the forthcoming anthology. He had written no new poetry recently, but "The Haunted Palace," "The Coliseum" and "The Sleeper" had a quality that kept them forever ageless.

Mr. Graham, meanwhile, was congratulating himself on his editor, who, within six months, had raised the circulation of the magazine from 5,000 subscribers to 20,000—and the list was still swelling. The "best pens" in the country did not wait to be coaxed to appear in *Graham's* pages—if not yet in the *Penn's*—and visiting notables, especially if they had a manuscript or an engraving to sell, made it a point to call at Third and Chestnut Streets. With the growing circulation the name of Edgar Allan Poe rang across the country—as editor and critic. The poet, and the author of a unique fiction, was as yet unrecognized by the public at large. Indeed, when during the summer of 1841 he suggested to Lea and Blanchard that they bring out a new edition of *Tales of the Grotesque and Arabesque,* they replied that they had not yet disposed of the first printing, which had failed to cover the expenses of publication. Even Poe's offer of a number of new and original tales did not entice them.

However, Graham, the epicure, was reaching out with both hands for the fruits of life—as, indeed, why not, when every morning his office desk was piled high with new subscriptions? Soon he installed himself and his wife in one of the finest houses in Philadelphia, on Arch Street, adjoining the residence and shop of a prosperous wine merchant. The furnishings, if not in impeccable taste, were lavish enough to impress the writers, artists and assorted bohemians whom he invited to his dinner parties, together with visiting celebrities. Wine and talk poured out in equal floods, while a huge crystal chandelier, which had once adorned a theater, twinkled with candle flames over-

[3] Griswold, *Memoir,* Vol. I. *Works of Edgar Allan Poe,* p. xxi.

head and duplicated its shimmer in the mirrors along the walls. Edgar, with Virginia strangely but becomingly dressed in some home-made creation, sat frequently among the guests. Mrs. Clemm, on those occasions, particularly whenever Edgar attended the dinners alone, made herself at home in the Graham kitchen, with her basket agape for the surplus of the banquet. The feasting over, she would see to it, gently but firmly, that Eddie was not sidetracked by his friends into further conviviality in some tavern.

Mr. Graham's generosity was much talked about, especially when, for the convenience of his dinner guests, he had a door broken through between his house and the wine merchant's. In that generosity, how-ever, he failed to include additional compensation for the man who had built up his magazine and swelled his bank account. While Mr. Graham was adding a fine team of grays and an elegant carriage to his gracious living, Poe was still drawing a salary of only $800 a year—$200 less than he had been getting at the *Messenger*. True, he was paid for his own writings, but not quite at the price that other contributors seemed to command. For one of his most recent short stories, which he considered among his best, Graham gave him $52, whereas Longfellow received $150 for his play, "The Spanish Stu-dent," and Cooper $1,000 for ten of his tales.

The dream of his *Penn* agitated Poe more than ever, yet dutifully he continued to solicit contributions from Longfellow, from Wash-ington Irving, Fitz-Greene Halleck, the foremost writers of the day, for another man's profit. Occasional discords arose between him and Graham on the contents of the magazine, which Poe found "namby-pamby"—a quality which the publisher approved for its appeal to the gentler sex, and which he reinforced by adding two "lady-editors" to his staff. However, Poe's reviews, like his treatment of Joseph H. Ingraham's *Quadroone,* served as an antidote. On that score, it was no use remonstrating with Poe. "*Quadroone* is, in my honest opinion, trash. If I must call it a good book to preserve the friendship of Prof. Ingraham—Prof. Ingraham may go to the devil." As the subscribers were obviously satisfied, Graham on that score gave Poe his way.

Edgar, however, felt increasingly disgusted with his circumstances, as he confessed to his friend Frederick W. Thomas, who had recently stepped into a comfortable government office in Washington. Poe had known Thomas for about a year, but mutual interests—Thomas had written a number of songs and published a successful novel, *Clin-ton Bradshaw*—had quickly sealed their friendship. Also, like Poe, Thomas, a New Englander, had been brought up in the South. There had been still another link, Thomas' friendship with Henry Poe, in

Baltimore, when the two had been rivals in a love affair, while Edgar was in the army.

A largehearted man, Thomas responded with quick sympathy to other people's afflictions whether hidden or visible, like his own. He had been crippled as a boy of eight when, on hearing the martial music of marching soldiers, he had run toward the window over a wet floor. The fall had kept him confined for over a year and left him, as he said without bitterness, a skeleton on crutches. Some five years earlier he had abandoned them for an ingenious contrivance that helped him to get about with less effort. Though he had not gone to college, he had studied law, while writing poetry at the same time. Like all thoughtful men, he had his dark periods. During one such mood, while wandering in dejection through the streets of Philadelphia, he was struck by a song that someone was playing. "The discovery that the song was mine,' 'Tis said that absence conquers love,' changed the whole current of my feelings," he confessed to Poe.

Now, thanks to his post, he had fewer moods of depression for, while scrupulously fulfilling his duties, he still had leisure for his writing. It was, as Poe saw it, an ideal situation for a man with literary inclinations. "From the bottom of my heart I wish you joy," he wrote his friend in congratulation. "You can now lucubrate more at your ease & will infallibly do something worthy yourself. . . . Would to God, I could do as you have done. Do you seriously think that an application on my part to Tyler would have a good result?" [4]

He was writing on the 26th of June, 1841, in answer to a kindly expression in a letter of Thomas' alluding to such a possibility. For Poe a mere wish instantly demanded realization so that, as he wrote on, the prospect of a government post, with its opportunity for easeful lucubration, became increasingly attractive. Although during the previous electoral campaign Poe, like Dr. Johnson, had probably cared as little for one party as for the other, he now informed Thomas that his political principles had always been with the existing administration. "I battled with right good will for Harrison, when opportunity offered," he declared in a safe generalization. "With Mr. Tyler I have some slight personal acquaintance. . . . For the rest, I am a literary man—and I see a disposition in government to cherish letters. Have I any chance?" By the time he reached the close, the post had become of the greatest urgency. "I am *really* serious about the office. If you can aid me in any way, I am sure you will." Even that was not enough, for he added, in a postscript: "It is not impossible that you

[4] Ostrom, p. 170.

could effect my object by merely showing this letter yourself personally to the President. . . ." [5]

Mr. Thomas interested himself on Poe's behalf and suggested that he come to Washington. But the man who had obtained the money for Mr. Graham's house, his chandelier, his grays and handsome turnout did not command the fare to take him to the capital, "saying nothing of getting back."

Meanwhile *Graham's* literally kept on increasing, in bulk as in number, thanks to Poe's stories, his articles, and his recently introduced popular feature, "Autography"—already tested in *the Southern Literary Messenger*—whereby, on the basis of the signature of a famous author, Poe ostensibly divined his temperament and character. Besides, he added a department on cryptography, or secret writing. For some five months he had been solving a series of cryptograms, sent in by the readers of *Alexander's Weekly Messenger*. He now defied the subscribers of *Graham's* to send him something he could not decipher, however unusual and arbitrary the characters employed. His challenges were accepted. Sales boomed. Graham called for rarer wines while Poe had to be content with the pride of his triumphs, which had no value at the butcher's and the baker's.

Still, his family was better off than it had ever been. Virginia not only had her harp but a little pianoforte as well, on which she would pick out the accompaniment for her songs. Poe was proud of her and had great confidence in her musical taste. During his correspondence with Mr. Thomas he had taken a song of his to Willig's for publication, but waited till it was out "that I might give you my opinion and Virginia's about its merits. . . . Virginia is very anxious to see it, as your 'Tis said that absence' &c is a great favorite with her." [6]

As Virginia grew in grace and beauty, Poe's adoration—for it was not love as it is generally understood—grew equally and was remarked upon by all who saw them together. Graham, whose eyes were ordinarily set upon material things, described it as a sort of rapturous worship of the spirit of beauty. Some, however, noting Virgina's youth and her almost childlike ingenuousness, could not understand it. The legend of the "child-wife" began to grow and many biographers even extended that childishness to Virginia's intellect, seeking to draw a parallel between her and the mentally retarded Rosalie. [7]

[5] *Ibid.*, pp. 170-171.
[6] *Ibid.*, p. 184.
[7] For this the Mackenzies were largely responsible by transmitting their antipathy toward Mrs. Clemm and Virginia to Mrs. Susan Archer Talley Weiss. Her *Home Life of Poe* has done much toward spreading the myth about Virginia.

"Undoubtedly, one of the chief factors in the non-success of Poe's life and its consequent unhappiness was his marriage . . ." wrote Mrs. Susan Archer Talley Weiss. "Mr. John Mackenzie, Poe's lifelong . . . friend, never hesitated to say that had Poe been left to himself the idea would never have occurred to him of marrying his little child-cousin. In no transaction of his life was his pitiable weakness more manifest than in this feeble yielding of himself to the dominant will of his mother-in-law. Had Poe remained single or have married another than Virginia, his regard for her would have continued what it had been in the beginning and what it remained to the end—the affection of a brother or cousin for a sweet and lovable child. . . . Mr. John Mackenzie might well have said, as he did, that Poe's marriage was the greatest misfortune of his life and a millstone round his neck, holding him down against every effort to rise. . . ." [8]

At one point snobbery also rears its head. "His imprudent and . . . unnatural marriage, cut him off from what would probably have been the highest happiness of his life, with its accompanying worldly and social advantages. . . . It deprived him of social position and social enjoyment; for his poverty-stricken 'home' was never one to which he could invite his friends; and he himself seems never to have found in it any real pleasure, but to have regarded it merely as a haven of refuge in seasons of distress. . . ." [9]

Those who saw the marriage from a less prejudiced view gave a different picture. Mr. Gowans, in New York, while rhapsodizing over Virginia's beauty, spoke of her devotion to Edgar as that of a mother for her first-born. To Dr. Chivers, a few years later, Virginia appeared as "a tenderhearted and affectionate woman—particularly to him whom she addressed with the endearing appellation of *My Dear!*" [10] Even Griswold, all too ready to disparage anything pertaining to Poe, described Virginia as a very amiable and lovely girl. A. B. Harris who, like many others, visited the Poe household, found Poe's wife, at twenty, "Fair, soft and graceful and girlish. Every one who saw her was won by her. Poe was very proud and very fond of her . . . and she in turn idolized him. She had a voice of wonderful sweetness and was an exquisite singer, and in some of their more prosperous days, when they were living in a pretty little rose-covered cottage she had her harp and piano." [11]

[8] Weiss, pp. 223-235.
[9] *Ibid.*
[10] Chivers, *Life of Poe.* Ed. Richard Beale Davis. (Original manuscript in the Henry E. Huntington Library, San Marino, Calif.)
[11] Quoted in Ingram, Vol. I, p. 221.

It must have been at about this time that Thomas Sully, who had painted a miniature of Poe in his Spanish cape and a suitably Byronic attitude, also portrayed Virginia in perhaps the only likeness of her from life, outside of a sketch Poe once made of her head.[12] In Sully's painting she is shown Ophelia-like, gathering flowers in a romantic setting of dense trees and far distances through which the light barely penetrates. By contrast the graceful young body, in a pale dress with a richly colored sash, illuminates the whole from its dominant position in the center, seeming to radiate light. The slope of the shoulders is grace itself. The arms and exquisite hands, the right holding a flower on which her gaze rests, the left supporting the folds of her sash, wherein a bird nestles on a bed of blooms, carry out the triangular composition on which the painting is based. Virginia's head, with its vast brow and heavy lids, its parted hair and sensitively molded cheeks, seems weighed down by some strange sorrow—a sorrow that permeates the picture like a tangible shadow. Consciously or not, Thomas Sully had imparted to the portrait Poe's dictum that a "certain taint of sadness is inseparably connected with all the higher manifestations of true Beauty" [13]—Beauty that must die. For Virginia was ill, how ill Poe did not know until, as always in his life, he was made cruelly aware of it.

One evening toward the middle of January, 1842, Poe was entertaining a few friends, among them his cousin Eliza Herring, now Mrs. Andrew Tutt. There was nothing Mrs. Clemm liked better than to preside over the tea and coffee urns while a fire burned on the hearth, the guests sat in the straight, flower-painted chairs, and the new member of the family, a tortoise-shell cat named Catarina for the pun in the name, basked in the warmth of the fireplace. The room glowed in the lamplight and was as cozy as Mrs. Clemm could make it with the few luxuries Poe had been able to provide, like a carpet of the crimson he described in "The Philosophy of Furniture," though not quite of the thickness which he thought *de rigueur*. In a corner stood Virginia's harp, to which, in the course of the evening, she was called upon to sing.

Dressed in a simple gown of white, her hair gathered in a Grecian knot and her large eyes half veiled, she looked to Poe like the embodiment of all that was pure and beautiful. Sweetly her voice rose, perhaps in that song of Thomas' which she liked so much, or maybe in Edgar's favorite "Come Rest in this Bosom." Suddenly the singing

---

[12] Reproduced in the *New York Times,* Sept. 22, 1930. The well-known three-quarter portrait was made after her death.

[13] Poe, "The Poetic Principle," *Works,* Vol. II, p. xvii.

choked; Virginia's hands went quickly to her throat and a stream of arterial blood gushed forth, staining the bosom of her dress. Edgar went at once for the doctor. The rest, appalled, did what they could to help. Even without medical confirmation Poe understood the gravity of the disease that had been the scourge of his family.

For several weeks he was crazed with despair and could neither write nor attend to the magazine. "You might imagine the agony I have suffered, for you know how devotedly I love her," he was at last able to write to F. W. Thomas. "But to-day the prospect brightens, and I trust that this bitter cup of misery will not be my portion. . . ." [14]

Early in March, however, a welcome distraction occurred with the arrival of Charles Dickens in Philadelphia. At thirty, "Boz" had already won world renown with his novels, which, with the nickname he had adopted, became household familiars in the English-speaking countries. An entertaining lecturer in the pristine heyday of the art, he had more engagements than he could fill, yet his peripatetic life did not in the least impede the flow of his extraordinary creativity that filled page after page of his journals and accreted into mammoth novels with not a dull paragraph in them. He had already published *Oliver Twist* and *The Old Curiosity Shop* and, most recently— in 1841—his novel, *Barnaby Rudge*. While it was running serially, Poe wrote a lengthy review of it in the *Saturday Evening Post*—May 1, 1841—from the first eleven chapters, and crowed in self-commendation for predicting the conclusion of the plot and the identity of the murderer. Dickens, it seems, had exclaimed at Poe's acuity: "The man must be the devil!" What Poe did not tell, however, was the impression the simple hero, Barnaby Rudge, had made upon him with his raven, Grip, that, huddled in a basket on his back, would croak: "Never say die!"

Once Dickens had settled down at the United States Hotel, where a political mob had gathered to greet him, against all protocol, Poe wrote requesting an interview and sent him his *Tales of the Grotesque and Arabesque*. Dickens responded cordially, though with perhaps a touch of pique at the parallel between his *Barnaby Rudge* and Godwin's *Caleb Williams,* which Poe, indulging his favorite sport, had pointed out.

Perhaps they carried on the discussion, the neat but rather seedy poet and the dandified visiting celebrity in the splendid dressing gown, his long wavy hair almost touching the scarf at his neck, his keenly intelligent eyes studying the strange man before him, so striking, seemingly so self-assured, yet somehow so lost.

[14] Letter of Feb. 2, 1842. Ostrom, p. 191.

Though their genius differed, they had at least one common interest, the necessity for effective copyright laws to protect the author, and this, together with their works, they must have discussed in the present, and at a subsequent, interview. At any rate, before Dickens left Philadelphia he had engaged himself to try to find a publisher for Poe's *Tales* in England and perhaps obtain for him some literary connection with an English magazine.

Unfortunately the friendship, so auspiciously begun, had an unhappy ending. Not long after Dickens' *American Notes* appeared, *Blackwood's* published a devastating review of it, signed Q.Q.Q. It was so much in Poe's tomahawk style that Boz assumed it had been written by him. On the last day of 1842, perhaps to relieve himself of all animus for the coming year, Dickens wrote to Professor C. C. Felton on the subject of his *American Notes:* "It has won golden opinions from all, except our friend in F—(Philadelphia) who is a miserable creature; a disappointed man in great poverty, to whom I have ever been most kind and considerate. . . ." [15]

The miserable creature whose poverty had been so obvious to the beloved of Fortune had more than sufficient reason for his otherwise unaccountable behavior—though it is not certain that he had written the review in *Blackwood's*. The very heart of his emotional security had recently been threatened. Death had given warning. The man whose imagination had dwelt so long in its realms was maddened by the menace to the being who was for him not only the Eleonoras, Ligeias, Morellas of his stories but, in the real world, his protection against its dangers. The pact of fidelity in "Eleonora" had not been wholly fiction.

Unable to cope with his anguish, Poe sought the usual escape. Graham now remonstrated with him, now tried to help. Sometimes, on a mild evening, he would take the Poes out driving in his carriage, when he would note how Virginia's slightest cough caused Edgar to shudder, how he never took his eyes off her, as if in hourly anticipation of her loss. "I felt all the agonies of her death—" Poe described his own reactions, "and at each accession of the disorder I loved her more dearly & clung to her life with more desperate pertinacity. . . . I became insane, with long intervals of horrible sanity. During these fits of absolute unconsciousness, I drank—God only knows how often and how much. . . ." [16]

Drink, unfortunately, brought out some latent aggressiveness which made him seek an outlet in quarrels. The assistant editor, Charles

[15] James T. Fields, *Yesterdays with Authors,* p. 142.
[16] Ostrom, p. 356.

Peterson, at *Graham's,* became his whipping boy, and heated arguments ensued, fanned on Peterson's side by resentment at the inferior position he had had to occupy since Poe's accession. What with Poe's unsteady habits and the disharmony in the office, Graham felt called upon to remonstrate with him. When he persisted, Graham took direct measures. One May morning, when Poe came into the office after a bout of "sickness," he found the Rev. Mr. Rufus W. Griswold sitting at his own desk. It did not take him long to realize that he had been supplanted—and by a man to whom he had offered friendship. Making for the door, he closed it behind him with finality.

Poe always believed that Griswold had been engaged by Graham to take his place, as indeed a letter of Graham's to the reverend gentleman, then assistant editor to Park Benjamin on New York's *New World* would indicate. "Have you fully determined to abandon the editorial chair? Or could you put it in your heart to locate in Philadelphia? Let me hear from you, as I have a proposal to make." [17] The letter bore the date of April 19, 1842. By the 3rd of May Griswold, evidently, had not only learned the nature of the proposal but had also accepted it. He was to receive $1,000 a year—$200 more than Poe. "We shall hope to see the light of your countenance soon," Mr. Graham had closed.

Poe's departure was therefore not the resignation that Graham wished to make it appear, but the dismissal which Poe, with justice, believed it to be. A manuscript letter of Griswold's to the Hon. G. C. Verplanck, written on the 2nd of November, 1842, further justifies Poe's assumption.

The undersigned has been associate editor of Graham's Magazine during the last half year, and will hereafter have the sole direction of it. Anxious to elevate its character and to make it creditable to the country, he has, with the approval of the proprietor, endeavored to secure for it contributors from the best American writers.

Mr. J. F. Cooper, Mr. Bryant, N. P. Willis, Thos. T. Hoffman, Professor Longfellow, T. C. Grattan and Richard H. Dana will furnish articles for every number of 1843.

Should you consent to write for it, the prices paid in the first class of foreign magazines will be promptly paid for your articles.

> With highest respect,
> Yr Obt Sevt
> RUFUS W. GRISWOLD. [18]

---

[17] Phillips, p. 706.
[18] Hitherto unpublished MS, New York Historical Society Library.

CHAPTER XX

-≫≫ • ≪≪-

Intimations of Insanity

ALTHOUGH Poe's editorship of *Graham's* ended with the May number, his friendship with its owner was not seriously affected, for he continued to publish in its pages. Still, the loss of his position, following so close upon Virginia's attack, brought about what could only be looked upon as a period of mental derangement. Anxiously he tried every remedy to help Virginia, even a nostrum, Jew's Beer, recommended by his cousin Eliza. Most of all he sought through every connection to secure some reliable post to compensate for his lost salary. Mr. Thomas was not forgotten, nor the possibility of a berth with the government. The loyal friend, accordingly, informed him of an expected opening at the Philadelphia Custom House.

"What you say . . . gives me new life," Poe responded with pathetic eagerness. "Nothing could more precisely meet my views. Could I obtain such an appointment, I would be enabled thoroughly to carry out all my ambitious projects." [1] The dream of the *Penn* almost became a reality in the urgency of his need.

He had written to Thomas on the 25th of May, 1842. A week later, even though the prospect was still as nebulous as before, Poe was informing another friend that he had the promise of a situation in the Custom House. He would receive the appointment upon the removal of several incumbents, he wrote hopefully but with scant knowledge of how slowly the mills of government revolved. "Please mention nothing of this," he added with the prudence of the too often disillusioned, "for, after all, I may be disappointed." [2] He ended the letter with the laconic information that Virginia was again dangerously ill with hemorrhage from the lungs.

He was not idle, for on the 4th of June he offered a new story simultaneously to George Roberts, of the *Boston Times and Notion* and to Dr. Snodgrass for his magazine. Although, as he explained to

[1] Ostrom, p. 197.
[2] *Ibid.*, p. 199.

Roberts, the tale was worth $100 to him, he was desirous of having it published in Boston for reasons of his own and would be willing to accept $50. To Snodgrass, for friendship's sake, he was willing to surrender it for $40—or was it as an inducement to the good doctor to execute for him a private vengeance? "Have you seen Griswold's Book of Poetry? It is a most outrageous humbug, and I sincerely wish you would 'use it up.' . . ." [3]

Neither Roberts nor Snodgrass would touch "The Mystery of Marie Roget," which appeared, of all unlikely places, in Snowden's *Ladies' Companion,* where it ran serially in three numbers. Poe described the story as a sequel to "The Murders in the Rue Morgue," though it had nothing to do with the exploits of the by now notorious orang-utan. Unlike most of Poe's tales, the new story was based on a sensational crime which had kept the papers supplied with thrills from the time of the sudden disappearance, in August, 1841, of pretty Cecilia Rogers, a young clerk at the tobacconist's shop of John Anderson, on Liberty Street, New York.

For days the papers had carried the usual rumors and assumptions. Cecilia had been seen in Weehawken, New Jersey, in the company of a man in a naval uniform. Impossible. She was a good girl, modest and home-loving. Besides, what would she be doing across the river, when she lived in New York? Speculation, among the baffled police and the amateurs in the editorial offices, kept the presses grinding out theories, one of them that Miss Rogers had probably fallen into the clutches of a criminal gang.

Then one day somebody discovered a female body floating on the Hudson. It was identified as that of the missing girl. The discovery roused the sleuth Edgar Allan Poe in his alter ego, Dupin. "Thus under pretence of showing how Dupin . . . unravelled the mystery of Marie's assassination, I, in fact, enter into a very rigorous analysis of the *real* tragedy in New York. . . . The press has been entirely on a wrong scent. In fact, I really believe, not only that I have demonstrated the falsity of the idea that the girl was the victim of a gang . . . but have indicated the *assassin.* . . ." [4] And indeed Poe had done so, for the man in the naval uniform, according to him, ultimately confessed to having caused the death of Cecilia Rogers through an attempt at abortion.

In its translation to the French metropolis Nassau Street, where Cecilia lived, becomes Rue Pavée Saint Andrée; Anderson is Monsieur Le Blanc; Weehawken is transmogrified into the Barrière du Roule,

[3] *Ibid.,* p. 202.
[4] Letter of June 4, 1842. Ostrom, pp. 201-202.

while the Hudson appears, of course, as the Seine. One thing Poe could not alter: the fixation of his creative imagination on dead or dying women, on fair mutilated bodies. Meanwhile, under the same roof where he was writing his tales—among them "The Mask of the Red Death," that compelling fantasy in scarlet and black whose every effect stresses the inevitability of final dissolution—were his aunt and the wife whom he believed to be dying.

All of a sudden, obeying some compelling impulse, he left Mrs. Clemm and Virginia, he left Philadelphia, and made his way to New York. He may have gone in search of employment, but soon a deeper motive emerged. His Baltimore sweetheart, Mary Devereaux, now married, lived in Jersey City. Her husband was working in New York. Poe looked him up and obtained the address. If Mary's husband noticed anything strange or overexcited in Mr. Poe he laid it to the artistic temperament. At any rate, during his escapade, Poe took the ferryboat for Jersey City.

Always a noticeable figure, he was all the more so, for he had lost his hat and his long wavy hair fluttered in disarray in the breeze of the moving boat. His black stock was awry; his eyes looked wild. As the boat neared the Jersey shore he could not recall Mary's address. In great agitation he went from passenger to passenger, up and down the boat, making inquiries, but no one could enlighten him. The crowd got off, but Poe stayed on, putting the same question to the people who boarded the ferry. Back and forth he shuttled, getting wilder and more insistent, the passengers shaking him off as a lunatic. At last he found a deck hand who knew Mary Devereaux but was reluctant to give her address. "I'll get it if I have to go to hell for it," menaced the crazed Poe. The deck hand gave it to him.

Poe found his way to Mary's house. She was out with her sister, but he was invited to wait. When they got back, he himself opened the door. Mary assumed at once by his looks that he was on one of his sprees.

"So you have married that cursed ——!" he greeted her. "Do you love him truly? Did you marry him for love?"

"That's nobody's business. That is between my husband and myself," she said.

"You don't love him," Poe insisted. "You do love me. You know you do."

Mary was mistaken in thinking that he had been drinking, although, even if he had been incited by alcohol, his reactions would have sprung equally from the same deep reservoir of fixations and primal desires. Through some obscure urge for self-preservation he had fled the house where he had been living so intimately with actual sickness and imaginary death; where he had described in such horrid detail the mangled bodies of a mother and daughter; where, more recently, he had been solving the sordid mystery of Cecilia Rogers, to seek the one woman toward whom he had reacted as a normal male. How else could even the brilliant Mr. Poe, who prided himself on his analyses of the human mind, explain his compulsive flight, which modern psychology recognizes under the name of *fugue?* His subsequent behavior at Mary's unveiled his subliminal motivations.

At table Poe and the two women were having tea. As he drained his cup, while they were conversing, he grew noticeably excited. There was dish of radishes on the table. Seizing a knife, Edgar began to chop them up in a frenzy, scattering the red pieces about in wild exhilaration. When this strange fit of violence subsided he asked Mary to sing for him "Come Rest in this Bosom." He then left the house and disappeared.

Meanwhile Mrs. Clemm and Virginia were in despair when all communication from him abruptly ceased. ("My dear little wife . . . began to fret . . . because she did not hear from me twice a day. . . . What it is to be pestered with a wife! . . ." he commented jocularly in a letter to his cousin Eliza, soon after that visit.)[5]

Thinking the worst, Mrs. Clemm set out to look for him. The clues led her to Jersey City. Mary told her the story of Poe's strange visit and stranger behavior, but she had no idea of where he could have gone. The alarm was sent out and the little community was alerted to be on the lookout for a hatless, sober-suited, unusual-looking stranger. The citizens then formed a searching party, with Mary and Mrs. Clemm in the lead. At last they came upon Edgar wandering, hallucinated, in the woods bordering the town. He had eaten nothing for days and looked and behaved, as Mary said, "like a crazy man." He who had always dreaded insanity had had his first brush with it.

The exact date of the escapade cannot be ascertained. Mary Devereaux placed it in the spring of 1842.[6] However, it was probably toward the latter part of June, for in his note to his cousin Eliza, on July 7, Poe had written: "About ten days ago . . . I was obliged to go to New York. . . ."[7]

Back in Philadelphia, Poe exerted himself once more to find employment and to gain subscriptions for his *Penn*. But he was sick and often delirious and Dr. John K. Mitchell was called upon to minister

[5] Ostrom, p. 209.
[6] *Harper's New Monthly Magazine,* March, 1899.
[7] Ostrom, p. 209.

to him as often as to Virginia. The tireless writer was unable to pen a line, and for over seven weeks even his correspondence lapsed.

Not long after this the Poes moved to Number 234 North Seventh Street, above Spring Garden, West Side, as Poe wrote explicitly to James Russell Lowell. The house, known as their Spring Garden cottage, was a small, three-story brick building facing Wistar Lane, in a sparsely populated section of Philadelphia, though near a main highway that led to the center of the city. The cross-streets boasted a lighting system of whale-oil lamps strung on chains between twenty-foot poles. However, they were lighted only on dark nights, when the moon was off duty. But then, the city was protected by the watch, with their staves and rattles and their reassuring cries of "Twelve o'clock, and all is well! Two o'clock, and a starlight morning!"

A large garden, belonging to the house, caught the earliest rays of the rising sun and three rows of windows let in the light. Overhanging the garden were the branches of a tall pear tree which had shed its blossoms and gave promise of plentiful fruit. Flowers bloomed everywhere. Yet for all the cheerfulness of nature, sickness and despair reigned within. An unfailing index of the family fortunes—a number of luxuries were missing from the furnishings, among them Virginia's little pianoforte. Her harp she kept upstairs in her low-ceilinged room under the roof, with its four square-paned windows and cozy open fireplace. Mrs. Clemm's bedroom was on the same floor, in the rear of the house.

Poe had the front room with its black-slate mantel and red carpet. It was there that, among his few books, his framed engravings—but no mirrors, which he abhorred—he would write, or entertain occasional visitors who, occupying the large horsehair mahogany sofa, listened to what even the envious Griswold described as Poe's "supramortal" eloquence.

At this time Poe was neither writing nor entertaining, and as he showed no signs of improving, Dr. Mitchell arranged for a change of scene for him. He knew Mr. and Mrs. Barhyte, proprietors of Barhyte Trout Ponds at the fashionable resort of New York's Saratoga Springs. He provided Poe with money and a letter of introduction and sped him on his way—alone.

Soon Poe, draped in his cape, his pale face shaded by his black, broad-brimmed hat, became a conspicuous figure as he drove about Saratoga Springs with Mrs. Barhyte in her carriage. A number of Philadelphians who were enjoying the waters at the resort recognized in the cloaked figure the former editor of *Graham's* and instantly apprised the gossip circles at home of the intrigue that was brewing between Mr. Poe and a married lady who was paying all his expenses, while his invalid wife was wasting away in the city of brotherly love. In time slander, issuing from the pen of the Rev. Mr. Griswold and hissed at as a "scandalous secret" by Thomas Dunn English, a bard whom Poe had not handled too gently in the days of *Burton's Magazine,* implied the worst.

Common literary interests, as it happened, formed the bond between Poe and Mrs. Barhyte, a member of the "starry sisterhood" of New York females who had abandoned their knitting needles in favor of the pen. Poe, however, had not known who she was until he happened to pick up a scrapbook from the mantelpiece of the Barhyte living room and found that "Tabitha," whose poems and articles appeared in the *New York Mirror,* was none other than his hostess. Their friendship ripened, Mr. Barhyte, who was proud of his wife, approving so cordially that he invited Poe to be their guest again the following summer.

Their son, a boy of eight or nine, was fascinated by the storybook gentleman with the Spanish cape and large hat, and nicknamed him "The Mexican." He would follow Poe about with mute worship on his walks and to the secret place which the Mexican liked best of all, a seat among the pines and hemlocks bordering the trout pond. There Poe would talk to himself and recite aloud, waving his arms excitedly. Most of the time it was something about a talking raven. One day the lad heard the Mexican ask the bird what its name was. "Nevermore," said the raven.

"Who ever heard of a bird with a name like that?" piped the boy.

The Mexican laughed and jotted something down. Later Poe told Mrs. Barhyte of the incident. He would include the boy's observation, he said, in the poem he was writing—as indeed he did, in the lines:

> For we cannot help agreeing that no living human being
> Ever yet was blest with seeing bird above his chamber door—
> Bird or beast upon the sculptured bust above his chamber door,
>   With such name as "Nevermore."

After the second visit Poe never returned again to the Barhytes, and to his seat among the pines, for Mrs. Barhyte died in April, 1844. Tabitha's last work was an article on "The Raven" in which her little son had unconsciously collaborated and which she had been privileged to discuss with the poet in one of its earliest forms.

Ever since Griswold had supplanted him, Poe had earned little from the articles which *Graham's* and other magazines occasionally printed, and the wolf seemed to have taken its stand permanently at his door. He wrote indefatigably, Mrs. Clemm taking the contributions to the various editors, but frequently coming back with the disheartening answer: "Not accepted." The basket which, for a happily prosperous period, she had carried for the family marketing, now went the rounds with her on friendly and—she hoped—gainful visits. At home Virginia was coughing more and more, each attack making Poe shudder as if her end had come.

The *Penn* had temporarily been abandoned, and the extremity of Poe's need was implicit in a letter he wrote to James Russell Lowell toward the close of 1842, offering himself as a regular contributor to the *Pioneer,* which the New England poet was about to launch. Its prospectus might have been copied from Poe's. Certainly Mr. Lowell's expressed aversion to the "enormous quantity of thrice-diluted trash, in the shape of namby-pamby love tales and sketches" which inundated the public every month in the popular magazines coincided almost word for word with Poe's condemnation of current periodical literature. He himself, while on *Graham's,* had more than once flared out impatiently against the namby-pambiness that Mr. Graham admitted both in its stories and its art. In his enthusiasm for Lowell's venture he pronounced: "That your success will be marked and permanent I will not doubt." [8]

Never had prophet more wrongly prophesied. The *Pioneer* started out courageously in January, 1843, persevered through a second issue, then expired with the third, amid general apathy on the part of the public, which continued to devour its preferred fare. Each number had contained something of Poe's. "The Tell-Tale Heart," one of his finest stories for its powerful impact, superbly achieved, dramatized madness, obsession and conscience as only Poe could. It had appeared in the January *Pioneer.* The second number printed "Lenore," the poem he had earlier called "A Paean." From its opening stanza it rang with solemn cadences new to poetry at that time, but very few heard or caught the rueful enchantment of its mourning for youth and beauty, dead.

> Come! let the burial rite be read—the funeral song be sung!—
> An anthem for the queenliest dead that ever died so young—
> A dirge for her the doubly dead in that she died so young—
>
> .   .   .   .
>
> For her, the fair and *debonair,* that now so lowly lies,
> The life upon her yellow hair but not within her eyes—
> The life still there, upon her hair—the death upon her eyes.

[8] *Ibid.,* p. 217.

The second number contained Poe's essay, "The Rationale of Verse." He was paid at the rate of $10 for each article. As a result of his unsuccessful venture, however, Lowell was left with a heavy debt upon his hands and wrote apologetically to Poe that he could not, at the moment, pay him. Poe responded with sympathy and warmth for one of his almost frigid reserve, calling him "My dear Friend"—an unwonted form of address—and commiserating with him in his misfortune. "As for the few dollars you owe me—give yourself not a moment's concern about *them.* I am poor, but must be very much poorer, indeed, when I even think of demanding them." [9]

The failure of the *Pioneer,* far from discouraging Poe in his desire for his own mouthpiece, revived his yearning, and on the 25th of February of that year he was sending his friend Thomas a prospectus of the *Stylus*—his *Penn,* revived and remodeled under better auspices—and informing him that he had at last been able to secure his great object: "a partner possessing ample capital and, at the same time, so little self-esteem, as to allow me entire control of the editorial conduct. He gives me, also, a half interest, and is to furnish funds for all the business operations—I agreeing to supply, for the first year, the literary matter. . . . We *shall* make the most magnificent Magazine as regards externals, ever seen. . . ." [10]

To Lowell he wrote that on the first day of July he hoped to publish the initial number. He was anxious, he said, to obtain a poem of Lowell's for that issue, but was too much concerned about his health—Lowell feared he was going blind—to press the request. When Lowell was in a condition to write, would he try to procure for him an article from Mr. Hawthorne, also for that same number?

Utopian though the scheme sounded for one so shadowed by ill luck, Poe had indeed succeeded in interesting Thomas Cottrell Clarke of the *Saturday Evening Post* in his grand project. He had not, however, abandoned the hope of a pleasant government sinecure which, according to him, he would have obtained the previous year but for the chicanery of an official, a certain Mr. Smith, at the Custom House—a Whig of the worst stamp, who would appoint none but Whigs. "As for me, he trialed me most shamefully," Poe complained to the faithful Mr. Thomas, who was more than ever anxious to place him in a soft berth." [11]

Mr. Thomas had already interested Robert Tyler, the President's son and a practicing poet, in the genius who had composed some of

[9] *Ibid.,* p. 231.
[10] *Ibid.,* p. 224.
[11] *Ibid.,* p. 218.

the most extraordinary works in the language and was such a wonder at cryptography, as a biographical article in the *Philadelphia Saturday Museum,* tactfully placed on Mr. Tyler's desk, could prove. It was one of the usual compositions with which Poe liked to mystify the world. He fathered it on one of his Philadelphia cronies, Henry Beck Hirst, a youth with a delicate lyrical gift, who published it, with improvements of his own. The portrait illustrating the biography did Poe so little justice that he felt obliged to explain to Thomas, with a hint of false modesty: "I am ugly enough, God knows, but not *quite* so bad as that." [12] Ugly or not, Mr. Tyler was impressed, and Thomas suggested that Poe come to Washington.

It was a great opportunity, both for Poe's prospects of a sinecure and, particularly, for the *Stylus*. With the support of so important a man as Tyler, especially if he got his father, the President, to endorse Poe, the subscriptions would be coming in by the hundreds; the magazine would be made. Mr. Clarke, influenced by the rosy expectations, advanced the money for the train fare to Washington and gave Poe a little besides.

He started out, probably on the 8th of March, with the highest hopes. On his arrival he went at once to Fuller's Hotel where Mr. Thomas had his bachelor lodgings. Unfortunately Thomas was ill. As he could leave neither his bed nor his room, Thomas entrusted Poe to his friend and colleague, Jesse E. Dow, editor of the *Daily Madisonian*.

With so much at stake, Poe, whose nervous organization was an aeolian harp at best, tried to keep himself under control. Mr. Dow did his duty faithfully, ushering Poe about and effecting introductions. In the evening he led him to the conviviality of Mr. Fuller's hostelry. There, against his better judgment, Poe drank some port wine, which immediately had its usual effect. He pulled himself together, however, and after a night's sleep went to the barber's for a shave and a haircut, to make himself presentable for the visit to Robert Tyler and an interview with the President at the White House. What a triumph for himself and the *Stylus* if he succeeded in obtaining presidential backing!

Although he had been in Washington less than a day, his money was already gone and he left the barbershop owing the "levy" fee. Nevertheless, he went about his business and, according to Mr. Dow, kept pretty steady. After that he again succumbed, so that when Mr. Dow escorted him to Robert Tyler's office, Poe's condition would have deceived no one.

[12] *Ibid.,* p. 223.

"My Dear Sir," Poe addressed Mr. Clarke on the 11th of March,
"I write merely to inform you of my will-doing—for, so far, I have
done nothing." The wry pun, if nothing else, betrayed his state of
mind. After mentioning Thomas' illness, he complained that his
expenses were more than he thought they would be. *"However,* all
is going right," he went on. "I have got the subscriptions of *all* the
Departments. . . . I believe that I am making a *sensation* which will
tend to the benefit of the Magazine. . . . Day after tomorrow I am to
lecture. Rob. Tyler is to give me an article. . . ." [13]

He was indeed making a sensation, but of quite a different order.
For some reason he had taken it into his head to wear his Spanish
cape inside out. Not content with that eccentricity, he also insisted
on criticizing the mustachios and beards of utter strangers. That
caprice nearly led to a fray when, while drinking juleps in the company of Matthew Brady and Dow, he persisted in unseemly mockery
of a Spanish gentleman's hirsute appendages.

Needless to say, the scheduled lecture never came off. On the
12th of March, the eve of that event, Mr. Dow, fearing serious consequences from Poe's behavior, wrote to Mr. Clarke, explaining as tactfully as possible what had happened and urging him to come for Poe.
"Should you not come, we will see him on board the cars bound to
Phila., but we fear he might be detained in Baltimore and not be out
of harm's way. I do this under a solemn responsibility. Mr. Poe has
the highest order of intellect, and I cannot bear that he should be
the sport of senseless creatures who, like oysters, keep sober, and
gape and swallow everything. . . ." [14] The trip to Washington, far
from a sensation, had been a crashing fiasco.

It was not Clarke but, as always, Mrs. Clemm, who was waiting
for her poor Eddie in the car office. At home Virginia's distress of
mind was even greater than Poe had anticipated. As for Mr. Clarke,
"He received me . . . very cordially & made light of the matter," Poe
informed Thomas and Dow, the day after his homecoming. A graveyard humor tinged the jocularity that concealed his remorse at so
disastrously killing all his chances. "Remember me most kindly . . .
to the Don, whose mustachios I *do* admire after all. . . . I would be
glad, too, if you would take the opportunity of saying to Mr. Rob.
Tyler that if he *can* look over matters and get me the inspectorship,
I will join the Washingtonians forthwith. . . . I think it would be a
feather in Mr. Tyler's cap to save from the perils of mint julap—&

---

[13] *Ibid.,* p. 227.
[14] Letter first published in Gill's *Life of Edgar Allan Poe.*

'Port Wines'—a young man of whom all the world thinks so well & who thinks so remarkably well of himself. . . ." [15]

Mr. Clarke, already forewarned by Mr. Dow's letter, decided prudently to wait and see before definitely committing himself to the partnership with Poe on the *Stylus*. By June of the year he had made up his mind, for on the 20th Poe wrote to Lowell: "Alas! my Magazine scheme has exploded—, or, at least, I have been deprived, through the imbecility, or rather through the idiocy of my partner, of all means of prosecuting it for the present. . . ." [16]

Poe, so far as Poe was concerned, was never at fault.

[15] Ostrom, p. 229.
[16] *Ibid.*, p. 234.

-»» • «‹‹-

Imagined Treasure and Grim Poverty

ALL told, it had been a distressing period for the ex-editor of *Graham's*. Nevertheless, despite discouragement and anxiety, or perhaps because of them, early in 1843 Poe had sat down to write a short story, "The Gold-Bug." It differed from the rest in that it had no Ligeias or Eleonoras in it, nor, for that matter, the least vestige of Poe's Usher self. It was an adventure, rather, a treasure-hunt tale, of the sort which would make the fame of Robert Louis Stevenson, waiting until mid-century to be born. In a way, it was also a story of detection, with William Legrand, of an ancient Huguenot family, substituting his French brother, M. Dupin, of Rue Morgue fame. No vague, gloomy landscape nor foreign city formed the background of the tale, but the tropical Sullivan's Island of Poe's soldier days, with its tall tulip trees, its strange flora and fauna, and its surviving legend of buried treasure. From these elements Poe concocted his story. His imagination did the rest, from the invention of his famous bug, of a brilliant gold color, with three jet-black markings on the back, giving it the look of a death's-head, to the discovery and deciphering of a cryptogram leading to the buried treasure.

What a trove that death's-head gold-bug led to! In his description the poverty-stricken author went beyond all bounds, piling into a chest, three and a half feet long, three feet broad and two and a half feet deep, the contents of a pantechnicon. "All was gold of antique date. . . . There were diamonds—some of them exceedingly large and fine—a hundred and ten in all, and not one of them small . . . three hundred and ten emeralds . . . and twenty-one sapphires. . . . The settings themselves appeared to have been broken up with hammers. Besides all this, there was a vast quantity of solid gold ornaments . . . eighty-three very large and heavy crucifixes; five gold censers of great value; a prodigious golden punch-bowl, and many other smaller articles which I cannot recollect. The weight of these valuables exceeded three hundred and fifty pounds avoirdupois; and in this estimate I have not included one hundred and ninety-seven superb gold watches. . . . We estimated the entire contents of the chest . . . at a million and a half dollars. . . ."

Yet all Poe could extract from Graham for this treasure was a paltry $52. The story, however, was destined for better fortunes. Soon after Poe had given it to Graham, he found that the *Dollar Newspaper,* which had its offices in the same building as the magazine, was announcing a contest, offering $100 for the winning tale. Poe had once been lucky. Why not try again? Knowing his need, Graham returned the story, taking out his payment in future articles.

"The Gold-Bug" won, and never had anything of Poe's achieved such immediate popularity. The *Dollar Newspaper* published it on the front page on June 28, 1843, illustrating it with a chiaroscuro of the discovery of the treasure, in an engraving by F. O. C. Darley, for whose work Poe had such admiration that he had chosen him for the honor of providing the pictures for the *Stylus,* once more in the process of being revived. The *Saturday Courier* then reprinted it in three installments and—unfailing index of success—the *Saturday Evening Post* cried plagiarism, charging that Poe had stolen it from Miss Sherburne's *Imogene, or the Pirate's Treasure.* As the only thing that the tales had in common was a treasure, Poe's rejoinder in the *Dollar Newspaper* quashed the accusation.

No hard feelings ensued between him and the *Post,* for on the 19th of August the magazine published "The Black Cat." It was again one of Poe's stories of sadistic, reasonless cruelty, perpetrated in fiction for the release of some pent-up, destructive urge, roused, perhaps, by work ill-rewarded, by misery and misfortune and a sense of not receiving his just returns in a world that preferred the sham to the genuine and compensated genius by poverty and persecution. A feeling of being hounded by disaster became a fixation. The panacea he would take to assuage it, and so enable him to work, only aggravated his disorder, after its temporary relief.

In his moods of violence he struck out against real and fancied enemies. Early that year the *Saturday Museum* had carried an excoriating review of Griswold's *Poets and Poetry of America,* then in its third edition. The anonymous reviewer lashed out in a style that by now was recognizable to all, scoffing at the literary pretensions of "Dr. Driswold" and leaving him nothing but a fool's cap in which to hide his diminished head. As if that were not enough, the reviewer added to the injury the insult of lauding Edgar Allan Poe to the skies. Griswold did nothing, for the time being, though he suspected the source.

Nevertheless, on the 11th of June, not long after this public flagel-lation, Poe wrote to him: "Can you send me $5? I am *sick* and Vir-ginia is almost gone. Come and see me. Peterson says you accuse me of a curious anonymous letter. I did not write it but bring it when you make the visit you promised to Mrs. Clemm. I will try to fix that matter soon. Could you do anything with my *note?* . . ." [1]

As with other Poe letters quoted by Griswold, this may have been tampered with by the reverend doctor, to the disadvantage of Poe. It would appear, however, that Griswold magnanimously presented himself at the Spring Garden cottage the following day.

A complex and ambivalent relationship subsisted between the two men, Poe resenting, while admiring, the seemingly sterling qualities of the anthologizing minister who had succeeded in profitably im-posing his taste upon literary America, at the same time wielding a power that could make or destroy a writer's reputation; Griswold recognizing the genius of Poe while envying it with the malice of the noncreative yet ambitious man. To compensate for what he lacked in talent he magnified moral conduct. In that he lorded it over the weak, irresponsible and, according to the unsigned but Griswoldian article on the poet's visits to Saratoga Springs, the immoral, Poe.

At that time Griswold was in a particularly virulent mood, as he had just been dismissed from *Graham's* for persecuting Charles Peter-son with anonymous letters for which he disingenuously blamed Poe. In the literary snake-pit of nineteenth-century America, the most moral could be the most corrupt. The two men did not arrive at an open breach, however, until the close of the year, when, on Novem-ber 25, Poe, who had taken to lecturing, expatiated on Griswold's anthology, culling gems from his own devastating reviews and im-provising others with an eloquence which, certainly on this occasion, Griswold could not have found "supra-mortal."

Poe's personal reputation had been steadily suffering in the Quaker City, which, from its polished doorknobs to the pastoral wooded banks of the Wissahickon, exalted outward decency. Mr. Poe's pec-cadilloes were unfortunately much too open, and Quaker respect-ability disapproved. The extent of his weakness had even reached his cousin William Poe, in Baltimore. "There is one thing I am anxious to caution you against and which has been a great enemy to our family," William Poe had written on May 15th of that year. "I hope, however, in your case, it may prove unnecessary—'a too free use of the Bottle.' Too many, and especially literary characters, have sought to drown their sorrows and disappointments by this means, but in

[1] Griswold, *Memoir*. Vol. I. *Works of Edgar Allan Poe,* p. xxi.

vain. . . ." [2] Poe, at the time, had needed money rather than advice.
As William Poe had not sent the $50 Edgar asked for, the homily did
not ring well in his ears.

For several years, ever since his meeting with the young Philadelphia lawyer Henry Beck Hirst, Poe had been frequenting a coterie
of advance-guard bohemians who, in their way, were protesting
against the smugness of the Quaker City. Hirst did it by putting
his best energies into writing poetry, when he was not wandering
along the Wissahickon collecting birds' nests or taking off for Bordentown, New Jersey, to brood upon the now-dimmed glory of the erstwhile King of Spain, Joseph Bonaparte. George Lippard, to whom
Hirst introduced Poe, was on the staff of the *Spirit of the Times.*
Lippard shook Philadelphia's composure by wearing his locks as
long as a woman's and by sporting costumes of no recognizable era.
His house, on Apple Street, was as stolidly respectable as any in
the city, but at night, through fellow feeling with the strays of
humanity, Lippard would take his carpetbag and seek out an old
wreck of an abandoned building near Franklin Square. There, among
the homeless, the sick, the poor and the despised, he would sleep or,
more often, ponder his novel: *The Quaker City, or The Monks of
Monk Hall.* Philadelphia was not grateful to him for it when it appeared, not because of its contents, which resembled the inflamed
Gothic imaginings of young Shelley in his *Zastrozzi,* but for the
phrase on the title page, "Wo unto Sodom," with which Lippard
branded the vice and the poverty concealed beneath the city's
respectability.

Of the two, Hirst was the closer friend, close enough to be invited
to the Spring Garden house for Sunday breakfast of waffles, prepared
by Mrs. Clemm, though the young man was not altogether approved
of. He was too fond of brandy, and Eddie was in danger, especially
when they visited together at Mr. Sartain's and other artists' houses,
where drinks were likely to flow freely. The two had a bond in their
poetry, however. Though Hirst could not compare with Poe, he still
had a lyrical gift which the master—Poe saw to it that the distinction between them was clearly marked—was quick to notice and
to praise. He especially liked a stanza in the disciple's "The Owl":

> And he calls aloud—"too-whit! too-whoo!"
>   And the nightingale is still,
> And the pattering step of the hurrying hare
>   Is hushed upon the hill;

[2] See Allen, p. 453.

And he crouches low in the dewy grass
As the lord of the night goes by,
Not with a loudly whirring wing
But like a lady's sigh.

"No one save a poet at heart, could have conceived these images," commented Poe, "and they are embodied with much skill. . . . The 'lord of the night' applied to the owl, does Mr. Hirst infinite credit—*if* the idea is original with Mr. Hirst." Their friendship was almost ruined by Poe's fixation. "Steal, dear Endymion," Poe said to him, "for very well do I know you can't help it; and the more you put in your book that is not your own, why the better your book will be:— but be cautious and steal with an air. . . ." [3]

The reviews Poe now wrote became increasingly atrabiliar. It was as if, because of his own hardships and what he keenly felt as inadequate recognition, he stinted others their meed of praise. The continued strain of his unsuccess, his gnawing poverty, the fatal blight on Virginia, and most of all, his consciousness of being under a curse that nothing could avert broke what will power he had. Friends and enemies alike noted his behavior, with varying reactions. He seemed to trust no one, to have faith in no one, beyond Virginia and Mrs. Clemm. Least of all did he trust himself—the man, not the artist, for of the artist he had not the least doubt. This insecurity about Poe, the man, is nowhere so patent as in the letter he wrote to Thomas G. Mackenzie, on April 22, 1843:

My dear Thomas:

About a fortnight ago I wrote to Peter D. Bernard, who married one of T. W. White's daughters, and made inquiry about 'The Southern Literary Messenger' but have received no reply. I am very anxious to ascertain if it is for sale, and if it is, I wish to purchase it (through my friends here). You wrote me some time ago that the heirs had not made up their minds respecting it. Would you do me the favor, now, to call upon Bernard, or on some of the other heirs, and inquire about it?

I can't imagine why Bernard did not reply to my letter. If the list is for sale I would make arrangements for its immediate purchase upon terms which would be fully satisfactory to the heirs. But do not let them suppose I am *too* anxious. By the bye, there may be some prejudice, on the part of the heirs, against me individually, on account of my quitting White—suppose then, you get some of your friends to negotiate for you and don't let me be known in the business at all. Merely ascertain if the list is for sale and upon what terms. Please oblige me in this matter as soon as possible, as I am exceedingly anxious about it. Tell Rose that Virginia is much

[3] *Works. Literati.* Vol. III, pp. 210, 212.

better, toe and all, and that she has been out lately, several times, taking long walks. She sends a great deal of love to all. Remember me kindly to the whole family and believe me,

Yours most truly,

EDGAR A. POE [4]

What emerges, besides Poe's anxiety to acquire, if not the magazine, at least the subscription lists, is his utter lack of confidence in obtaining his object were he in any way known to be involved in the transaction. Let his friends obtain his ends for him through subterfuge, if need be. Yet even his friends could not be depended upon. They forgot about one. They stopped writing. "How does it happen that in these latter days I never receive an epistle from yourself?" he had complained to Dr. Snodgrass. "Have I offended you by any of my evil deeds?—if so how? Time was when you could spare a few minutes occasionally for communion with a friend. . . ." [5]

Those who knew him noted the change in him. "Edgar A. Poe . . . has become one of the strangest of our literati," Lambert A. Wilmer wrote to a fellow poet in May, 1843. "He and I are old friends,— have known each other since boyhood, and it gives me inexpressible pain to notice the vagaries to which he has lately become subject. Poor fellow! he is not a teetotaller by any means, and I fear he is going headlong to destruction, moral, physical and intellectual." [6]

Wilmer wrote from genuine feeling, with pity for the disintegration taking place before his eyes. Griswold too depicted the closing scene of the Philadelphia period, a Sophoclean tragedy of triumph and disaster, which the minister saw rather as a morality play. "He was at all times a dreamer—dwelling in ideal realms—in heaven or hell— peopled with the creatures and accidents of his brain. He walked the streets, in madness or melancholy, with lips moving in indistinct curses, or with eyes upturned in passionate prayer, (never for himself, for he felt or professed to feel, that he was already damned, but) for their happiness who at the moment were objects of his idolatry;—or, with his glances introverted to a heart gnawed with anguish, and with a face shrouded in gloom, he would brave the

---

[4] This letter, which is to be found in the *Catalogue of the Gluck Collection of Manuscripts and Autographs of the Buffalo Public Library*, July, 1899, was graciously called to my attention by Mr. Herbert Cahoon, Curator, Autograph MSS of the Pierpont Morgan Library. It is not included in John Ward Ostrom's exhaustive *Letters of Edgar Allan Poe;* nor to my knowledge has it appeared in any Poe biography.

[5] Manuscript in the Pierpont Morgan Library, June 4, 1842.

[6] Original in Boston Public Library.

wildest storms. . . ." [7] It was stirring pulpit oratory, but through the lightning and thunder Poe's self emerges.

Once again, during this desperate period, Poe sought a publisher for another collection of his tales, now amplified by some of his finest. No one would chance it. At last he found a listening ear in William H. Graham, who had his offices on Chestnut Street. He did not venture on the volume *Phantasy Pieces,* which Poe had in mind, but he was willing to send out a trial balloon in a pamphlet containing two or three stories. If it proved successful, the rest could be brought out in the same way in a uniform serial edition, *The Prose Romances of Edgar A. Poe,* each booklet to sell at 12½ cents a copy.

The first number, bearing the name of Poe as the author of "The Gold-Bug," etc. etc., contained "Murders in the Rue Morgue" and "The Man That was Used Up." Few buyers were tempted to dip into the small change in their pockets. The pamphlet wasted its allure on the desert air of the few bookshops that handled it, and was allowed to expire. No second number followed.

In the stringency of his situation Poe was compelled to ask Lowell for the money owed him by the defunct *Pioneer*. It was only $10 but it represented salvation if, alas, only for the moment. He had published little in 1843, though he compensated for the paucity by the excellence of "The Gold-Bug" and "The Black Cat," each a masterpiece in its genre. Then the source seems to have gone dry, except for "The Raven," on which he had been working in 1843 and which was still to occupy him for several years, in his search for perfection.

The spring of 1844 saw only the publication of the descriptive idyll, "Morning on the Wissahiccon," one of his best evocations of beauty in nature, and two stories, "A Tale of the Ragged Mountains" and the burlesque, "The Spectacles." Again, in the first tale, he drew on the nature he observed, as distinguished from the mood landscapes of his Ushers and Eleonoras. This time it was the mountain country of his Charlottesville days, though the story was as far removed from normal experience as an opium dream could make it. Indeed, the protagonist, Bedloe, started out for a walk in the Ragged Mountains only after taking a dose of morphine. The dream that followed, however, assumed a supernatural tinge when Bedloe re-enacted in it the incident which had brought about his death in a previous existence. Neither this tale nor "The Spectacles" could rank among Poe's best. Indeed, the latter, a tediously drawn-out grotesquerie of a near-sighted youth, who falls in love with a crone whom he thinks the

[7] Griswold, *op. cit.,* p. liv.

most ravishing nymph alive, irritates and annoys long before the author's mistaken sense of humor arrives at what he considered a devastatingly clever solution.

None of these stories appeared in *Graham's*. In March of 1844, however, it carried a review which, in its excessiveness of praise, made one wonder what had possessed the critic, ordinarily so chary of it. It concerned the long poem, *Orion*, by Richard Hengist Horne, an English versifier and eccentric who for some time had been corresponding with Elizabeth Barrett. "The farthing epic," people began calling *Orion*, after Horne set its price within the reach of all but with the proviso that it should not be sold to anyone who mispronounced the title. Though it had received encomiums in England, no one had placed it, as Poe did, among the most sublimely imaginative works in the realm of poetical literature. "It is our deliberate opinion that in all that regards the loftiest and holiest attributes of the true Poetry, 'Orion' has *never* been excelled. Indeed, we feel strongly inclined to say that it has never been equalled. . . ."

Alas for the famous, whose letters are preserved. Poe's criticism, it appears, had not been wholly objective. On the 15th of that same month Poe had sent a letter to Cornelius Mathews of New York— with a note and a small parcel for Mathews' friend, the author of *Orion*. The parcel contained the manuscript of "The Spectacles," which, now that Dickens was no longer exerting himself in favor of the American author, Poe was entrusting to Mr. Horne's good offices in England. Indeed, Dickens had fallen out of Poe's grace. "Have you seen the article on 'American Poetry' in the 'London Foreign Quarterly'?" Poe inquired of Lowell. "It has been denied that Dickens wrote it—but, to me, the article affords so strong internal evidence of his hand that I would as soon think of doubting my existence. . . . Among other points he accuses myself of 'metrical imitation' of Tennyson, citing . . . passages from poems which were written and published by me long before Tennyson was heard of. . . ." [8]

Poe guilty of imitation? Preposterous! Yet not long after this disavowal he was turning over in his mind the incidental internal rhymes and the lilting metre of "Lady Geraldine's Courtship," a poem by Mr. Horne's friend, Miss Barrett, which had roused considerable interest in England and was also to stir America, through Mr. Cornelius Mathews, who had been making the poetess known to the New World since 1842.

Her "romance of the age," as Miss Barrett subtitled her first-person narrative of the love of a highborn lady for a poet of low

[8] Letter of March 30, 1844. Ostrom, p. 246.

degree, becomes tedious to the modern reader after the first ten of its ninety-two stanzas, not to mention the conclusion, which required eleven more. Still, though Miss Barrett had written the major part of the ballad in one day, to fill up blank pages in the two-volume edition of her works then in preparation, there was vigor in the telling.[9] She had, besides, a cadenced and often subtle melody with a daring in the rhymes—she matched *certes* with *virtues*—which was effective, though startling. One stanza, the fourth in the conclusion, had particularly struck Poe:

With a murmurous stir uncertain, in the air the purple curtain
    Swelleth in and swelleth out around her motionless pale brows,
While the gliding of the river sends a rippling noise forever
    Through the open casement whitened by the moonlight's slant repose.

Whether because of the color of the curtain or the echoed music, or both, Poe's "Raven," which had hopped out of Barnaby Rudge's basket to inhabit Poe's imagination, became the richer, thanks to Miss Barrett, for some borrowed strains and at least one line:

And the silken sad uncertain rustling of each purple curtain . . .

In the life of everyday, borrowing, unfortunately, was less simple. Dependable sources, like William Poe, were drying up. Editors now often sent Mrs. Clemm away with a discouraging answer. One day Poe went himself to *Graham's* with a copy of "The Raven," copied out in his clear, beautiful hand. Graham turned it down. In desperation the poet pleaded with him, more on the grounds of his family's woeful situation than on the poem's merits, of which, however, he had no mean opinion. Graham shook his head.

Something in Poe's manner must have given him pause. Calling together his editors, the clerks, and even the printers and their devils, he had Poe read the poem to them. He read as he alone could read, but the faces of his listeners were if possible blanker after the last "Nevermore" than they had been in the beginning. What made the procedure even more humiliating to Poe was the presence of Mr. Godey, the editor of the *Lady's Book,* who had happened to drop in. The reading over, someone passed round the hat, without a word. Poe went home to Mrs. Clemm with $15, wrung by pity, if not by his genius.

Under the sting of such experiences Poe's pride reared to insane hostility against the world, life, circumstances, fate. As usual under

---

[9] See *Letters of the Brownings to George Barrett.* Edited by Paul Landis with the assistance of Ronald E. Freeman, p. 122.

such conditions, he would seek escape by fleeing from reality. "His dissipation was too notorious to be denied," recalled John Du Solle, at that time editor of the *Spirit of the Times,* "and for days, and even weeks at a time, he would be sharing the bachelor life and quarters of his associates. . . ."[10]

Du Solle was describing one of Poe's darkest periods, the early months of the unpropitious year 1844, when everything seemed to be going against him. Unhappily, Du Solle was not the only one to notice Poe's disintegration. In his discouragement and rebellion Poe was making more of a sensation than he had done in Washington. Life in Philadelphia was no longer possible. Mr. Poe was too well known. In fact he was notorious.

Little by little the Spring Garden house was denuded, first of the remaining luxuries, then, one by one, of the necessities, till its very name became a mockery in that bitter winter of penury. Poe had not been able to obtain another editorial post in Philadelphia. The *Stylus* seemed hardly likely to provide him with one. Again he turned his eyes toward New York. At least there he was known only for his works.

Early in the morning of April 6, Edgar and Virginia said good-by to Mrs. Clemm, who would be joining them after disposing of what little they had left, gave a farewell pat to Catarina and started off with their luggage for the Walnut Street Wharf, to wait for their train. The driver wanted Poe to pay a dollar, which he refused to do, quite understandably, since he was starting out with only $11 for himself and Virginia. After giving a boy a levy to put their trunks in the baggage car, he went with Virginia to the Depot Hotel and there they glanced through the *Ledger* and the *Times* till they heard the locomotive come chugging, to the clanging of its great brass bell. At about seven o'clock the two, peering out of the red-plush curtained windows, gave a look of farewell to Philadelphia as the train started off.

There was speculation about Mr. Poe's sudden departure among those who knew him. "I happen to know why," Thomas Dunn English wrote, "and there were several others who knew all about it. . . . As its recital would do no good to anyone, the whole affair shall be buried with me."[11]

English was no doubt referring to the Saratoga vacations, which had created such a scandal and had made Poe unpopular with Phila-

[10] Weiss, p. 99.

[11] English, "Reminiscences of Poe," *The Independent,* Oct. 22, 1896.

Part Four

CHAPTER XXII

-»» • «««

"*The Bird Beat the Bug, Though, All Hollow*"

IT was raining hard when the steamboat which the travelers had taken at Perth Amboy docked in New York. Moving their luggage to the ladies' cabin, Poe left Virginia in charge, in the company of two other ladies, while he went in search of lodgings. On the way he met a man selling umbrellas and bought one for 25 cents. Walking up and down the familiar quarter he stopped at No. 130 Greenwich Street, which appeared to be within his means. It was not a bad-looking building, with its brownstone steps, porch and pillars. He engaged a room, did a little bargaining, and then hired a hack to fetch Virginia, who was astonished at seeing him back so soon, and with so much accomplished.

The following morning, soon after breakfast, Poe wrote to "dear Muddy" all their little adventures and described the house in detail. He sounded like a schoolboy on a holiday, like a bridegroom on a second honeymoon—just he and "Sis" together, after eight years. While he wrote in their quiet back room, Virginia was busy with needle and thread, mending his pants, which he had torn against a nail the night before. Providently he had gone out before bedtime, to buy a skein of silk, a skein of thread, two buttons, a pair of slippers and a tin pan for the stove. The house was old and looked "buggy," he admitted to Mrs. Clemm; the landlady very chatty and the board the cheapest he had ever known, considering the central situation of the house and the *living*. That amazed him most of all. "I wish Kate could see it—she would faint," he alluded to their feline retainer. "Last night, for supper, we had the nicest tea you ever drank, strong & hot—wheat bread & rye bread—cheese—tea-cakes, a great dish of elegant ham, & 2 of cold veal, piled up like a mountain and large slices—3 dishes of cakes, and every thing in the greatest profusion. . . . For breakfast we had excellent-flavored coffee, hot & strong. . . . I wish you could have seen the eggs—and the great dishes of meat. . . . Sis is delighted, and we are both in excellent spirits. She has coughed hardly any and had no night sweat. . . ." [1]

This was not the stylist, not the arbiter of fashion describing the harmony of crimson and gold—without mirrors—of his favorite décor. He was just Eddie, just Buddy, using the speech of ordinary life to the woman with whom there was no need of pretense of any kind. He was simply her boy, talking her language as unaffectedly as she did herself. Between the lines, especially in the rhapsody on the landlady's bountiful table, one read admissions of very lean times, too frequently experienced.

Already, the morning after the Poes' arrival, the financial pinch was making itself felt and, characteristically, he set out to resolve it in his accustomed way. He had only $4.50 left. "Tomorrow I am going to try & borrow 3$—so that I may have a fortnight to go upon. I feel in excellent spirits & haven't drank a drop—so that I hope soon to get out of trouble. The very instant I scrape together enough money I will send it on. . . . Sissy had a hearty cry last night, because you and Catterina weren't here. . . . Be sure & take home the Messenger to Hirst. We hope to send for you *very* soon." [2]

It was, undoubtedly, the first letter Poe was writing in New York and already the painful arithmetic had begun. He had brought with him, however, a piece of writing which, if the editor agreed to his suggestions, would make him, Poe, return to the literary world of New York with a bang and earn him some money besides. One day, therefore, he walked down the brownstone steps of his boarding house and made his way to the office of the *New York Sun*. The editor fell in with Poe's plan, which he carried into effect on Saturday, the 13th of April, 1844, when the early morning issue of the paper carried the sensational headlines:

"*Astounding News!* By Express Via Norfolk. The Atlantic Crossed in THREE DAYS. Signal Triumph of Monck Mason's Flying MACHINE! ! !—Arrival at Sullivan's Island, near Charleston, S.C., of Mr. Mason, Mr. Robert Holland, Mr. Henson, Mr. Harrison Ainsworth, and four others, in the STEERING BALLOON *VICTORIA* after a passage of SEVENTY-FIVE HOURS from Land to Land.— Full Particulars of the VOYAGE! ! !" Besides, the *Sun* baited the reader with the promise of a detailed account of the Atlantic flight in a ten-o'clock extra.

Before long the amazed Gothamites were pouring into the square near the *Sun* building. From all directions they came, forcing their

---

[1] Ostrom, p. 252.
[2] April 7, 1844. Ostrom, p. 252.

way, blocking the streets and alleys and every approach. Ten o'clock struck but the extra was not ready. The people waited, however, while the crowds grew frenzied with excitement. Finally, toward noon, the newsboys began coming out with the extra edition. It was snapped up within minutes. Poe, incognito in the crowd, saw with saturnine amusement people disputing the paper among themselves and paying as much as a half dollar for a copy.

"The great problem is at length solved!" read the lucky possessors. "The air, as well as the earth and the ocean, has been subdued by science, and will become a common and convenient highway for mankind. *The Atlantic has been actually crossed in a Balloon* . . . and in the inconceivably brief period of seventy-five hours from shore to shore!"

Who could disbelieve such an assertion when the very editor expressed his amazement by his lavish use of exclamation points? And who could fail to commend the zeal of the *Sun*'s agent, Mr. Forsyth, in Charleston, S.C. who rushed to the scene to make such an historic scoop for his paper? What is more, Mr. Forsyth took the trouble to transcribe the combined journals of the fliers into a detailed, day-by-day account of remarkable conviction and excitement. *"We are in view of the low coast of South Carolina,"* it closed. "The great problem is accomplished. We have crossed the Atlantic—fairly and *easily* crossed it in a balloon! God be praised. Who shall say that any thing is impossible hereafter?" "Who, indeed!" answer the future generations, for whom a transatlantic flight of less than fourteen hours has become commonplace?

Poe had not written wholly from imagination. In 1837 Monck Mason and his small group had actually attempted a flight from Dover to Weilburg, in Hesse-Nassau, in their balloon, "Nassau." They had kept a meticulous log which was later published and which Poe, as acquisitive as a magpie for any shining object, was quick to appropriate.

For the moment Poe basked in the sensation he had created and his ego, so badly crushed by circumstances, expanded anew. People were again talking about him. The population of sophisticated New York had been royally gulled by him. Of course there were many who took the whole thing amiss; but if they had not been intelligent enough to detect the hoax it was the fault of their own stupidity. Had they had any perception, the pun in the name of the reporter, Forsyth (Foresight?) should have warned them. Anyway, the article brought Poe some welcome cash and caused his presence in New York to be remarked—enough, perhaps, to enable him to find a magazine post and settle down in the city where, as he wrote to Lowell, he intended living for the future.

Some of the "Balloon Hoax" money went to Mrs. Clemm, this time to help get her and Catarina out of exile. Mrs. Clemm, on her part, had been zealously disposing of the last few remaining objects, so zealously indeed that when she went to Leary's Book Store to sell the odds and ends of books that Eddie had left behind she also included the bound volume of the *Southern Literary Messenger,* which Poe had reminded her to return to Hirst. It was a sizable tome, worth $5. Unfortunately, it did not belong to Hirst but to William Duane, from whom he had borrowed it for Poe.

The circumstances, innocent enough to begin with, created an embarrassing misunderstanding among the three men concerned, and added fuel to the fire of gossip wherein the good Philadelphians had been immolating Poe's reputation. How shocking of Poe to sell a book that did not belong to him—for such was the assumption not only of Hirst and Duane, but of everyone who came to know of the affair. In vain Poe, in all sincerity, wrote to Duane that Mrs. Clemm had returned the book to Hirst's office. Indeed, she said she had left it there with one of Hirst's brothers. "Most probably it was deposited in a book-case, and thus over-looked and forgotten. May I trouble you to send for it?" Poe wrote to Duane.[3]

At this, Duane went to Hirst and showed him Poe's letter. Cried the indignant Endymion: "A damned lie!"—which was nothing less than the truth, though Poe did not know it. In her guilt-consciousness of what she had done, especially since it was having such unpleasant consequences, Mrs. Clemm, while shielding herself in a fib, was placing the innocent Poe in a very unfavorable light.

The matter dragged on for nearly eight months, during which, through Leary the bookseller, Mr. Duane traced the missing *Messenger* to Richmond from where, after passing through various hands, it found its way again to Mr. Duane, who had to ransom it for $5. There was no balm, however, for Poe's smarting reputation. It was one of those small troubles growing out from the *one* trouble of poverty, as Poe had once remarked to Lowell. On that ground alone Mrs. Clemm may be forgiven for this and other inconveniences which she brought upon Poe.

With the few worldly goods she had salvaged, Mrs. Clemm and Catarina—occupying the capacious basket in transit—arrived in New York. They may have enjoyed the bountiful fare at the Greenwich Street boardinghouse for a while, but by the summer the whole family

[3] Ostrom, p. 264.

had moved to the country, to a farm five miles north of the city, along the Bloomingdale Road. Poe had earned a little money by placing two new stories, "The Oblong Box" and "Thou Art the Man," in *Godey's,* and by acting as correspondent at large for the Pennslyvania *Columbia Spy.* For it he wrote brief articles ranging in interest from the various sites and sights in Mannahatta—*"Why* do we persist in *de-euphonizing* the true name?"—to the spuriously "Egyptian" architecture that was springing up everywhere.

An inveterate gadabout, he went in search of views as enthusiastically as Gibbon in Rome, climbing the summit of the white shot tower on the East River at Fifty-fifth Street, to enjoy the almost illimitable prospect, or riding the buses—the Red Birds, the Yellow Birds. "When you visit Gotham, you should ride out the Fifth Avenue, as far as the distributing reservoir, near Forty-third Street," he advised.[4] "The prospect is particularly beautiful." To the north one saw the Yorkville reservoir, while southward the city spread before one's eyes, to the Battery and the crowded Harbor. Poe made no comment on the crenelated Saracenic architecture of the new reservoir which the municipal government, carried away by the current craze for foreign flimflam, had seen fit to duplicate and reduplicate in armories, firehouses and public buildings. Poe was less reticent in his article on the Harbor, which, for natural beauty, he thought superior to anything in the Northern Hemisphere. "But . . . the Gothamites have most generously disfigured it by displays of landscape and architectural taste. More atrocious *pagodas,* or what not . . . were certainly never imagined. . . . If these atrocities appertain to taste, then it is taste in its dying agonies. . . ."[5]

Strangely enough, the man whose imagination was furnished with castles of decaying splendor missed nothing of the seamier aspects of the city. Like another observant peripatetic, the twenty-five-year-old Walt Whitman—fresh-cheeked, large, all-embracing, lover of populous pavements, "dweller in Mannahatta, my city," Poe noted its contrasts. Here, in the lower part of town, were the villas of the rich, built to resemble foreign palaces, their draped, gilt-furnished interiors graced by ladies in the latest Godey fashions, each occupying three yards of space with her hoops and flounces. There, not too far away, amid the rocky sterility of the unbuilt section, were the shanties of the Irish squatters.

"I have one of these *tabernacles* (I use the term primitively) at present in the eye of my mind," he wrote. "It is, perhaps, nine feet

[4] Now the site of the New York Public Library.
[5] *Columbia Spy,* June 18, 1844.

by six. . . . The whole fabric (which is of mud) has been erected in somewhat too obvious an imitation of the Tower of Pisa. A dozen rough planks, 'pitched' together, form the roof. The door is a barrel on end. . . . A dog and a cat are inevitable in these habitations; and, apparently, there are no dogs and no cats more entirely happy.

"On the eastern or 'Sound' face of Mannahatta . . . are some of the most picturesque sites for villas to be found within the limits of Christendom. . . ." [6]

The juxtaposition of shanty and villa was not without purpose, though Poe was not ordinarily given to pointing a moral. His own circumstances had not altered significantly; he had merely removed them from one city to another. As yet he had not found a regular post—the tomahawk man had scalped too many New York literati—and despite his assiduous free-lancing, the returns barely kept the family alive. Sometimes, to Mrs. Clemm's chagrin, part of the precious earnings were dissipated in Sandy Welsh's cellar, or similar haunts—a waste which, bad in itself, was infinitely worse for the consequences it had upon Poe. It was therefore with mute thanksgiving that she prepared for the removal of the family to the new dwelling, early in July. Perhaps there, in the country, Virginia might improve and Eddie be removed from temptation.

In days when the Forty-third Street reservoir was considered to be on the edge of town, Patrick Brennan's house was distinctly rural. Its dooryard faced the Bloomingdale Road and, beyond the undulating slopes and green fields, the wide silver sash of the Hudson—bounded on the opposite brink by the Jersey shore.[7] Patrick Brennan was indeed lord of all he surveyed, for he owned two hundred sixteen acres, some of which he cultivated with vegetables and fruits for the New York market.

The house itself, set on a rocky ledge, descended from the Revolutionary era and was said to have sheltered Washington and his men. It had the simple architecture of the period, without columns or ostentation, and consisted of the main original building of two stories, with a gabled roof, to which was attached a smaller extension, following the same lines. Shade trees surrounded it; but quite close to the house, so close that its delicate drooping branches formed a canopy over the roof, was a giant weeping willow. According to tradition, the

---

[6] *Doings in Gotham,* by Jacob E. Spannuth. With introduction by T. O. Mabbott.

[7] Today the house would be located at 84th Street, between Broadway and Amsterdam Avenue.

tree had grown from a shoot of the willow planted over Napoleon's tomb at St. Helena.

The Brennan family welcomed their tenants, for whom they had made a special concession, since they ordinarily did not take boarders. Besides Mr. and Mrs. Brennan there was a daughter, Martha, a blue-eyed Irish beauty of fifteen, and in her train came various younger brothers and sisters, not to mention a nondescript population of cats, dogs and other pets. The house was large, however, the grounds were extensive and the food proved to be excellent as well as plentiful. All told, it was at last a pleasant haven which, they all hoped, would do Virginia good. Mrs. Clemm had a room in the lower part of the house, from where it was convenient to have a little gossip with Mrs. Brennan or help her about the kitchen, when she, Muddie, was not occupied with scissors and paste, clipping, arranging and filing everything by, or about, Eddie—one of her duties about which Poe was very particular. Edgar and Virginia occupied the garret under the eaves of the extension to the main house, but he had his study on the floor below.

It was a spacious room and, certainly, the closest approximation he had ever achieved of the ideal chamber he had once described. Though not oblong, it was well proportioned, with three small-paned windows of heavy French glass against the gusts blowing in from the Hudson, and two more in the rear, looking out upon the wooded country. Along one side was an open fireplace with a finely carved mantel.[8] A touch of Old World refinement prevailed in the furnishings provided by an earlier tenant, an ex-officer of Napoleon's who had fought in his campaigns and, like his emperor, had gone into exile after defeat. Faded prints of past military glory still hung upon the walls. Pieces of massive furniture were disposed here and there, while heavy hangings carried out the Empire theme. By an odd circumstance a bust of Pallas, which had also belonged to the Frenchman, stood upon a shelf over a door leading to the hallway. Behind it a transom of small panes of smoked glass filtered the light. A bookcase, a writing table and chair completed the poet's study.[9]

In such peaceful surroundings, away from the "rum palaces and gin hovels" of the city which Poe had earlier criticized Mayor Harper for closing on the Sabbath, he worked as never before. "The Raven," amplified by new stanzas, with every allusion, every musical nuance

[8] Now in the Hall of Philosophy, Columbia University.

[9] Details from General James R. O'Beirne, who married Martha Brennan. *New York Mail and Express,* April 21, 1900.

calculated to intensify the total effect of the recurring theme of love and loss, was nearing completion.

The poem began with a disarming casualness in colloquial speech which, in its unaffectedness, might have come from the lips of Mrs. Clemm:

> Once upon a midnight dreary, while I pondered, weak and weary,
> Over many a quaint and curious volume of forgotten lore,
>> While I nodded, nearly napping, suddenly there came a tapping,
>> As of some one gently rapping, rapping at my chamber door.

Nothing could have been better calculated to put the unwary reader at his ease. Then, cunningly, in the very next stanza, comes the premonitory shock:

> Ah, distinctly I remember it was in the bleak December,
> And each separate dying ember wrought its ghost upon the floor.
>> Eagerly I wished the morrow;—vainly I had sought to borrow
>> From my books surcease of sorrow—sorrow for the lost Lenore . . .

The *dying ember,* that word *ghost,* become the key motifs of a symphony of terror, vanished happiness, fatality and hopeless, never-ending despair, which gain in poignancy by the almost flippant introduction of the Raven.

> "Sir," said I, "or Madam, truly your forgiveness I implore;
>> But the fact is I was napping, and so gently you came rapping,
>> And so faintly you came tapping, tapping at my chamber door,
> That I scarce was sure I heard you"—here I opened wide the door;—
>>> Darkness there and nothing more.

Darkness there and nothing more. Even before its materialization the bird of doom assumes its quality of darkness. The remaining stanzas play upon the main theme, each adding its suspense, terror and wonder to the final, hopeless, unalterable word.

> And the Raven, never flitting, still is sitting, still is sitting
> On the pallid bust of Pallas just above my chamber door;
>> And his eyes have all the seeming of a demon's that is dreaming,
>> And the lamplight o'er him streaming throws his shadow on the floor;
> And my soul from out that shadow that lies floating on the floor
>>> Shall be lifted—nevermore!

With a poet's prescience he had envisioned the future. Yet never had Virginia looked so well. The simple life at the Brennans' agreed with her. She had a lighthearted companion in Martha during the long hours that Edgar spent at his writing and she was free of the worry of watching at the window for him to come home, as she used to do in the city, often only to throw herself upon the bed in tears. Eddie was not drinking now. When he had done writing she would help him paste the sheets of manuscript together, top and bottom, till they formed a strip yards in length, which would then be gathered together into a roll. It was her one contribution to his work, other than that of providing his imagination with the prototype of his heroines.

Poe too had profited by his change of scene. He was writing much, if not less morbidly. Always, either directly or tangentially, his works touched upon his deep-seated terrors and fixations. In the eyes of the Brennans, however, he seemed to be a hard-working, devoted "son" and husband who, with his pretty wife, would sit of an evening at the west windows to watch the sun disappear behind the Jersey palisades. They noted too that the grave young gentleman had a way with children, to witness the devotion of their young son Tom, who dogged his steps as, swinging his cane, Poe made for the woods or, going in the opposite direction, strode toward the Hudson and his favorite seat, a rocky ledge which was known as Mount Tom. Often, in fascination, the boy would watch him trace strange designs on the powdery soil, and then come home and tell his parents about it.

In the study the things Poe traced in his copperplate hand were of a quite different order, to judge by the publications of that year. One story, "The Premature Burial," described with excruciating realism the sensations of a man who had been buried alive, though in the end it turned out to be a "vision," as Poe called it, conjured up by the man's confinement in a low, narrow berth on a sloop. Through his writings Poe may have achieved catharsis for his gruesome imaginings. Nevertheless, death, and the sensations of death-in-life, he exploited to the hilt. In another tale, "The Oblong Box," wherein a valuable painting was ostensibly secreted, proved in reality to be a coffin containing a corpse. Only "Thou art the Man," a satirical skit on the methods of detection, and "The Literary Life of Thingum Bob, Esq." were in the burlesque vein—his preferred method of getting even with a society for which he had nothing but contempt. None of these "articles," as he called such pieces, possessed his true genius.

One work of that year, the poem "Dream-Land," was purest Poe. Like a lullaby, it opened with a strophe which, in the poem's original form, he repeated, like a wistful refrain:

> By a route obscure and lonely,
> Haunted by ill angels only,
> Where an Eidolon, named NIGHT
> On a black throne reigns upright,

> I have reached these lands but newly
> From an ultimate dim Thule—
> From a wild weird clime that lieth, sublime,
> Out of SPACE—out of TIME.

It was the ultimate dim Thule of his true abode which he described, with chasms and caves and Titan woods, and mountains toppling into shoreless seas—the apocalyptic landscape of his tormented spirit:

> By the grey woods,—by the swamp
> .   .   .   .   .   .
> By the dismal tarns and pools
>   Where dwell the ghouls,—
> By each spot the most unholy—
> In each nook most melancholy,—
> There the traveller meets aghast
> Sheeted Memories of the Past—
> Shrouded forms that start and sigh
> As they pass the wanderer by—
> White-robed forms of friends long given,
> In agony, to the Earth—and Heaven.

Death, always death and the departed that, somehow, had greater hold upon him than the living—until they too were dead. Death which, at about the time that he was composing "Dream-Land," he endeavored to explore through "Mesmeric Revelation," his application of the current fad of the hypnotic trance, brought on by mesmerism. In his tale, however, his object in inducing this condition on a man suffering from the very disease that was consuming Virginia was to discover, by questioning his subject, the truth of immortality. The conclusion? Poe cleverly skirted it. "The sleep-waker. . . fell back upon his pillow and expired. . . . Had he . . . during the latter portion of his discourse, been addressing me from the region of the shadows?"

By the end of the year the poem in which he had been previsioning the loss of Virginia—Lenore, Eleonora, names denoting radiance, light—was nearing the ultimate perfection for which he always strove. Time and again he had seen Virginia on the brink of expiring and something of himself had died with her. Witnesses at such times told of the terrible effect of those crises upon him. In composing "The Raven" he was courageously facing the loss he must someday endure. Perhaps, too, by externalizing his secret terrors he was gathering the strength to bear them sanely once they became realities.

He sold the poem to George H. Colton, who edited the *American Review,* but it first appeared on January 29, 1845, in N. P. Willis' *New York Mirror,* perhaps as Poe's gesture of gratitude to its editor. Poe had been working for Willis as his assistant since October, 1844, after Mrs. Clemm had called upon him in distress, begging employment for her son-in-law who, she said, was very ill. As Willis was then about to convert his weekly *Mirror* into a daily, he had taken on Poe and given him a desk in a corner of the office. There the poet had sat from nine in the morning until the paper went to press, discharging his duties, uncomplaining, unsmiling, as if he had never done anything else.

Poe liked Willis, envied him, and was annoyed by his "society" airs. In early youth Willis had met Byron's last mistress, La Guiccioli, and had never got over having drunk tea with her. His poem *Melanie,* Byronic to the last syllable, had dealt, of course, with incestuous love. Willis was therefore irritated whenever he read anything as intangibly out of space, out of time as Poe's "Dream-Land," which, on his first encounter with it, he had flung into the fire, watching it burn with devilish glee. A kindhearted man, he fancied himself, in his editorial chair, as another ruthless Christopher North. A shy man, he liked to fascinate the gentler sex and get into quarrels with conspicuous males. In spite of their divergent characters, Poe and Willis got along together and, in time, even became friends.

In his editorial capacity Mr. Willis prefaced "The Raven," which appeared on the front page, with a few words in his typical style: "In our opinion, it is the most effective single piece of 'fugitive poetry' ever published in this country; and unsurpassed in English poetry for subtle conception, masterly ingenuity of versification, and consistent sustaining of imaginative lift and 'pokerishness.' . . ." [10]

Fugitive it was, in an unintended sense—it was a runaway success. Other papers copied it. Everybody talked about it. People who had not been aware of Poe except as the perpetrator of the "Balloon Hoax" now knew him as a poet. The "starry sisterhood" who foregathered in the salons of the literary minister Orville Dewey, of Thomas Lawson, and of the erudite Miss Anna C. Lynch, now took to mentioning his name at their gatherings and discussed the possibility of inviting the author of "The Raven" to their readings. At last Edgar Allan Poe had the fame for which he had always hungered. The $10 he received for the poem, however, did not go far in providing daily bread.

In his "Philosophy of Composition" Poe was to give a cold ac-

[10] *New York Evening Mirror,* Jan. 29, 1845.

→≫ • ≪←

CHAPTER XXIII

Poe and Some Poets

POE was riding the crest and loving every exhilarating moment of it. Luck, so relentless toward him, seemed at last to be smiling; at any rate, the new year augured well. Early in January, 1845, Poe had resigned from the *Mirror* in the hope of a post on the *Broadway Journal,* which two New Englanders, Charles F. Briggs, a friend of Lowell's, and John Bisco, a novelist, had launched on the 4th of January. That they were favorably disposed was evident in the fact that the first two numbers contained a criticism of Elizabeth Barrett, by Poe. The success of "The Raven," not long afterward, certainly weighed with them in Poe's favor. Anyway, in the issue of February 22, Briggs and Bisco announced that thereafter Edgar Allan Poe would be associated with the editorial department of their journal. "As his name is of some authority," Mr. Briggs wrote to Lowell, "I thought it advisable to announce him as an editor. . . ." [1] Poe was paid at the rate of a dollar per column. To be nearer his office in the "city" he moved his family to a small apartment at 195 Broadway.

It had not been without preliminary misgivings that Briggs had engaged Poe. The inevitable rumors had been circulating about him in journalistic circles and Briggs was prejudiced against him before they met. "For my own part I did not use to think well of Poe," he confessed to Lowell, "but my love for you and implicit confidence in your judgment, led me to abandon all my prejudices. . . . The Rev. Mr. Griswold, of Philadelphia told me some abominable lies about him, but a personal acquaintance with him has induced me to think highly of him. Perhaps some Philadelphian has been whispering foul things in your ear about him. . . ." [2]

However, "The Raven" had everybody "raven-mad," as Mr. Briggs punned. From America it winged its way across the Atlantic to England, where, too, it had its readers all agog. "Orion" Horne read it

---

[1] Briggs to Lowell, March 8, 1845. Woodberry, p. 227.
[2] Letter of March 19, 1845. Woodberry, p. 229.

and, of course, Elizabeth Barrett, who received it from the author himself. A copy also fell into the hands of young Dante Gabriel Rossetti, whom it was to spur to emulation in "The Blessed Damozel." At least so Rossetti told Hall Caine. "I saw that Poe had done the utmost that it was possible to do with the grief of the lover on earth, and so I determined to reverse the conditions and give utterance to the yearning of the loved one in Heaven." [3] It is interesting to observe that neither Poe's Lenore nor Rossetti's Damozel had left the world when their lovers translated them to a higher sphere.

Meanwhile the year continued favorable to Poe, who saw the realization of several of his wishes. The previous autumn, after a silence of years, he had written to Professor Anthon to approach the Harpers for him once more. He had enough tales, Poe wrote, to make five of the ordinary novel volumes. He knew he had no claim upon Anthon's attention, not even that of personal acquaintance, "But I have reached a crisis in my life, in which I sadly stand in need of aid. . . ." [4] The kindly professor could not withstand such a plea, but he had no success with the Harpers, who had not forgotten the affair of the *Conchologist's First Book.* "They have *complaints* against you, grounded on certain movements of yours," wrote Anthon, with as much tact as possible. [5]

Wiley and Putnam, however, saw their opportunity, and in the summer of 1845 they brought out *Tales* by Edgar A. Poe. The small volume was not the imposing set which Poe had envisioned nor did it contain the stories he would have chosen. Still, the dozen tales formed a representative selection, although to capture popular interest the publishers had leaned more heavily on the ratiocinative, rather than on the imaginative, genius of Poe.

Considering the enemies he had made by the virulence of his reviews, it was to be expected that, now they had their chance, the critics would take their revenge. Indeed, the *American Review* expressed the fear that Poe's reputation would not add to the success of the volume. The consensus, however, was favorable. The public bought the book, and for the first time Poe received royalties—eight cents on every copy sold. England, too, found much to praise in the volume, although the ladylike author of *Proverbial Philosophy,* Martin Farquhar Tupper, while admiring "Murders in the Rue Morgue," turned with relief to "A Descent into the Maelström," whose turbulence, at least, was elemental.

---

[3] P. H. Baum, ed., *Poems, Ballads and Sonnets* of D. G. Rossetti.
[4] Ostrom, p. 271.
[5] Letter of Nov. 2, 1844. Griswold Collection, Boston Public Library.

From her invalid's room at 50 Wimpole Street, the already famous Miss Barrett followed every current of the literary stream and commented on it to her many correspondents. On the 12th of May, 1845, she took up her pen and wrote to "Orion" Horne: "Your friend, Mr. Poe, is a speaker of strong words. . . . But I hope you will assure him . . . that I am grateful for his reviews and in no complaining humour at all. As to the 'Raven' . . . There is certainly a power—but it does not appear . . . the natural expression of a sane intellect. . . . The rhythm acts excellently upon the imagination, and the 'nevermore' has a solemn chime about it. . . . The 'pokerishness' (just gods! what Mohawk English) might be found fatal. . . . Besides—just because I have been criticised, I would not criticise . . . there is an uncommon force and effect in the poem. . . . But Mr. Poe, who attributes the 'Oedipus Coloneus' to Aeschylus (*vide* review on me) sits somewhat loosely, probably, to his classics." [6]

It is the letter of a woman, rather, of a poet, in a pique—and with justification, to judge by the review, in *two* installments at that, with which Poe had inaugurated his accession to the *Broadway Journal.* The extraordinary thing about it all was that Poe admired Miss Barrett. He had hailed her as a poet worth a dozen of Tennyson and six of Motherwell in the second number of the *Evening Mirror,* and only a month since, in that same paper, he had said of her: "We do not believe there is a poetical soul embodied in this world that—as a centre of thought—sees further out toward the periphery permitted to the angels. . . ." [7] Even now, in his first paragraph, he declared: "Of all the friends of the fair author, we doubt whether one exists, with more profound—with more enthusiastic reverence and admiration of her genius, than the writer of these words." But, he went on, "It is for this very reason, beyond all others, that he intends to speak of her *the truth.*"

The book under review was the American edition of Miss Barrett's *The Drama of Exile and Other Poems.* Already the press, wooed by Miss Barrett's prefatory praise of "the great American people," had responded in kind, much to Poe's annoyance. "All that anybody can say or think, and all that Miss Barrett can *feel* respecting it," he said of a dithyramb in a new monthly, "is, that it is an eulogy as well written as it is an insult well intended." He set out to remedy that insult, and with such zest that, by the time he had done with the *Drama of Exile,* Miss Barrett, as well as Adam and Eve, were glad to be out of the reach of his fulminations.

[6] Original in Boston Public Library.
[7] *Evening Mirror,* Dec. 7, 1844.

The *Drama,* he complained, opened with a palpable bull: " 'Scene, the outer side of the gate of Eden, shut fast with clouds'—(a scene out of sight!)—from the depth of which revolved the sword of fire, self moved . . .'. These are the 'stage directions' which greet us on the threshold of the book. We complain first of the bull: secondly, of the blue-fire melo-dramatic aspect of the revolving sword, which, if steel, and sufficiently inflamed to do service in burning, would, perhaps, have been in no temper to cut; and on the other hand, if sufficiently cool to have an edge, would have accomplished little in the way of scorching a personage so well accustomed to fire and brimstone and all that, as we have good reason to believe Lucifer was. . . ." [8]

Here was Dupin, assuming the functions of the critic. In paragraph after paragraph he pointed out the *niaiseries*—the critic here used the French word—both in the *Drama* and in the poems. Now and then, as Poe, he saw excellence in individual lyrics, yet even here he found that if they burned with divine fire, it was only in scintillations. "The Cry of the Children" he praised without reserve for "a horror sublime in its simplicity—of which a far greater than Dante might have been proud."

What of "Lady Geraldine's Courtship" that had helped to feather a certain Raven? "With the exception of Tennyson's 'Locksley Hall,' we have never perused a poem combining so much of the fiercest passion with so much of the most ethereal fancy, as the 'Lady Geraldine's Courtship' of Miss Barrett. We are forced to admit, however, that the latter work *is* a palpable imitation of the former, which it surpasses in plot . . . as much as it falls below in artistical management. . . ." [9] So the magpie, by rumpling the nest, seeks to conceal its stolen jewel.

After such candor on the part of her critic, Miss Barrett found little solace in being told in the final paragraph: "Her poetic inspiration is of the highest—we can conceive nothing more august." [10]

However, on the very day, January 11, 1845, that the second installment of Poe's review appeared, Miss Barrett sat down to answer a letter which had come the day before. "I love your verses with all my heart, dear Miss Barrett," the letter began, and after an embarrassed peroration, went on, "I do, as I say, love these books with all my heart—and I love you too." It was signed Robert Browning.[11]

[8] Griswold, Ed. *Poe, Works* Vol. III, p. 405.

[9] *Ibid.,* p. 412.

[10] *Ibid.,* p. 424.

[11] *Letters of Robert Browning and Elizabeth Barrett, 1845–1846,* Vol. I, pp. 1-2.

"These books" contained the very poems with which Mr. Poe was dealing in his extraordinary fashion. Still, however peculiar Poe's admiration for Miss Barrett, it was sincere, as he demonstrated when, the following November, Wiley and Putnam brought out a companion volume to the *Tales—The Raven and Other Poems*. Its dedication read:

To the Noblest of her Sex, To the Author of "The Drama of Exile" To Miss Elizabeth Barrett Barrett of England I dedicate this volume with the most enthusiastic admiration and with most Sincere Esteem.

Poe's volume contained thirty-one poems and sold at 31 cents a copy. At a penny a poem the public had its money's worth.

Of course the first thing Miss Barrett did on learning of the dedication was to communicate her feelings to Browning. "And think of Mr. Poe, with that great Roman justice of his (if not rather American!) dedicating a book to one and abusing one in the preface of the same. He wrote a review of me in just that spirit—the two extremes of laudation and reprehension, folded in on one another. You would have thought that it had been written by a friend and foe, each stark mad with love and hate and writing the alternate paragraphs. . . ." [12] Her feminine subtlety had caught that ambivalence in her admirer which was, unfortunately, so much part of his nature.

On receiving Poe's book, she again informed Browning: "I see that the deteriorating preface which was to have saved me from the vanity fever produceable by the dedication is cut down and away—perhaps in this particular copy only." [13]

At the same time she wrote to her friend and cousin, John Kenyon: "What is to be said, I wonder, when a man calls you 'the noblest of your sex'? 'Sir, you are the most discerning of yours.' " [14]

In writing to Poe, urbanity mingled with coyness superseded candor. The dedication, she said, was too great a distinction, conferred by too generous a hand. "After which imperfect acknowledgment of my personal obligation, may I thank you as another reader would—thank you for this vivid writing, this power which is felt? Your 'Raven' has produced a sensation—a 'fit horror'—here in England. Some of my friends are taken by the fear of it, & some by the music—I hear of persons haunted by the 'Nevermore'—and one acquaintance of mine who has the misfortune of Possessing a 'bust of Pallas,' never can bear to look at it in the twilight. I think that you

[12] *Ibid.*, Vol. I, p. 307.
[13] *Ibid.*, Vol. I, p. 384.
[14] *Letters of E. B. Browning*, Ed. F. G. Kenyon, Vol. I, p. 249.

will like to be told that our great poet Mr. Browning, the author of 'Paracelsus' & the 'Bells and Pomegranates,' was struck much by the rhythm of that poem. . . ." [15]

This was the balm Poe needed for his too easily wounded ego. Yet even Miss Barrett's generous dose was not thick enough to satisfy him. At a time when he felt the necessity for a bit of puffery, he sent to Joseph M. Field a few quotations for insertion in his paper, among them Miss Barrett's which, in Poe's version, had been transformed into a "rave." "The world's greatest poetess, *Elizabeth Barrett Barrett,* says of Mr. Poe: 'This *vivid* writing!—this power *which is felt!* 'The Raven' has produced a *sensation*—a 'fit horror'—here in England. . . . I hear of persons absolutely haunted by the 'Nevermore.' Our great poet, Mr. Browning, the author of 'Paracelsus,' 'The Pomegranates' etc. is enthusiastic in his admiration of the rhythm. . . ." [16]

One thing Poe betrays in connection with Browning, whose greatness Elizabeth Barrett had so early recognized. It is Poe's ignorance of that poet's work when he copies as "The Pomegranates" the title which Miss Barrett had correctly given. Obviously Poe had no idea whether it referred to a poem, a long opus, or a collection of lyrics. True, Browning had still to gain popular recognition, but his little pamphlets of *Bells and Pomegranates* issued at his family's expense, already included many of his finest works. Somehow he did not interest Poe, who may not even have read him. At any rate, Browning had the distinction of being excluded from Poe's literary notice and from the oddly assorted company of some fourscore literati, whom he treated in the course of his life and of whom very few are now remembered. Oddly enough, Emerson, too, does not appear, while Longfellow received notice only in a series of violent broadsides, fired off from Willis' *Evening Mirror* and continued relentlessly in the *Broadway Journal.*

Poe, who so delightedly put Miss Barrett's praise to his own use, would have been less than pleased by the expression of her *private* opinion to Browning. "Oh, and I send you besides a most frightful extract from an American magazine sent to me yesterday . . . on the subject of mesmerism—and you are to understand, if you please, that the Mr. Edgar Poe who stands committed in it, is my dedicator . . . whose dedication I forgot, by the way, with the rest—so, while I am sending, you shall have his poems with his mesmeric experience and decide whether the outrageous compliment to E.B.B. or

15 MS in New York Public Library.
16 Ostrom, pp. 319-320.

the experiment of M. Vandeleur [Valdemar] goes furthest to prove him mad. There is poetry in the man, though, now and then, seen between the great gaps of bathos. . . . 'Politian' will make you laugh —as the 'Raven' made *me* laugh, though with something in it which accounts for the hold it took upon people such as Mr. N. P. Willis and his peers—it was sent to me from *four* different quarters besides the author himself. . . . Some of the other lyrics have power of a less questionable sort. For the author, I do not know him at all . . . and in my opinion, there is more faculty shown in the account of that horrible mesmeric experience (mad or not mad) than in his poems. . . . Most horrible!— Then I believe so much of mesmerism, as to give room for the full acting of the story on me. . . ." [17]

So poets may deceive each other.

That account of the mesmeric experience which had so horrified Miss Barrett was "The Facts in the Case of M. Valdemar," published in the *American Review* in December, 1845. With his flair for the sensational, Poe had taken a subject which at the time held people between fascination and wonder, and concocted what he presented as an actual experiment in mesmerism. Being Poe, he was not content with any ordinary subject. No person had as yet been mesmerized *in articulo mortis.* Would it be possible to mesmerize a person in that condition? For how long could death be arrested in the process? These and other questions the narrator set out to answer, with the co-operation of the dying M. Valdemar.

The result exceeded anything Poe had ever done, in its credibility and horror, a horror all the more gripping for the scientific detachment with which the experiment was carried out to its appalling conclusion. Indeed, Poe had succeeded so well in his realistic presentation that the account was taken for fact. In London a pamphlet, selling at threepence, called the story "Mesmerism in Articulo Mortis" and gave it as the astounding and horrifying narrative of an actual happening. In France the compiler of the *Dictionnaire des Superstitions Populaires,* the Abbé Migne, wrote, under the subject of magnetism: "We cannot abandon this question of animal magnetism without apprising our readers of an extraordinary . . . happening which was much talked about in the scientific world." Here he translated "The Facts in the Case of M. Valdemar." [18]

Poe's satisfaction in so royally taking in the public, especially the

---

[17] *Letters of Robert Browning and Elizabeth Barrett, 1845–1846,* Vol. I, pp. 428-429.

[18] Rémy de Gourmont, *Promenades littéraires,* pp. 378-379.

English, set him up in his self-esteem. He luxuriated in the sense of power it gave him. He was intoxicated by the sound of his name on everyone's lips. For more than a year now he had managed to get himself noticed, not so much by the publication of his works—"The Raven" and the Valdemar story excepted—as by the clamor he had raised by his attack on Longfellow.

He had started it in the *Evening Mirror* in 1845, when he had noticed or, rather, "used up" an unpretentious little anthology of poems, *The Waif*, edited by Longfellow. His parting shot betrayed the reason for his rancor. "We conclude our notes on 'The Waif' with the observation that, although full of beauties, it is infected with a *moral taint*—or is this a mere freak of our own fancy? We shall be pleased if it be so; but there *does* appear, in this little volume, a very careful avoidance of all American poets who may be supposed especially to interfere with the claims of Mr. Longfellow. These men Mr. Longfellow can continually *imitate* (*is* that the word?) and never even incidentally commend." [19]

The moral taint was, of course, plagiarism. The poets who interfered with Mr. Longfellow's claims were chiefly Poe and, by implication, such men as Lowell and Bryant, who had also been excluded. A number of Longfellow's friends came to his defense, pointing out that the anthology, by its very title, had merely collected the waifs and strays of literature, the songs of the humble, the anonymous poets. Poe stuck to his charge and for a number of issues attack and defense filled the columns of the *Mirror*, with Willis straddling both sides. Finally he chose for the victim and published a note declaring himself against the disparagement of Longfellow. In atonement for his part in it, Willis made room in his paper for a lengthy article in which one "Outis"—Greek for "Nobody"—picked up the cudgels for Longfellow with a will.

Poe, meanwhile, had gone over to the *Broadway Journal*, remarking to Mr. Briggs that Willis was too Willisy for him. While paying his critical compliments to Miss Barrett, Poe was also giving close attention to the "Outis" article and pondering his rebuttal. A clever fellow, that "Outis." Borrowing Poe's own methods, he had turned them against him, in the matter of parallels.

"I have before me an anonymous poem," he wrote, "which I saw some five years ago, entitled 'The Bird of the Dream' . . . The author was awakened from sleep by the song of a beautiful bird, sitting on the sill of his window . . . the sweet notes . . . brought to his remembrance, the sweeter voice of his lost 'Clare.' He says:

[19] E. A. Poe, *Works*, Vol. III, p. 292.

And thou wert in my dream—a spirit thou didst seem—
  The spirit of a friend long since departed;
Oh! she was fair and bright, but she left me one dark night—
  She left me all alone, and broken-hearted. . . .

My dream went on, and thou went on a warbling too,
  Mingling the harmonies of earth and heaven;
Till away—away—away—beyond the realms of day—
  My angel Clare to my embrace was given. . . .

Sweet bird from realms of light, oh: come again to-night
  Come to my window—perch upon my chair—
Come give me back again the deep impassioned strain
  That tells me thou hast seen and loved my Clare.

"Now I shall not charge Mr. Poe with plagiarism," "Outis" went on. "Ten to one, he never saw this before. But let us look at the *'identities'* that may be made out between this and 'The Raven.' *First,* in each case, the poet is a broken-hearted lover. *Second,* that lover longs for some hereafter communion with the departed. *Third,* there is a bird. *Fourth,* the bird is on the poet's window. . . ." One by one, "Outis" added up the parallels to the number of fifteen. "Moreover," he continued, "this poem contains an example of that kind of repetition which I have supposed the critic meant to charge upon Longfellow as one of his imitations—*Away—away—away,* etc. I might pursue it further. But I will not. Such criticisms only make the *author* of them contemptible, without soiling a plume in the cap of his victim. . . ." He went on, nonetheless, with poise and urbanity, and concluded: "I scarcely remember an instance where the resemblances detected were not exceedingly far-fetched and shadowy, and only perceptible in a mind pre-disposed to suspicion, and accustomed to splitting hairs." [20]

Poe would scarcely have been in character had he not seen a pointed allusion to himself in the last few words. Maintaining that no gentleman should degrade himself to *ex parte* argument, he retorted: "I shall not insult Outis at the outset, by assuming for a moment that he (Outis) is weak enough, to suppose me (Poe) silly enough, to look upon all this abominable rigmarole as anything better than a very respectable specimen of special pleading." [21]

He then proceeded to detect resemblances and to split hairs through five issues of the *Broadway Journal,* repeating the charges he had made earlier and adding new fuel to the fire. He must con-

[20] *Ibid.,* Vol. III, pp. 290-299.
[21] *Ibid.,* Vol. III, p. 299.

vince the world that in "The Spanish Student" Longfellow had stolen from *Politian*. Poe then chose as an example the scene wherein the heroine sits reading and muses aloud on her woes, and printed with it Longfellow's variant on the subject. The treatment of Poe's Lalage was as different from Longfellow's Preciosa as were the temperaments of the two poets, but to Poe, hipped on the subject, it was all arrant robbery—even to the stage directions, which he sought, not too convincingly, to turn into parallels. By the end of Poe's diatribe the worst that could be proved against Longfellow was that he was guilty of the sin of didacticism in his poems, and that he wrote hexameters.

Longfellow kept himself above the fray. He never penned a line or spoke a word against Poe. Once only, when neither praise nor blame could have touched Poe, he wrote with profound understanding: "The harshness of his criticisms, I have never attributed to anything but the irritation of a sensitive nature, chafed by some indefinite sense of wrong.' " [22]

Meanwhile Mr. Briggs, in spite of the success of the *Broadway Journal,* was writing uneasily to Lowell about his uncomfortable editor. "He has latterly got into his old habits and I fear he will injure himself irretrievably." [23]

As it happened, Lowell had seen it for himself when, on a recent visit to New York, where Page was painting his portrait, he called upon Poe. He found him a small man, with a clammy-white face but fine dark eyes and a fine head, though it receded sharply backwards from the brows. He noted Poe's formality and a certain pompousness. He also had the impression that Poe was soggy with drink—as if he had been holding his head under a pump to cool it. Mrs. Clemm, who did not once leave the room during the visit, he thought rather ordinary and uncultivated. He made no mention of Virginia. Poe, for his part, was also disappointed. "He was not half the noble looking person that I expected to see," he confided to another visiting poet, Dr. Thomas Holley Chivers.[24]

Meanwhile disaffection on the *Broadway Journal* increased. Poe who had no great opinion of anyone else's talents, yearned for full control of the magazine, from which poverty alone kept him. Mr. Briggs, who had at first rejoiced in the man who had built up his publication, now looked for the flaws which, alas, were all too evident. "Poe's mother-in-law told me that he was quite tipsy the day you called

[22] *Southern Literary Messenger,* November, 1849.
[23] Letter of June 29, 1854. Woodberry, p. 234.
[24] Chivers, *Life of Poe.*

upon him," he wrote to Lowell, "and that he acted very strangely. He was to have delivered a poem before the societies of the New York University a few weeks since, but drunkenness prevented him. He has been frequently carried home in a wretched condition. I am sorry for him. He has some good points, but, taken altogether, he is badly made up." Now that the floodgates of his grievances were open, he poured them all out. "He talks about dactyls and spondees with surprising glibness; and the names of metres being caviare to nine men out of ten, he has gained a reputation for erudition at a very cheap rate. He makes quotations from the German, but he can't read a word of the language." He had written this on the 16th of July, 1845. On the 21st of August Mr. Briggs was still complaining. "You have formed a correct estimate of Poe's characterless character. . . . He cannot conceive why the world should not feel an interest in whatever interests him, because he feels no interest himself in what does not personally concern him. Therefore, he attributes all the favor which Longfellow, yourself, or anybody else receives from the world as an evidence of the ignorance of the world. . . . He has no reverence for Homer, Shakespeare or Milton. . . . The Bible, he says, is all rigmarole. . . ."[25]

The relationship had quite obviously reached the breaking point. As it was, by this time both Mr. Briggs and Mr. Bisco had had enough of the *Journal*. First the one and then the other stepped out, Mr. Bisco relinquishing his rights to Poe on a promissory note of $50, signed by Poe and endorsed by Horace Greeley. Thus, on October 24, 1845, Poe had his own magazine. It was neither the *Penn* nor the *Stylus,* but he could make of it what he wished.

One day, in that same October, young Walt Whitman was lured into Niblo's Garden to hear a song recital by the Cheney Quartette, three young men and their sister, the children of a New Hampshire preacher who conducted singing classes in the country districts of his state. Whitman listened to their fresh, native notes and his great chest expanded as he heard the voice of America singing. When he reached home he sat down to write: "Great is the power of Music over a people! As for us of America, we have long enough followed obedient and child-like in the track of the Old World. We have received her tenors and her buffos . . . listened to and applauded the songs made for a different state of society—made, perhaps, by royal genius, but made to please royal ears likewise; and it is time that such listening and receiving should cease. The subtlest spirit of a nation is expressed through its music—and the music acts reciprocally on the

[25] Woodberry, pp. 234-238.

nation's very soul. . . ." He wrote on, pouring out his plea for the encouragement of native music. "There are two kinds of singing—heart-singing and art-singing. That which touches the soul and sympathies of other communities may have no effect here—unless it appeals to the great heart of humanity itself. . . ." [26]

There was one editor in whom he knew he would find a responsive note. He sent the article, "Art Singing and Heart Singing" to Poe, who published it in the *Broadway Journal* with a comment of his own: "It is scarcely necessary to add that we agree with our correspondent throughout." O wonderful accord, between Israfel and the New Adam! In the same issue Poe, characteristically, aimed a squib in the direction of the Transcendentalists: "The Frog Pond seems to be dried up—and the frogs are, beyond doubt, all dead—as we hear no more croaking from that quarter." So much for *that* native singing.

The *Broadway Journal,* alas, was soon to sing a swan song of its own, but not before Walt Whitman came to see Poe about his piece and perhaps to talk about future contributions. "Poe was very cordial, in a quiet way, appear'd well in person . . . very kindly and human, but subdued, perhaps a little jaded." [27]

Poe had reason to be subdued and even a little jaded. Virginia had been acutely ill. He himself was sick and depressed and, as he wrote to Mr. Duyckinck while requesting financial aid for the *Journal:* "I really believe that I have been mad—but indeed I have abundant reason to be so. . . ." [28] In his desperation he suspected a deliberate attempt on the part of "one or two" persons to involve him in ruin by destroying the *Journal.* Fitz-Greene Halleck lent him money. Griswold, too, helped to tide him over with $50. Others ignored his requests. Some, like Horace Greeley, he could not approach again as he had not been able to pay back the original loan. Nor was Poe ever to reimburse him. Greeley took it philosophically, if also wryly. A gushing youth once wrote him for any autograph of Poe's that Greeley might possess. "I promptly responded as follows," Greeley wrote in his *Recollections of a Busy Life:* " 'Sir—among my literary treasures, there happens to be exactly *one* autograph of . . . Edgar A. Poe. It is his note of hand for fifty dollars, with my indorsement across the back. It cost me exactly $50.75 (including protest) and you may have it at half that amount. . . .' That autograph, I regret to say, remains on my hands. . . ." [29]

[26] *Broadway Journal,* Nov. 29, 1845.
[27] Whitman, "Broadway Sights," *Specimen Days.*
[28] *Bulletin* of New York Public Library, VI (January), 1902.
[29] *Recollections of a Busy Life,* pp. 243-244.

CHAPTER XXIV

->>> · <<<-

The Lion among the Doves

ON THE 7th of May, 1846, Elizabeth Barrett, with a little feline purr, picked up one of her well-sharpened goose quills and wrote to Browning: "To-day I had a book sent to me from the poetess Mrs. Osgood. Did you ever hear of the poetess Mrs. Osgood? . . . and her note was of the very most affectionate, and her book is of the most gorgeous, all purple and gold—and she tells me . . . that I ought to go to New York, only 'to see Mr. Poe's wild eyes flash through tears' when he reads my verses. It is overcoming to think of, even . . . isn't it?" [1]

How did it happen that the poetess Mrs. Osgood addressed Miss Barrett, in the first place, and sent her a copy of her gorgeous volume, all purple and gold? The rather personal allusion to Mr. Poe's wild eyes gave the clue. Indeed, it was not unlikely that Mr. Poe himself had suggested that Mrs. Osgood speed her book to Miss Barrett, through whom—who knows?—it might reach London's literary circles. Certainly the mention of Mr. Poe had not been altogether casual.

As it was, Poe had become aware of Mrs. Frances Sargent Osgood early in 1842, when he published a story of hers in the March number of *Graham's* and her verses in subsequent issues. She was the daughter of a Boston merchant, Joseph Locke, and one of a talented family of children whom their proud parents encouraged. Her brother, A. A. Locke, was a well-known journalist. She herself had enjoyed the precocious glory of having her poems published in Mrs. Child's popular *Juvenile Miscellany*.

As a sentimental young woman of twenty-three she fell in love with a painter of twenty-six, Samuel S. Osgood, while he was working on her portrait and, like Othello with another Desdemona, beguiling her hours with tales of his adventures. They married and soon afterward went to live in London, where Mr. Osgood had many valuable connections, made during his years at the Royal Academy. Rogers, the

[1] *Letters,* 1845–1846, Vol. II, p. 133.

273

banker poet, was attracted by the fresh New England flower who breathed poetry as well as looked it. Others of his influential circle shared his admiration, so that when Mrs. Osgood's little volume, *A Wreath of Wild Flowers from New England,* came out it enjoyed its moment of fame. The Osgoods then returned to Boston, where, in 1841, Mrs. Osgood, still exploiting her floral theme, published *The Poetry of Flowers and Flowers of Poetry.* There was a certain sensibility in her lyrics, a feminine charm that overcame frequent deficiency of music; but she had vigor in her extended work, as in *The Daughters of Herodias,* which Poe had also taken for *Graham's.*

The Osgoods had been living for some time in New York and were already part of the intellectual circle whose ruling deity was the formidable bluestocking, Miss Anna C. Lynch. She was thirty years old, tall, slender, with fair looks, a fearless tongue and a withering stare for those beneath her intellectual, social or political demands. Not for her the poetic triflings of her sisters-in-letters on the tender sentiment. *She* plucked the lyre on such themes as "Bones in the Desert" and Italy's struggle for freedom, while, as for prose, nothing less would do than the production of a *Handbook of Universal Literature.* That, however, did not see the light until 1860, when she was the wife of Professor Vincenzo Botta. In comparison, even the extraordinary achievements of Margaret Fuller, as daring in her manner of life as in her works, seemed diminished.

The temple of the goddess was a large double parlor on Waverly Place. Fires glowed in hearths at both ends of the apartment, which had a certain austerity in the simplicity of its furnishings in an era that, in its clutter, liked to demonstrate the fullness of its purse. On her literary evenings Miss Lynch, flowingly dressed, would take her place at a corner near one of the fireplaces and welcome the guests as they were ushered in by a pert little maid of twelve. The lions and lionesses of the moment were certain to be present, happy to purr by Miss Lynch's fire or, at her invitation, to let out a lordly roar for the edification of the less distinguished guests.

Patriot martyrs of other countries were also welcome. There was Pietro Maroncelli, a short, slight Italian who bore the marks of his long imprisonment in his prematurely whitened hair and beard. One of his legs, gangrened by his shackles, had been amputated in the Spielberg prison. Back in his cell, he tapped on the wall to let his fellow prisoners in the adjoining cubicle—Silvio Pellico and Felice Foresti—know that he had survived. He had recently translated Pellico's *Le Mie Prigioni* into English, adding details from his own experience. Poe noted the animation on his worn features whenever he spoke of Italy, struggling to freedom from under Austria's heel.

Miss Margaret Fuller would often be there, an ardent advocate for Italy's liberation, her lustrous fair hair framing a plain but arresting face, her lips beautiful when in repose but most often agitated by her endless talk on the "Infinite me" which Lowell was to put into his *Fable for Critics:*

> She will take an old notion and make it her own
> By saying it o'er in a sibylline tone;
> Or persuade you 'tis something tremendously deep
> By repeating it so as to put you to sleep.
> And she well may defy any mortal to see through it
> When once she has mix'd up her infinite *me* in it.

Only when discoursing on Italy in chains did she forget her transcendentalism to predict the glory of the freedom that was to be. Some predictions she would not herself have believed—her marriage in Italy to the young Marquis Angelo d'Ossoli; their heroic role on the Roman barricades; a son of her own.

Other remarkable women adorned the Waverly Place gatherings— Mrs. E. Oakes Smith, who was taking up the cudgels for the emancipation of her sex, and handsome Mrs. Cora Mowatt, author of a scintillating little play, a social satire called *Fashion.* She was about to produce it herself—a daring thing for a woman to do, and which had all the starry sisterhood aflutter. Last but not least there, too, sitting on a footstool, would be found little Mrs. Osgood, her face upturned to the speaker of the evening, her wide eyes beaming their admiration from a face that had the look of an Italian *madonnina,* by one of the lesser painters. Thomas Dunn English, not overly sympathetic, perhaps because Mrs. Osgood chose to sit at his feet and cramp his position, described her as doing "the infantile act."

Poe had become aware of Frances Sargent Osgood for more than her poetry. Her small, graceful person, her exotic look, her gray, luminous, expressive eyes appealed to him. It was not with wholly impersonal appreciation that on the 28th of February, 1845, when he lectured on American Poetry at the Society Library, he singled her out, with N. P. Willis and Thomas Holley Chivers, for his illustrative recitations.

The *Tribune,* reporting the lecture the following day, did not like his renditions. "His lecture gained nothing from the graces of his elocution," it said, "and in one or two instances we thought the Poets suffered more from his recitation of their verses than from his most savage criticism. . . ."

The latter, of course, had been reserved for Longfellow, whom Poe was still ruthlessly attacking. "We are rather ashamed to add," the reporter resumed on another tack, "that this Lecture by a Poet and critic of genius and established reputation, was listened to but by some three hundred of our four hundred thousand people. Any dancing dog or summersetting monkey would have drawn a larger house."

Not impervious to Poe's compliments to him, N. P. Willis returned them in the *Evening Mirror,* on March 12, when he reviewed the lecture. "He becomes a desk—his beautiful head showing like a statuary embodiment of discrimination. His accent drops like a knife through water, and his style is so much purer and clearer than the pulpit commonly gets or requires that the effect of what he says, besides other things, pampers the ear." Perhaps Willis understood what he was writing. No one else did.

Poe's public tribute to herself had not escaped Mrs. Osgood. When, therefore, a few days later he sent her through Willis a copy of "The Raven" for her opinion, she read it eagerly. "Its effect upon me was singular," she wrote, "so like that of 'wierd, [*sic*] unearthly music,' that it was with a feeling almost of dread, I heard he desired an introduction." For all her premonition, the temptation was too strong. She met Poe through his innocent intermediary in the drawing room of the Astor House, where Willis lived. "With his proud and beautiful head erect, his dark eyes flashing with the elective [*sic*] light of feeling and of thought, a peculiar, an inimitable blending of sweetness and hauteur in his expression and manner, he greeted me, calmly, gravely, almost coldly . . ." she described their first meeting.[2]

It was not long before the coldness melted and the calm changed to that nervous exaltation which Poe experienced whenever erotically aroused. Mrs. Osgood, with her blend of childlikeness and passion, exerted a spell over sensitive natures, for not only Poe, but the Rev. Mr. Griswold, had succumbed to it. In a volume of Leigh Hunt's poems which Griswold had presented to her, he had inscribed:

> Would I were anything that thou dost love,
> A flower, a bird, a wavelet or a gem.

Her fascination must indeed have been potent to inspire such strange desires.

However it was, not long after that first meeting between Poe and

[2] Griswold, *Memoir,* Vol. I, *Works,* p. liii.

Mrs. Osgood, the *Broadway Journal* began publishing a series of amorous lyrics. The first appeared in the issue of April 5, 1846, and bore the title, "So Let it Be, To ————." It was by a lovelorn Violet Vane and its burden pleaded for friendship, if not love:

> Perhaps you think it right and just,
>   Since you are bound by nearer ties,
> To greet me with that careless tone,
>   With those serene and silent eyes. . . .
>
> The fair fond girl, who at your side
>   Within your soul's dear light doth live,
> Could hardly have the heart to chide
>   The ray that friendship well might give. . . .

On April 12 verses signed Frances S. Osgood, but bearing the stamp of Violet Vane, begged the reluctant one, among other things, to "write *from your heart to me*," and later, under the pseudonym of Kate Carol, gushed forth with "The Rivulet's Dream."

Poe, who had been remarkably prudent so far, at last addressed a few lines "To F————" which had earlier served for other fair ones:

> Beloved! amid the earnest woes
>   That crowd around my earthly path—
> (Drear path, alas! where grows
> Not even one lonely rose)—
>   My soul at least a solace hath
> In dreams of thee, and therein knows
> An Eden of bland repose.

As an afterthought, he added an "impromptu" to Kate Carol:

> When from your gems of thought I turn
> To those pure orbs, your heart to learn,
> I scarce know what to prize most high—
> The bright *i-dea,* or bright *dear-eye.*[3]

It was hardly the response of an impassioned male, but the reticence existed only in print. As it was, literary gossips had already begun to whisper. Before the end of the summer they were going full blast. Under the excitation of so ardent a flame Poe was often "not himself." Mrs. Clemm thought it rather unfortunate, for at that very time Dr. Thomas Holley Chivers, who had been one of the few to respond to the *Penn* project, was visiting in New York and often called upon Eddie.

[3] *Broadway Journal,* April 26, 1845.

Dr. Chivers was one of those products of nature designed to be a genius but who, through some flaw in his components, wavered between brilliance and eccentricity. Thanks to his father, a Georgia planter rich in land and slaves, Chivers studied at the Transylvania University and took his degree in medicine. He preferred painting and writing poetry to practicing his profession, however. He also had an inventive mind back of his tremendous brow rising in an irregular arch above his earnest, too earnest, eyes. Out of that mind, besides some of the most peculiar poetry that America was ever to read, also came practical and profitable inventions—among them a machine for unwinding the fiber from the cocoons of the silkworm.

Poe had first noticed Chivers in the *Southern Literary Messenger.* Later he also treated him to an "autography" which was hardly flattering to the Shelley-mad Chivers, who thought himself Ariel's American incarnation. On his manifesting interest in the *Penn,* Poe's attitude toward him altered, especially when he found the Georgian not averse to lending him money now and then. An epistolary friendship began in 1840, but it was not until the summer of 1845, when the Poes were still boarding at 195 East Broadway, that Chivers called upon them.

By then Chivers had acquired a certain, if dubious, reputation for his curious poems which, at their best, sounded like inferior Blake and at their worst like the lucubrations of a madman intoxicated with sound. Yet he could be capable of grandeur, as in his lines on the Mississippi:

> We look on thy bosom, but cannot control
> The terror that strikes from the heart to the soul!
> We know thee unique in the East and the West,
> Who look'st in a calm like a lion at rest!

One of the best and one of the worst poets in America, Poe had called him; but he also found that even his worst nonsense—and Chivers had plenty of it—had an indefinite charm of sentiment and melody. Still, the most solicitous concern for his *Penn* or his *Stylus* could not blind Poe to such gems as Chivers' "To Allegra Florence in Heaven," voicing the grief of a father for his lost child:

> As an egg when broken, never can be mended, but must ever
> Be the same crushed egg for ever, so shall this dark heart of mine
> Which though broken still is breaking, and shall never more cease aching
> For the sleep which hath no waking—for the sleep that now is thine.[4]

[4] Woodberry, "Poe-Chivers Papers." *Century Magazine,* February, 1903, p. 557.

Simple and literal-minded, in spite of his noble dome, Chivers saw no reason for not using the homely analogy of a cracked egg and a father's broken heart. Indeed, he was proud of it, as of his metre, which he was certain Poe had stolen for "The Raven." Furthermore, was there not a "never more" in this stanza? For the present Chivers said nothing about it, since Poe was kind enough to review his booklet, "The Lost Pleiad and Other Poems" in the *Journal,* where he described it as "the honest, fervent utterance of an exquisitely sensitive heart which has suffered much and long. . . . The poet seems to have dwelt among the shades of the tombs, until his very soul has become a shadow. . . . The thesis . . . is *death* of beloved friends. . . ." [5]

In that thesis poet and reviewer had much in common. Poe, however, could not follow him in his eccentricities and floridities of style. Once, in all seriousness, Chivers expostulated: "When will this world learn Charity—that fairest, most beautiful Daughter of Religion of whom Christ became so enamoured, that he not only died for her, but took her up into Heaven where he now enjoys her as his wife." [6]

Of Poe himself Chivers left a portrait certainly unique in style, yet somehow capturing the man. "I would say that he was the Greek Prometheus chained to the Mount Caucasus of demi-civilized Humanity, with the black vulture of Envy feeding on his self-replenished heart. . . . His countenance was tropical in its aspect—precisely the reverse of his heart, which like the fountains of Solomon, had long been kept sealed up, as something sacred, from the vulgar gaze of the world. . . . His digestion was always good—which is *prima facie* evidence that he *was never a student.* . . . His voice was soft, mellow . . . as the prismy-lipped Shell when mumuring of its never-tiring reminiscences of the ever-sounding Sea. . . ." [7]

Too humorless a man to strive for effect at the expense of truth, Chivers may be trusted in his reports of his impressions which, discounting the peculiarities in which they are couched, are at the very least sincere.

It was during the first week of their acquaintance that Chivers, walking down Nassau Street, saw the familiar figure of Poe "tottering from side to side as drunk as an Indian, while at the corner of Ann I saw a man standing on the steps of either a Whiskey Shop or a Restaurant, spouting at the top of his voice in his praise . . . calling him the *Shakespeare of America.* As soon as he met me, he grasped me

[5] *Broadway Journal,* Aug. 2, 1845.
[6] MSS, Huntington Library.
[7] MSS, Huntington Library.

by the coat collar, exclaiming, 'By G——d! Here is my friend now! Where are you going? Come, you must go home with me.'" [8]

Chivers took him by the arm and they were going in the direction of East Broadway when Poe, seeing Lewis Gaylord Clark talking with another man, attempted to pull himself away from Chivers' grasp, determined to attack Clark for some adverse comments upon him in the *Knickerbocker*. "No, Poe," said Chivers. "You must not do so while walking with me."

"I will, by G——d," he continued, dragging Chivers along.

On seeing Poe's fierce determination Clark's companion made off as discreetly as possible. Chivers feared the worst when Poe suddenly offered Clark his hand. "Why, Poe! Is this you?" exclaimed Clark.

"Yes, by G——d! This is Poe," he replied. "And here's my friend Dr. Chivers from the South." Suddenly he said, in a belligerent tone: "What business had you to abuse me in the last number of your magazine?"

"Why, by G——d, Poe!" exclaimed Clark, sidling off toward the curb. "How did I know the article referred to was yours? You had always attached your name to all your articles before, and how in Hell did I know it was yours?"

While talking Clark had cunningly bowed himself off, leaving the two men in the middle of Nassau Street. Hooking his arm in Chivers' with an air of triumph, Poe chuckled: "A damned coward, by G——d!" and, pulling his companion along, walked on till they came to Chatham Street. Suddenly he stopped short. "I am now going to reveal to you the very secrets of my heart," he said. "I am in the d——dst amour you ever knew a fellow to be in all your life and I make no hesitation in telling you about it—as though you were my own brother. But, by G——d! don't say anything about it to my wife—for she is a noble creature, whom I would not hurt for all the world."

"Well, what is it, Poe?" asked Chivers. "I'm anxious to hear it. Where is the lady with whom you're so in love?"

"In Providence, by G——d!" he said. "I've just received a letter from her, in which she requests me to come on there this afternoon on the four o'clock boat. Her husband is a painter—always from home—and a damned fool at that!"

Poe said no more, for before they got to East Broadway he was so far gone that Chivers had all he could do to keep him from falling

[8] This and the following scenes have been derived from the *Poe-Chivers Papers* at the Henry E. Huntington Library. Parts have been published as Chivers' *Life of Poe,* edited by Richard Beale Davis.

in the street. Just as they were staggering up the steps of the house, Chivers saw Virginia looking out of the window. Seeing her husband in that condition, she quickly drew her head back. When they got upstairs she had locked herself in her room. Mrs. Clemm met him at the door, exclaiming gently: "Oh, Eddie! Eddie! Eddie, come here my dear boy! Let me put you to bed."

She took off his coat and helped him onto the bed, covering him with the counterpane. "Oh, dear Dr. Chivers!" she said, with tears in her eyes. "How I have prayed that my poor Eddie might not get in this way while you were on here. But I knew when he went away from here this morning that he would not return in his right senses. Oh, I do believe that the poor boy is deranged! His wife is now at the point of death with bronchitis and cannot bear to see him! Oh, my poor Virginia! She cannot live long!"

She poured out all her troubles, yet was careful to call Virginia's disease by a less fearful name than consumption. "My poor child!" she went on, relieved to have a sympathetic ear. "He has been here in bed for a whole week with nothing in the world the matter with him—only lying here pretending to be sick, in order to avoid delivering the poem promised, before one of the literary societies. . . . Now he is in this deranged state again. My poor child! What will become of her?"

Virginia, in her despair over her husband's condition, did not show herself during Chiver's visit.

When he called the following day, Poe was not there, but on the next, Chivers found him in bed, saying he was sick, though there was nothing the matter with him. Hiring a carriage, Chivers coaxed him out for a ride. As they were jogging along the doctor teased him about his fair inamorata. Looking as shamefaced as any adolescent under similar circumstances, Poe, "walling up his eyes under the narrow brim of his hat," denied being involved with any woman, either in Providence or anywhere else.

The following afternoon, on going to call on him again, Chivers met Poe dressed in his best, walking toward the *Journal* office, from which he then intended going to Providence. He had not the least coin in his pocket and borrowed $10 from Chivers, swearing him not to breathe a word of his adventure to Virginia or to Mrs. Clemm. *Someone,* he said, had written him to come and he was obliged to go, but he promised to be back next day. Mrs. Osgood had won.

Her poems in the *Broadway Journal* now became more impassioned, more incautious. She signed them with her own name. On September 6, on the front page, appeared her "Echo-Song":

I know a noble heart that beats
   For one it loves how 'wildly well!'
I only know for *whom* it beats;
   But I must never tell!
      Never tell! . . .

I know a smile that beaming flies
   From soul to lip, with rapturous glow,
And I can guess who bids it rise,
   But none—but none shall know! . . .
      None shall know. . . .

The irony of it was that many did know, and those who merely surmised found confirmation for their suspicions in the novelette, *Ida Grey,* published by Mrs. Osgood in *Graham's,* in August, 1845. "No:—I will not attempt to deny it. She was a coquette—a desperate one—a coquette by nature—yet wild, reckless, wayward and often heartless as she appeared—everybody seemed to love her, and to be happy in her presence. . . . She was the veriest sunbeam that ever gladdened the weary, weary world with beauty and light. . . . She was a privileged person, too, and was not to be judged by common rules." So the story opened, in the words of one who had known Ida Grey. At twenty-four—Mrs. Osgood had made herself ten years younger— she was a widow. Though she had loved her husband in her way, "he was a sort of cypher in the world—scarcely more a cypher dead than alive."

One night, at a brilliant party, Ida's gaze was riveted on a distant part of the room. Then she blushed deeply. A little later there approached "a remarkable looking man, whose face once seen could never be forgotten. . . . His keen grey eyes were bent with singular earnestness upon her face, and though his manner and expression were coldly courteous, there was a peculiar depth in his tone which only some strong emotion could have given it."

It was as close a description of the meeting and the man as fiction would allow. In the story Ida Grey dies, but she conveniently leaves a journal which traces the progress of her love. It is so detailed, so deeply felt, so true to what actually happened, that Mrs. Osgood had merely transposed to fiction what had been fact.

"I have seen him as last!—him of whom I have read and heard so much. . . . I knew that he had heard much of me, and had sought an introduction. . . . I was foolish enough to expect that he would meet me frankly and cordially, and that we should be friends at once. But no! he was strangely distant. We spoke but a few formal words, and then we parted—parted! ah no; we shall never part again. Our souls are one forever. Yes! cold and careless as he seems, he loves me—or *will* love me. . . . He is married. His wife, they say, is cold and does not love him. . . . If destiny had willed her to love him, he would have loved *her*—and do I not know that he is *my* destiny? She will find hers hereafter."

Disposing of the wife in this cavalier fashion, Ida Grey revels in her love. "He had written to me words of almost divine passion. . . . He feels . . . that God has sent him to me—to calm my heart—to spiritualize my being—to wean me from the world. . . ." [9]

Poe, meanwhile, still enjoying the fame that "The Raven" had brought him, was often in demand for lectures and readings. In July of that year he had been requested by the Rutgers Institute to read the winning poem in a competition that had been held among the refined young females of that school. For the occasion the commencement exercises were taking place at the Rutgers Street Church, and a number of distinguished guests, among them Henry T. Tuckerman, had been invited. As editor of the *Boston Miscellany* he was both flattered and feared by the literary confraternity, though he would have preferred their appreciation, even their envy, for his Petrarchan sonnets and the refined chastity of his style. The vulgar brutes, however, labeled his stiffness *tuckermanity* and ridiculed it whenever they could. Poe disliked him—first of all, because Tuckerman had refused his "Tell-Tale Heart" for the *Miscellany;* secondly, because he was a Frogpondian. Respecting the amenities of the occasion, however, they shook hands cordially and forgot their differences.

While the beaming parents jammed the pews of the church, Poe, rising from his place on the platform among the professors, lent his famed voice to the reading of an innocuous screed that seemed to have won for its length, more than for its merit. It was a well-publicized affair, however, the *Mirror* of July 19, 1845, devoting to it no fewer than seven pages. Such publicity offered Poe the incense that his self-esteem required to offset the uncertainties deep within, which found expression when he had been drinking. To an acquaintance who met him shortly after his success Poe, obviously not himself, declared that he would soon be reading "The Raven" before Queen Victoria.

He was invited, instead, by the no less exalted Boston Lyceum—not, however, to deliver his famous Bird, but to read a new poem for the occasion. The date was set for the 16th of October, giving Israfel several months during which to draw accords from his heart-

[9] *Graham's Magazine,* August, 1845.

strung lute. Unhappily, inspiration would not come. As the weeks passed and he had not yet produced a line, he took to his bed, where Chivers had found him.

Earlier that year, in the preface to *The Raven and Other Poems,* Poe had written: "With me poetry has been not a purpose, but a passion; and the passions should be held in reverence; they must not— they cannot at will be excited with an eye to the paltry compensations, or the more paltry commendations, of mankind." What amounted to an order for a poem dried up the wellsprings, like an intellectual drought.

In his frustration Poe turned to Mrs. Osgood. Her facile pen was soon gushing out a Niagara of lines. But, alas, they would not do. Anyone could have told instantly that the voice was not Israfel's.

In July Poe had published in *Graham's* "The Imp of the Perverse," a story in which, with subtle insight, he analyzed the injurious impulse that makes human beings do the very thing that leads to their destruction, however earnestly they seek to avoid it. Prompted by the imp, Poe decided to read before the Boston Brahmins a work as transcendental as any they could produce: "Al Aaraaf." Despair at his sterility, as well as arrogant defiance of the school he detested, suggested his choice.

Accordingly, on the 16th of October, Poe, among other distinguished men, occupied the platform of the Lyceum, while Mr. Caleb Cushing, who preceded him, was terminating his address. The audience, as Poe could see, was large and distinguished. It was also enthusiastic, to judge by the applause it gave the speaker.

When his turn came, Poe rose. Instead of beginning his reading, he perorated for some fifteen minutes on the evils of didactic poetry— poetry with a moral being a favorite with the Transcendentalists. Not content with this breach of etiquette in his hosts' domain, he declared that a didactic poem was no poem at all, thus throwing out a great deal of Emerson and of other transcendental worthies. He then commenced to read "Al Aaraaf."

"If he uttered poesy in the first instance, it was certainly of a most prosaic order," wrote Miss Cornelia M. Walter, editor of the *Boston Transcript,* the following day. "The audience listened in amazement to a singularly didactic exordium, and finally commenced the noisy expedient of removing from the hall, and this long before they had discovered the style of the measure, or whether it was rhythm or blank verse. . . . Another small poem succeeded. This was 'The Raven'—a composition probably better appreciated by its author than by his auditory. . . ." To leave no doubt of Mr. Poe's reception by the Bostonians, Miss Walter headed her article *A Failure.*

In vain Poe elaborately sought to contradict her in the *Broadway Journal,* in the facetious tone he usually employed to conceal a hurt. The failure rankled. To have *his* poem described as didactic capped the injury. Miss Walter's attack was part of a plot against him, he was certain. "The adorable creature has been telling a parcel of fibs about us, by way of revenge for something that we did to Mr. Longfellow (who admires her very much). . . . The Bostonians have no soul. They have always evinced toward us individually, the basest ingratitude for the services we rendered them in enlightening them about the originality of Mr. Longfellow."

As for the poem—did the Bostonians imagine he would have put himself to the trouble of composing an original work for them? "We did not. We had a poem . . . lying by us—one quite as good as new—one, at all events, that we considered would answer sufficiently well for an audience of Transcendentalists. *That* we gave them—it was the best that we had—for the price. . . . The poem is what is occasionally called a 'juvenile poem.' . . . We wrote it, printed it and published it, in book form, before we had fairly completed our tenth year. . . . It did well enough. . . ." [10]

After Miss Walter's reception, it was a welcome relief for the ruffled Raven to return to his admiring doves and his poetic exchanges with the chosen one. If any still had doubt of the liaison between poet and poetess, they had clarification in the poem, "To ——" which Mrs. Osgood prefaced with the motto from "Israfel," a name which had but one association.

> I cannot tell the world how thrills my heart
> To every touch that flies thy lyre along,
> How the wild Nature and the wondrous Art
> Blend into Beauty in thy passionate song—
>
> But this I *know*—in thine enchanted slumbers
> Heaven's poet, Israfel,—with minstrel fire—
> Taught thee the music of his own sweet numbers,
> And tuned—to chord with his—thy glorious lyre.

By a freak of chance Mrs. Osgood's lines, addressed to one American immortal, found themselves directly above the essay on "heart singing" by another whose immortality still lay before him, Whitman.

[10] *Broadway Journal,* Nov. 1, 1845.

CHAPTER XXV

Three Valentines

SINCE 1844 Poe had been working on a poem, "Eulalie," altering and improving it in his customary fashion. In July, 1845, at the height of his involvement with Mrs. Osgood, he published it in the *American Review*. It was not, however, addressed to her.

> I dwelt alone
> In a world of moan,
> And my soul was a stagnant tide,
> Till the fair and gentle Eulalie became my blushing bride—
> Till the yellow-haired young Eulalie became my smiling bride.
>
> Ah, less—less bright
> The stars of the night
> Than the eyes of the radiant girl!
> And never a flake
> That the vapour can make
> With the moon-tints of purple and pearl,
> Can vie with the modest Eulalie's most unregarded curl—
> Can compare with the bright-eyed Eulalie's most humble and careless curl.
>
> Now Doubt—now Pain
> Come never again,
> For her soul gives me sigh for sigh,
> And all day long
> Shines, bright and strong,
> Astarté within the sky,
> While ever to her dear Eulalie upturns her matron eye—
> While ever to her young Eulalie upturns her violet eye.

Eulalie—"the sweet spoken"—was Virginia, the young wife, still beloved, still the embodiment of his ideal of beauty—Virginia, mature now in her womanhood and upturning to him her "matron eye." The publication of "Eulalie," besides affirming his love for her, gave to the literary coterie—the Mrs. Ellets, the Mrs. Lewises, who hoped

for critical or other favors, yes, even to Mrs. Osgood—a clear understanding of his dedication to his wife.

Indeed, Mrs. Osgood, unlike other women in her situation, had no
illusion of herself as being the great love of Poe's life, however much
she deluded herself in her writings. When, at Virginia's urging, Mrs.
Osgood was admitted into the close little household, she had occasion to note the relations between husband and wife. "Of the charming love and confidence that existed between his wife and himself,
always delightfully apparent to me, in spite of the many little poetical
episodes, in which the impassioned romance of his temperament impelled him to indulge. . . . I believe she was the only woman whom
he ever truly loved." [1] She had a just perspective on her own poetical
episode with the poet who, until the demise of the *Broadway Journal,*
had traced its course in the magazine. Although her own poetical
source kept gushing as freely in December as it had in the spring,
Poe's had frozen. He had to resort to the printing of an Italian sonnet by Fabio Galeota to tell her how he counted every moment till
he could fly toward her glorious orbs. [2]

A change, however, had also come over Mrs. Osgood's muse, ex-
plicable by the appearance, on December 13, of certain verses where
hers should have been. They were signed Elizabeth E. Ellet, a poetess
whose feline claws had been reaching out toward Poe, even though
she was married to a famous professor of chemistry. The verses,
headed "Coquette's Song," left no doubt whatsoever as to whom they
were addressed. Their meaning, moreover, was certainly explicit.

> Ah, yes—gentle sir—I will own
>   I ne'er saw perfection till now;
> That I never—no never—have known
>   A smile such as yours—I'll allow.
> And your eyes—Oh, they speak to the soul
>   With their glances as bright as the day
> But *I* mean to keep my heart whole—
>   So away with your love-vows—away.
>
> .   .   .   .
>
> No, no—I assure you 'tis vain
>   To sigh and to plead and to woo;
> But I'll own, if I *could* wear a chain,
>   I would have it—yes—woven by you.

The sentimental charade went on, as Poe, the Orpheus, disputed
by the two Bacchantes, gave each a fair hearing. The next issue of

[1] Griswold, *Memoir.* Vol. I, *Works of Edgar Allan Poe,* p. liii.
[2] *Broadway Journal,* Dec. 6, 1845.

the *Journal* carried in the first column Mrs. Osgood's "To the 'Lady Geraldine,' " reproving Mrs. Ellet for her treason to one who had always been her friend. Besides,

> Was it so blest—my life's estate—
> That you with envy viewed me?
> Ah, false one! could you dream my fate,
> You had not thus pursued me.

> Perhaps when those who loved me once
> Beguiled by you have left me,
> You'll grieve for all the hopes of which
> Your whispered words bereft me.

The demise of the *Journal* with the issue of January 3, 1846, put an end to the poetic exchange, though not to the gossip it had elicited. Despite the assumed names, everyone in Miss Lynch's circle, at the gatherings of the Greeleys and Margaret Fuller, in the parlor of Mrs. Sarah Anna Lewis, the Brooklyn poetess who kept in evidence a bust of Pallas with a stuffed raven perched upon it—everyone was more than aware of the identity of each person concerned, and each reacted according to his or her involvement with the participants in that public drama.

Of them all, only Virginia and Mrs. Clemm, being closest to the protagonist and knowing him best, had the right perspective, though not without qualms. Now and then Virginia would accompany her husband to some literary soirée. The guests were struck by the vivacity of her expression, though none remarked upon anything she ever said. Quiet, modest, the reflection of Edgar's brilliance sufficed for her. Amid those fashionable women, dressed in the extravagant furbelows of the moment, she made a quaint yet striking figure in her homemade gown of some crimson stuff, trimmed with yellow lace—colors no doubt chosen by Poe.

Mrs. Clemm never appeared in the elegant world. Indeed, she would have jarred like a clucking, scratching, provident hen in those cotes of plump, sleek-plumaged doves. She preferred it when they called upon her at home—like dear Mrs. Osgood and Mrs. Ellet. Then she would pour out the tale of the family's poverty and hardship, while discreetly presenting a metaphorical basket to receive whatever might drop into it.

Of course intrigue would play its part, the jealous Bacchantes keeping eyes and ears open for any advantage on the part of a rival in the favors of their Orpheus. With the cunning of her need Mrs.

Clemm played upon these rivalries. In that loyal clan, huddled in narrow rooms—as now at 85 Amity Street—Poe had no secrets and Mrs. Clemm no reticence in reading the intimate correspondence of amorous females.

Virginia, incapable of jealousy in the simplicity of her devotion, made friends with Eddie's admirers and, in Mrs. Osgood's case, actually encouraged her for the good influence she seemed to exert upon him. "Virginia, his sweet wife, had written me a pressing invitation to come to them," wrote Mrs. Osgood of one of these visits. "I found him just completing his series of papers entitled 'The Literati of New York.' 'See,' said he, displaying, in laughing triumph, several little rolls of narrow paper . . . 'I am going to show you, by the difference of length of these, the different degrees of estimation in which I hold all you literary people. . . . Come, Virginia, help me!' And one by one they unfolded them. At last they came to one which seemed interminable. . . . 'And whose lengthened sweetness long drawn out is that?' said I. 'Hear her!' he cried, 'just as if her little vain heart didn't tell her it's herself!' "[3]

The breach following the *Journal* revelations soon healed and the friendship was resumed, although without its earlier fervor. Mrs. Osgood had come out of it chastened—but also relieved. At the very height of the affair, when Poe had been joining her in Providence, in Boston, in Lowell—where she sought as much to escape him as to lure him—she had been warned by feminine misgivings that he might prove an importunate responsibility which, in her situation as a married woman with children, she was reluctant to assume. Through it all her husband had been an indulgent, perhaps indifferent "cypher." She had to extricate herself somehow. With feline cunning she had made her first effort as early as the Providence meeting when she had tried to lead him, on a moonlight night, to the house of a spiritual sister, Mrs. Sarah Helen Whitman, a poetess, ethereal, of frail health, well-to-do, and a widow. Poe, however, refused to go there, and with such obstinacy that the lovers had their first quarrel.

In the reconciliation following the *Journal* serial, Mrs. Osgood made sure that, while still retaining Poe's friendship, she chastised him for the "Lady Geraldine" interlude and discouraged further resumption of intimacy. To that end she encouraged the lovelorn Rev. Mr. Griswold, who had long been panting at her dainty heels. Poe, evidently, took notice and protested, for she defended her fickleness in "Caprice," which *Graham's* printed in February, 1846.

[3] Griswold, *Memoir, op. cit.,* p. liii.

> Reprove me not that still I change
>   With every changing hour,
> For glorious nature gives me leave
>   In wave and cloud and flower. . . .
>
> 'Tis true you played, on feeling's lyre,
>   A pleasant tune or two;
> And oft beneath your minstrel fire
>   The hours in music flew. . . .
>
> Be less—thou art no love of mine—
>   So leave my love in peace!
> 'Tis helpless woman's right divine,
>   Her only right, Caprice.

Undeterred, Poe responded with a valentine, spelling out her name in the first, second and succeeding letters of the lines. Its reading at Miss Lynch's on February 14, 1846, was much appreciated, though oddly enough the poet misspelled the lady's middle name as Sergeant, instead of Sargent. Mrs. Osgood, too, had honored the day of the patron saint of lovers, but in her verses her own name was intertwined with that of a certain reverend gentleman.

There was still another valentine composed on that day, and for one of the principals; but it was neither read at Miss Lynch's nor published in a newspaper. It was lovingly written, in a clear hand, and the first letters spelled the name Edgar Allan Poe.

> Ever with thee I wish to roam—
> Dearest my life is thine.
> Give me a cottage for my home
> And a rich old cypress vine,
> Removed from the world with its sin and care
> And the tattling of many tongues.
> Love alone shall guide us when we are there—
> Love shall heal my weakened lungs;
> And Oh, the tranquil hours we'll spend,
> Never wishing that others may see!
> Perfect ease we'll enjoy, without thinking to lend
> Ourselves to the world and its glee—
> Ever peaceful and blissful we'll be.
>   Saturday February 14, 1846

The verse is halting, the expression of the utmost naïveté; yet Virginia's untutored lines stir the heart by their very awkwardness. "Give me a cottage for my home, removed from the world and the tattling of many tongues," she asks of the man whom other women claimed.

"Love alone shall guide us . . . love shall heal my weakened lungs." It is the cry of a feeling, sensitive woman, in love with her husband, wanting him for herself. These lines alone are sufficient to give the lie once for all to the legend of the "child-wife," of little Virginia who never grew up.

Virginia's pathetic allusion to her weakened lungs was an understatement; her hope of healing, a vain dream. Her mother and her husband had learned to live with her disease and did all they could to help. They knew there was no cure. Poe had met Dr. Valentine Mott and Mrs. Marie Louise Shew, a capable nurse. He also knew Dr. John Wakefield Francis, who used to frequent the salons of the literati. They may have been called upon in times of crisis—particularly Dr. Francis, a short, florid, stout man in his late fifties, with tangled gray locks and literary pretensions, who had treated Poe on several occasions.

With the coming of spring the Poes left Amity Street and sought refuge in the Turtle Bay section, as the boarders of Mr. and Mrs. John L. Miller, friends of the Brennans. The farmhouse, situated in what is now 47th Street and Second Avenue, consisted of two stories, with a brick basement and an attic of three rooms, the middle one high-ceilinged, the other two with a roof that sloped to within three feet of the floor.[4] It was here that the Poes lodged.

Though it was not the cottage that Virginia dreamed of, it was at least removed from the tattling of many tongues, and if it lacked its cypress vine, it made up for it by the blaze of red honeysuckle at the end of the front porch and by the syringa bushes on the north. An orchard of apples, pears, apricots and cherries, all in bloom, contrasted with the dark row of Lombardy poplars bordering the place. In the middle of the garden, in a clump of lilacs, a marble "monument" marked the street and avenue.

The Millers, simple people, lived comfortably on their farm with their children, one of whom was Sarah, a favorite with Poe, and the boy Le Fevre, then about ten years old. "I remember the first night they were at our house," recalled Le Fevre. "Mrs. Clemm took her lamp, it was a brass one burning oil. . . . My mother could not remember her name. 'It is Clem, think of Clams, it may help you to remember.' And Virginia, that is Mrs. Poe, had a dreadful cough, was very pale and seldom left the house, was very quiet and always looked pleasant. Mrs. Clemm was tall and dignified, always cheerful except

---

[4] Description derived from a typewritten letter of J. Le Fevre Miller, son of the Millers, to his great-niece, Mrs. Mabel E. Heine. It is dated Sept. 26, 1922. In the archives of the New York Historical Society.

when [she] got talking to my mother (who was always a sympathetic listener) of her troubles. She did not always approve of the way 'Eddie' acted and I heard her tell my mother how Eddie let his wife go home from a literary meeting alone while he escorted a Mrs. —— home as he said to Virginia it was necessary to show Mrs. —— courtesy on account of her standing in literary society, and Virginia the timid child would go several blocks crying and trembling with fear all the way." [5]

In these vivid words one can almost hear Mrs. Clemm as she confided her troubles to a sympathetic heart, and the bitterness of the mother against the Mrs. —— whose favor had to be propitiated at the expense of her poor, timid Virginia.

Le Fevre also recalled that Poe was very intemperate at the time. One day, while intoxicated, Poe took Mr. Miller's rowboat and went to his favorite swimming place, the cluster of islands just south of Blackwell's. Suddenly he began to shout for help, saying that he was drowning. When two fishermen went to his rescue he became abusive and said that if he had a "screw auger" he would dive under their craft and sink them. "I never liked Mr. Poe's eyes, but Mrs. Poe had beautiful large loving eyes. . . . I never liked Mr. Poe. I think he didn't like little boys, he never tried to be friendly with me and I was afraid of him and kept out of his way. He liked my sisters and gave one of them [Sarah] a small Chinese puzzle of carved ivory." [6]

At that time Poe was still writing for *Godey's* the series of articles on New York personalities, *The Literati,* in which he combined critical opinion of their works with character sketches. Great and small, they found their place in the design—from the Rev. Mr. George Bush, professor of Hebrew at the University of New York, through Richard Adams Locke, known for his "Moon Story," a skillfully perpetrated hoax from which Poe had learned a thing or two when he launched his famous "Balloon." Charles F. Briggs, James Aldrich, Margaret Fuller, whose *Woman in the Nineteenth Century* Poe described as "nervous, forcible, thoughtful, suggestive, brilliant"; N. P. Willis, Catherine M. Sedgwick and the poetess Mary E. Hewitt—all were there. So, of course, was Frances Sargent Osgood, whose "lengthened sweetness," with generous excerpts from her poetry, took up five times the space allotted to Poe's good friend Professor Anthon and twice that given to Fitz-Greene Halleck. Poe quoted with particular appreciation the love passages of her "Elfrida, a Dramatic Poem," written in her girlhood, singling out the line spoken

[5] *Ibid.*
[6] *Ibid.*

by Elfrida to the hero, Edgar: "When but a child I saw thee in my dreams!" Commented Poe: "The woman's soul here shrinks from the direct avowal of want of love for her husband and flies to poetry and appeals to fate, by way of excusing that infidelity which is at once her glory and her shame." [7] His own entanglement with the poetess was still far from over.

The first article of the series appeared in May, 1846. It aroused so much interest that the whole edition of *Godey's* was immediately exhausted and the publisher found himself in the improvident position of receiving hundreds of orders that he could not fill. To satisfy the disappointed, the article was reprinted in the June number. Letters began to come from the readers, some praising, some protesting Poe's treatment of his subjects. In the matter of a critic's honesty, Poe had but one opinion: Courtesy was out of the question. A critic, he maintained, should have "the boldness to praise an enemy and the more unusual courage to damn a friend." [8] He was lavish of both praise and damns in the more than three dozen sketches which appeared from May through October. From the perspective of more than a century, except where the more unusual courage failed before the claims of the heart, his estimates remain just.

Again Poe had struck a rewarding vein, though the profits were not for his purse. While the publisher pocketed the gains from the soaring circulation, Poe had to be content with the usual modest rates. Thus, although he worked through illness, emotional upheavals and recurring depression, he was unable to extricate himself from debt and incurred new obligations. Ironically, while his name was on everyone's lips and the press busied itself in reactions to *The Literati,* Mr. Godey charged the author $10 for one of his replies which he, Mr. Godey, instead of printing in his magazine, farmed out on the *Spirit of the Times.*

Throughout the spring of 1846 Poe's letters alluded repeatedly to ill-health. That April the Literary Societies of the University of Vermont had elected him Poet for their anniversary celebration, but Poe had to decline the honor. Several months later he again refused, on the grounds of continued illness, a similar invitation on the part of Pennsylvania's Dickinson College. As it was, he had enough cares to keep him in a turmoil, with such consequences as had been apparent even to the Miller boy. At the bottom were two chronic anxieties, Virginia's slow dying and his unappeasable poverty. For neither did there seem to be a remedy, no matter what care he and

---

[7] *Works of Edgar Allan Poe,* Vol. III, pp. 89-90.
[8] *Ibid.,* Vol. III, p. 286.

Mrs. Clemm gave Virginia, no matter how hard he drove himself. At times he would work through the night, goading his nervous system with cup after cup of strong coffee. Unmerciful disaster always had the upper hand.

His usual compulsive protests were the inevitable reaction to his anxieties. Then Mrs. Clemm would have two invalids on her hands: her daughter choking for breath in her paroxysms; Eddie delirious, crying for opium. It was by this time a vicious chain of habit: anxiety breaking Poe's will for the alcohol he had again and again resolved never to touch, then his craving for opium, to allay the reactions brought on by the liquor.

Despite Mrs. Clemm's valiant efforts to keep her secrets at home, they were, alas, all too public. Chivers, in sympathy for the man he both admired and envied, had tried to help by appealing to his better nature. "What would God think of that Angel who should condescend to dust his feet in the ashes of Hell?" he inquired of Poe.[9] The poet had taken the question to heart, at least for a while, and had assured Chivers: "I have not touched a drop of the 'ashes' since you left N.Y.—& I am resolved not to touch a drop as long as I live." That had been on August 29, 1845, and the resolution had been frequently broken. Now, nearly a year later, on the 22nd of July, 1846, Poe was writing him: "It has been a long while since any artificial stimulus has passed my lips. When I see you . . . this is a topic on which I desire to have a long talk with you. I am done forever with drink—depend upon that—but there is much more in this matter than meets the eye. . . ."[10]

That "much more" he revealed to a young admirer, George W. Eveleth, a medical student of Phillips, Maine, who had evinced an interest in the *Stylus* and with whom he had begun a correspondence during his editorship of the *Broadway Journal*. The youth, in his earnest and ingenuous interest, did not hesitate to ask questions that would have given pause to older and wiser heads, and Poe had responded with, for him, extraordinary candor. In one of his letters Eveleth asked if Poe could hint at the "terrible evil" which had motivated his irregularities. "Yes; I can do more than hint," the poet replied. "This 'evil' was the greatest that can befall a man. Six years ago, a wife whom I loved as no man ever loved before, ruptured a blood-vessel in singing. Her life was despaired of. I took leave of her forever & underwent all the agonies of her death. She recovered partially and I again hoped. At the end of a year the vessel broke

[9] MS letter in the Huntington Library.
[10] Ostrom, p. 326.

again—I went through precisely the same scene. . . . Then again—again—again & even once again at varying intervals. Each time I felt all the agonies of her death—and at each accession of the disorder I loved her more dearly & clung to her life with more desperate pertinacity. . . . I became insane, with long intervals of horrible sanity. During these fits of absolute unconsciousness I drank, God only knows how often or how much. As a matter of course, my enemies referred the insanity to the drink rather than the drink to the insanity. . . ." [11]

The confession revealed self-knowledge as well as awareness of the workings of the psyche, long before its study had become a science. However, the inimical world which saw only the evil and not its motivations, misunderstood and condemned. Perhaps it was as much to protect their privacy from the prying of friends and enemies alike, perhaps to give Virginia the cottage she longed for, that the Poes and their petted Catarina left Turtle Bay in midsummer for the seclusion of the country.

"I am living out of town about 13 miles, at a village called Fordham, on the rail-road leading north," Poe wrote to Chivers. "We are in a snug little cottage, keeping house. . . ." [12] There is a note of comfort in that "keeping house," a sense of the intimacy of home, after the nomad existence in borrowed rooms in other people's houses.

The modest dwelling that he had discovered on one of his rambles consisted of one story and an attic, and had been built in the early part of the century for people of small means. The shingled roof with its chimney at one end, sloped steeply to the low wide attic windows. The main floor was of a cozy height that let in the sunshine through the square-paned windows and, in the fall and winter, retained the warmth from the hearth, framed by its plain white mantel. Originally the ground floor had consisted of two rooms, like the attic, but a kitchen had been added, with its own fireplace and chimney.

Woods and orchards gave the land about the cottage a delightfully rural aspect, though civilization reared its bulwark about a mile and a half away, at Williamsbridge, where the railway station linked the modest Eden with New York. Learning, too, had set up its temple in the vicinity, when the College of St. John had risen on the Rose Hill property, once the vast acreage of the family of Richard Corsa, which had also owned the cottage till March, 1846, when it was bought by John Valentine. From him Poe leased it for $8 a month.

Country lanes and paths radiated from the neighborhood of the

[11] Letter of Jan. 4, 1848. Ostrom, p. 356.
[12] Ostrom, p. 325.

cottage in almost every direction, a lure for Poe, who loved losing himself for hours, ambling through the woods. A walk that soon became a favorite led him along the footway of the Croton Aqueduct, then in the process of construction. Crossing the highroad near the Dutch Reformed church, he then traversed wood and meadow till he reached High Bridge. There the lover of grand prospects would dominate the distant view of New York, diminished by distance, over the Harlem flatlands.

The cottage itself was like a small island, bounded on the east by a line of lilacs concealing the roadway. A cherry tree lifted its branches high over the bushes. Beyond, in the large, sloping garden, maples spread their shade over a rocky mound which Poe soon chose as a hideout for himself and his thoughts.

Somehow, doubtless with the help of friends—for the Poes had left a bed with the Millers in lieu of rent—they made their small cottage habitable. They had a rocker with a cane back, a small settee, a few chairs and a looking glass. There was also Virginia's little bedstead, whose round knobs at the corners of the end boards had to be sawed off on one side to make it fit under the low slope of the attic roof. Poe's writing table stood before the windows in the small parlor. A hanging shelf on the wall held the few books Poe treasured —presentation copies, among them those of Elizabeth Barrett, recently become Mrs. Robert Browning.

If the furnishings were spare, the place was spotlessly clean and made cheerful by the flowers on the table and the pot of geraniums in the fireplace. The wide grounds about the house were mowed into a velvety greensward, shaded by ancient trees, while flowering vines clung about the porch. The place breathed happiness and peace; yet that valentine-card setting was to see enacted scenes more harrowing than any that the House of Usher had ever witnessed.

CHAPTER XXVI

→» · «←

"Her High-born Kinsman Came"

IN THEIR seclusion poverty was their first guest and it came to stay, although Mrs. Clemm and even Virginia, whenever she could, tried to earn a little money by sewing knickknacks and doing some fancy knitting which they disposed of in a neighborhood notions store. "In the meantime the flocks of little birds of prey that always take the opportunity of illness to peck at sick fowl of larger dimensions, have been endeavoring with all their power to effect my ruin. My dreadful poverty, also, has given them every advantage. In fact, my dear friend," Poe wrote to Chivers, "I have been driven to the very gates of death and despair more dreadful than death. . . ." [1]

Poe had always suffered from delusions of persecution. In Philadelphia he had been certain that he was the victim of his friend Wilmer's slanders and nothing could convince him that it was not so. Later he fixed upon Griswold, which did not prevent Poe from exposing himself to one he did not trust by appealing to him for loans. Now, though this time with cause, it was Thomas Dunn English on whom he swore to be avenged.

The two had become acquainted in Philadelphia and exchanged amenities by printing each other's works in their magazines. However, on writing his *Godey's* sketch on English, Poe not only followed his perverse streak, this time inspired by the nickname Thomas Done Brown, which Lippard had fastened upon the young poet, but he also justified his ruthlessness in revenge for the uncomplimentary report of his Boston lecture which English had printed in the *Evening Mirror*. In it, among other things, English had reproved Poe for his "Al Aaraaf" reading and also accused him of committing an act unworthy of a gentleman by accepting money for his performance. On one occasion, when Poe was in liquor, a state in which he always found English particularly irritating, they had even come to blows. Then, in the *Evening Mirror* of May 30, 1846, English wrote of him: "Some of

[1] Letter of July 22, 1846. Ostrom, p. 326.

297

the students in Dr. Arthur's grammar school made a pilgrimage to Bloomingdale to gaze upon the asylum where Mr. Poe was reported to be confined, in consequence of his great mental efforts having turned his brain. . . ." It was a cruel thrust to one tormented by fear of insanity, though that allusion did not affect Poe as much as the ridiculous description of him which followed. "Mr. Poe is 39. . . . In height he is about 5 feet 1 or two inches. . . . His face is pale and rather thin; eyes gray, watery and always dull . . . mouth not very well chiselled . . . his tongue shows itself unpleasantly when he speaks earnestly . . . forehead rather broad, and in the region of ideality decidedly large . . . which gives his head upon the whole, a balloonish appearance, which may account for his supposed light-headedness."

Hurt in his vanity, Poe wrote to his friend Joseph M. Field to defend him. "All that I venture to ask of you . . . is to say a few words in condemnation of it, and to do away with the false impression of my personal appearance it *may* convey, in those parts of the country where I am not individually known . . . I am 33 years of age," he declared, lopping off four of his thirty-seven years.[2]

In a sense English had done a *literati* sketch of him in advance of the one Poe was about to write: "Thomas Done Brown." Under that title Poe did him up brown with a vengeance. The gentleman, Poe said, was ungrammatical—he used to blame his mistakes on the printer—and given to the vice of plagiarism. Carried away by his sense of humor Poe went much further than English's unimportance demanded or required.

"Mr. Brown," he wrote, "had for motto on his magazine cover, the words of Richelieu,

> —Men call me cruel:
> I am not:—I am *just.*

Here the two monosyllables 'an ass' should be appended. They are no doubt omitted through 'one of those d——d typographical blunders.' . . . Mr. Brown," he added, "has at least that amount of talent which should enable him to succeed in his father's profession—that of a ferryman on the Schuylkill. . . ."[3]

Soon after the appearance of the sketch, the irate English responded with an article in the *Mirror,* prefixed with the headline: *The War of the Literati. Mr. English's Reply to Mr. Poe. A Terrific Rejoinder!* Far from terrific, the rejoinder was vulgar: "Others have converted the

[2] Ostrom, p. 319.
[3] *Works, Literati,* Vol. III, 103-104.

paper on which his sketches are printed to its legitimate use"—; it was also libelous in that, among much else, English alleged: "A merchant of this city has accused him [Poe] of committing forgery." [4]

Poe's reply to English was published on the 10th of July in the *Spirit of the Times*. Apart from Poe's discerning a "family resemblance between the whole visage of Mr. English and that of the best-looking but most unprincipled of Mr. Barnum's baboons," it was honest and manly, Poe admitting his own besetting frailty. "Never, even, have I made attempt at extenuating a weakness which is (or by the blessing of God, *was*) a calamity. . . ." The grave allegation of forgery he forcefully denied, having traced its source to Edward J. Thomas, the merchant involved. It had all been a misunderstanding on the part of a third party whose assertion Mr. English had accepted without question. Now in possession of the facts, Poe instituted a suit for libel against the *New York Mirror*.

This, however, was only one of the many events that came to disturb the idyllic peace of Fordham. One day Mr. H. F. Harrington, a relative of Mrs. Osgood's, came from Albany to call on her and found her about to get into a hack, accompanied by another lady author. She was going to carry some articles of comfort, she told him, to Mrs. Poe, who was ill at Fordham. "When she returned," wrote Mr. Harrington, "she described Mrs. Poe's condition to me—how that the poor wife, neglected, penniless, lay dying on a comfortless bed in a cottage that lacked many of the commonest essentials of domestic need . . . and was dependent on her friends for ministrations. . . ." [5]

Mrs. Osgood was not alone in her excursions by hack, or train, or private carriage. Now that Eurydice was facing death, the Bacchantes fought one another for the privilege of ministering to her, thus winning the gratitude, perhaps more, from the bereaved Orpheus. Mrs. Clemm, however, looked upon the Osgood visits, too frequent and too long, with a jaundiced eye and, though by this time she had grown accustomed to Eddie's platonics with this or that pretty woman, she sensed something here that might have justified the gossip which the all-too-public flirtation in the *Journal* had aroused. Still, she put on a pleasant countenance and thankfully accepted whatever love or friendship brought, whether through Mrs. Osgood or through the other writing women whom Eddie had noticed in *Godey's*.

There was the very kind Mrs. Mary Gove,[6] mesmerist, Sweden-

---

[4] *New York Mirror,* June 23, 1846.
[5] *New York Critic,* Oct. 3, 1885.
[6] Later Mrs. Nichols.

borgian, phrenologist and homeopathist, and also writer of magazine
articles. She had received a mere half page in the *Literati* series, but
she was grateful. Margaret Fuller brought sympathy, together with a
sharp eye for the proprieties, though for herself she scorned them.
Like the rest came the Brooklyn poetess, Sarah, or "Estelle," Lewis,
as she preferred to be called. Poe had not included her among the
literary sisterhood, but she knew that he would write about her; there
were ways of obtaining one's purpose through the unresisting door
of poverty, especially when Mrs. Clemm was its keeper. With the
others also arrived Elizabeth Oakes Smith and Mrs. Elizabeth Frieze
Ellet, whose "Coquette's Song" had challenged Mrs. Osgood's priority
over Poe's affections. He had placed her among the starry ones in a
mere paragraph which said, rather ambiguously: "She first made her
debut . . . as the writer of 'Teresa Contarini,' a five act tragedy which
had considerable merit, but was withdrawn after its first night of
representation at the Park. . . . The ill success of the play had little
effect in repressing the ardor of the poetess. . . . In person, short and
much inclined to embonpoint. . . ." [7]

Despite such forthrightness Mrs. Ellet still languished for the writer
from whom someday she hoped to elicit more flattering words. In
the meantime she ingratiated herself with Mrs. Clemm by filling her
ready ear with gossip and oiling her palm with contributions. There
was not one among the women, except perhaps for Margaret Fuller,
who, while dispensing charity, did not envision its returns in golden
words.

Mrs. Ellet desired more than words. In short, she was ambitious
to supplant Mrs. Osgood as the predilected of Israfel. One day, while
on her errand of mercy at Fordham, she came upon a letter of Mrs.
Osgood's addressed to Poe, and immediately began to express her
opinion of the lady to the already prejudiced Mrs. Clemm. Finding
a ready listener for her own grievances, Mrs. Clemm poured out her
misgivings and, in her expansiveness, read aloud various passionate
purple passages from Mr. Osgood's missives, which Mrs. Ellet thoroughly enjoyed. She was not one to keep such choice gossip secret,
especially when it involved the reputation of so cherished a member
of the sisterhood.

One day, however, she herself had a rude shock. She had just
gone into the sitting room of the Poe cottage when she heard voices
and laughter in the next room. As she listened, she recognized tender
sentences from one of her own letters, read out in the unmistakable
voice of Mrs. Clemm and greeted with the laughter of Virginia and

[7] *Works. Literati*, pp. 202-203.

Mrs. Osgood. Striding into the room, she snatched the letter from them and was ready to make a scene, but she had no defense against laughter. She had her revenge, nonetheless. With feigned indignation she let the world know how one's delicate secrets—she particularly mentioned Mrs. Osgood's—were violated in the Poe household.

Before long three graces, rather, three Eumenides—Mrs. Ellet herself, Margaret Fuller, and Miss Anna C. Lynch—presented themselves at the small door under the vine-clad porch in Fordham. Poe happened to be at home and they told him their errand. They had come to reclaim Mrs. Osgood's letters. At a loss to understand why such a request was made, and in such public fashion, Poe, stung by Mrs. Ellet's jealousy and the length to which she had carried it, broke out with the remark that she had better look after her own correspondence.

He had no sooner uttered the words than he regretted them, for, he argued with himself, although Mrs. Ellet must be conscious of her own baseness, she still had a right to reproach him for having betrayed her confidence.[8] He handed over the Osgood letters. After the women had gone, he also made a packet of Mrs. Ellet's effusions, over which, it must be confessed, Virginia and Mrs. Osgood had had many a laugh. He addressed them to the sender and, himself, left them at her door.

The woman, scorned, reacted in typical fashion. Pretending that she had not received the letters, she sent her brother and brother-in-law to demand them of Poe, who, in his hyperexcited state, was almost driven mad by the persecution and an intolerable sense of wrong. Mrs. Ellet would not be appeased. Anonymous letters filled with slander and malice began arriving for Virginia, who, though tortured by them, was not deceived, knowing their source. Through all the pettiness, the rivalries, the intrigues, she never doubted Edgar's love nor her own beneficent influence over him. "My dear Heart," he called her, and the name was more than a metaphor.

It was no childish charade that the boy John Le Fevre Miller had witnessed between husband and wife when they were boarding with his parents. "One day, when Mrs. Poe was very sick she said to 'Eddie' . . . 'Now, Eddie, when I am gone I will be your guardian angel, and if at any time you feel tempted to do wrong, just put your hands above your head, so, and I will be there to shield you. . . .' "[9] The words and gesture were true to the character of Virginia, toward whom, in his periods of weakness, Poe became the child of the child.

[8] Letter of Nov. 24, 1848. Ostrom, p. 407.
[9] See Phillips, p. 1111.

She was and remained what the other women aspired to be, his comforter and his inspiration. "In my last great disappointment," he had written her, one day, when he had had to be in town overnight for a business interview, "I should have lost my courage *but for you—* my little darling wife you are my *greatest* and *only* stimulus now. . . . Be assured until I see you, I will keep in *loving remembrance* your last words and your fervent prayer! . . ." [10]

It was during this hectic summer that Rosalie Poe, who had not seen her brother for some years, decided to pay him a visit. When she arrived she found only Virginia and Mrs. Clemm, who explained that Eddie was away on a business trip, but that he would soon return. Mrs. Clemm had never liked Rosalie. There were those letters with their "secret" which had caused Eddie so much grief, and there was Rosalie herself, now thirty-six, but with the intelligence of a twelve-year-old. She was a very perceptive and even uncannily shrewd twelve-year-old, however, who would startle one with the depth of her observation.

Still, Rosalie was someone to whom to pour out one's troubles, and Mrs. Clemm did so, bewailing the fact that poor Eddie had been taken ill and needed money at once. Would Rosalie lend her a few dollars to send him? Rosalie gave her the money. She also bought a few supplies for the bare cupboard from the market wagons that furnished the neighborhood.

When Eddie came home at last he was so ill that he was put to bed at once, Mrs. Clemm scolding and wailing at the same time. It was hard to tell who was more in need of help, Virginia, lying quietly in her bed, or Eddie, "talking out of his head," as Rosalie put it, and crying for morphine. It was some days before he was better, and then he sat down at his secretary and began to work. When he grew tired Mrs. Clemm would take his place and continue to write while he dictated. She had learned to imitate his handwriting so perfectly that it was hard to tell where the one ended and the other resumed.

Rosalie, brought up in the comfortable Mackenzie household, was distressed by her brother's poverty. On her return to Richmond she told of how one day Mrs. Clemm was carefully inking the worn seams of his suit, while he read his manuscript to her. He read everything to Mrs. Clemm, even while she was cooking or doing the laundry, when he would take his place on a settle outside the kitchen door and unroll his manuscripts. Through all this Rosalie had felt like an outsider. "Aunt Clemm and Virginia," she told the Mackenzies,

[10] Letter of June 12, 1846. In the original the words "disappointment" and "fervent" are misspelled. Ostrom, p. 318.

"cared for nobody but themselves and Edgar." Still, she left with Virginia the jewel box which she had inherited from her mother.

As the summer waned and the journey from town began to lose its pleasant air of an excursion, the visits from the literary ladies became less frequent. Mrs. Osgood had sought refuge from scandal with her Harrington relatives in Albany. Mrs. Ellet was content to continue her persecution from a distance. Others, seeing small benefit to be gained in a literary way from a man who was not publishing, hugged the comfort of their own firesides.

It was a lonely time, broken by the occasional visits of Father Edward Doucet, a young Jesuit priest from St. John's College, or by some kindly housewife who had been made acquainted with the needs of the family by Mrs. Clemm, who would sometimes stop at a neighborly door to "borrow." She had been observed, too, filling her basket in the summer season with dandelion greens from the meadows—her family was so fond of them! Now she could dig up only a few turnips from the fields planted for the cattle.

It must have been at this distressing time that she called on William Cullen Bryant, then editor of the *New York Evening Post,* on the chance of obtaining help, for on the 14th of September Bryant had burst out in a letter to his wife: "I have been run down with beggar women." He mentioned particularly "Mr. Poe's mother-in-law, who says her son-in-law is crazy, his wife dying, and the whole family starving." [11] It is doubtful that Bryant's unflinching rectitude allowed him to help the family of a man whose morals he abhorred.

Unexpectedly the Poes had visitors from the city: Mrs. Mary Gove, George Colton, who had bought "The Raven" for his *American Review,* and another man. Mrs. Gove, who was meeting Virginia for the first time, could not help marveling at the contrast between the small Mrs. Poe, who looked so very young and whose pale face and brilliant eyes gave her an unearthly look, and the stalwart woman who was her mother and, the visitor observed, appeared to be a sort of universal Providence to her strange children. With a woman's eye she noted the neatness and gentility of the modest cottage, the kitchen floor scrubbed as white as wheaten flour, the check matting in the sitting room, the hanging shelf with the precious volumes. On her remarking upon them Poe drew from his inside pocket a letter he had received from Elizabeth Barrett Browning and read it to his visitors. It was probably the epistle whose praise he had augmented for purposes of *réclame*—but what did it matter? A poet had compli-

[11] Quoted by H. Braddy, *Philological Quarterly,* Vol. XVI, 1937.

mented him—a rare event in a grudging world—and he was unhappy and in need of encouragement in this dark period of his career.

As it happened, more visitors arrived and all strolled away into the woods, where someone proposed a game of leaping. Poe had a' ways excelled in the sport and he had no difficulty in outdistancing them all, while Mrs. Gove watched. Alas, in a triumphant leap he burst his gaiters and the game ended. An unspoken anguish fell over the company and none dared to follow the wretched man as he went back to the cottage. Mrs. Gove, however, had left something in the house and went in to get it. "The poor old mother," she noted, "looked at his feet with a dismay that I shall never forget. 'Oh, Eddie!' said she, 'how did you burst your gaiters?' Poe seemed to have come into a semi-torpid state. . . . 'Do answer Muddie,' said she coaxingly." [12]

Mrs. Gove explained how the accident had occurred, whereupon Mrs. Clemm drew her into the kitchen. Would Mrs. Gove speak to Mr. Colton about the poem of Eddie's which she had carried to that gentleman a week ago? "If he will only take that poem, Eddie can have a pair of shoes." Mrs. Gove promised that the poem would be taken, although she and Mr. Colton had already read it and had not been able to make head or tail of it. However, the poem, thanks to Mrs. Gove, was paid for at once. "It bought the poet a pair of gaiters, and twelve shillings over." [13]

Something during this visit had distressed Mrs. Gove as much as the sight of Virginia, who, when she coughed, seemed ready to expire. It was a bobolink which Poe had caught and was training to captivity. There it was, in a cage hanging from a nail in the trunk of a cherry tree and hopping in fierce protest from one side of its prison to the other. Mrs. Gove pleaded for its liberty, but Poe stood there, impassive, his arms crossed, as he stared at the tormented bird. He then said curtly: "You are wrong. He is a splendid songster . . . and he will delight our home." [14] Perhaps deep within Poe saw an analogy between the imprisoned bird and Israfel, also a splendid songster, caught in a crueler cage of poverty and humiliation, and whose voice was for the moment stilled.

In the early autumn there were fair days when Virginia could go out into the sunlight. The lawns were still green and the cherry trees reddening with fruit. On one such day she was standing under the laden branches, holding out her white apron as Edgar, perched on one of the sturdy limbs, flung down clusters of the bright red cherries.

[12] Mary Gove Nichols, *Sixpenny Magazine*, February, 1863.
[13] *Ibid.*
[14] *Ibid.*

Virginia was laughing lightheartedly when suddenly the laughter choked in a cry and Edgar saw a crimson stream stain the white apron. Leaping down, he took her up in his arms and carried her into the house. From then on Virginia seldom left her bed, which was brought down from the attic into the small room off the parlor.

It was there that Mrs. Gove would come to chat with her, always marveling at her look of a disrobed spirit and at her disturbing beauty. A sense of strangeness, of the uncanny, seemed to pervade the cottage and its inhabitants. It extended even to the cat, who made Mrs. Gove nervous and almost afraid. It would always leave its cushion to greet her, and she had to talk to it and pet it before it would retire to its place. Poe, it seems, was Catarina's favorite and it was he who would let her out and bring her in at night. According to Mrs. Clemm, the devoted animal would refuse to eat whenever he was away.

What with Poe's agony on witnessing Virginia's suffering, what with his own wrecked health, he found it hard to undertake sustained creative work and therefore produced the brief, informative paragraphs of curious knowledge, observations on life and letters—the "Marginalia," which he had introduced into the *Democratic Review* and continued to feature in the other magazines under his editorship. The January, 1846, issue of *Arthur's Ladies' Magazine,* however, had contained "The Sphinx," an unusual piece of didacticism for one so opposed to it in art. The narrator had escaped New York during the cholera epidemic at the invitation of a friend who had a cottage in the country. While there, as he was gazing out of the window, he was horrified to see a monstrous creature, with a strange death's-head design on its breast, come gliding down the hill. Certain that it foreboded either his death or an attack of insanity, he confided his fears to his host. That sensible man took out a book on lepidoptera and showed him that the monster had been nothing more dangerous than a tiny insect, the Death's-headed Sphinx, which the onlooker had magnified by seeing it at too close a range. The same was true of Democracy, said the host. The distance of the epoch of its diffusion had to be considered before its effects could be judged—an extraordinary allowance from Edgar Allan Poe, who had earlier expressed himself with such violence against the Mob.

Then, in April of the same year, *Graham's* published "The Philosophy of Composition," Poe's analysis of his method in writing "The Raven." The fine frenzy, the ecstatic intuition which poets claimed, had had nothing to do with it or, for that matter, with any of his compositions. "The work proceeded, step by step, to its

completion with the precision and rigid consequence of a mathematical problem. . . ." [15]

At this time, while jotting down paragraphs of "Marginalia," he
was also working perfunctorily on a study of American letters, partly
culled from his *Literati* and augmented by his critical judgments. He
planned to call it *Literary America*. However, while striking such
feeble sparks he was waiting for the true fire. He knew it would come,
and when it came, he was certain it would illumine the world. At
present, in his abysmal dejection, it stirred within him as a craving
for fame, the same old hunger which he had appeased with his blatant
hoaxes and sensational tricks. By some means, any means, he was
determined to hew his way into the ranks of the immortals.

Still, he was unwilling to admit this to the world. "I write from
a mental necessity," he told Mrs. Gove, "to satisfy my taste and my
love of art. Fame forms no motive power with me. What can I care
for the judgment of a multitude, every individual of which I despise?" [16] Subsequently, he told her the truth. "I said to you when
you were here last, that I despised fame. It is false. I love fame—
I dote on it—I idolize it—I would drink to the very dregs the glorious intoxication. I would have incense ascend in my honour from
every hill and hamlet, from every town and city on this earth. Fame!
Glory!—they are life-giving breath, and living blood. No man lives
unless he is famous! . . ." [17]

As it happened, he had been offered a few intoxicating whiffs of
that incense in France, in November of 1845, when Alphonse Borg-
hers translated "The Gold-Bug" which created a sensation when it
appeared as "Le Scarabée d'Or" in the *Revue Britannique,* which drew
its material from British and American publications. Now, at the
very time that Poe was confessing his love of fame, all of Paris was
agog over the orang-utan affair and the murders in the Rue Morgue.
Furthermore, M. Forgues—"Old Nick"—who had appropriated Poe's
orang-utan, now atoned for the theft by a long and appreciative review
of his *Tales* in the important *Revue des Deux Mondes*.[18] Hearing confused rumors of these happenings, Poe was elated and sent out his
misinformation wherever he thought it would help him.

The most significant encounter of his genius with European fame
he was, however, never to know: the meeting of his tales with the
twenty-six-year-old Charles Baudelaire when he came across a trans-

[15] *Works,* Vol. II, p. 261.
[16] *Ibid.*
[17] *Ibid.*
[18] Oct. 15, 1846.

lation of "The Black Cat" in the socialist paper, *Démocratie Pacifique*, on the 27th of January, 1847. This translation, with others that followed, were the labor of love of Mme. Isabelle Meunier, an English girl and the wife of Victor Meunier who was dedicated to the communistic theories of Fourier which at the time also appealed to Baudelaire. Instantly the young French poet felt a kinship with the American, an immediate identification of their creative personalities. Baudelaire knew English well through his mother, who was part English and had taught him the language. Yet it was not the mere turn of phrase that struck Baudelaire, but rather the process of thought, the very choice of subject. "I found poems and tales that I had myself conceived, in a vague, confused and disorganized way, which, however, Poe had succeeded in organizing and bringing to perfect completion." [19]

Poe took possession of him as if he, Baudelaire, had been one of his characters and depended upon his creator for his existence. He collected every magazine he could find that contained Poe's works and sought the acquaintance of Americans in the hope of gleaning some little fact about his idol. He literally beatified Poe. Toward the close of his life he made a vow in his private diaries "To pray to God, every morning—to God who is the source of all strength and righteousness, to my father . . . and to Poe, as my intercessors." [20] Of the eight published volumes left by Baudelaire, three were his translations of Poe. He never wrote his biography; but of all who have sought to fathom the mystery of Poe, Baudelaire came closest to the truth of the man and the poet, in the introductory essays to his translations.

Yet he too was baffled by Poe, the erotic male, and made the comment that in his tales there is never any love. Certainly, in the stories there is a total absence of sensual love; but the almost hypnotic fixation of the lover for the total spiritual assimilation of Ligeia, for the ultimate penetration of her mystery, goes beyond mere physical possession, for it would absorb the very soul and by some perverse means reach a consummation beyond the merely physical. It was not that there was no love, but that the love Poe sought, both in reality and in his life of the imagination, lay beyond human attainment, or was attainable only at the cost of sanity.

While Poe was being discovered in France he was passing through the most desolating period of his life. Let Mrs. Gove question whether as a critic he had always been honest or whether for a consideration

[19] Baudelaire, *Corréspondance Générale*, Vol. III, p. 41.
[20] Baudelaire, *Œuvres Posthumes*, "Journaux Intimes," p. 135.

he had not sometimes given unmerited praise. "If he (the critic) were placed on a rack, or if one he loved better than his own life were writhing there, I can conceive of his forging a note against the Bank of Fame, in favour of some would-be poetess, who is able and willing to buy his poems and opinions," he had answered her. "Would you blame a man for not allowing his sick wife to starve?" [21]

Even granting such concessions, it was soon apparent to Mrs. Gove that vigorous measures had to be taken if the Poe family was to survive. Within the brief interval since her last visit it was as if, with the winter, doom had descended upon them all. It was bitter cold. In the little downstairs bedroom Virginia was lying on the bed, not on a mattress but on straw, though with a snow-white counterpane and sheets; so much, at least, Mrs. Clemm had been able to provide. Edgar's West Point greatcoat was wrapped about her shivering body and she was hugging Catarina to her breast for warmth. The wise animal lay there quietly, as if aware of its helpfulness. Edgar and Mrs. Clemm were holding her chilled hands and feet.

On returning to the city Mrs. Gove immediately enlisted the help of Mrs. Marie Louise Shew, to whom Poe was already known. Mrs. Shew's practical knowledge of medicine—she was the daughter of a doctor—and her nursing experience would be invaluable to Virginia in what were obviously her last days. Mrs. Shew went at once to Fordham, taking along a feather bed, clothes and other necessities, while Mrs. Gove reawakened the sympathy of the literary ladies. They came to the rescue at once, Mrs. Osgood even writing to her sister-in-law, Mrs. Locke, in Massachusetts, presenting Poe's dire distress.

Somehow, through the well-meant efforts of the charitable band, the poet's terrible need achieved more notoriety than he desired, when, on the 15th of December, the *New York Morning Express* printed an appeal which, for all its tact, was mortifying to his pride.

"We regret to learn that Edgar A. Poe and his wife are both dangerously ill with the consumption, and that the hand of misfortune lies heavy upon their temporal affairs. We are sorry to mention the fact that they are so far reduced as to be barely able to obtain the necessaries of life. . . . We hope that the friends and admirers of Mr. Poe will come promptly to his assistance in his bitterest hour of need."

Poe learned of the appeal through an anonymous letter, probably from Mrs. Ellet, addressed to Virginia. It enclosed a clipping from the *Morning Express,* as well as another, attacking Poe.

"That my wife is ill, then, is true," Poe wrote to Willis, "and you may imagine with what feeling I add that this illness, hopeless from

[21] Mrs. Mary Gove Nichols, *Sixpenny Magazine,* February, 1863.

the first, has been heightened and precipitated by her reception . . . of anonymous letters. . . . Of the facts, that I myself have been long and dangerously ill, and that my illness has been a well understood thing among my brethren of the press, the best evidence is afforded by the innumerable paragraphs of personal and literary abuse with which I have been latterly assailed. This matter, however, will remedy itself. At the very first blush of my new prosperity, the gentlemen who toadied me in the old, will recollect themselves and toady me again. . . . I am getting better, and may add—if it be any comfort to my enemies—that I have little fear of getting worse. The truth is, I have a great deal to do; and I have made up my mind not to die till it is done." [22]

Whether as a result of the appeal or from private subscription among Poe's friends, Mrs. Shew brought the family $60—not a large amount, yet six times what the celebrated "Raven" had earned its Elijah. Poe had difficulty in swallowing his pride, but he had to submit to the terms which society, even at its best, imposes upon indigent genius: a meager handout at the cost of great humiliation.

The sympathetic Mr. Willis drew from the newspaper announcement a text for a proposal close to his heart, and the day after Christmas he offered it in his *Home Journal*. Here was Poe, "one of the finest scholars, one of the most original men of genius, and one of the most industrious of the literary profession . . . whose temporary suspension of labor, from bodily illness, drops him immediately to a level with the common objects of public charity. There was no intermediate stopping-place, no respectful shelter where, with the delicacy due to genius and culture, he might secure aid. . . ."

He offered a humane solution for the still-existing problem of the independent artist who, when he cannot create, must starve. Unfortunately it did little to ameliorate Poe's immediate need.

Meanwhile at Fordham Mrs. Shew alternated between Virginia's bedside, where the racked body seemed to find peace only after the terrible fits of suffocation, and the anguished Poe, who was driven insane by each attack. Quiet, competent, with sympathy yet with common sense, Loui, as Mrs. Clemm called Mrs. Shew, accomplished her tasks, consulting Dr. Valentine Mott and keeping him informed of her patients' progress. She was not deceived about Virginia's condition, which had grown worse with the winter. At last, toward the close of January, 1847, she communicated her fears to Mrs. Clemm, who notified friends and relatives. Very few came. In fact, none of the literary ladies braved the thirteen miles to Fordham in the cold.

[22] Letter of Dec. 30, 1846. Ostrom, pp. 338-339.

Virginia knew she had not much longer to live, but 'her sole concern was for Edgar. "Darling, darling Muddy, you will console and take care of my poor Eddy—you will *never, never* leave him?" she implored. "Promise me, my dear Muddy, and then I can die in peace." [23]

On the 29th of January Mary Devereaux was expected. Perhaps to give Virginia the illusion of receiving her friends, but more probably to keep her warm, she was carried into the parlor and propped up on an armchair near the fire. It was there that Mary Devereaux found her, with no little surprise, with Edgar beside her. The only other relative who came to call was Eliza Herring.

That day Mrs. Shew, foreseeing the end, had gone to New York to make the inevitable preparations. Poe, who had grown increasingly dependent upon her, sent her a note. "Kindest—dearest friend— My poor Virginia still lives, although failing fast and now suffering much pain. May God grant her life until she sees you and thanks you once again! Her bosom is full to overflowing—like my own—with a boundless—inexpressible gratitude to you. Lest she may never see you more —she bids me say that she sends you her sweetest kiss of love and will die blessing you. But come—oh come tomorrow. . . ." [24]

Among the things Mrs. Shew brought from the city the following day was a beautiful linen dress for Virginia.

She found her lying in bed, with Eliza sitting beside her. Suddenly Virginia slipped her hand under her pillow and drew out a picture of Edgar and the little jewel casket that had once belonged to his mother. These she gave to Mrs. Shew. Then she took two faded letters from a portfolio and begged Mrs. Shew to read them aloud. They were from Frances Allan, who had written them to Edgar after he had left Richmond, and cleared him of blame in the break with his foster father. It was as if, knowing she was dying, Virginia were exonerating Edgar of the least blame, before confiding him to a woman who might perhaps be his guardian angel when she herself had gone.

That night, the 30th of January, 1847, "her high-born kinsman came"—the Angel of Death, who had wooed her for so long—and bore her away from Edgar and the world. She was twenty-four when she died, the age of Poe's mother and of his brother Henry.

[23] Mrs. Clemm to Annie Richmond, July 9, 1849. Ingram, *Edgar Allan Poe,* Vol. II, pp. 222-223.
[24] Ostrom, p. 340.

→》》 • 《《←

Ulalume

MRS. SHEW saw to the last offices. She dressed Virginia in the white linen gown, and the worn body, now still at last, was laid in the coffin. In the midst of her grief Mrs. Clemm was comforted by the beautiful linen—not plain cotton—that clothed her daughter for the last journey. The casket was placed upon Poe's writing table, between the windows of the parlor, and there Virginia lay for friends and neighbors to see, pale as she had been in life, with her still-beautiful face framed in her glossy hair, combed smooth on either side of the brow. It was strangely fitting that she, who had inspired so much of Poe's work, should rest for the last time upon that pedestal.

Now that the death which Poe had so long experienced had occurred, he was like one in a state of shock. Mrs. Shew watched over him anxiously. She took his greatcoat off Virginia's bed and put it out of sight, to spare him painful thoughts, and quietly, efficiently ministered to him almost without his knowing. All the while that Virginia lay in her casket he refused to look upon her face. But someone there, perhaps at the request of Mrs. Clemm, who had no picture of her daughter, painted in water colors a portrait of the dead girl. The head leaned toward the right, its Canova modeling still unmarred by death. The unknown artist copied that serene brow, the rounded cheeks which disease had not wasted, the heavy lids, and the faint upcurving of a smile about the lips. The closed eyelids, however, were too painful a reminder of death, and the artist later lifted them halfway and painted in the pupils. This attempt at giving the portrait a semblance of life only intensified its macabre quality. It became that representation of life-in-death which Poe had so eerily portrayed in the struggle of Ligeia to invade the body of Rowena, of Morella to relive in her child.

The day of the burial dawned "ashen and sober" and a chill wind blew. The wedding ring was taken from Virginia's finger, the funeral service read and the coffin nailed down. The procession then left the

311

house: Mrs. Clemm, Edgar in his West Point cloak, for he had no other, Mrs. Shew, the Valentines and a few neighbors. Mr. and Mrs. S. D. Lewis from Brooklyn, N. P. Willis and his partner had also come for the burial. Mary Devereaux remained at the cottage, to receive anyone who might arrive. No one came. Mrs. Osgood was in Albany. It was too bitter cold a day for the New York ladies to incommode themselves for such a trip.

The casket was carried to the Reformed Dutch Church. As Poe had no grave plot and no money to buy one, Virginia was laid in the vault of Dennis Valentine, near the rear porch of the church.

No sooner was the tension of years released by the finality of death than Poe broke down. Mrs. Shew diagnosed his illness as brain fever and kept Dr. Mott informed. The patient's pulse, she reported, beat only ten regular beats and then intermitted. "I decided that in his best health he had lesion of one side of the brain, and as he could not bear stimulants or tonics, without producing insanity, I did not feel much hope that he could be raised up from brain fever brought on by extreme suffering of mind and body . . . until exhaustion and lifelessness were so near at every reaction of the fever, that even sedatives had to be administered with extreme caution. . . ." [1]

Dr. Mott went to Fordham and confirmed Mrs. Shew's suspicion of the brain lesion. They tried to keep the patient quiet but they could not control the outpouring of reminiscences, ambitions and anxieties that agitated him in his delirium. When alone with Mrs. Shew he told her of how, in his youth, he had wandered all over Europe and become involved in the most extraordinary adventures. In Spain he had fought a duel. Tearing off his shirt he bared his left arm and shoulder to show the scar he still carried from that fray. A Scottish nurse had tended him, he said, but he would not reveal her name. With growing excitement he told of his journey to France, and the resulting adventures in Boulogne, in Paris. While in that city he had mingled with the famous literary men of the day and had found time to write a novel which appeared under the name of Eugène Sue. She must write everything down, he begged her, all his thoughts and fancies, for he had promised them to many greedy publishers. If he did not satisfy them, they would say that he did not keep his word and if he should die they would take their revenge by inventing all sorts of evil things about him.

Under her protective concern, her competence and sympathy, Poe slowly recovered. Mrs. Shew represented strength and security. She

[1] Mrs. Shew to Ingram, Vol. II, pp. 115-116.

was a young Mrs. Clemm, attractive and independent, who had been an angel of mercy to Virginia, a savior to him. He remembered something she had said to him in one of his crises, "that nothing could or would save him from a sudden death, but a prudent life, of calm, with a woman fond enough—and strong enough to manage his work. . . ." [2]

It was rash advice to have given one in Poe's weakened and susceptible condition. For the present, however, he was still too much overwhelmed with grief to think of achieving his salvation by those means.

Want was still hounding the Fordham cottage when suddenly help came, with the settlement of Poe's suit against the *Mirror,* on the 22nd of February. As Mr. English did not appear in court, the case went by default and the *Mirror* had to award damages of $225. So Thomas Done Brown unwittingly brought Poe more money than any one of his works had ever earned him.

Mrs. Clemm set about making purchases to replace the necessities which poverty had compelled her to sell. A new tea service supplanted the broken crockery, a real carpet covered the floor. After the period of mourning the cottage was hospitably open to friends and neighbors —yet not without arousing criticism. Cornelius Mathews, who had been invited to tea, could not help feeling offended in his sensibilities on seeing Mrs. Clemm, in the luxury of a new dress, presiding over a handsome silver pot, at a table heaped with dainties—so soon after her daughter's death. Others probably noticed a ring, made up of two gold circlets joined together, which Poe had recently begun wearing. He had had it made from Virginia's wedding band and from Mrs. Clemm's, soon after he won his suit. It was never to leave his finger, nor was it to reveal what obscure symbolism of troth and fidelity lay concealed in it.

With the renewal of health and hope, Poe turned again to the *Stylus.* Once more the old prospectus, brought up to date, was put to use in soliciting subscriptions. He knew that unless he had the editorship of a magazine, preferably his own, he could not hope to publish enough to support himself and Mrs. Clemm. As it was, the flame of inspiration had scarcely been flickering. However, on the 13th of March, 1847, the *Home Journal* contained a poem of his, in blank verse: "To M.L.S.———."

It was a throbbing apostrophe to his good angel, a paean of gratitude and devotion, full of abstractions in capital letters and coined phrases that had long worn thin:

[2] Ingram, *op. cit.*

Of all who hail thy presence as the morning—
Of all to whom thine absence is the night—

.   .   .   .

Of all who, on Despair's unhallowed bed
Lying down to die, have suddenly arisen
At thy soft-murmured words, "Let there be light!"

.   .   .   .

Of all who owe thee most—whose gratitude
Nearest resembles worship—oh, remember
The truest—the most fervently devoted,
And think that these weak lines are written by him—
By him who, as he pens them, thrills to think
His spirit is communing with an angel's.

These admittedly weak lines, however, implied more than they said, as Mrs. Shew and those familiar with Poe's technique of literary courtship were quick enough to divine. As it was, the scandal over the Osgood affair, despite the lady's protracted seclusion, had not died down, and feeling in the genteel coterie was still antagonistic to Poe. Mrs. Shew took alarm, but she was too sensible to betray it. She had given Poe advice and he was acting upon it. In vain she had told him repeatedly that she knew nothing about literature, that she was much too familiar with the suffering and tragedy of life to sympathize with imaginary evils. In the dependence of the sick soul upon its healer, Poe had fixed upon her for the health of his mind and body.

Without actually discouraging him, Mrs. Shew, in order to distract him and also to give him a sense of reciprocating her many services, set him to interior decorating. She lived in a pleasant section of New York, at 51 Tenth Street, within sound of the clanging bells of Grace Church, on Broadway. Whether the idea was her own or her family's, it was decided that the music room and library needed re-doing. Supplying Poe with money, she gave him full discretion to make the new purchases.

The house, unlike the overfurnished interiors of the time, evidenced taste and culture. Coming from the plain Fordham cottage, Poe could not but be impressed by the large painting over the piano—"A masterpiece indeed deserving a place in a palace or a church," he commented. Remembering his essay on domestic aesthetics he approved of the scroll design of the drawing-room carpet, and rhapsodized over his predilected color scheme of crimson and gold, so effectively carried out. He was also charmed to see, for a change, the piano and harp uncovered. "I wondered that a little country maiden like you had developed so classic a taste and atmosphere," he complimented Mrs. Shew.[3] By exercising her subtle influence she gradually became his "dear friend Louise," and on the basis of friendship her door remained open to him.

Indeed, what Poe sought in his relationships with women was the abstract, the ideal, image of love, which was more potent than any creature of flesh and blood because, unlike the physical being, it could not be destroyed. Already, with his first poem to Mrs. Shew, he had converted her to an angel. It may have been this, as much as Mrs. Shew's knowledge of his ambiguous nature, that gave her warning. Chivers, with the vision of the "fool of God," had also glimpsed Poe's mystery. "He was tired of the world, and Hell itself would have been a better place for him than the society of heartless men. He had long before ceased to believe in men—and women, tortured as he was by doubtful misgivings, had but very few charms for him." [4]

These "doubtful misgivings" Virginia, while alive, had shielded from the world. His public flirtations had cast dust in the eyes of the prying. Psyche from the regions which are Holy Land had been his first love. It was that Psyche whom he sought and would seek in all the women who mistakenly believed him to be in love with themselves. Except for the incident related by Mary Devereaux and the heated period of his relations with Mrs. Osgood, which had frightened her away, his passion had been of the mind or, as he would have preferred, of the soul.

Baudelaire, who, while speculating on the sexual urge in his private notebooks, was unconsciously analyzing his own attitudes, wrote: "The more man cultivates the arts the less he indulges in sex. Another, more and more perceptible division, is created between the spirit and the brute. Only the brute knows how to have sex, and sex is the lyrism of the people. To fornicate is to aspire to enter into another being, whereas the artist never comes out of himself." [5]

What applied to Baudelaire uncannily fitted the alter ego he had recognized in Poe, with the difference that, while in himself the brute and the spirit never ceased their struggle, in Poe their division began almost as soon as the sexual urge had asserted itself. In Virginia he had found the woman who satisfied the needs of his dual nature, both by fulfilling his spirit through her innocence and beauty and by chastening the brute—in the beginning by her youth, later because

[3] Letter of May, 1847. Ostrom, p. 350.

[4] *Poe-Chivers Papers.* Huntington Library.

[5] From the manuscript in the possession of M. Armand Godoy. Quoted by Princess Marie Bonaparte in her study of Poe. Translation of passage by F.W.

of her precarious health. Her loss now left him exposed to the challenges and perils of an alien world.

At first his own grave illness, following Virginia's death, had confined him to the cottage, to the very bed where she had died. Later, on his recovery, he began to resume his long walks, drawn by a plot of ground and a tomb. Starting off from the cottage, he would trace the same path as on that drear day in February, through an alley of cypress, past marshlands where the rains left their waters in dim lakes overhung with fog that reminded him of the Scottish weirs of his boyhood. Then along the Kingsbridge Road he walked, the ground rising higher till he reached the Dutch church. Skirting round its side, he went toward the rear porch, walked some thirty paces to the east, and stood by the tomb of Dennis Valentine that also held the body of Virginia. In the same way, as a boy, he had made his pilgrimages to the grave of Helen.

At home he read and reread those writings in which Virginia's spirit lingered. He always associated her with gardens and flowers and idyllic seclusion. Perhaps to keep fresh the memory of the Fordham countryside, he reworked his earlier "Landscape Garden" into "the Domain of Arnheim" by putting into it some of the familiar country.

One day he came across a manuscript copy of his "Eulalie," and the weight of his loss overpowered him. In pencil he traced on the reverse of the sheet:

> Deep in the earth my love is lying
> And I must weep alone.[6]

The name Eulalie reawakened echoes of the past, bringing poignantly to his consciousness the depth of his bereavement and, with it, the guilt of real or intended infidelities, if not of the flesh, certainly of the spirit. Eulalie, Eleonora: the names of beauty, of light which he had always associated with Virginia blended into still another name, stranger and more magical than either, yet combining the loveliness of the first and the radiance of the second—Ulalume, derived from *eu*, fair or beautiful, and *lume*, from *lumen*, light. Not that Poe, as he maintained, pursued his work as if he were a mathematician, allowing no room for inspiration or intuitive promptings. The name for his poem, "Ulalume," may have suggested itself unconsciously at first, as he turned over in his mind the related Eulalie and Eleonora. It would also have been true of him, however, to

---

[6] The manuscript was discovered by Victor H. Palsits, Curator of Manuscripts at the New York Public Library, between the pages of an old album.

evolve it with the methodicalness of a scientist. In either case, he still possessed the genius to imbue it with mystery and magic.

> The skies they were ashen and sober;
>   The leaves they were crisped and sere—
>   The leaves they were withering and sere;
> It was night in the lonesome October
>   Of my most immemorial year;
> It was hard by the dim lake of Auber,
>   In the misty mid region of Weir—
> It was down by the dank tarn of Auber,
>   In the ghoul-haunted woodland of Weir.
>
> Here once, through an alley Titanic,
>   Of cypress, I roamed with my Soul—
>   Of cypress, with Psyche, my Soul.
> These were days when my heart was volcanic
>   As the scoriac rivers that roll—
>   As the lavas that restlessly roll
> Their sulphurous currents down Yaanek
>   In the ultimate clime of the pole—
> That groan as they roll down Mount Yaanek
>   In the realms of the boreal pole.

With broken rhythms, as of a voice choked with sobs, and with the repetitiveness of the hallucinated who cannot absorb at once the evidence of their senses, the poet sets the spectral atmosphere of that night in the lonesome October when, with Psyche, his Soul, he retraces the path that he, Poe, had so often followed, through the cypress alley and across the mist-shrouded swamps.

> Our talk had been serious and sober,
>   But our thoughts they were palsied and sere—
>   Our memories were treacherous and sere—
> For we knew not the month was October,
>   And we marked not the night of the year—
>   (Ah, night of all nights in the year!)
> .   .   .   .
>
> And now, as the night was senescent
>   And star-dials pointed to morn—
>   As the star-dials hinted of morn—
> At the end of our path a liquescent
>   And nebulous lustre was born,
> Out of which a miraculous crescent
>   Arose with a duplicate horn—
> Astarte's bediamonded crescent
>   Distinct with its duplicate horn.

And I said—"She is warmer than Dian:
      She rolls through an ether of sighs—
      She revels in a region of sighs:
She has seen that the tears are not dry on
      These cheeks, where the worm never dies,
And has come past the stars of the Lion,
      To point us the path to the skies—
      To the Lethean peace of the skies—
·   ·   ·   ·   ·   ·   ·

But Psyche, uplifting her finger,
      Said—"Sadly this star I mistrust—
      Her pallor I strangely mistrust:—
Oh, hasten!—oh, let us not linger!
      Oh, fly!—let us fly!—for we must."
In terror she spoke, letting sink her
      Wings till they trailed in the dust . . .

The allegory is simple. While tormented by grief and his memories, the poet sees in the coming morn a nebulous light, and there before him rises Astarte, goddess of love and passion. "She is warmer than Dian," he pleads with Psyche—warmer than the goddess of chastity, and comes with love to comfort him, whose tears are not yet dry. But in terror Psyche, the Soul, bids him fly from that pale star of temptation. He urges:

"Let us on by this tremulous light!
Let us bathe in this crystalline light!
Its Sybilic splendor is beaming
      With hope and in beauty to-night . . .
·   ·   ·   ·   ·   ·   ·

Ah, we safely may trust to its gleaming,
      And be sure it will lead us aright . . ."
·   ·   ·   ·   ·   ·   ·

Thus I pacified Psyche and kissed her,
      And I tempted her out of her gloom—
      And conquered her scruples and gloom;
And we passed to the end of the vista,
      And we stopped by the door of a tomb—
      By the door of a legended tomb;
And I said—"What is written, sweet sister,
      On the door of this legended tomb?"
She replied—"Ulalume—Ulalume—
      'Tis the vault of thy lost Ulalume!"

Then my heart it grew ashen and sober
      As the leaves that were crisped and sere . . .

What mystery lay in the vault with the lost Ulalume to make the poet's heart grow ashen after he had conquered Psyche's scruples? Was it the recollection of his promise to Eleonora-Virginia, never to supplant her in his heart? Or was it some secret, known only to her and to him, which the innocent and adoring wife had carried with her to the grave? That the poem held something intensely personal is betrayed by the anonymity he sought for it, not only when it appeared in the *American Whig Review,* in December, 1847, as "To — — —. Ulalume, A Ballad," but also when he sent a copy of the magazine containing it to the ever-friendly Willis, with the request that he reprint it, *without his name.* "I do not care to be known as its author just now," he wrote, "but I would take it as a great favor if you would copy it in the H.J., with a word of *inquiry* as to who wrote it. . . ." [7]

Poe's love of mystification as well as his flair for publicity no doubt played their part in such self-effacement, but more personal reasons are implied in his not caring to avow authorship just then. The three dashes of the dedication point, as usual, to some emotional involvement over which a semitransparent curtain must be drawn. Whose name did they conceal? Perhaps that of Marie Louise Shew, whom he was still courting hopefully, if platonically, despite her reluctance? But he had written her a poem of no fewer than nine stanzas, "The Beloved Physician," which in her fear of being compromised she would not allow him to print, even though an editor had offered him $20 for it. Humbly Poe apologized for having dared to voice his adoration in a poem. "You must know *and be assured* of my *regret,* my *sorrow,* if aught I have written has hurt you! My *heart* never *wronged you.* I place you in *my esteem* in all solemnity beside the friend of my boyhood, the mother of my school fellow, of whom I told you, and as I have repeated in . . . the 'Beloved Physician,' as the truest, tenderest of this world's most womanly souls, and an angel to my forlorn and darkened nature. . . ." [8]

Among the eligible there was also Mrs. "Estelle" Anna Lewis, who was often to be found resting her embonpoint on a chair in the Fordham kitchen, gossiping with Mrs. Clemm, pumping her, and hopeful of catching a glimpse of the poet who, whenever forewarned of her coming, fled to the woods, cursing all literary bores. Nevertheless, prudence dictated that he immortalize her in verse, for the Lewises were always good for financial help in exchange for his improvement of Mrs. Lewis's poems or an occasional puff in the magazines. He wrote the sonnet "An Enigma" for her, a skillful acrostic but a poem

[7] Letter of Dec. 8, 1847. Ostrom, p. 354.
[8] Ostrom, p. 374.

as mediocre as the subject whose "dear names" lay concealed within it. "Estelle" could not have been pleased, for he used her real name, Sarah, in it and also accompanied it with a note which closed "with all the affection of a brother."

There was still another candidate, once loved and by no means forgotten: Frances Sargent Osgood, to whom at this time his thoughts may have turned, as, it would seem, they did. Again her relative, H. F. Harrington, is the informant of the event which he places roughly in 1847, at any rate, after Virginia's death. Mr. Harrington was then returning to Albany after an absence in New York.

"Mrs. Osgood, who . . . was on a visit to my family, related that while I had been gone Poe had sought an interview with her alone in my parlor, and in passionate terms had besought her to elope with him. She described his attitudes as well as reported his words—how he went down on his knee, and clasped his hands and pleaded for her consent; how she met him with mingled ridicule and reproof, appealing to his better nature, and striving to stimulate a resolution to abandon his vicious courses; and how finally he took his leave, baffled and humiliated, if not ashamed." [9]

Whatever the name the initials concealed, whatever the truth of Mrs. Osgood's account to Harrington, Poe, after Virginia's death, was like a waif in search of affection, even more, of security. Mrs. Clemm, innocent yet cunning, encouraged the ladies who, from one motive or another, wooed her to obtain favors from him. In the small parlor, preferably in the cozier intimacy of the kitchen, sly little plots were hatched, promises given that Eddie would notice this or write that. Then, very discreetly, tokens of gratitude would change places from elegant purses to Mrs. Clemm's pocket.

Poe had not published much. Since "The Cask of Amontillado" in *Godey's* for November, 1846, he had done little that brought in money. He was not so often on people's lips, although his new story, an exposition of a cruel revenge was, in its absolute marriage of idea and execution, as near perfection as art could attain. From the murderer's opening vow of vengeance to the jingle of the carnival bells of the walled-up victim, answered by the sardonic *In pace requiescat* of the triumphant villain, there was not one syllable that, like the minutest stone in a perfect mosaic, could have been found superfluous to the design. Poe's skill in the tale had now reached its peak.

His spirits, on the other hand, had never been lower. It was as if, with the loss of Virginia, his whole moral structure, the very cornerstone of his security, had collapsed and he was reaching out wildly anywhere, everywhere, for support. The least word of pity from any

[9] Harrington, *The Critic,* Oct. 3, 1885.

woman, whether married or not, made him attach himself to her, believing he had found at last the one Mrs. Shew had advised him to seek. Led on by her undiminished kindness, he still deluded himself that she would eventually yield. At any rate, in the *Columbia Magazine* for March, 1848, he once again endeavored to win her to his ideal passion with the lines "To — — —." He spoke of gentle sounds,

> Two words—two foreign soft disyllables—
> Italian tones, made only to be murmured
> By angels dreaming in the moonlit "dew
> That hangs like chains of pearl on Hermon hill"
> Have stirred from out the abysses of this heart
> Unthought-like thoughts that are the souls of thought,
> Richer, far wilder, far diviner visions
> Than even the seraph harper, Israfel
> (Who has "the sweetest voice of all God's creatures"),
> Could hope to utter. And I! my spells are broken . . .

Nevertheless, he had succeeded in conveying the foreign soft disyllables, "Io t'amo." Mrs. Shew became alarmed. On her next visit to the cottage she took along John H. Hopkins, a student at the General Theological Seminary—a man whom Poe did not like. He detected a touch of conventional coldness in Mrs. Shew's "Good morning" and in her hurry to open the kitchen door to find Mrs. Clemm, while leaving him with Mr. Hopkins, who stood smiling and bowing at the madman, Poe.

From their first meeting Poe had felt an antagonism in the youth who, indeed, feared that Mrs. Shew's duty to God and her family was being compromised by her association with a man who publicly avowed his pantheistic, nay, atheistic, theories. He based his prejudice on Poe's indiscriminate airing of a tremendous theory that he was propounding "of the physical, metaphysical and mathematical—of the material and spiritual universe—of its essences, its origin, its creation, its present condition and its destiny. . . ." [10]

Perhaps to disprove to herself Mr. Hopkins' prejudices against Poe's atheism, Mrs. Shew, one night, took Poe to a midnight service, probably in Grace Church. She noticed that he followed the service like a churchman, and, holding one side of her prayerbook, sang the Psalms in an agreeable tenor. Gravely, he then listened to the sermon, on the sympathies of the souls with their wants. However, at the words "He was a man of sorrows and acquainted with grief" he suddenly broke down. Excusing himself, he told Mrs. Shew that he would wait for her outside, and quickly slipped out.

[10] *Works. Eureka*, Vol. II, p. 117.

->>> • <<<-

Eureka

"I AM about to make an effort at re-establishing myself in the literary world," Poe wrote to Willis on the 22nd of January, 1848, "and I *feel* that I may depend upon your aid." He was once again seriously planning to start the *Stylus* and, since he needed a list of at least four hundred subscribers, he proposed to get some of the subscriptions in person by going south and west. "In order to get the means of taking the first step, I propose to lecture at the Society Library, on Thursday, the 3rd of February . . . I have chosen a broad text—'The Universe.' " [1]

Grandiose thoughts had always seethed behind that great brow. As a mere boy he had set his "Al Aaraaf" in the universe of stars. Throughout his life he had nurtured lofty schemes which, if not attained, he had invented. Always there had been his aspiration toward superhuman achievement. Now nearing the end of his fourth decade Poe, as poor as ever, if not poorer, had reached a crisis of exaltation that bordered the maniacal. He had done many things to gain attention in his life. They were not enough, for others with far less talent than himself had obtained as much fame, indeed, more. He must distinguish himself in a way that would put all the so-called thinkers of America to shame—Emerson with his Transcendentalism and his Oversoul, and all the other petty philosophers who claimed revelation.

Eureka. "I have found it." Certainly Poe believed in his discovery. From his youth he had had intimations of the workings of nature, obscurely felt and sometimes converted into poetry. He had always kept his mind open to the mysterious stirrings of what people called the supernatural. Thus, when Andrew Jackson Davis, the Seer of Poughkeepsie, claimed spiritual revelation for his "Principles of Nature," which offered a solution of the mystery of the universe, Poe had been one of the first to make the trip to see him. For Poe, the visionary,

[1] Ostrom, p. 359.

there was nothing extraordinary in that the spirit should force the prison of the flesh and attain the world beyond. It was one of the mystical currents of the times and he escaped it no more than did Elizabeth Barrett Browning, or Walt Whitman, who was ever to be moved by night, sleep, death and the stars.

Poe saw much of the night and the stars in his Fordham wanderings, while Death had been his familiar since childhood. Indeed, it appears it was still with him, for on meeting Poe, the Seer of Poughkeepsie beheld his body entirely enveloped in the shadow of Death that went before it. In "Al Aaraaf" Poe had already linked Death with the stars. During his nocturnal observations of the heavens from the cottage porch of a summer evening, or on some clear autumn night, the mystery of that grandeur had not failed to thrill a mind always alive to such stimulus. One starry vision, the pale Astarte, had found its fixed place in "Ulalume." The whole firmament now bade him reveal its secret.

This aspiring after the sublime had intensified after the death of Virginia, when, succeeding the brain fever, his mind experienced a strange exaltation. His delusions of grandeur now began to take on abnormal proportions. Mrs. Shew's young Mr. Hopkins was appalled one day when, on his protesting the pantheism he detected in Poe's theory of the universe, the poet, with flashing eyes and an expression of scornful pride, exclaimed: "My whole nature utterly *revolts* at the idea that there is any being in the Universe superior to myself!"

For much of 1847 Poe had been elaborating *Eureka,* expounding his theory to the long-suffering Mrs. Clemm, who, if she did not understand a word of it, had the good sense not to show it. Up and down of a starry night they would pace the lawn, Poe's arm about Muddie's waist, while he laid mind and soul open to supernal influences, till, exhausted and ready to fall, Mrs. Clemm led him back into the cottage. He would then go to his writing table and set down his ideas, while Mrs. Clemm, dozing wearily in a chair, would start up every hour or so to give him a cup of hot coffee. Then again she would sit by him, relieving him by her presence of the terrors of the night, which he dreaded now as much as in his childhood. At three or four in the morning he would put down his pen and go to bed. But even so Mrs. Clemm had to follow him, to stroke his forehead till that restless brain was calm and sleep closed his eyes. She would then quietly slip out and sink down upon her bed.

By 1848 Poe was ready to present his *Eureka* with authority. On the evening of the 3rd of February the doors of the Society Library opened to the public that had ventured out in bad weather to hear

Edgar Allan Poe discourse on "The Cosmogony of the Universe." A scattering of some sixty individuals sat shivering in the chill auditorium. Poe rose, went to the lectern and fingered the bulky manuscript. He looked handsome, pale, poetically grave in his black suit and stock. He began to speak, rather, to read, in his rich, expressive voice. First of all, he announced the theorem that he sought to demonstrate: that "in the Original Unity of the First Thing lies the Secondary Cause of all things, with the Germ of their Inevitable Annihilation." In illustration of the idea, he went on, he proposed "to take such a survey of the Universe that the mind may be able really to receive and to perceive an individual impression"—and, accordingly, he limited the Universe to include only the Universe of Stars. (!)

The lecture lasted over two hours. After the statement of his thesis he made an imaginary excursion, in his insufferable comic vein, to the year 2848, to give a perspective on contemporary thought. Whether his audience was amused by his Aries Tottle for Aristotle or by his puns on Bacon and Hogg, it is too late to discover. It was left in no doubt, however, that both Aristotle and Bacon, with their deductive and inductive methods of reasoning, were not only centuries, but aeons, away from the intuitiveness, checked, of course, by experiment, which he, Poe, advocated and practiced. As he continued, his serio-comic digression appeared to have been delivered for the sole purpose of impressing upon the world the words: "I care not whether my work be read now or by posterity. I can afford to wait a century for readers when God himself has waited six thousand years for an observer. . . ." He did not mention, however, that those words, almost to the syllable, had originally been penned by Kepler, after discovering his famous Third Law.

From there Poe then proceeded to his abstruse theories, expounded in meticulous detail. "Thought is its self-cognizance, and with some little equivocation, it may be said that no fog of the mind can well be greater than that which, extending to the very boundaries of the mental domain, shuts out even those boundaries themselves from comprehension." Much of that fog interfered with his audience's comprehension, unfortunately, or at least with the reporters', some of whose comments he felt called upon to answer.

He had started out with the proposition that because Nothing was, therefore Everything is; that gravity is only a mode of manifesting the tendency of all things to return to their original unity. That the law of gravitation is the necessary result and sole possible mode of equable *irradiation* of matter through space. That the Universe of Stars as distinguished from the Universe of Space is limited. That matter, springing up from Unity, sprang from Nothingness—that is, was created. That all will return to Nothingness in returning to Unity.

On the whole his audience remained overawed, impressed and mystified. Mr. Poe had certainly done a great deal of reading and thinking. Eminent names—Laplace, Pascal, the Baron de Bielfeld, Newton—punctuated the discourse. The great Idea, however, found few minds vast enough to comprehend it. Poe remained unshaken in the tremendousness of his revelation. In his total absorption he abandoned the pursuit of Astarte to lose himself in the Universe of Stars. He must give his Great Idea to the world.

He approached George P. Putnam, late of Wiley and Putnam, but now a publisher on his own account. Sitting opposite Mr. Putnam, who was behind his desk in his office, Poe fixed his eyes earnestly upon him and began to expound his discoveries, which, he said, were a matter of the greatest importance to the world. It was not enough to publish *Eureka* in the usual small edition. Fifty thousand copies should be the minimum to begin with. Later Putnam could follow it with a larger printing.

Mr. Putnam eventually agreed to risk publication, starting with a modest five hundred copies. A cautious man, he did not involve himself too deeply financially either. For his book of revelation Poe received an advance of $14—plus a shilling to take him to Fordham—for all of which he had to sign a document that read: "Received of George P. Putnam Fourteen Dollars money loaned, to be repaid out of the proceeds of the Copyright of my work entitled 'Eureka, a Prose Poem'; and I hereby engage, in case the sales of said work do not cover the expenses . . . to repay the said amount of Fourteen Dollars; and I also engage not to ask or apply for any other loans or advances from said Putnam in any way, and to wait until January, 1849 for the statement of account as above, before making any demand whatever. Edgar A. Poe, New York, May 23, 1848." The statement was further witnessed and signed by Maria Clemm and Marie Louise Shew.[2]

Eureka was dedicated to Alexander von Humboldt, the German scientist who had dealt with cosmic theories. It was also addressed "To the few who love me and whom I love—to those who feel rather than to those who think—to the dreamers and those who put faith in dreams as the only realities . . . *What I here propound is true:*—therefore it cannot die:—or if by any means it be now trodden down so that it die, it will 'rise again to Life Everlasting.' . . ."[3]

[2] Original in Koester Collection.
[3] *Works. Eureka*, Vol. II, p. 117.

Here rings distinctly a note of exaltation that cannot but alarm. Here is messianic fervor which, as one reads on in the "prose poem," rises to the fever pitch of megalomania. Poe, recently, had taken to quoting a statement of Bielfeld's which, of course, had found its way into *Eureka:* "We know absolutely nothing of the nature or essence of God:—in order to comprehend what he is, we should have to be God ourselves." [4] Further on, the *should be* has become an affirmation. "Each soul is, in part, its own God—its own Creator." The closing lines assert the ultimate fact: "Think that . . . Man, for example, ceasing imperceptibly to feel himself Man will at length attain that awfully triumphant epoch when he shall recognize his existence as that of Jehovah." [5] It is to be assumed that Poe had already reached that triumphant epoch.

For all its seething chaos *Eureka* was not without flashes of poetical sublimity. Speaking of the atoms of the Universe, he said: "If I venture to displace, by even the billionth part of an inch, the microscopical speck of dust which lies now upon the point of my finger, what is the character of that act upon which I have adventured? I have done a deed which shakes the Moon in her path, which causes the Sun to be no longer the sun, and which alters forever the destiny of the multitudinous myriads of stars that roll and glow in the majestic presence of their Creator." [6] Only Whitman at his best was to reach for, and attain, such heights.

Eureka fell on a sluggish public. Still, the edition ultimately found purchasers and an additional printing of two hundred fifty copies was required. The criticisms began to appear. Inevitably, none of them satisfied Poe. Some he took the trouble to answer, particularly the one by a "Student of Theology" in Charles F. Hoffman's *Literary World* for July 29, in which he suspected the hand of the young gentleman "with the turn-down shirt collar," as he called Mr. Hopkins. Pointing out the Student's misquotations and distortions, Poe took particular exception to the statement that his theory was only Laplace's all over again. "I have only to say that no gentleman can accuse me of the disingenuousness here implied. . . . The *ground* covered by the great French astronomer compares with that covered by my theory, as a bubble compares with the ocean on which it floats. . . ." [7] Let the Student of Theology swallow *that,* if he could.

Poe had reached such a point that he could not accept criticism,

[4] Quoted in French on p. 132 of *Eureka.*
[5] *Ibid.,* p. 214.
[6] *Ibid.,* p. 142.
[7] Ostrom, p. 380.

however well intended. He even lost his sense of humor when, in Lowell's *A Fable for Critics,* witty, sly though good natured, satire on the American literary scene, he found the lines:

> Here comes Poe with his Raven like Barnaby Rudge,
> Three fifths of him genius and two fifths sheer fudge,
> Who talks like a book of iambs and pentameters
> In a way to make people of common sense damn meters;
> Who has written some things quite the best of their kind,
> But the heart somehow seems all squeezed out by the mind . . .

The heart squeezed out by the mind also stung for the fragment of truth in the observation. Altogether the words of the once "dear friend" irritated him. What was Lowell's "fable" but "a dish of skimmed-milk-and-water"? he wrote to his old friend F. W. Thomas. "Miss Fuller, that detestable old maid—told him, once, that he was 'so wretched a poet as to be disgusting even to his best friends.' That set him off at a tangent and he has never been quite right since. . . . Lowell is a ranting abolitionist and *deserves* a good using up." [8] For that purpose he sent a review of the "Fable" to the *Southern Literary Messenger.*

His delusions of grandeur, his nervous irritability, had manifested themselves long before this, with his collapse following Virginia's death. To her unquestioning, unalterable love he had been what he believed himself to be—a genius far above the popular idols who enjoyed their brief day in the sun only to die, like the ephemera that they were. In his spiritual and physical decadence he had to bolster himself up to survive; hence *Eureka,* hence his last passionate effort to establish the *Stylus,* to attain that position of power which now became the very breath of his life.

With the new spurt of publicity from his *Eureka* lectures, the moths of the salons were once more fluttering about him. The radiance he shed, however, like that of the stars of his universe, extended far beyond the immediate orbit, reaching Providence, where, in 1845, he had strolled on a moonlit night with Mrs. Osgood, nearly to the doorstep of Mrs. Helen Whitman.

One day, late in 1847, Mrs. Whitman received a letter from Miss Lynch, relating literary gossip and adding: "Last year on the evening of Valentine's day . . . I had a Valentine party; that is, there were Valentines written for all present. . . . The best of them were selected and read, and some of them afterwards published. I am going to have another this year . . . and I want to know if you will not help me . . .

[8] *Ibid.,* pp. 427-428.

I will mention the names of some that I expect . . . and if you will write you can select your victims from the list. . . ." [9] She suggested C. F. Hoffman, Halleck, Horace Greeley and Tuckerman, with a few others.

Mrs. Whitman eagerly set pen to paper. In her enthusiasm she produced a Valentine poem of forty-eight lines. It was not addressed to any of the names suggested by Miss Lynch, but to Edgar Allan Poe, who had not been on the list. Making a fair copy of her poem, Mrs. Whitman dated it February 14, 1848, and sent it to New York. On that evening the doves and swans were all aflutter as they listened to the stanzas from Providence.

> Oh! thou grim and ancient Raven,
>   From the Night's plutonic shore,
> Oft in dreams, thy ghastly pinions
>   Wave and flutter round my door—
> Oft thy shadow dims the moonlight
>   Sleeping on my chamber floor . . .
>
> From thy wing, one purple feather
>   Wafted o'er my chamber floor
> Like a shadow o'er the heather,
>   Charms my vagrant fancy more
> Then all the flowers I used to gather
>   On 'Idalia's velvet shore.'
> Then, Oh! Grim and ghastly Raven!
>   Wilt thou to my heart and ear
> Be a Raven true as ever
>   Flapped his wings and croaked, 'Despair?'
> Not a bird that roams the forest
>   Shall our lofty eyrie share.[10]

Poe was delighted with the verses. Oddly enough, for one so susceptible to flattery, he made no immediate response. At that time, however, Poe was in the throes of his worship of his "beloved physician." He was also at the lowest ebb of his powers and, consequently, in no mood for such exchanges as Mrs. Whitman's overture indicated. Mrs. Osgood, on the other hand, quickly wrote to her, vicariously titillated by the promise of the entanglement which she had tried to bring about. "I see . . . your beautiful invocation has reached 'The Raven' in his eyrie and I suppose ere this, he has *swooped* upon your little *dove-cote* in Providence. May Providence protect

[9] James A. Harrison and Charlotte F. Dailey, *Century Magazine,* January, 1909.

[10] *Century Magazine,* January, 1909.

you if he has! He is in truth 'A glorious devil, with large heart and brain.' " [11]

Poe, however, had not budged from New York. Moody and love-lorn, he was haunting Mrs. Shew's comforting presence. One day in the spring, while having tea with her in the conservatory of her house, he complained of the blight that seemed to have fallen over his creative faculties. He longed to write a poem, but nothing would come. He was nervous and overwrought, so much so that the sound of the Grace Church bells, which just then began ringing, struck him with almost physical pain. Wisely Mrs. Shew sought to distract him. Pen and ink were handy. She took a sheet and wrote upon it, "The Bells, by E. A. Poe." Then, below, she added, "The little silver bells . . ."

Taken in by her compassionate ruse, he picked up the pen and added six lines, completing the stanza. Then she wrote "The heavy iron bells . . ." Again Poe met the challenge in a longer stanza. Absorbed now, he went on, adding more stanzas. The effort, however, seemed to exhaust him and he could not write another word. As it was suppertime, they went upstairs, but Poe appeared so spent that Mrs. Shew led him to her brother's bedroom, where he soon sank into a sleep so profound that she sent for Dr. Francis. He examined the sleeping man. "He has heart disease, and will die early in life," he said.[12] The good doctor was only confirming what Mrs. Shew had long known: that, and the threat of insanity.

Poe eventually finished "The Bells" after working and reworking the verses to the form in which they have rung through generations, in the cadences of the elocutionists.

In June of that year, when Poe finally acknowledged Mrs. Whitman's valentine with a poem of his own, he had already lost hope of ever winning his "beloved physician" to any relation other than friendship, and even that, thanks to the young gentleman with the turn-down collar, had cooled. Indeed, there was a valedictory note in the last sentence of the letter Poe had written Mrs. Shew earlier that month: "I will try to overcome by grief for the sake of your unselfish care of me in the past, and in life or death, I am ever yours gratefully & devotedly." [13]

The Raven, however, had not allowed Sarah Helen Whitman's poem to remain unanswered for so long. If inspiration failed, he still had backlog enough to keep the fire from dying. Taking a volume of his Wiley and Putnam *Poems*, he tore out the page containing "To

[11] Caroline Ticknor, *Poe's Helen,* p. 48.

[12] Ingram, Vol. II, p. 155.

[13] Ostrom, p. 374.

Helen," underlined the words *on desperate seas, long wont to roam,* and sent it in March, like a harbinger of spring, to Mrs. Whitman.

Meanwhile he had been making discreet inquiries about the new Helen. From Miss Lynch he learned many things about her romantic character which both absorbed him and aroused his curiosity. Miss Lynch spoke of them as eccentricities, but in his infatuated mood Poe detected remarkable resemblances between thoughts, traits and sentiments which till then he had believed peculiar to himself. From that moment a profound sympathy with the poetess took possession of him. Immediately he began to read whatever he could find of her verses and deemed them beyond question poetry—*instinct with genius.* Everything he learned about the lady only whetted his curiosity. However, his vanity was piqued by Mrs. Whitman's silence. Not a line had come from her. Was it marital fidelity that kept her from answering? For, somehow, he seemed to have gathered from Miss Lynch that Mrs. Whitman was a wife, and a happy one. But, then, how explain her valentine?

At last, in mid-June, not long after his last poignant plea to Mrs. Shew, he sent Mrs. Whitman, anonymously, a new poem, also called "To Helen." In it he elaborated upon his reminiscence of his glimpse of her, that summer night when, at the urging of Mrs. Osgood, he had come by her house.

> I saw thee once—once only—years ago:
> I must not say *how* many—but *not* many.
> It was a July midnight; and from out
> A full-orbed moon, that, like thine own soul, soaring.
> Sought a precipitate pathway up through heaven,
> There fell a silvery-silken veil of light,
> With quietude, and sultriness, and slumber,
> Upon the upturn'd faces of a thousand
> Roses that grew in an enchanted garden,
>
> .   .   .   .
>
> That gave out, in return for the love-light,
> Their odorous souls in an ecstatic death . . .

From its opening the poem is studied, impersonal, lacking the fervid spontaneity, the intensity, of the fifteen sublime lines of the first "To Helen." Then the compelling spark had sprung from the heart, kindling to inspiration. Here in the new "Helen," almost five times as long, the fire had cooled to the temperature of the moonlight that overlaid it. In the early poem it was Helen herself who was the giver of light. In the new, the light had fallen from the cold goddess.

But now, at length, dear Dian sank from sight,
Into a western couch of thunder-cloud;
And thou, a ghost, amid the entombing trees
Didst glide away. *Only thine eyes remained;*
They *would not* go—they never yet have gone;

.   .   .   .

They follow me—they lead me through the years.

.   .   .   .

They fill my soul with Beauty (which is Hope) . . .

Poe had woven the essential texture from his imagination. There never had been a rose garden, nor a violet bank, which he also introduced, for only a simple court stretched behind the Whitman house. Mrs. Whitman, according to her own statement, had probably stood in the doorway looking out upon the night, as she sometimes did when she could not sleep. The poem, however, contained several clues which betrayed that Poe had been smitten: the *ecstatic death* of the nonexistent roses; Helen's face upturned *in sorrow;* the fascination exerted by her eyes—all lures that he could not resist.

The already predisposed Mrs. Whitman was enchanted, but again she exercised her delaying method, enjoying the pleasure of the fisherman who, to be sure of the game, allows the fish to dangle on the hook before pulling it in. At last she answered. As only poetry could worthily respond to Poe's sentiments, she penned a throbbing screed which, among much else, confessed:

A low bewildering melody
Is murmuring in my ear
Tones such as in a twilight wood
The aspen thrills to hear . . .
And gazing on night's starry cope
I dwell with "Beauty which is Hope."

For Mrs. Whitman it was the beginning of an overwhelming experience which she had scarcely dreamed of in writing that fateful valentine. Though her birth date was the same as Poe's—January 19—she had preceded him by six years, making her forty-five years old in 1848. She traced her descent from Celtic-Norman origins and in her maiden name, Power, she sought, and convinced herself that she had found, a common root with that of Poe. Indeed, she saw everywhere fatidic links and the workings of predestination.

As a girl she had been attached to her father, who, however, seemed to have been attached to nothing, least of all to his home.

True, his capture by the British, during the War of 1812, and his three-year imprisonment had been none of his doing; but his alone was the choice of adventuring for nearly twenty years before he thought of returning home and of dying, at last, on the comfortless bosom of Mrs. Power.

Sarah Helen was thoughtful, sensitive, with a leaning toward the spiritual, rather, the spiritualistic, which had become more pronounced as she grew older. Marriage to John W. Whitman, a young lawyer from Massachusetts, did not alter her perceptibly. After five connubial years he died, leaving her a widow at thirty. When she began corresponding with Poe she was living with her mother, Mrs. Nicholas Power, and with Susan Anna, an eccentric sister, in their home on Benefit and Church Streets. The Sunday evening functions which the neighbors attended in the Benefit Street house involved communion with the other world. While the hushed women sat in a circle in the parlor, Mrs. Whitman, in a black silk dress, low slippers and a black veil trailing from her hair to the floor, brought them messages from their dear departed.

In her family circle and, for that matter, in Providence itself, Mrs. Whitman was considered quite extraordinary. First of all, she was a poetess. That, however, did not impress her neighbors as much as did her power to cross the barriers of the other world and commune with spirits. She had a mystical look which she emphasized by draping her small, shapely form—one could not call a *body* anything so ethereal—in flowing garments, and by always wearing a filmy scarf that floated behind her in the breeze. Hanging from her neck, on a narrow black velvet ribbon, she wore an unusual ornament, a tiny coffin carved out of some exotic wood—perhaps a *memento mori* to one who, the doctors said, had heart trouble. Mrs. Whitman further emphasized her frail hold on life by shutting out all that was too vivid for her sensitive nerves: too bright a light, too loud a sound. Also, to attenuate the impact of reality, she had taken to soothing her delicate senses by inhaling occasional whiffs from a handkerchief soaked in ether.

Her face, with its thoughtful eyes, set wide apart, could have been thought beautiful. The brow, broad and serene, gave it a noble look, while the ringlets clustering about the temples and descending along the cheeks framed it in frivolous beguilements. Still, with all the feminine softness, there was a line of willfulness in the compressed lips, a hint of spirit about the wide nostrils. Mrs. Whitman *was* ethereal, but by no means unaware of reality.

Meanwhile Poe, in New York, had been trying to raise money for his trip south. Just then Mrs. Osgood's sister-in-law, Mrs. Ermina Jane Locke, with whom he had also initiated a sentimental correspondence, wrote to him from Lowell, where she had obtained a lecture for him at Wentworth Hall. He needed every cent he could raise. Therefore, instead of flying to Providence, he left Mrs. Whitman in the company of Beauty which is Hope and set out for Massachusetts.

The trip was not wholly disinterested. In his last letter to Mrs. Locke, of whom he knew very little, he had written: "You will not suspect me of affectation, dear friend . . . merely because I find it impossible to tell you *now*—in a letter—what that one question was which I 'dare not even ask' of you. . . . Tell me only of the ties—if any exist—that bind you to the world:—and yet I perceive that I may have done very wrong in asking you this:—now that I have asked it, it seemed to me the maddest of questions, involving, possibly, the most visionary of hopes." [14]

He had written this on the 19th of May, before his lines to Mrs. Whitman but also before his rueful valedictory to Mrs. Shew. He was obviously in an abnormal state, lost and despairing and ready to cling to anyone who offered the least sympathy. Evidently he had not forgotten Mrs. Locke's "beautiful lines" to him, enclosed in a letter to N. P. Willis, in the grim winter when his poverty had become public knowledge.

One can readily imagine the tenor of his anticipation on his way to Lowell. Alas, when he arrived at Wamesit Cottage, a weird, ramshackle wooden-Gothic edifice on the Concord River, reality crushed all illusion. Instead of another Mrs. Osgood, he saw a matron who revealed all of her forty-three years and had nothing of the poetic about her, no inspired look of the eyes, no appealing melancholy. He also found that she had a husband—he had expected her to be widowed— as well as four children. She was a good hostess, however, though meddlesome, and took great pride in her literary lion whom she enjoyed exhibiting to her neighbors.

Poe's lecture, on "The Poets and Poetry of America," drew all of Lowell's intellectuals on July 10. His procedure was the same as usual—some expository talk and then his reading or, rather, declaiming of a few chosen poems which, it was noted, he almost sang to bring out their music. Everyone, particularly the ladies, remarked how much the poet he looked, how seldom he smiled, and how he never laughed. The *Lowell Advertiser* noticed him favorably the following day.

[14] *Ibid.,* p. 367.

Through Mrs. Locke Poe became acquainted with the Richmonds, who lived nearby and who may have been distantly related to her, for Mrs. Richmond had been born Locke Heywood. Mrs. Richmond—Annie—was twenty-eight, enthusiastic, vivacious and eager to take up everything and everyone novel, from the latest fad to the newest lion. Her husband, Charles, engrossed in his paper manufacturing business, was proud of her interests, shared some of them, and good-naturedly indulged her. With them lived Sarah Heywood, Annie's sister, a girl of eighteen. Amos, a brother, who taught school in Westford, often came to visit.

Poe did not set down his impressions of Annie until later, but the effect of the meeting had been immediate. "A figure advanced to the threshold . . . slender, or rather slight, and somewhat above the medium height. As she approached, with a certain *modest decision* of step . . . I said to myself, 'Surely here I have found the perfection of the natural, in contradistinction to artificial *grace* . . .' So intense an expression of *romance,* perhaps I should call it, or of unworldliness, as that which gleamed from her deep-set eyes, had never so sunk into my heart of hearts before. . . ." [15]

The impression must have sunk deep, for after his lecture, instead of devoting his evening to his host and hostess, he went to the Richmonds' and spent the remainder of the night there, as well as part of the next day. Amos Heywood, who was present, listened wide-eyed, with the rest, to Poe's reminiscences—of how he was the offspring of a runaway match; how he had been adopted by a very rich uncle who, because he had no children, wished to make him his son. But then the uncle marrried a young woman who, seeing in Edgar an obstacle to her being sole heir, quarreled with him and succeeded in driving him away. Poe also told of his marriage to his cousin. Although he loved her with an undivided heart, he could not think of her as his wife, or as anything other than his sister. He spoke of her death with tears running down his cheeks.[16]

In Providence, meanwhile, Mrs. Whitman waited.

[15] "Landor's Cottage," *Works,* Vol. I, p. 414.
[16] Frederick W. Coburn, "Poe as seen by the brother of 'Annie.'" *New England Quarterly,* September, 1943.

CHAPTER XXIX

Helen of a Thousand Dreams

DESPITE the attraction, Poe did not stay long in Lowell, for on July 14 he sent a note to Dr. Chivers, at his hotel, through the indefatigable Mrs. Clemm, inviting his friend to spend the weekend in Fordham as he, Poe, intended to leave for the South on Monday. Perhaps Dr. Chivers went back on the cars with Mrs. Clemm. Perhaps at Fordham the two men who, in some ways, were remarkably sympathetic, recited their old and new poems to each other. It may be, too, that Poe confessed the new stirrings of love which, together with the gossip the doctor had gathered from the literary crew, made him shake his moral head and later pronounce, in the true Chivers accent, that Poe married Venus Urania in early life but that afterwards he committed adultery with Venus Pandemos.

With the money from the lecture and whatever else he had been able to scrape together, Poe set out for Richmond, hopeful of obtaining a good part of the five hundred subscriptions he counted upon for the *Stylus*. He was absent from home nearly three weeks, but whether or not he wrote to Mrs. Clemm, no letters exist. Indeed, the whole interlude would remain obscure except for a number of lurid but illuminating flashes contained in the correspondence of John R. Thompson, editor of the *Southern Literary Messenger*. Some Poe biographers have found Thompson's revelations so distressing that they have tried in vain to invalidate his testimony. A few have even endeavored to cancel from the record this visit of Poe's to Richmond. Unfortunately Mr. Thompson's two letters and Poe's own testimony of his being in Richmond at the time are irrefutable.

According to Thompson's letter of October 17, 1848, to the poet, Philip Pendleton Cooke, Poe had by then left Richmond. "He remained here about three weeks, horribly drunk and discoursing 'Eureka' every night to the audiences in the Bar Rooms. . . . I was very anxious for him to write something for me, while he remained here, but his lucid intervals were so brief and infrequent that it was

335

impossible. 'The Rationale of Verse' I took—more as an act of charity than anything else, for though exhibiting great acquaintance with the subject, it is altogether too bizarre for the general reader. . . ." [1]

In the other letter, to E. H. N. Patterson, written more than a year later, Thompson amplified his recollections of the visit. Poe, he learned, had been spreeing for about a fortnight "in one of the lowest haunts of vice upon the wharves. . . . When I reached the purlieus of this abandoned quarter, I learned that such a person had indeed been there, drunk . . . and that he had gone a few hours previous, without hat or coat, to the residence of Mr. John MacKenzie . . . alone and on foot. The next day he called on me with Mr. MacKenzie. . . . I did all I could to restrain his excesses and to relieve the pressure of his immediate wants . . . but no influence was adequate to keep him from the damnable propensity to drink. . . . He spoke of himself as the victim of pre-ordained damnation, as *l'ame perdue*. . . ." [2]

Poe in one of the lowest haunts of vice upon the wharves? The description may have been the exaggeration of a teetotaler for the pubs in the less respectable part of town; but that Poe had been drinking during this visit is more than likely. He had set out in an abnormal state of exaltation, induced partly by *Eureka,* with which he hoped to astound Richmond. He was, moreover, spinning in a vortex of emotions, involving at least three women—Mrs. Shew, Mrs. Whitman and Mrs. Richmond. Then, on his arrival, his unstable organism, shaken by inescapable memories—of the Allans, of Elmira—sought strength in the "ashes" he had sworn never to touch.

Beyond visiting the Mackenzies, Rosalie and a few friends, he did nothing during the Southern visit to justify it. Interest in the *Stylus* proved negligible. Poe distinguished himself for nothing but his insobriety and for quarreling with the editor of the *Examiner,* John M. Daniel, whom he challenged to a duel.

Back in Fordham, he recalled some neglected business. He had failed to answer Mrs. Whitman's verses, which, through a series of delays had not reached him until toward the end of his stay in Richmond.

"Dear Madam—" he addressed her on the 5th of September. "Being engaged in making a collection of autographs of the most distinguished American authors, I am, of course, anxious to procure your own, and if you would so far honor me as to reply . . . I would take it as a *very especial* favor." He signed it Edward S. T. Grey. [3]

---

[1] Quoted by Allen, Quinn, etc. Original in Koester Collection.
[2] Original letter, dated Nov. 9, 1849, in the Pierpont Morgan Library.
[3] Ostrom, p. 379.

It was certainly an odd thing to do after what had passed between him and the lady; but Mrs. Whitman, penetrating the disguise, merely interpreted it as Poe's way of finding out whether she was still in Providence. She did not answer him. Poe thereupon obtained a letter of introduction from Miss Maria J. McIntosh, a literary lady who knew them both. "I feel much obliged to Mr. Poe for permitting me thus to associate myself with an incident so agreeable to both of you," she wrote slyly to Mrs. Whitman.[4]

On the 21st of September Poe presented himself at the door of the Benefit Street house which his poetic fancy had surrounded with roses and banks of violets. He was led into the parlor and there waited for Mrs. Whitman to appear. At last, after a suitable interval, she glided into the room. They gazed at each other. Instantly Poe was struck by her eyes and at once believed himself unalterably in love. She was his fate, his predestined one. "As your eyes rested appealingly for one brief moment upon mine, I felt, for the first time in my life, and tremblingly acknowledged, the existence of spiritual influences altogether out of the reach of reason. I saw that you were *Helen—my* Helen—the Helen of a thousand dreams—she whose visionary lips had so often lingered upon my own in the divine trance of passion. . . ."[5]

In the wings, unobserved but observing, sharp-witted old Mrs. Power kept her eyes and ears open. She was not sure of this man Poe's intentions, nor did she know anything about his morals or the state of his pocketbook. For all his dignified looks he might be one of these adventurers who preyed upon well-to-do widows. As for the peculiar Susan Anna, perhaps she was turning over in her mind some lines to celebrate this novel visitation, as she had memorialized the sudden reappearance of her father, when she had commented:

Mr. Nicholas Power left home in a sailing vessel bound for St. Kitts,
When he returned, he frightened his family out of their wits.

Poe and Helen—he had instantly called her by that name—succeeded in being alone on several occasions during this visit. He had left Fordham like a battle-worn knight, sick of the struggle and eager to fling himself at the feet of the merciful lady of Providence. He had nothing to offer except his genius and, as he called it, his love. In reality he was making a final effort to alleviate his relentless poverty. This, however, he would not admit. His exalted nature forbade. He had persuaded himself that he was in love with Helen. He had been

---

[4] Harrison, *Century Magazine*, January, 1909.
[5] Ostrom, p. 387.

in love with her from the moment he had read her verses. Having convinced himself, he tried to convince her that their meeting had been preordained in Heaven.

One day the two went out for a walk to Swan Point Cemetery, far out in the country. Hand in hand they strolled in the shade of the cypresses in the burial ground and then sat down side by side near a low nameless grave. Deeply affected, as always in the presence of death, Poe, his arm encircling Helen's waist, asked her to marry him.

"Helen, I love now—now—for the first and only time," he said, and no doubt believed the lie. That evening, and again the next, they talked about their feelings for each other, while Helen paced about the room, or sat beside him, or stood with her hand on the back of his chair, in studied attitudes. "My brain reeled beneath the intoxicating spell of your presence, and it was with no merely human senses that I either saw or heard you. It was my soul only that distinguished you there. I grew faint with the luxury of your voice and blind with the voluptuous lustre of your eyes," he wrote on his return to Fordham.[6]

Helen's voice, however, talked solid sense for a mystic. "You will perhaps attempt to convince me that my person is agreeable to you— that my countenance interests you:—but in this respect I am so variable that I should inevitably disappoint you. And, again . . . you are not, perhaps, aware that I am many years older than yourself. . . . I can only say to you that had I youth and health and beauty, I would live for you and die with you. *Now,* were I to allow myself to love you, I could only enjoy a bright, brief, hour of rapture and die—perhaps. . . ." [7]

"Ah, beloved, beloved Helen the darling of my heart—my first and my real love," he countered, "may God forever shield *you* from the agony these your words occasion me! . . ." [8]

The dialogue of their emotions went on. Could not her terrible disease be conquered? [9] A nervous disorder, when exasperated by ether, he told her, might give rise to the symptoms of heart disease, and even deceive the most skillful physicians. "On my bosom could I not still the throbbings of your own? . . . At your feet—if you so willed it—I would cast from me, forever, all merely human desire, and clothe myself in the glory of a pure, calm and *unexacting* affection. . . . You would get better, and finally well. And if *not,* Helen,—if not—if you

---

[6] *Ibid.,* p. 387.
[7] Mrs. Whitman to Poe. Ostrom, pp. 388-389.
[8] *Ibid.,* p. 389.
[9] She survived Poe by twenty-nine years.

died then at least would I clasp your dear hand in death, and willingly, —*oh, joyfully*—*joyfully*—*joyfully*—go down *with* you into the night of the Grave." [10]

Such morbid exaltation—twelve pages of it—would have warned another, but Helen was as much in love with death as he. Poe's infatuation excited her, for she could not yet believe it was love. As for herself, she thrilled to him, to his person, to his words, but she knew too much about his amorous escapades, his irresponsible ways, to commit herself. In her scrupulous honesty she had not even allowed herself to say or write "I love you," despite his pleading, so that when he returned to New York he was in an agony of uncertainty. Her reluctance stung him and made him want her all the more. What had begun as a sentimental adventure had become a deep involvement.

Sympathizing with his hurt, Helen endeavored to make him understand that her hesitation was not without reason. "How often have I heard men and even women say of you—'He has great intellectual power, but *no* principle—*no* moral sense.' " It was one of the least of the accusations. Some presumed to suggest in all earnest that Virginia had died of the neglect and unkindness of her husband, that by her death he might be inspired to immortal elegies.[11]

In his next letter Poe decided to bare his soul, to cleanse her mind of the evil she had heard of him. To that end he marshaled the facts and, concentrating upon what he sought to achieve, twisted them to his purpose. "By the all-divine love I bear you . . . and by the God who reigns in Heaven, I swear to you that my soul is incapable of dishonor—that, with the exception of occasional follies and excesses which I bitterly lament, but to which I have been driven by intolerable sorrow . . . I can call to mind no act of my life that would bring a blush to my cheek—or to yours. If I have erred at all . . . it has been on the side of what the world would call a Quixotic sense of the honorable . . . of the chivalrous. . . . It was for this species of luxury that, in early youth, I deliberately threw away from me a large fortune, rather than endure a trivial wrong. It was for this that, at a later period, I did violence to my own heart, and married, for another's happiness, where I knew that no possibility of my own existed.—Ah, how profound is my love for you, since it forces me into these egotisms for which you will inevitably despise me! Nevertheless I must now speak to you the truth or nothing." [12]

If ever Poe had need of holding his hands above his head and in-

[10] Ostrom, pp. 389-390.
[11] See Gill, pp. 132-133
[12] Ostrom, p. 393.

voking the protective spirit of Virginia it was now, when, for a desperate expediency, he maligned himself and her. Still, there was reason
for it. In her poem Helen had written:

> I think of thee and thy lone grave
> On the green hill-side far away.

She must not feel that Virginia's grave would stand between them.
But, then, he was underestimating its power.

Yet, after protesting his love, Poe turned unsubtly to a subject
which lay at the bottom of his devotion, as much as the virtues he
saw in Helen. "I heard something, a day or two ago, which . . . withers
forever all the dear hopes upspringing in by bosom. . . . I *dreaded*
to find you in worldly circumstances superior to mine. So great was
my *fear* that you were rich, or at least possessed of some property
which might cause you to *seem* rich in the eyes of one so poor as I
had always permitted myself to be—that, on the day I refer to, I had
not the courage to ask my informant any questions concerning you.
. . . The horror with which . . . I have seen affection made a subject
of barter, had, long since—long before my marriage—inspired me
with the resolution that, under *no* circumstances, would I marry
where 'interest' as the world terms it, could be suspected as, on my
part, the object of the marriage. . . ." [13]

Mrs. Whitman was uplifted by such candor, even though it had
never occurred to anyone so spiritual that Poe could have desired her
for her comfortable situation. Mrs. Power, however, had other views
on the matter, and they coincided to a remarkable degree with those
which the overscrupulous suitor was disclaiming. She said nothing
but kept her eyes and ears open whenever Poe came to call.

Both mother and daughter would have been aghast had they
learned of the visits Poe had been making to Mrs. Richmond in the
village of Westford and of the impassioned letters—spiritual, of course
—which he was even then sending her. From his first meeting with
Annie he had been powerfully affected, and his immediate outpouring of his life history revealed his eagerness to bridge at once the
years which had separated them. When he called on her again he was
deeply in love with her. They took walks together to the hills and,
back at the cottage, when they were all sitting by the fire in the early
autumn chill, he would hold her hand in his, saying not a word, while
the old wall clock ticked the rhythm of their pulses. Mr. Richmond
understood. He knew his wife and trusted her. In his silent man's way
he also understood Poe.

[13] Ostrom, p. 395.

At either the first, or the second, meeting, Poe had avowed his adoration to Annie. "So long as I think that you *know* I love you, as no man ever loved woman . . . *so* long no worldly trouble can ever render me absolutely wretched. But oh, *my darling, my* Annie, my own sweet *sister* Annie, my *pure* beautiful angel—*wife* of my soul—to be mine hereafter & *forever in the Heavens*—how shall I explain to you the bitter anguish which has tortured me since I left you?" [14]

It is impossible to tell when the pledge of a union in the Heavens had been given. Whenever it was, it did not deter Poe from pursuing his suit of Helen of a Thousand Dreams. One evening—the date is uncertain—Mrs. Whitman invited a large gathering to meet Poe and enjoy the privilege of listening to him. The guests arrived and took their places along the two sides of the parlor, while their hostess and Mr. Poe sat at opposite ends of the room. The *conversazione* began with Mr. Poe introducing the subject, a discussion between himself and Mrs. Whitman on the poetic principle. All fixed their gaze upon the author of "The Raven," whose gleaming eyes, even more than what he said, held them. The spell was not broken when Mrs. Whitman took up the subject in her dulcet tones. While they discoursed, Poe's eyes were riveted on Mrs. Whitman's and hers upon his, in mutual fascination. They became visibly more and more agitated. At one point Poe rose from his chair and, holding out his arms, walked in the direction of Mrs. Whitman, who had also risen and was moving toward him. In the center of the room they met. Enfolding her in his embrace, he kissed her, then led her back to her chair. They were now betrothed in the eyes of the world.

It was a conditional engagement, for, although Mrs. Whitman had long since reached the age of discretion, Mrs. Power still dominated her. Moreover, Helen herself, either from scruples of conscience or from some doubt she may still have entertained of Poe's intentions, had not committed herself irrevocably. With her it was a question of Poe's character, of his weaknesses, his drinking which, for her sake, he swore to overcome. Moreover, she was not sure it was love that she felt for him. As she confessed, years later, her feeling for Poe had not really partaken of the character of love. It was, as she put it, "something at once more intimate and more remote—a strange inexplicable enchantment that I can neither analyze nor comprehend." [15]

The worldly-wise Mrs. Power, on the other hand, comprehended

[14] Letter of Nov. 16, 1848. Ostrom, p. 401.
[15] Stanley T. Williams, "New Letters about Poe," *Yale Review*, July, 1925.

all too well. She was inflexibly opposed to her daughter's binding herself to a penniless man who, she was convinced, was after her money, and she made no effort to disguise her dislike and mistrust. In spite of her daughter's pleas she made it clear that she would never give her consent to the marriage.

The self-deluded lovers, meanwhile, were building up their pathetic deceptions from different motives and in accordance with their peculiar natures. Into Helen's empty life had suddenly come not only the knight of her dreams but a god. Indeed, like a priestess of some occult art she juggled the letters in the name Edgar Poe and produced "A God-Peer." By this exaltation she too was exalted, for had not Poe elected her above all women? Had he not written: "It was . . . when I thought of *you*—that I dwelt exultingly upon what I felt that I could accomplish in Letters and Literary influence. 'I will erect,' I said, 'a prouder throne than any on which mere monarch ever sat; and on this throne she—*she* shall be my queen.' " [16]

Meanwhile Mrs. Whitman still refrained from saying the words for which Poe had long been waiting—that she loved him, that she would be his. At last, late in October or early November, Poe had word from her; but her letter was still noncommittal. He had a date to lecture in Lowell in November. Probably on the 2nd of the month, distraught by the state of indecision in which she had kept him, and further agitated by his emotional involvement with Annie, he set out on his trip, informing Helen to expect him on Saturday, November 4. "Oh how powerless is the pen to express such feelings as now consume me! May the God of Heaven protect you until I clasp you to my heart," he wrote her, signing himself "Your Edgar." [17]

What followed was a Poe nightmare, but in real life and with himself as the protagonist. First he went to see Annie Richmond. He was about to take the irretrievable step of binding Mrs. Whitman to a sacred promise, and he was telling this to the woman whom he loved, or believed himself to love, above every other being on earth. What was he to do? Weak and incapable of making up his mind, he pleaded with Annie to guide him. Loving and pitying the man who was clutching so desperately for someone to save him, she advised him according to her womanly understanding. He must speak out to Mrs. Whitman, have her declare herself once for all. But these were hardly the words he wanted to hear. For him, at that time, the greatest bliss lay in his nearness to her, "My Annie, whom I so madly, so dis-

---

[16] Ostrom, p. 396.

[17] This is the only fragment that remains of the original letter. Ostrom, p. 399.

tractedly love." Still, for her sake and on her persuasion, he promised to say the words that were to be said, though his heart revolted. Before leaving, he clasped her to his heart, saying to himself: "It is for the last time, until we meet in Heaven." [18] Then he exacted a promise, a *holy* promise: that she come to him when he was dying.

Thoughts of death, . . . death itself, like the shadow which Davis the Seer had seen enveloping him, pursued him all the way to Providence. He could remember nothing distinctly until he arrived there on November 4, his mind mercifully blacking out his despair. At the hotel he went to bed, but he could not sleep and he wept through the night which broke hopelessly into dawn. In spite of his promise to Annie he could not muster up the resolve to go to Mrs. Whitman and wrest from her the pledge that would bind her to him forever. It was not Helen of a Thousand Dreams whom he wanted, but Annie, his *"pure, virtuous, generous, beautiful, beautiful sister Annie!"* [19]

Dressing hurriedly on the morning of the 5th, he went out for a brisk walk, hoping to clear his mind, but his torment remained with him. He then bought two ounces of laudanum and, instead of going to his hotel, took the cars to Boston. There he wrote Annie a letter. "I told you how my struggles were more than I could bear—how my soul revolted from saying the words which were to be said—and that not even for your dear sake could I bring myself to say them." [20] After writing the letter and informing Annie where she could find him in fulfillment of her promise, he swallowed half the laudanum and hurried to the post office, intending to take the rest when she arrived. By the time he reached the post office he no longer knew what he was doing, for he had miscalculated the strength of the drug. The letter was never sent.

By chance, someone he knew found him and took care of him. After his stomach had rejected the laudanum, Poe was himself again —calm and, to the casual observer, sane, as he commented with tragic self-knowledge. At any rate, he was well enough to be sent back to Providence. Now the dreaded interview had to be faced. He had avoided an appointment with Mrs. Whitman on the 4th, when she was expecting him, and he made it impossible on the 5th, by fleeing to Boston and attempting suicide. One morning he finally summoned up enough resolve to go to her. He presented himself on her doorstep at such an impossibly early hour that he was not admitted. First of

[18] Letter of Nov. 16, 1848. Ostrom, p. 401.
[19] Ostrom, p. 403.
[20] *Ibid.,* p. 401.

all, it would have been too unconventional; secondly, Mrs. Whitman was certain that he had been intoxicated in Boston, and so had broken his promise to her.

He then sent her a note, addressing her as *dearest* Helen. He was very ill, he told her, so much so that he must go home, if possible. If she would say stay, he would try to do so. "If you cannot see me— write *one word* to say that you *do* love me and that, *under all circumstances,* you will be mine. Remember that these coveted words you have never yet spoken—and, nevertheless, I have not reproached you. . . ." [21]

In reply, she sent him word at his hotel that she would meet him at the Athenaeum in half an hour. Despite the cool, classical surroundings, Helen was not in the most ingratiating of moods. Friends never wearied of cautioning her against marrying a man like Poe, and only recently she had received a letter from one of his associates in New York repeating the warning. She faced Poe with the accusations and, the better to strike home, read him part of the letter. Poe listened, visibly wounded by all that was being heaped upon his head, and, saying that when they met again it would be as strangers, he abruptly left her.

That evening, flinging promises to the winds, he went to the bar of his hotel to try to drink himself to forgetfulness but only succeeded in bringing on a night of delirium. Next day, still in great mental distress, he reappeared at the Benefit Street house. Mrs. Whitman was in her room, from where she heard him crying out to her mother that his salvation for time and eternity depended upon her, Helen. His tones rang through the house. Never had she heard anything so awful, awful even to sublimity, as she described them.

Mrs. Power saw that the situation was more than she could manage and sent for a physician, Dr. O. H. Oakie. He found signs of brain fever and ordered the half-crazed poet to be taken to the house of Mr. W. J. Pabodie, a friend of Poe's. Helen, unable to nerve herself to see him, had listened in terror for nearly two hours to his cries.

When she finally made her appearance, Poe clung to her so desperately that when she pulled herself away he was clutching a fragment of her dress in his hand. The scene had a moving effect upon her, influencing her enough to assure Poe of their engagement, on condition that he maintain his promises of reform. With that understanding they parted and on the 14th of November, thanks to Mr. Pabodie, who took care of him until his recovery, Poe returned to Fordham.

Mrs. Clemm hardly recognized him—he was so ravaged by his re-

[21] Letter of Nov. 7, 1848. Ostrom, p. 399.

cent tribulations. One, certainly, his suicide attempt, he must have kept from her. Yet a record survives of his extreme agony, a daguerreotype taken a few days after he had swallowed the laudanum. His hair is matted and damp over his forehead. The eyes, scarcely able to focus, are those of one who has seen hell. Anguish distorts the face as if from some spiritual cataclysm that somehow also affects the clothes, disordered, rumpled and awry. With all that, there is still beauty in that face where good and ill are visibly at war.

He had sent Helen a note which he wrote while the boat was being made fast to the wharf and in the interval of waiting for the Fordham train. It was as brief and loving as he could make it, but it hardly rang with conviction. There was much more sincerity in the admission: "That I am not supremely happy, even when I feel your dear love at my heart, terrifies me. What can it mean?" [22]

He answered the question in his letter to Annie two days later, the 16th of November. "Ah, Annie! Annie! my Annie!—is your heart *so* strong?—is there *no* hope!—is there *none?*" he cried, after telling her of his engagement and the laudanum episode. He felt that he must die if he went through with the marriage, but how could he retract with honor? "Ah *beloved,* think—think for *me* & for yourself—do I not *love* you Annie? do you not *love* me? . . . It is not much that I ask, *sweet sister Annie*—my mother & myself would take a small cottage at Westford—oh *so* small—so *very* humble. . . . I would labor day & night, and with industry, I could accomplish *so* much Annie! it would be a Paradise beyond my wildest hopes . . . I would hear from you continually . . . & our dear mother would be with us & love us both. . . ." [23]

Unconsciously he was recalling the closely knit unit of Mrs. Clemm, himself and Virginia. It was at this time that he wrote "Landor's Cottage." While describing Annie and their first meeting in this idyl, he placed her where his longing wished her to be, in the little Fordham house.

Understandably perturbed by the revelations in Poe's letter, Annie did not answer immediately. When, after the lapse of a week, Poe had not heard from her, he wrote to her sister Sarah. "If there is any pity in your heart reply immediately to this letter, & let me know *why* it is, I did not hear from Annie— If I do not hear from her soon I shall surely die—I fancy everything evil . . . & that she no longer loves me or cares for me. . . ." [24] What made the silence worse was

[22] Ostrom, p. 400.
[23] *Ibid.,* p. 402.
[24] Letter of Nov. 23, 1848. Ostrom, p. 406.

Annie's neglect to answer two letters which Mrs. Clemm had also written her in the interval.

On the 24th, the day after his appeal to Sarah, Poe wrote to Mrs. Whitman, who had sent him several communications, one of them containing a poem, "Arcturus— Written in October." It was an invocation to the star; more deeply, it was the confession of her troubled spirit.

> Hast thou not stooped from heaven, fair star! to be
> So near me in this hour of agony?—
> So near—so bright—so glorious, that I seem
> To lie entranced as in some wondrous dream,
> All earthly joys forgot—all earthly fear,
> Ringed in the light of the resplendent sphere:
> Kindling within my soul a pure desire
> To blend with thine its pale candescent fire. . . .

"In a little more than a fortnight, dearest Helen," Poe began, "I shall once again clasp you to my heart:—until then I forbear to agitate you by speaking of my wishes—of my hopes, and especially of my fears. You say all depends on my own firmness. If this be so, all is safe—for the terrible agony which I have so lately endured—an agony known only to God and to myself—seems to have passed my soul through fire and purified it from all that is weak. Henceforward I am strong:—this those who love me shall see—as well as those who have so relentlessly endeavored to ruin me. . . ." [25] The old persecution mania had been revived by Helen's saying that she had been tortured by reports about him.

After the first affectionate words, he became absorbed in self-justification, with his own concerns. As for the poem, after saying it was truly beautiful, he set out to correct it. "There is obvious tautology in 'pale candescent.' To be *candescent* is to become *white* with heat. Why not read—'To blend with thine its incandescent fire?' . . ." [26] Gratefully Helen adopted his improvement. Beyond that, there was little in the letter to gratify her heart. Poe was aware of it, for two days later he apologized that his words might have seemed cold, perhaps even selfish.

He had another reason for writing her again so soon. "Was I right, dearest Helen, in my first impression of you . . . in the idea that you are ambitious? If so and *if you will have faith in me,* I can & will satisfy your wishes and your desires. . . . When I see you I will explain all—as far, at least, as I dare explain *all* my hopes even

[25] Ostrom, pp. 406-407.
[26] *Ibid.,* p. 408.

to you. Would it not be 'glorious,' *darling,* to establish, in America, the sole unquestionable aristocracy—that of the intellect—to secure its supremacy—to lead & control it? All this I *can* do, Helen, & will —if you bid me—and aid me. . . ." [27]

He was, of course, referring to the *Stylus,* once more resurgent, for only the previous week he had written to Frances Allan's brother, Edward Valentine—"during my childhood, you were very kind to me"—for the loan of $200 to help him start the magazine. Meanwhile his sole earnings came from his sporadic lectures. As it happened, in the middle of December he received an invitation, his fifth, to lecture at the Franklin Lyceum, in Providence, on Wednesday the 20th, and promptly wrote to *"My own dearest* Helen" about it. However, he added that, since he could not be in Providence before Wednesday morning and since he had to get some sleep after he arrived, he would not be able to see her until the afternoon. "My mother sends her dearest love and says she will return good for evil & treat you *much* better than *your* mother has treated me," he closed with a little sting.[28]

In New York, meanwhile, the news of the engagement was being noised about. One of the first reactions was a visit from Mrs. Osgood to Mrs. Whitman. One can only guess at Mrs. Osgood's motives; that they were of the most altruistic, Mrs. Whitman was convinced, considering her dear friend's affectionate interest and solicitude for her welfare. At Mrs. Osgood's request, Helen promised to repeat to Poe many of the things the lady had told her during the interview, although she, Helen, had a feeling that their tendency would be to increase Mrs. Osgood's influence over him, while perhaps weakening her own.

At the New York station, as he set out, Poe encountered Mrs. Ellet, the last person he would have wished to see. "Mr. Poe, are you going to Providence to be married?" she inquired.

"It is a mistake," he said. "I am not going to be married."

"Why, Mr. Poe, I understand that the banns have been published," she persisted.

"I cannot help what you have heard, my dear Madam, but mark me, I shall not marry her." [29]

Poe was indeed approaching the marriage with foreboding—loving one woman yet binding himself to another. It was too late, however, for him to retract with honor, as he had told Annie.

In Providence, too, there were misgivings, particularly on the part

[27] *Ibid.,* p. 410.
[28] *Ibid.,* p. 412.
[29] Griswold, *Memoir,* pp. xlv-xlvi.

of Helen's mother and her relatives, who had been doing their utmost to break off the match. If Mrs. Power could not prevent the union, she was resolved at least to protect her daughter's interests. Accordingly, when the marriage contract was drawn up, Mrs. Whitman legally transferred the bulk of her estate, worth more than $8,000 in money and mortgages, to her mother. Had not Poe averred that under no circumstances would he marry where interest could be suspected in his motives?

Poe, with the rest, signed his name as witness, but he was affronted and angered by so vulgar a measure to protect Helen's money. Yet, the thought could not help insinuating itself:—how much a thousand dollars could have accomplished for the *Stylus* and toward the establishment of the aristocracy of the intellect. Had he not proved himself a leader of that aristocracy by drawing 1,800 individuals to his Providence lecture? "And such applause!" he crowed to Annie, in a note.

His triumph may have induced Mrs. Whitman to arrive at a decision, for on the 23rd of December she allowed him to write to the Rev. Dr. Crocker to publish the banns. Simultaneously Poe informed Mrs. Clemm: "We shall be married on Monday, and will be at Fordham on Tuesday on the first train." [30] For some odd reason he did not sign the brief note.

The previous day, however, he had affixed his signature to a last-minute document, a sort of codicil to the one he had signed on the 15th of the month. It read: "Whereas a marriage is intended between the above named Sarah H. Whitman and the subscribed Edgar A. Poe—I hereby approve and assent to the transfer of the property in the manner proposed in the papers of which the preceding are copies." He was not allowed the minutest loophole through which to slip a grasping finger.

The one firm condition Helen had set upon the marriage was that Poe promise never to touch liquor. That afternoon, soon after Poe had written, but not yet delivered, the note to Dr. Crocker, she went to meet Poe at the library, where someone handed her a note. In it a well-meaning friend informed her that her fiancé had been drunk that very morning, warned her against the imprudent marriage, and retailed a number of scandalous acts of which Poe had recently been guilty. Among other matters, the informant mentioned Poe's passion for Mrs. Richmond at Lowell, which was scandalizing the whole town.

With a feeling of helplessness, of incapacity in the struggle that confronted her, Helen faced Poe with the accusations the moment they arrived at her house. In vain he sought to justify himself. The

[30] Ostrom, p. 412.

evidence for some of the allegations was too strong. Then and there, while he was still pleading with her, Helen countermanded the note to Dr. Crocker. While she listened to Poe's explanations and denials she felt a kind of marble calm. "Nor was I, at that bitter moment, unsolaced by a sense of relief," she admitted, "at being freed of the intolerable burden of responsibility which he had sought to impose upon *me.*" [31] Indeed, it took more than a mystical poetess, it took a grand, simple Mrs. Clemm to assume that burden and make of it the glory of her life.

"My mother," added Mrs. Whitman, "had a brief interview with Mr. Poe which resulted in his determination to return immediately to New York." [32] One can only imagine the hard facts and harder words that the termagant, solicitous for her fledgling of forty-five, hurled at the unworthy poet when, at her request and in the company of Mr. Pabodie, he confronted her later that afternoon in her parlor.

During the interview there was a sudden whiff of ether in the air as Helen floated in, holding the drenched handkerchief to her nostrils with one hand, while with the other she returned to Poe a bundle of papers and manuscripts which he had left in her keeping. Then, sinking back upon a couch, she covered her face with the handkerchief, praying for unconsciousness to spare her the anguish of that parting. It was mercifully brief, but not brief enough for Mrs. Power, who, fearful that her daughter would again fall under the influence of Poe's serpent wiles, was speeding him off with unceremonious words.

"You hear how I am insulted!" he appealed to Mr. Pabodie.

In vain he endeavored to rouse Helen from the torpor into which she had sunk. At last, falling upon his knees beside her, he entreated her to speak to him. "One word! But one word!" he repeated.

She lay there, in her cloud of ether, incapable of speech. At length she whispered, "What can I say?"

"Say that you love me, Helen."

"I love you," she said.

The two men left the house together. In half an hour the erstwhile "God-Peer" was on his way back to New York, the taunts of Mrs. Power still ringing in his ears.

[31] "New Letters about Poe," *Yale Review,* July, 1925.
[32] *Ibid.*

Tributes to the Living and the Dead

THE humiliation of the Providence episode rankled, but in the end, despite the injury to Poe's self-esteem, it effected a catharsis. The whole literary world by this time knew, or thought it knew, all about it and gossip spread like a monsoon from Providence to New York, gathering fact and fiction on its way in a great cloud of confusion. In Westford Annie staunchly championed Poe, even against her husband, who had allowed himself to be influenced by the rumors. In New York it became the topic of wry comment among those who knew one or both parties.

"I know a widow of doubtful age will marry almost any sort of white man," Greeley, who had not yet heard of the break, wrote to Griswold, "but this seems to me a terrible conjunction. Has Mrs. Whitman no friend within your knowledge who could faithfully explain Poe to her?" [1] Like Greeley, everyone who knew the poet had something to say.

In Providence itself, because of the face-saving version authorized by Mrs. Whitman, feeling was strong against Poe. Through the intangible wires that gossip commanded even before the invention of the telegraph, every syllable of Helen's apologia reached Annie, who promptly imparted it to Poe. "I will not repeat *all* her vile & slanderous words—you have doubtless heard them—" she wrote, "but one thing she says that I cannot *deny* though I do not believe it—viz— that you had been *published to her once,* & that on the Sat. preceding the Sabbath on which you were to have been published for the *second time,* she went herself to the Rev. Mr. Crocker's, & *after stating her reasons for so doing,* requested him to stop all further proceedings." [2]

The implications of Mrs. Whitman's act, if indeed she had been guilty of it, were certainly injurious to Poe. "My own *faithful* Annie! How shall I ever be grateful enough to God in giving me, in all my

[1] Harrison, *Life and Letters of Edgar Allan Poe,* p. 290.
[2] Quoted in Poe's letter to Mrs. Whitman, Jan. (21?), 1849. Ostrom, p. 420.

adversity, so true, so beautiful a friend! . . ." he replied. "From the bottom of my heart I forgive her all, and would forgive her even more. . . . That her friends will speak ill of me is an inevitable evil—I must bear it. In fact, Annie, I am beginning to grow wiser and do not care so much as I did for the opinions of a world in which I see . . . that to act generously is to be considered as designing, and that to be poor is to be a villain. I must get rich—rich. . . . But of one thing rest assured, Annie—from this day forth I shun the pestilential society of *literary women*. . . ." [3]

In the letter he enclosed another, his last, to Mrs. Whitman, asking Annie to read it and to show it to those she trusted, and then to seal it with wax and mail it from Boston. To an abstract "Dear Madam," once Helen of a Thousand Dreams, Poe quoted the slander which he had heard. "Your simple disavowal is all that I wish— You will of course write me immediately on receipt of this—only in the event of my not hearing from you within a few days will I proceed to take more definite steps. . . . I blame no one but your Mother. . . . So far I have assigned no reason for my declining to fulfil our engagement— I had none but the suspicious & grossly insulting parsimony of the arrangements into which you suffered yourself to be forced by your Mother. . . . It has been my intention to say simply, that our marriage was postponed on account of your ill health. . . ." [4]

He promised to show Annie Mrs. Whitman's answer, but she was deprived of that satisfaction, for none ever came. Helen's silence hurt Poe's pride. "My opinion is, that her mother (who is an old devil) has intercepted the letter and will never give it to her," he decided.[5] Helen had received it, however, but she had her own reasons for not answering. She had loved Poe, the one vitalizing but shattering force in her life, and she never forgot him or ceased to love him. Her poems to him, "Arcturus in April," following "Arcturus in October," "Resurgemus," "The Portrait," a sonnet sequence "Our Island of Dreams," with many others, were the thread with which, a mournful Penelope, she wove to the end the fabric of her one great passion. If she never replied to Poe, it was for fear of a renewal of the harrowing scenes. Poe, too, after the unanswered letter, held his peace.

Although, after his return from Providence, he had been plagued by distressing headaches, he had set to work again. For once circumstances seemed to favor him. "I am *so* busy now, and feel so full

[3] Ostrom, pp. 417-419.
[4] *Ibid.*, p. 421.
[5] *Ibid.*, p. 425.

of energy," he wrote exultingly to Annie. "Engagements to write are pouring in upon me every day." [6] The remark was largely wishful, but he had been very active. He had sent fifty pages of "Marginalia" to the *Southern Literary Messenger* and "Landor's Cottage" to another magazine. On February 7 he finished one of his cruelest short stories of revenge, as effective as "The Cask of Amontillado" if without its perfection as art. He called it "Hop-Frog." "You would never guess the subject (which is a terrible one) from the title," he remarked to Annie.[7]

Poe had found the germ of the plot in a retelling of an incident from Froissart's *Chronicles,* in the *Broadway Journal* in 1845. It was the familiar account of the gruesome accident at the court of Charles VI, when, during the festivities following a state marriage, Charles and five of his nobles disguised themselves as satyrs and joined the merrymakers, the king leading his companions, who were linked with chains. Suddenly the pitch and flax of the improvised costumes caught fire, and the satyrs, held by their chains, were burned alive.

Poe kept only the masquerade and the fiery death in his story. His king was a cruel tyrant who took pleasure in mocking his jester, Hop-Frog, for being a dwarf and a cripple, and who plied him with wine, to enjoy its effect upon the fool.—"It excited the poor cripple almost to madness," the author noted.— Hop-Frog put up with the insults to himself, but when the king flung a glass of wine in the face of a young girl, a dwarf, whom Hop-Frog loved, he planned his devilish revenge. In the guise of a rare jest, Hop-Frog induced his victims to disguise themselves as orang-utans—Poe was not one to ignore an animal that had brought him success—and lured them to a spectacular death, high up in the air, where they formed a flaming chandelier of human bodies. Who knows what private vengeance Poe was wreaking vicariously through his art?

The story was taken by the Boston weekly *The Flag of Our Union.* Accustomed to publishing in the most prominent magazines, Poe was apologetic about his new connection—not a very respectable journal, perhaps, in a literary point of view, as he told Annie. But it paid him $5 a page, and the same price for a sonnet, too. Besides, Park Benjamin and Mrs. Sigourney were represented in its pages, and so was Mrs. Osgood.

Poe was soon contributing to it regularly. In the issue of April

[6] *Ibid.,* p. 419.
[7] *Ibid.,* p. 426.

14, 1849, appeared his bow to the gold rush, "Von Kempelen and his Discovery," a convincing account of a successful experiment in the age-old dream of converting base metal into gold. The wonder had occurred in Bremen, though the successful alchemist, well known to the narrator, had been born in Utica, New York. With this story Poe had intended to perpetrate another hoax and had offered it as such to Evert A. Duyckinck. "My sincere opinion is that nine persons out of ten . . . will *believe* the quiz (provided the design does not leak out before publication) and that thus, acting as a sudden, although of course a very temporary, *check* to the gold-fever, it will create a *stir* to some purpose. . . ."[8] Duyckinck, however, had not cared to create that stir.

Two weeks later, *The Flag* published Poe's lines "For Annie," which also came out in the *Home Journal* on the same day but in an improved version. Then, on the 7th of July, appeared at last a long-deserved tribute to Mrs. Clemm: the sonnet "To my Mother." It was a simple, personal poem, devoid of artifice, deeply felt and of a sincerity that spoke instantly to the heart, having sprung from the heart.

> Because I feel that, in the Heavens above,
>   The angels, whispering to one another,
> Can find, among their burning terms of love,
>   None so devotional as that of "Mother,"
> Therefore by that dear name I long have called you—
>   You who are more than mother unto me,
> And fill my heart of hearts, where Death installed you
>   In setting my Virginia's spirit free.
> My mother—my own mother, who died early,
>   Was but the mother of myself; but you
> Are mother to the one I loved so dearly,
>   And thus are dearer than the mother I knew
> By that infinity with which my wife
>   Was dearer to my soul than its soul-life.

Here, as in all his communications with Mrs. Clemm, he was her Eddie, speaking the speech of their daily living, letting elevation of thought and feeling transmute it to poetry.

"For Annie" is also in the same idiom; but here, in the short panting lines, the rhythm is of one struggling for breath, after a shattering crisis—of one who has stepped beyond the threshold of human experience and comes back, babbling incoherently, to tell of it. It is

[8] Letter of March 8, 1849. Ostrom, p. 433.

an account, mingled with fantasy, of his near-death from laudanum—
with Annie there, however, keeping her promise at his deathbed.

> Thank Heaven! the crisis—
>   The danger is past,
> And the lingering illness
>   Is over at last—
> And the fever called "Living"
>   Is conquered at last.
>
> .   .   .   .   .   .
>
> And I rest so composedly,
>   Now, in my bed,
> That any beholder
>   Might fancy me dead—
> Might start at beholding me,
>   Thinking me dead.
>
> .   .   .   .   .   .
>
> The sickness—the nausea—
>   The pitiless pain—
> Have ceased, with the fever
>   That maddened my brain—
> With the fever called "Living"
>   That burned in my brain.
>
> And Oh! of all tortures
>   *That* torture the worst
> Has abated—the terrible
>   Torture of thirst
> For the naphthaline river
>   Of Passion accurst—
>
> .   .   .   .   .   .
>
> My tantalized spirit
>   Here blandly reposes,
> Forgetting, or never
>   Regretting, its roses—
>
> .   .   .   .   .   .
>
> For now, while so quietly
>   Lying, it fancies
> A holier odor,
>   Commingled with pansies—
> With rue and the beautiful
>   Puritan pansies.

And so it lies happily,
  Bathing in many
A dream of the truth
  And the beauty of Annie—
Drowned in a bath
  Of the tresses of Annie.

.   .   .   .   .   .

And I lie so composedly,
  Now, in my bed,
(Knowing her love)
  That you fancy me dead—

.   .   .   .   .   .

But my heart it is brighter
  Than all of the many
Stars in the sky,
  For it sparkles with Annie—
It glows with the light
  Of the love of my Annie—
With the thought of the light
  Of the eyes of my Annie.

His spiritual purgation was now achieved—or so he thought—with the fever of living and the thirst for passion sublimated at last by the pure love of Annie.

The printing of the poem served a practical purpose as well, by laying the rumors of the scandalmongering Mrs. Locke, who, out of jealousy, maligned Annie to Poe and at the same time tried to prejudice Annie's husband against him. For a time she almost succeeded, which distressed Poe for several reasons. He and Mrs. Clemm had been contemplating a move to Lowell, which Mrs. Locke's mischief now made impossible. Then, Poe had also thought of having the Richmonds, or perhaps Annie's parents, board Mrs. Clemm during the trip south which he was contemplating for the summer.

As usual, the wear and tear upon his emotions, together with the demands of the sudden spurt of productivity upon his energy, produced the expected result. Mrs. Clemm nursed him, but even she was alarmed by the gravity of the attack. "I thought he would *die* several times," she wrote to Annie. "God knows I wish we were both in our graves—it would, I am sure, be far better." [9] Edgar must have been very sick indeed to discourage that staunch soul.

Poe tried to make light of it to Annie, saying that he had not

[9] Ingram, Vol. II, p. 215.

been so much ill as depressed in spirits. But he admitted that he had never been in such a state of gloom, aggravated by a secret terror that he would never see her again. There were other reasons for discouragement. That year, which had begun so promisingly, now suddenly altered. All his prospects, his hopes, were frustrated. First, the *Columbia Magazine* failed, followed by Post's *Union* from which he had his principal income. Then the *Whig Review* was forced to stop paying for contributions, and the *Democratic* as well. To crown all, the *Southern Literary Messenger,* which owed him money, could not pay. "No doubt, Annie, you attribute my *'gloom'* to these events —but you would be wrong. It is not in the power of any mere *worldly* considerations, such as these to depress me. . . . No, my sadness is *unaccountable,* and this makes me the more sad. I am full of dark forebodings. . . ." [10]

Still, his depression had not dammed his inspiration. "I have written a ballad called 'Annabel Lee,' which I will send you soon," he told her in the same letter.

He had penned his tributes to Annie and Mrs. Clemm, the living whom he loved; now, in "Annabel Lee," he recalled once again his more beloved dead. It was as if, in the foreboding that oppressed him, he wished to reaffirm, before it was too late, his love for them. He sent "Annabel Lee" and "For Annie" to Griswold, who already had "Lenore," for the tenth edition of *Poets and Poetry of America,* where they would have a longer life than in their fugitive appearance in a magazine. "In one of your editions, you have given my sister's age instead of mine," he reminded Griswold. "I was born December, 1813," he insisted, ignoring the ascertainable fact that by then his mother had been dead two years.

It may be he was longing for the lost happiness of youth, that youth with its discovery of love which had been the theme of his "Eleonora," in the Valley of the Many-Colored Grass, by the waters of the River of Silence, where he had called upon the Mighty Ruler of the Universe to witness his vow of eternal fidelity. That vow he had broken again and again; he had even perjured his love. "Annabel Lee" was his atonement, his reassertion to Virginia that she had always been the one he loved.

The Valley of the Many-Colored Grass here becomes a kingdom by the sea.

[10] Letter of April 28(?), 1849. Ostrom, pp. 437-438.

I was a child and *she* was a child,
  In this kingdom by the sea;
But we loved with a love that was more than love—
  I and my ANNABEL LEE;
With a love that the wingèd seraphs of heaven
  Coveted her and me.

And this was the reason that, long ago,
  In this kingdom by the sea,
A wind blew out of a cloud, chilling
  My beautiful ANNABEL LEE;
So that her high-born kinsman came
  And bore her away from me,
To shut her up in a sepulchre
  In this kingdom by the sea.

The rhythm, dirge-like, recalls the tolling of a buoy in the ceaseless ebb and flow of the sea; recalls the slowing or accelerated heartbeat in the broken verses; and reality attains the remoteness of a ballad. Nevertheless, reality is unmistakable in that wind that blew out of a cloud, in that chill—bronchitis, as Mrs. Clemm called her daughter's malady—that killed Annabel Lee.

But our love it was stronger by far than the love
  Of those who were older than we—
  Of many far wiser than we—
And neither the angels in heaven above,
  Nor the demons down under the sea,
Can ever dissever my soul from the soul
  Of the beautiful ANNABEL LEE.

For the moon never beams, without bringing me dreams
  Of the beautiful ANNABEL LEE;
And the stars never rise, but I feel the bright eyes
  Of the beautiful ANNABEL LEE;
And so, all the night-tide, I lie down by the side
Of my darling—my darling—my life and my bride,
  In the sepulchre there by the sea,
  In her tomb by the sounding sea.

Throughout, the repetition of "the kingdom by the sea," of the name of Annabel Lee, the recurrence of *love,* of *sepulchre,* the internal rhymes, are like the obsessions of a tortured mind that will not exorcise its memories, but rather treasures them for the supreme ecstasy of the imagined communion in the final lines.

With the cessation of Poe's sources of income, once again Mrs. Clemm had to resort to her techniques of subtle ingratiation. Stella Lewis was now the privileged one—the other ladies had long ago ceased coming—who made helpful trips to the cottage or entertained Poe and Mrs. Clemm in her house on Dean Street, Brooklyn. Sylvanus Lewis, it seemed, was as much taken as his wife with the poet, to whom he was grateful for certain literary services in preparing Stella's "Child of the Sea" for publication. Such transactions were always tactfully handled between the Lewises and Mrs. Clemm, the vulgar lucre never touching the poet's palm.— "Would you blame a man for not allowing his sick wife to starve?"— Virginia was beyond human needs, but Mrs. Clemm still had to be clothed and fed.

Suddenly, late in April, Poe received a letter from a complete stranger, a certain Edward H. N. Patterson, from Oquawka, Illinois, which flung wide the door toward the realization of his long-cherished dream of the *Stylus*. He lost no time in answering, for, as it was, Patterson's communication had been lying unclaimed in the West Farms post office for more than four months. "We must aim high— address the intellect—the higher classes . . . and put the work at $5: —giving about 112 pp . . . with occasional wood engravings in the first style of art," Poe wrote him on the 30th. Intoxicated with the possibilities, he went on: "There is no earthly reason why, under proper management, and with energy and talent, the work might not be made to circulate, at the end of a few years, 20,000 copies—in which case it would give a clear income of 70 or 80,000 dollars. . . ." [11] To get the magazine started he proposed taking a tour west and south, lecturing on the way, to pay expenses. In three months he guaranteed at least a thousand subscriptions.

Edward Howard Norton Patterson rejoiced on obtaining a favorable response from the great Mr. Poe. A quiet, eager youth, just come of age, he had inherited a small weekly, the *Oquawka Spectator,* which his father had founded and carried on until his death. The elder Patterson, a Virginian, had been an enlightening influence in tiny Oquawka, which had scarcely expanded beyond its few houses and the usual stores since its founding some twenty years earlier. Through his paper he had brought news of the outer world to the small community, and on its returns he had managed to give his son an education and leave him a comfortable inheritance besides.

Poe had no idea of Oquawka, but probably envisioned wide-open spaces as extensive as his dreams. Within a week he had an answer from Patterson, agreeing to most of his suggestions but cutting down

[11] Ostrom, p. 440.

the number of pages to ninety-six. Poe was to enjoy entire editorial control and make his own bargains with contributing authors, while he, Patterson, would bear the expenses of publishing. The profits would be shared equally. Meanwhile Poe was to select a title and send it to him immediately.

Poe did not reply until the 23rd of May, so that he could think long and carefully on Patterson's proposals. "Your residence at Oquawka is certainly one of the most difficult of these difficulties. . . . Is it not possible to put on the title-page 'Published simultaneously at New-York & St. Louis'—or something equivalent. . . . Upon the whole, I say *Yes* to your proposition." With the letter he enclosed the title page which he had designed for the *Stylus,* a title which he said should be adhered to. He intended leaving that very day for Boston and Lowell, to remain a week, and soon afterward he would start for Richmond, whither Patterson was to direct his letter to him in care of Mr. Thompson of the *Southern Literary Messenger.* Meanwhile he would do what he could for the magazine in Boston and Virginia. "I must ask you to advance half of the sum I need to begin with—about $100. Please, therefore, enclose $50 in your reply, which I will get at Richmond." [12] It was a very modest request, considering the $80,000 of his expectations from the *Stylus.* A more significant demand he made in an offhand manner—that Patterson reprint "For Annie" from the clipping he was enclosing, in some paper in either St. Louis or Oquawka.

Poe may not have left for Lowell on that very day, but he did visit the Richmonds during the early part of June. However, he was back in New York by the 9th, refreshed in spirit by the never-failing warmth of the Westford household and Annie's strange power to soothe him. But something had happened during his stay which caused him keen mortification—the return of his draft on *Graham's Magazine.* The reason, he took pains to explain to Annie, was that the articles on which he drew had not yet been received. His pride was sorely injured, for he enclosed the publisher's reply to his letter of inquiry. "I cannot tell you, darling, how sad I felt about parting from dear Sarah so coldly as I was forced to do. . . . Tell her I hope to see a great deal more of her when I return to Lowell. . . . And now Heaven forever bless you, my darling— Your own Eddie." [13]

Poe had originally planned to raise enough money to take him to Richmond and there collect Patterson's $50, which was waiting for him. As usual, he had overestimated his prospects and was forced to

---

[12] *Ibid.,* p. 444.
[13] Letter of June 16, 1849. Ostrom, pp. 447-448.

write Mr. Thompson to forward the letter and send him $10 besides. In the meantime his departure had to be deferred from day to day, while he waited for the money to arrive.

It came at last. Mrs. Clemm made all the preparations, packed Eddie's belongings to which he added the manuscripts of his two lectures and, locking the door of the cottage behind them, the two took the train and then the ferry to Brooklyn, where the Lewises were expecting them. It was the 29th of June. Poe would be leaving for Richmond on the morrow.

The Lewises, as usual, made them welcome. There may have been a warmer degree of cordiality than ever, for only the day before Poe had done Stella another of his many literary services. He had written to Griswold that in his opinion the article in *Female Poets of America* did not quite do justice to their common friend, Mrs. Lewis. He had therefore prepared a longer article which he hoped Griswold would substitute for the old one. "I would reciprocate the favor when, where, and *as* you please. . . . The MS. is ready. I will leave it sealed with Mrs. L. who is unaware of my design—for I would rather she should consider herself indebted to *you* for the favor. . . ." [14] It had all been arranged very neatly, very discreetly, and neither saw the other's blushes. It was also understood that after Edgar's departure Mrs. Clemm would be staying with the Lewises for a while.

The summer had begun badly for New York. Sporadic cases of cholera had been reported and as the season progressed the death tolls mounted. "Since you left, as you will have heard, my darling boy died of cholera," Horace Greeley wrote to Bayard Taylor, on August 16. "He was first taken at 2 or 3 o'clock in the morning, and died at 5 P.M. the same day. The world looks very dark to me since . . . 200 deaths per day in the city for some time, but they are now slowly diminishing. . . ." [15]

On the morning of the 29th of June Poe was ready to leave. There were the usual tears and handshakes, the reiterated words of farewell at the front door, and Mrs. Clemm's gloomy fears, which did not fail to communicate themselves to Edgar.

"Dear Stella, much beloved friend," he said, taking Mrs. Lewis' hand. "You truly understand and appreciate me— I have a presentiment that I shall never see you again. . . . If I never return," he added, according to her, "write my life. You can and will do me justice." [16] Here, certainly, Stella's imaginings supplanted truth. There is greater

[14] Letter of June 28, 1849. Ostrom, pp. 450-451.
[15] From the original manuscript in the New York Historical Society Library.
[16] For this farewell scene see Ingram, Vol. II, pp. 216-217.

plausibility in the account of Sylvanus, her husband: "He was hopeful; we were sad; and tears gushed in torrents as he kissed his 'dear Muddie' and my wife 'good-bye.' . . ." [17]

It was after eleven o'clock. Mrs. Clemm accompanied Edgar to the Battery and saw him to the steamer, the *John Potter,* readying itself for its daily run, at noon, for South Amboy. From there Poe would be taking the train to Philadelphia. The signal sounded. Now came another tearful parting, another embrace. "God bless you, my own darling mother," he said, as she was leaving. "Do not fear for Eddie. See how good I will be when I am away from you, and will come back to love and comfort you." [18] Mrs. Clemm returned to the Lewises'.

The *John Potter* soon made its way down the Bay with its conglomerate passengers, some to stop at South Amboy, others, like Poe, to make the train connection. There is always a convivial atmosphere among men traveling together. Conversations are begun, drinks are offered. Poe had money in his pocket—if not all, at least a good part of Patterson's $50. Either on board or in the interval between the docking and his taking the train at South Amboy, something must have happened. Certainly, by the time he found himself in the cars bound for Philadelphia, he was no longer sane. The comforting influence of Mrs. Clemm receded farther and farther as the train jogged on; Poe's mind, in nightmare tumult, began tormenting him with his latent fears. He was certain that the men who were sitting a few seats back of him were plotting to kill him. They were talking very low, but he could hear them distinctly, planning how they would do away with him and then throw him off the platform.

Somehow he reached Philadelphia. There, for two or three days, he wandered, lost in the realm of his own confusions. Then, one afternoon he suddenly showed up at John Sartain's with only the clothes on his back, as his carpetbag had been lost or stolen. The artist, in his engraving room, was aghast at the unexpected apparition of the haggard man whose eyes were starting with terror. "Mr. Sartain, I have come to you for a refuge and protection," said Poe. "Will you let me stay with you? It is necessary for my safety that I lie concealed for a time." [19]

Sartain, continuing with his engraving as if nothing were the

[17] Sarah Sigourney Rice, *A Memorial Volume,* p. 86.
[18] Ingram, Vol. II, p. 221.
[19] For this and what follows see John Sartain, *Reminiscences of a Very Old Man,* pp. 196-217.

matter, listened to Poe's wild tale of the plotters. He had given them
the slip, he said, at the Bordentown station, where he remained in
hiding till the cars moved on again. Sartain tried to reason with him.
What motive could those strangers have had in wanting to take his
life?

"It was for revenge," said Poe.

"Revenge for what?" inquired Sartain.

"Well, a woman trouble," he said.

As they talked on, Sartain began to perceive a change in the trend
of Poe's thoughts, from fear of being killed to the idea of suicide.
He was quickly on his guard, therefore, when Poe suddenly remarked
that it was his mustache that gave him away. "Will you lend me a
razor, that I may shave it off?"

Sartain told him that he had no razor, as he never shaved, but
he offered to remove the mustache with scissors, which he did.

Toward nightfall Sartain saw that Poe was getting ready to go
out. On his asking where he was going, Poe answered: "To the
Schuylkill." He was wearing Sartain's slippers, into which he had
changed because his own shoes, badly worn down at the heel, had
chafed his feet. So shod, he started off, Sartain following on the
pretext that the view would be beautiful in the moonlight. At Ninth
and Chestnut Streets they took an omnibus. During their conversation
Poe remarked that after his death he wanted Sartain to see to it that
his portrait, painted by Osgood, should go to his "mother."

They left the bus a little short of Fairmount and walked in the
darkness toward the bridge, Sartain being careful to keep on Poe's
left and guiding him till they ascended the steep flight of steps that
led almost to the top of the reservoir. There they rested on a seat at
the landing, where Poe "in a calm, deliberate, measured utterance,"
inducted him into his fearful world of nightmare. Imagination and
reality mingled inextricably in the still-crazed mind.

He had been confined in a cell in Moyamemsing prison overnight,
Poe said, on the charge of trying to pass a $50 counterfeit note—an
allusion, perhaps, to Patterson's $50, counterfeit because it was no
good to him since he had wasted, or lost, it. From his prison window,
he said, he looked out on the battlemented granite tower, and on the
parapet he saw against the sky a young woman, "brightly radiant,
like silver dipped in light, either in herself or in her environment, so
that the cross-bar shadows thrown from my window were distinct
on the opposite wall. From this position . . . she addressed to me
a series of questions, in words not loud but distinct, and I dared

not fail to hear or to make apt response. Had I failed . . . the consequences to me would have been something fearful. . . ." [20]

An attendant, it seems, then took him for a walk about the place, he told Sartain. Suddenly they came to a caldron full of burning spirits. The man asked him if he would not like to take a drink, but Poe declined. "Had I said yes, what do you suppose would have happened?" Poe asked Sartain. "Why, I should have been lifted over the brim and dipped into the hot liquid up to the lip, like Tantalus. . . . But you see, again I escaped the snare. So at last, as a means to torture me and wring my heart, they brought out my mother, Mrs. Clemm, to blast my sight by seeing them first saw off her feet at the ankles, then her legs to the knees, her thighs to the hips, and so on." [21]

At this point the horror of his own imaginings threw him into a sort of convulsion. Fearful that Poe, in his derangement, might try to leap from the height into the depths below, Sartain remained on his guard and finally lured him down the steep stairway, holding cautiously to the handrail. Once he got Poe back home he tried to put him to bed, but Poe kept crying for laudanum. At last, to quiet him, Sartain gave him a small quantity, made a bed for him on a sofa, and himself stretched out on three chairs to watch over him during the night.

The following day Poe took off on his own, spent a few hours in the fields and then returned to Sartain's, saying he had come to the conclusion that perhaps his visions had all been delusions created by his imagination. It had cleared his mind, he said, to lie upon the grass with his face buried in it, while he inhaled its fragrance and the good smell of the earth. Then again he left without warning. Somehow he found his old friend, George Lippard, who, with Charles Chauncey Burr, now looked after him for a few days.

It was probably from Lippard's that he wrote to Mrs. Clemm on the 7th of July, 1849—his first letter to her since his departure. Its contents, his error in dating it from New York instead of Philadelphia, and his agitated handwriting were not calculated to reassure her, who as it was had been driven to distraction with worry.

For some reason she had left the Lewises' soon after Edgar's departure and had returned to Fordham, where she waited anxiously for some word from him. When, after ten days, nothing had come, she confided her anxiety to Annie Richmond. "Eddy was obliged to go through Philadelphia, and how much I fear he has got into some

[20] *Ibid.*
[21] *Ibid.*

trouble there. . . . Oh, if any evil has befallen *him,* what can comfort me? . . ." [22] Poe's letter, when she finally received it, after it had lain for days at the Lewises', in whose care he had sent it, confirmed her forebodings.

"I have been *so* ill—have had the cholera, or spasms quite as bad, and can now hardly hold the pen," he wrote, concealing the truth, yet perhaps really believing he had had the cholera. "The very instant you get this, *come* to me. The joy of seeing you will almost compensate for our sorrows. We can but die together. It is no use to reason with me *now;* I must die. I have no desire to live since I have done 'Eureka.' I could accomplish nothing more. . . . I was never *really* insane, except on occasion where my heart was touched. I have been taken to prison once since I came here for getting drunk; but *then* I was not. It was about Virginia." [23]

Efforts have been made to turn the Moyamemsing prison incident to a delusion, but Poe not only told it to Sartain soon after the event but repeated it to Mrs. Clemm when he was sober. Sartain, who made inquiries about it, wrote: "I learned later that when his turn came in the motley group before Mayor Gilpin, some one said, 'Why, this is Poe, the poet,' and he was dismissed with the customary fine. . . ." [24] There was probably truth, however, in Poe's declaration that *then* he had not been drunk, but crazed with thinking of Virginia, whose radiant vision had come to warn him.

His money was gone. Lippard, however, solicited Poe's friends for help, but only Sartain, Burr, L. A. Godey and S. D. Patterson contributed, making up the sum of $10. Burr got Poe a steamboat ticket as far as Baltimore. The rest of the journey Poe would have to manage by himself. Before his departure his lost valise turned up at the Philadelphia railroad depot, but when he opened it he found, to his despair, that the manuscripts of his two lectures had been stolen.

On Friday, the 13th of July, Charles Chauncey Burr saw him safely off to the cars, after which the poet would proceed by boat to Baltimore.

[22] Ingram, Vol. II, p. 222.
[23] Ostrom, p. 432.
[24] Sartain, *op. cit.*

CHAPTER XXXI

"Down the Valley of the Shadow"

THAT same evening of July 13, Poe took the steamer from Baltimore to Richmond, his forebodings deepening as he sailed farther south. The following morning he jotted a note to Mrs. Clemm. "I am so homesick I don't know what to do. I never wanted to see anyone half so bad as I want to see my own darling mother. It seems to me that I would make any sacrifice to hold you by the hand once more, and get you to cheer me up, for I am terribly depressed. . . ." [1]

In Richmond he took a room at the American Hotel. Indeed, considering his condition as he described it that Saturday night, the 14th, he could not have shown himself even at the Mackenzies', his closest friends. He was so ill that he longed for sleep, but he would not go to bed until he had reassured Mrs. Clemm of his safe arrival. "Oh, my darling Mother, it is now more than three weeks since I saw you —[it was only two]—and in all that time your poor Eddy has scarcely drawn a breath except of intense agony. Perhaps you are sick or gone from Fordham in despair, or dead. . . ." He wrote her of the stolen lectures, and of the kindness of Burr— "Never forget him, Mother, while you live"—yet, strangely, he had wiped all of Sartain's care from his mind. "I got here with two dollars over—of which I inclose you one. Oh, God, my Mother, shall we ever again meet? If possible, oh COME! My clothes are *so horrible,* and I am *so ill.* Oh, if you *could* come to me, *my mother. . . ."* [2]

There is an almost frantic insistence in that "Come" in his letters to Mrs. Clemm, as if he dreaded that she would forsake him. On the day she had left the Lewises', she had called on a rich friend who, when Mrs. Clemm told her of her present situation, advised her to leave Poe. "Any one to propose to *me* to leave my Eddy—what a cruel insult! No one to console and comfort him but me; no one to nurse

---

[1] Ostrom, p. 453.
[2] *Ibid.,* p. 454.

him and take care of him when he is sick and helpless! . . ." [3] On this night, alas, she was not with him, and he knew the full misery of her absence.

In his wretched condition he was in dire need of friends and to whom could he go if not to the Mackenzies? John may have contributed to Poe's wardrobe for, surely, the single dollar Edgar had left could not have remedied his appalling state. Rosalie may have helped with needle and thread and the Mackenzie servants with soap and water. At any rate, Poe was in better spirits and rational enough to judge his recent behavior more accurately when he again wrote to Mrs. Clemm on July 19. He had been totally deranged, he said, although he had not been drinking. "All was hallucination, arising from an attack which I had never before experienced—an attack of *mania à potu.* May heaven grant that it prove a warning to me for the rest of my days." [4] In other words, he had had *delirium tremens* and had come out of it considerably chastened. To Edward Patterson, who, meanwhile, had been concerned about the fate of the *Stylus,* Poe repeated the story of his cholera from which, he added, he barely escaped with his life. In his brief note he made no mention of the magazine, and to spare his pride declared he had just received Patterson's $50.

He had been trying to interest his old friends in the *Stylus,* however, and most of them promised to help. Richmond's attitude, noticeably better during his previous visit, was cordial now, and even respectful. He was famous, after all. Not only had he written a book on the universe so profound that few could pretend to understand it, but he had also produced "The Raven" that made his name re-echo wherever English was spoken. His name as lecturer, too, had spread, and everybody who had heard him before now wished to hear him again, while those who had neglected the first opportunity were eager to make up for it. A lecture was therefore arranged for him in the Concert Rooms of the Exchange Hotel, for August 17, on "The Poetic Principle."

Everybody attended. Despite the loss of the manuscript—or had he found it?—Poe acquitted himself so well, both in his exposition and in his incidental recitations, that the audience responded with such applause as had never been heard in those halls. There was only one discordant voice in the hosannas from the press—that of Mr. Daniel, whom Poe had challenged to a duel on his last visit. Still, Daniel had nothing but praise for the lecture itself. It was Poe's

[3] Letter of July 9, 1859, to Annie Richmond. Ingram, Vol. II, pp. 222-223.
[4] Ostrom, p. 455.

recitation that he disliked. He made one observation that revealed unusual perspicacity. "Had Mr. Poe possessed talent in the place of genius, he might have been a popular and money-making author. He would have written a great many more good things than he has; but his title to immortality would not and could not be surer than it is. . . ." [5] In Poe's present state of exaltation nothing but unadulterated praise would satisfy.

Despite the success of the lecture, the returns were pitiable, as the fee for the tickets had been only 25 cents. Still, he became the lion of the day. Strangers asked for his autograph and invitations came from the "best" houses for him to recite "The Raven." He visited Mrs. Julia Mayo Cabell, Miss Eliza Lambert, General Lambert's sister; he saw friends of his Allan days, who were accepting him again—the Poitiaux, the Strobias. But though he was invited out a great deal he often did not attend for lack of a dress coat. His extraordinary looks formed the topic of feminine conversation, especially the mesmeric quality of his eyes, so luminous and compelling. "What *awful* eyes Mr. Poe has," remarked a lady to Miss Susan Archer Talley, a young woman whom Rosalie had taken her famous brother to meet. "It makes my blood run cold to see him slowly turn and fix them upon me when I am talking." [6]

The fascination had not failed to recapture the heart of his first love, Elmira—Mrs. A. Barrett Shelton, now a widow with an adolescent son and an estate from the dear departed worth $50,000. Some time after Virginia's death, a well-meaning Richmond friend had written to Poe, hinting at a possible renewal of the old romance, but at the time Poe had other involvements. Things were different now.

One day, after he had sufficiently recovered from his recent seige, he went to call on Mrs. Shelton. While he was waiting in the parlor, a servant went upstairs to announce the visitor. "I went down and was amazed to see him—but knew him instantly." Mrs. Shelton recalled. "He came up to me in the most enthusiastic manner and said, 'Oh! Elmira, is it you?' " Since it was Sunday and Mrs. Shelton, who had developed a rigorous piety, would not let even a meeting with her first love keep her from church, she gave Poe short shrift and told him to call some other time. When Poe did call again, he renewed his addresses. "I laughed at it; he looked very serious, and said he was in earnest and had been thinking about it for a long time.

[5] *Richmond Examiner*, Aug. 21, 1849.
[6] Susan Archer Talley Weiss, "Last Days of Edgar A. Poe," *Scribner's Monthly*, March, 1878.

Then I found out that he was very serious and I became serious. I told him if he would not take a positive denial he must give me time to consider of it. And he said a love that hesitated was not love for him. But he sat there a long time and was pleasant and cheerful." [7]

Poe went to see Elmira frequently after that, and though Mrs. Shelton never admitted to an engagement, she allowed that there was a "partial understanding." Richmond, however, spoke of it as an engagement.

For Poe, marriage to Elmira meant, among other blessings, the establishment of his magazine, under his own control and in a patrician $5 format. Indeed, there had been a rift on the subject between him and Patterson, who insisted on a cheaper issue. "The mere ideas of a '$3 Magazine' would suggest namby-pamby-ism and frivolity," Poe wrote tersely on August 7. In the same epistle he also disengaged himself of a long-standing appointment in St. Louis, telling Patterson that he was still too feeble to travel.[8]

As he had written to Eveleth, a few weeks earlier, he was awaiting the *best opportunity* for issuing the magazine, and if by waiting until the day of judgment he perceived increasing chances of ultimate success, until the day of judgment he would patiently wait. That day, as far as the project was concerned, had now arrived, or so he believed. Elmira, however, thought differently. Officious friends, noting the renewal of the romance, had early warned her that the impecunious Poe might be much more interested in her money than in her mature charms. Indeed, the practical, hard-featured, matter-of-fact woman, once the wistful Elmira of Poe's youthful drawings, was scarcely the realization of a poet's dream, though in the zeal of his wooing he may have tried to persuade her that she was his "lost Lenore." Notwithstanding, he soon found himself confronted with the same financial manipulations that had so humiliated him in Providence. To protect her son's interests, Elmira declared her intention of securing her property so that Poe would have no control of it. Affronted, he withdrew. For a while their relations cooled so noticeably that when, after his lecture at the Exchange Hotel, everyone expected Poe to escort Mrs. Shelton, who had been sitting prominently in front, he passed her by without a word and joined the Talley family.

Poe was then living at the old Swan Tavern, once Richmond's fashionable hotel. It was a long, low, seasoned structure, near the Capitol and not far from Duncan Lodge, the handsome new house

---

[7] "Notes of a conversation between E. V. Valentine and Mrs. Shelton." In Valentine Museum, Richmond.

[8] Ostrom, p. 457.

which the Mackenzies had been occupying for some five or six years. From there it was no distance to Talavera, the home of Poe's new friends, the Talleys, particularly young Susan, who wrote and questioned the great man with the pertinacity of a Boswell. She was deaf—some say mute—but she was able to communicate. In compensation, her other senses had extraordinary acuity.

Poe became her all-absorbing interest. Finding her sympathetic, he threw off all pose. "He had a pallid and careworn look . . . somewhat haggard," she described him. "He wore a dark mustache . . . not entirely concealing a slightly contracted expression of the mouth and an occasional twitching of the upper lip, resembling a sneer. This sneer, indeed, was easily excited. . . . There was in it nothing of ill-nature, but much of sarcasm. . . ." [9] Susan also made an uncannily penetrating discovery. She found that, although Poe was quick in his intuitive insight to character, he was strangely deficient in knowledge of human nature.

She left an amusing vignette of the trials Poe had to bear from the peculiar fancies of Rosalie. One night, while he was reciting "The Raven" for a gathering at Duncan Lodge, Rosalie sleepily entered the room and perched herself upon his knee. He went on, undeterred, till he came to the line, "And the raven never flitting, still is sitting, *still* is sitting . . ." when he meaningfully rested his eyes on the burden on his knee. "The effect," said Miss Talley, "was irresistible."

The amusements were not all of this nature. Temptation, in hospitable Richmond, was ever present, and he could not always resist it. On one occasion John Mackenzie, now a doctor, had seen him through one of his delirious sieges at the Swan Tavern. In belated repentance Poe swore he would never succumb again, but not long afterward he relapsed. This time his friend, Dr. Gibbon Carter, was summoned from his office on Broad Street. Alarmed by Poe's condition, he and Dr. Mackenzie removed him to Duncan Lodge, where he could be cared for. The second bout must have been akin to the *mania-à-potu* of Philadelphia, for Dr. Carter spoke to him sternly and with brutal directness, warning him that another such indulgence might prove his last. Poe was all contrition and with tears in his eyes swore never again to give way to temptation. To make good his promise, he took the pledge in the Shockoe Hill Division of the Sons of Temperance. The *Richmond Whig* was quick to announce the great reformation.

Perhaps as a result of it Mrs. Shelton once more looked upon Poe with favor. She also saw with approval that he spent a good part of

[9] Weiss, "Last Days of Edgar A. Poe," *Scribner's Monthly,* March, 1878.

his day in the offices of the *Richmond Examiner,* assisting his erst-while critic, Mr. Daniel.

Early in September, Mrs. Shelton decided to retire to the country for a few days. Perhaps she could not resist the effect of Poe's hand-someness in his white linen suit, black velvet vest and his planter's straw hat, with its jaunty band. However it was, during that first autumnal week Mrs. Shelton gave him her promise of marriage. A week later Poe left for Norfolk to deliver a lecture at the Academy on the 14th. Both the public and the press acclaimed him with en-thusiasm. His luck had at last turned.

While in Norfolk he visited some old friends, the Ingrams. He had, of course, to recite. Among the poems he read "Ulalume" for the obscurity of whose last stanza he apologized. Little Susan Ingram, with the temerity of the young, spoke up when he had finished. "It is quite clear to me," she said, "and I admire the poem very much." Next day Poe sent her a copy of it, in his own beautiful script, the whole rolled up into a scroll. On another visit, while walking with her, he remarked on the fragrance of orris root on her clothes. "Do you know what it makes me think of?" he said. "My adopted mother. Whenever the bureau drawers in her room were opened there came from them a whiff of orris root, and ever since, when I smell it, I go back to the time when I was a little boy." [10]

Many things, especially in and about Richmond, took him back to his boyhood—the old house on Tobacco Alley, the garden where he had walked with Elmira, the grounds where he knew a secret patch of white violets that came up every spring. There were also places, linked with persons he had known, some whom he had loved. Miss Nancy Valentine he did not go to see. She had never written to him, nor ever cared to know about him, after he had left the Allans. But he did knock at the door of Catherine Poitiaux, Frances Allan's god-child who had not wished to see him on his previous visit to Rich-mond.

"Old friend," he now greeted her, "you see, I would not be denied." He did not stay long. As he stood on the steps to say good-by, Catherine asked him when they would meet again. While he spoke it seemed to her that a gray shadow, such as she had seen only on the faces of the dying, passed across his countenance. His eyes gazing gravely into hers, he answered her question: "In the words of my Raven, perhaps Nevermore."

Mrs. Shelton returned to town on the 17th of September. Poe spent the evening with her. She was still cautious, though before going to

[10] Susan V. C. Ingram, *New York Herald,* Feb. 19, 1905.

the country she had vaguely talked of visiting Fordham. At that time the possibility had alarmed Poe, who suggested instead that Mrs. Clemm take the packet to Richmond—although he did not say what she would use for money. Poor Muddy, during his absence, had received nothing from him except one of the "two dollars over" with which he had arrived in Richmond. In her state of inanition Mrs. Clemm had been compelled to write to Griswold for a small loan, after which she had had no choice but to return to the hospitality of the Lewises.

"Could we be happier in Richmond or Lowell?" Poe had inquired in that same letter, "for I suppose we could never be happy at Fordham—and Muddy, I *must* be somewhere where I can see Annie. . . . I think, upon the whole . . . it would be better for you to say that I am ill, or something of that kind, and break up at Fordham, so that you may come on here . . . but I want to live *near Annie*. . . . Do not tell me anything about Annie—I cannot bear to hear it now—unless you can tell me that Mr. R. is dead.—I have got the wedding ring—and I shall have no difficulty, I think, in getting a dress-coat." [11]

Poe still had the wedding ring, and now it was likely that he would use it, for Elmira's caution seemed to melt before the immediate presence. "I think she loves me more devotedly than any one I ever knew," he declared to Mrs. Clemm, "and I cannot help loving her in return." [12]

The surest token of Elmira's conquest came, however, in the letter she wrote to Mrs. Clemm on the 22nd of September, soon after Edgar had left her. "I am fully prepared to *love* you, and I do sincerely hope that our spirits may be congenial. . . . Edgar spoke frequently of . . . his Virginia, for which I love him but the more. . . . I remember seeing Edgar & his lovely wife, very soon after they were married. . . . I shall never forget my feelings at the time— They were indescribable, almost agonizing. . . . I remembered that I was a married woman, and banished them from me. . . . It is needless (I know) for me to ask you, to take care of him when he is, (as I trust he soon will be) again restored to your Arms—'I trust a kind Providence' will protect him and guide him in the way of truth, so that his feet slip not. . . . It has struck 12 O'Clock, and I am encroaching on the Sabbath, and must therefore conclude— 'Good Night Dear Friend' and May Heaven bless you, and shield you. . . ." [13]

[11] Ostrom, pp. 458-459.
[12] Letter of Sept. 18, 1849. Ostrom, p. 461.
[13] Harrison, *Poe*, Vol. II, MS in Pratt Library.

Mrs. Shelton had alluded to many things in her long screed, but she made no mention of the nuptials, set for October.

On the 24th of September Poe once again delivered his lecture at the Exchange Hotel. This time the price of admission was higher. Nevertheless, the public flocked to hear him, impelled in part by the rumor of the renewed love affair and the coming marriage which, to Poe's annoyance, had been made public by Mr. Daniel.

Richer by the receipts from his lecture, Poe decided to leave for New York on the 26th, first stopping, on the way, in Philadelphia for a bit of business which had come up. A certain Mr. St. Leon Loud, the husband of a Philadelphia poetess, had recently called upon him, offering him $100 to edit the lady's poems. Of course Poe accepted the offer.

"*If possible* I will get married before I start—but there is no telling," Poe wrote Mrs. Clemm. He then made a strange request. "Write immediately in reply & direct to Phila. For fear I should not get the letter, sign no name & address it to E.S.T. Grey Esqre. . . . The papers are praising me to death. . . ." In a postscript he added: "Be sure & preserve all the printed scraps I have sent you & keep up my file of the Lit. World." [14]

Philadelphia evidently still held some real or imagined menace which, by using his alias, he hoped to avert. Fate, alas, has seldom been known to come where it leaves its most conspicuous calling card. At the time of his writing to Mrs. Clemm Poe also sent a letter to Dr. Griswold requesting that, in case of his sudden death, Griswold become his literary executor.

The day of the 25th of September Poe spent in preparing for his departure and in making farewell calls. That evening he went to the Talleys, who were giving a party. He was in excellent spirits. The past few weeks spent with his Richmond friends, both old and new, he said, had been among the happiest he had known in many years. He was eagerly looking forward to the future and expressed the hope that when he again left New York he would also leave behind him all the troubles of his past.

He talked freely and intimately with the Talleys in a small sitting room, while the rest of the guests were entertaining themselves in the parlor. In the course of the evening he showed the Talleys a letter he had just received from Dr. Griswold, who declared himself to be highly flattered by Poe's request. "My friend Dr. Griswold," Poe called him, happy that his future lay in such hands.

The guests dwindled as the night progressed, but Poe stayed on,

[14] Letter of Sept. 18, 1849. Ostrom, p. 461.

seeming reluctant to leave. At last, after all had gone, he said his good-bys. The Talleys saw him to the door and stood on the portico as he walked away. After a few steps he turned round and lifted his hat again in a final adieu. "At that moment a brilliant meteor appeared in the sky directly over his head, and vanished in the east," Miss Talley noted. "We commented laughingly upon the incident, but I remembered it sadly afterward." [15]

He did not return to the Swan Tavern but spent the night at Duncan Lodge. For a long time he sat at the window of his room, pensively smoking, and then, very late, went to bed. Poe had evidently stored at the Mackenzies' his little old ironbound black leather trunk which had first accompanied him to the university and followed him on his various peregrinations, for, in the morning, he had it sent to the Swan Tavern. Then, saying good-by to Rosalie and Mrs. Mackenzie, he left for town with John Mackenzie and Dr. Gibbon Carter. On his way out Edgar had accidentally broken a lamp, at which Rosalie delivered herself of the only comment anyone ever remembered—that no complaint should be made, as it was broken by a poet.

Poe spent the day attending to last-minute business, calling at editorial offices and disposing of manuscripts. He left "Annabel Lee" with Thompson at the *Messenger*. "A little trifle that may be worth something to you," he said. Incidentally, he had already sold the poem to Sartain and, as Sartain later found out, to three other publishers besides.

In the evening Poe paid his farewell visit to Elmira. He did not look well; in fact, he complained of feeling quite sick. Elmira felt his pulse and knew at once that he had a high fever. Under the circumstances she did not think it probable that he would be starting out early next morning, as he planned. She felt wretched about him all night after he left her and hoped against hope that he would delay his departure.

From Elmira's house Poe went directly to Dr. Carter's office, perhaps following her advice that he be looked at before setting out. Dr. Carter was not at home. Poe sat waiting for him, idly reading the paper. When, after about an hour, the doctor had not yet returned, Poe went to the cane stand where he had left his walking stick and, in his muddled state, took away Dr. Carter's malacca sword cane instead.

As it was night, he walked the short distance to Sadler's restaurant and had a late supper. The company was congenial. The time passed cheerfully in talk and conviviality. Then, at four in the morning, two of the men, strangers to Mr. Sadler, accompanied Poe to Rockett's Landing and put him on the steamer. Later, like nearly all who testified for Poe, everyone who had been with him at Sadler's swore he had not "drank a drop." Yet neither Poe nor his escorts had given the least thought to his luggage, so carefully packed, which remained behind at the Swan Tavern, while the voyager sailed away toward Norfolk and the steam packet that would take him to Baltimore.

If Poe made his connections, he disembarked at Spear's Wharf at about seven o'clock in the morning of September 28. Had he wished to go at once from Baltimore to Philadelphia he could have taken the train at nine o'clock the same morning. For some reason he did not, for he showed up that afternoon at the house of Dr. Nathan C. Brooks in a noticeably intoxicated state. Not finding Brooks at home, Poe wandered off. Then, for five days, he vanished as completely as if the earth had engulfed him.

On the 3rd of October, in the late afternoon, Poe's old friend, Dr. J. E. Snodgrass, was handed a note, in pencil, on coarse paper, bearing that day's date. "Dear Sir," it read. "There is a gentleman rather the worse for wear, at Ryan's 4th ward polls, who goes under the cognomen of Edgar A. Poe, and who appears in great distress, & he says he is acquainted with you, and I assure you, he is in need of immediate assistance. Yours, in haste, Jos. W. Walker." [16]

Judging by his note, Mr. Walker, a compositor on the *Baltimore Sun,* seemed to have no notion of who the derelict with the "cognomen" of Edgar A. Poe might be. He recognized him as a gentleman, however. Human sympathy did the rest. Certainly, if it was Walker who found him stretched, semiconscious, upon a broad plank across some barrels on the sidewalk, in a dismal October rain, he could not have conceived that there lay one of the two or three men in the forefront of American letters.

Dr. Snodgrass, who lived nearby, hastened to Cornelius Ryan's place. Poe, by then, had been taken inside. He was sitting in an armchair in the barroom, his head sunk forward. He was haggard, unwashed, unkempt. "His expansive forehead . . . and . . . soulful eyes for which he was so noticeable when himself . . . were shaded from view by a rusty, almost brimless, tattered and ribbonless palm leaf hat. His clothing consisted of a sack coat of thin and slazy black alpaca ripped more or less at intervals of its seams, and faded and soiled, and pants of a steel-mixed pattern of cassinette, half-worn and

[16] Harrison, *Poe,* Vol. I, p. 327.

badly fitting. . . . He wore neither vest nor neck cloth, while the bosom of his shirt was both crumpled and badly soiled. . . ." [17]

For Poe to appear without vest or black stock, almost the insignia of his calling, indicated foul play. He had not a penny in the clothing that had been substituted for his. The hat was the planter's Panama which he had worn in Richmond, but there must have been violence at some point for it to have become so battered. Strangely enough, as Poe slumped in that armchair in a stupor, he was still clutching Dr. Carter's cane. That he had it at all—an irresistible lure to any thief—indicated that it may have served him in self-defense.

Whatever had happened, it was now imperative to get him to a hospital at once. Someone called a hack and Dr. Snodgrass, with Poe's uncle, Henry Herring, who, with Poe's other relatives, had been notified, took the unconscious man to the Washington College Hospital. There, at about five o'clock, that Wednesday afternoon, Poe was admitted and placed in charge of the resident physician, Dr. J. J. Moran.

To the young doctor—he was twenty-seven—the pitiful tatterdemalion was no different from other human wreckage brought in for his ministrations. Mr. Poe, whoever he might be, needed him, and he served him with sympathy and kindness. There was little enough anyone could do for him in his state except to remove his vile tatters and put him to bed. Mercifully he remained unconscious until three o'clock the next morning.

Now the coma was succeeded by delirium and a tremor of the limbs. He was aware of no one about him but kept up a constant talking with imaginary objects on the walls. Dr. Moran noted his ghastly pallor and the perspiration that drenched his person. Despite all efforts to quiet him, he continued delirious so that when his cousin Neilson Poe called with a change of linen for him he was not allowed into the sickroom. The morning of the second day Poe became calmer.

Dr. Moran, who had left orders with the nurses to summon him as soon as the patient could talk, went to his bedside at once. He questioned him about his family and relatives, but for some time could get no coherent answers. Finally Poe told him that he had a wife in Richmond—in his pathetic imaginings the marriage to Elmira had already taken place—but he had no idea of when he had left that city nor could he tell what had become of his trunk and his clothes.

"Wishing to rally and sustain his now fast sinking hopes, I told him I hoped that in a few days he would be able to enjoy the so-

---

[17] J. E. Snodgrass, "The Facts of Poe's Death and Burial," *Beadle's Monthly,* March, 1867.

ciety of his friends here . . ." Dr. Moran noted. "At this he broke out with much energy, and said the best thing his best friend could do would be to blow out his brains with a pistol—that when he beheld his degradation he was ready to sink into the earth. . . ." [18]

Since, after his contrition, Poe seemed to want to doze, Dr. Moran left him. When he returned he found Poe in a violent delirium, resisting the efforts of two nurses to keep him in bed. He remained delirious through Saturday evening, when he began calling: "Reynolds! Reynolds!" his mind perhaps wandering to the unknown seas which Reynolds had sailed, and from them to the grandeur of his own vision of ultimate extinction, as the chasm threw itself open to receive him and there arose that "shrouded human figure, very far larger . . . than any dweller among men. And the hue of the skin of the figure was of the perfect whiteness of snow."

All through the night, until early Sunday morning, Poe's anguished summons rang out in the hospital room. Dr. Moran then noted a decided change. As if enfeebled from exertion, Poe seemed at last to find rest. It was only for a short time. Then, gently moving his head, he said, "Lord help my poor soul," and spoke no more.

Early that spring Poe had published a brief lyric, "Eldorado." In the guise of an allegorical quest for the land of gold, Poe was writing about Poe.

> Gaily bedight
> A gallant knight,
> In sunshine and in shadow,
> Had journeyed long,
> Singing a song,
> In search of Eldorado.
>
> But he grew old—
> This knight so bold—
> And o'er his heart a shadow
> Fell as he found
> No spot of ground
> That looked like Eldorado.
>
> And, as his strength
> Failed him at length,
> He met a pilgrim shadow—
> "Shadow," said he,
> "Where can it be—
> This land of Eldorado?"

[18] Letter from Dr. Moran to Mrs. Clemm, Nov. 15, 1847. Woodberry, 1885 edition, pp. 343-345.

> "Over the Mountains
> Of the Moon,
> Down the Valley of the Shadow,
> Ride, boldly ride,"
> The shade replied—
> "If you seek for Eldorado!"

Poe had now found it, in a room of a charity hospital. Dr. Moran noted that it was five o'clock of Sunday morning, October 7, 1849.

Poe had died alone. Annie, whom he had pledged to come to his deathbed, was far away. Mrs. Clemm, who, had she known, would have trudged the distance barefoot, was confidently waiting for her Eddie to come for her. Elmira—it was difficult to know about Elmira. It may be she was too much absorbed in her religious observances to give more than a passing thought to a sinner of whom she had her doubts. When it was safe to speak truthfully she replied to the question of whether she had been engaged to the poet: "I was not engaged to Poe when he left here . . . but I do not think I should have married him under any circumstances." [19]

Now, on that Sunday in October, the corpse of Edgar Allan Poe was lying on a hospital bed. As none of the Baltimore relatives came forward to give him a decent burial, Dr. Moran, though poor, ordered a coffin at his own expense. It was of plain poplar, unlined, with neither plate nor handles. The young medical students contributed what they could spare—a coat, trousers, a vest, a neckcloth. He was to be buried the following day.

As soon as it was known that Edgar Allan Poe lay dead at Washington College Hospital, newspapermen, people who had known him, made their way there. Dr. Moran suddenly realized that he had been attending greatness unawares. Mrs. Moran, who had taken pity on Poe and had been very kind, now sewed a neat muslin cover for the coffin, to conceal the starkness of the wood. The casket was then carried to a large room in the Rotunda. So many came to see the dead poet that the funeral was put off till Tuesday, October 9.

Though so many had come to gaze at him, some to ask for a lock of his hair, only a handful followed him to the grave. It was already dug for him near General Poe's, in the old Presbyterian Cemetery, where his brother Henry also had been laid, eighteen years before him. Dr. Snodgrass stood by the graveside with Neilson Poe and Mr. Herring and a few others, while the Rev. W. T. D. Clemm read the funeral service and the sexton, George Spence, waited, in readiness

[19] E. V. Valentine's notes on his conversation with Mrs. Shelton. Valentine Museum.

for his office. As on the day of Virginia's burial, "the skies, they were ashen and sober." Now, however, it was really October, the month whose name recurred like a funeral knell in "Ulalume."

On the very day of Poe's burial the *New York Evening Tribune* carried an obituary notice occupying the third and fourth columns of the second page. Starkly it opened: "Edgar Allan Poe is dead. He died in Baltimore the day before yesterday. This announcement will startle many, but few will be grieved by it. The poet was known, personally or by reputation, in all this country; he had readers in England, and in several of the states of continental Europe; but he had few or no friends. . . ." Farther on, it continued: "His imagery was from the worlds which no mortals can see but with the vision of genius. . . . He was at all times a dreamer—dwelling in ideal realms— in heaven or hell. . . ."

In a contradictory fashion, now praising the man and his work, now holding him up to contumely, the notice went on and on—an outpouring of rankling resentments at last released, of envious admiration perforce rushing out. It was, as Miss Barrett had said of Poe's review of her poetic drama, the work of a friend and foe, each stark mad with love and hate. Toward the end the animus conquered and the dead man, who had scarcely reached a higher Court, was condemned here below. "Though he regarded society as composed altogether of villains, the sharpness of his intellect was not of that kind which enabled him to cope with villainy, while it continually caused him by overshots to fail of the success of honesty. He was in many respects like Francis Vivian in Bulwer's novel of 'The Caxtons.' 'Passion, in him, comprehended many of the worst emotions which militate against human happiness. You could not contradict him, but you raised quick choler; you could not speak of wealth, but his cheek paled with gnawing envy. . . . There seemed in him no moral susceptibility and . . . little or nothing of the true point of honor. . . .' "

The article, signed "Ludwig" was by Rufus W. Griswold, to whom Poe, unlucky in death as he had been in life, had so hopefully entrusted his future fame.

–»» • «‹‹–

Epilogue

IN RETRACING Poe's days, from the time he left Richmond to his departure from the world, the author has adhered to ascertainable fact, documented by the immediate testimony of those who were with the poet before the end. Stress is laid upon *immediate* for the reason that, as Poe's fame increased through the years and the world was eager to know everything about him, Dr. Moran, Dr. Snodgrass and others, who had come in on the last act of the tragedy, very humanly succumbed to the temptation not only of magnifying their roles but of exercising their imaginations on the lecture platform and for the press. In the course of the decades Dr. Moran's once simple account of Poe's last days became a full-dress production, including dialogue and stage effects. Dr. Moran now told of taking Poe's hand in his left, and with his right pushing back the "raven black locks of hair," while the dying poet declaimed: "O God! Is there no ransom for the death-less spirit? . . . He who arched the heavens and upholds the universe, has His decrees legibly written upon the frontlet of every human being, and upon demons incarnate." The glassy eyes then rolled back and Poe vanished to the realm of the spirits.[1]

Dr. Snodgrass also lectured, and published two accounts which grew more fantastic with the years. The only credible piece of evidence remains his description of Poe's condition when found at Ryan's Fourth Ward polls. To what realm other than fiction can one consign his later account of coming upon Poe in an eating house kept by an Irish widow, of going out with him and of their being seized by two men who took them to a mysterious hideout, where they were confined through the night? Next day, after drugging their victims, the kidnapers—still according to Snodgrass—hauled them off to the polls in their almost unconscious state and had them vote again and again. Dr. Snodgrass was not seriously affected by the treatment, but the poet succumbed. At this the kidnapers, commenting that it was

[1] See John W. Robertson, *Edgar Allan Poe.*

379

foolish to drag about a dead man, called a hack, thrust Poe into it, and ordered the driver to take him to Washington College Hospital. "I myself saw Poe thrust into the hack, heard the order given, and saw the vehicle drive off," the doctor solemnly swore, forswearing truth at the same time.

Ever since, devoted biographers have clung to the theory of the kidnaping and the drugging by politicians, to clear Poe of being charged with a vice that was really a disease. It is true that on the 3rd of October, 1849, Baltimore was holding an election for members of Congress. But there is no shred of evidence to support the theory that Poe had been "cooped" or, for that matter, drugged, and marched about from poll to poll as a "repeater." Moreover, the cooping would not explain the loss of his clothes and the substitution of the "slazy black alpaca" nor the ripping up of his planter's hat.

There is, on the contrary, a convincing plausibility in Griswold's objective account. "Arriving in Baltimore . . . he went into a tavern to obtain refreshment. Here he met acquaintances who invited him to drink; all his resolutions and duties were soon forgotten; in a few hours he was in such a state as is commonly induced only by long-continued intoxication; after a night of insanity and exposure, he was carried to a hospital. . . ." [2]

It was, in other words, a repetition of what had occurred again and again in Poe's life. In his senseless state he may have fallen into the clutches of unscrupulous individuals who robbed him of clothes and money, substituted cast-offs to give him the look of a derelict, and cast him out into the street in the cold October night. No doubt he had struggled, as his hat was torn and ribbonless and his sack coat ripped at the seams. That he clutched his cane to the end means that he had to use it in self-defense—in vain.

Dr. Moran indicated with rare delicacy the cause of Poe's death in the opening words of his letter to Mrs. Clemm of November 15, 1849: "Presuming you are already aware of the malady of which Mr. Poe died, I need only state concisely the particulars. . . ." Besides, Poe's outburst of self-recrimination and his suggestion that his best friend blow out his brains with a pistol point to himself as the one to blame for the *degradation* into which he had sunk.

It must have been from someone who had seen the "Ludwig" obituary that Mrs. Clemm learned of Edgar's death, for she wrote at once to N. P. Willis, who had always been an understanding friend. "I have this morning heard of the death of my darling Eddie. . . . Can you give me any circumstances or particulars . . . Oh! do not

[2] Griswold, *Memoir,* Vol. I, p. xlvi.

desert your poor friend in this bitter affliction. . . . Ask Mr. —— to come, as I must deliver a message to him from my poor Eddie. . . . I need not ask you to notice his death and speak well of him. I know you will. But say what an affectionate son he was to me, his poor desolate mother. . . ."[3]

The poignancy of the final request moved Willis and inspired his rejoinder to "Ludwig" in the *Home Journal* on the Saturday following the death of Poe.

Desperate, Mrs. Clemm also wrote to Neilson Poe. She told him she never had any peace when Eddie was away from her, but this time her fears had been cruelly confirmed. Neilson Poe replied at once, stiffly, though with sympathy, giving her the details as he knew them, from his first visit to the hospital to Edgar's burial. He would be glad at all times to hear from her, he assured her, and to alleviate the sorrows to which that dispensation might expose her; he only wished his ability was equal to his disposition. With that, Neilson Poe, rather, Judge Poe, felt his duty had been accomplished.

Fortunately Mrs. Clemm had less passive, if more emotional, sympathizers, in the women Poe had left behind. Annie Richmond wrote her at once, calling her "darling mother." She said that her own heart was breaking and begged her to come to Lowell, to stay as long as she pleased. Mr. Richmond, too, was willing. Then came a letter from Mrs. Shelton, who had learned of Poe's death through a Richmond paper. He had now become "our dear Edgar . . . the *dearest* object on earth to me."[4] But she extended no invitation to her "dear and afflicted friend" to share her grief in Richmond. Mrs. Lewis and her considerate Sylvanus, however, offered Mrs. Clemm their home.

She went first to Annie Richmond, who had, incidentally, asked her to bring any writings of Poe that she might have—everything he had written being *so dear* to her. Perhaps Mrs. Clemm obliged with a sheet or two of noncommittal manuscript. True to an understanding she had had with Edgar, she adhered to it. "When I heard of my Eddie's death, I was at Fordham, and then I acted as I *well* knew he would have wished me to do. I destroyed all the letters he had received from his *female* friends, and many others of a private nature. . . ."[5] Among the latter had been the mysterious packet of correspondence left as a melancholy heritage by Elizabeth Poe to her son.

It may be that Mrs. Clemm, who had always been hounded by the

[3] Willis, "Death of Edgar A. Poe," Griswold edition, *Works of E. A. Poe,* Vol. I, p. xix.
[4] Woodberry, "Poe-Chivers Papers," *Century Magazine,* February, 1903.
[5] *Ibid.*

fear that she would end her days in the poorhouse, had hoped to have a home with the Richmonds; but she did not stay with them long. It was one thing to have sheltered the famous Poe, but quite another to take on his indigent aunt as a permanent guest. The Richmonds had a daguerreotype taken of her, however, and thus kept her, in effigy—her patient face framed by her dark hair and white widow's cap, her set smile of resignation, and the unending sorrow in her eyes. They did not neglect her, however, for ten years later Mrs. Clemm was writing to Helen Whitman: "You ask if dear Annie 'still cherished the memory' of dear Eddie, indeed she does, and how sweetly she cherishes it, by her continued kindness and love to me. . . ." [6] It was quite another matter with Mrs. Shelton. "She has not been the friend to me that you have, and she is *rich, too,* but I will not blame her. . . ." [7]

Meanwhile the "Ludwig" obituary—rather, Griswold's attack on Poe—roused the dead poet's friends to his defense. John R. Thompson wrote extenuatingly of Poe's faults in the *Messenger;* Lambert Wilmer lashed out against the calumniator, calling Poe his critic's superior, morally and intellectually. When George R. Graham first saw the article in Poe's *Works,* edited by Griswold, he published a defense of his friend. "Accompanying these beautiful volumes," he wrote of the obituary notice, "it is an immortal infamy—the death's head over the entrance to the garden of beauty. . . . Mr. Griswold does not feel the worth of the man he has undervalued. . . . They were for years totally uncongenial, if not enemies. . . . Literature with [Poe] was a religion; and he, its high-priest, with a whip of scorpions scourged the money-changers from the temple. In all else he had the docility and kind-heartedness of a child. . . . Could he have stepped down and . . . made himself the shifting toady of the hour, and with bow and cringe, hung upon the steps of greatness . . . he would have been feted alive, and *perhaps,* been praised when dead. . . . I think I am warranted in saying to Mr. Griswold, that he must review his decision. It will not stand the calm scrutiny of his own judgment, or of time. . . ." [8]

It remained for N. P. Willis to give "Ludwig" the most effective answer. He published it in his own *Home Journal,* on October 20, with the title, "Death of Edgar A. Poe." While allowing Rufus W. Griswold his say,—for Willis called him by his name—he answered the accusations one by one from its own knowledge of Poe, whose

[6] J. A. Harrison, *Century Magazine,* January, 1909.

[7] *Ibid.*

[8] *Graham's Magazine,* March, 1850.

personality he likened to the ancient fable of two antagonistic spirits
imprisoned in one body, each having complete mastery by turns. He
granted Poe's faults, but he also left beyond doubt the qualities which
Griswold denied Poe—humility, willingness to persevere, capability
for cordial and grateful friendship. Most of all, Willis extolled the
devotion binding the Poe household, under the ministering of Mrs.
Clemm. "It was a hard fate that she was watching over. Mr. Poe wrote
with fastidious difficulty, and in a style too much above the popular
level to be well paid. . . . Winter after winter, for years, the most
touching sight to us . . . has been that tireless minister to genius,
thinly and insufficiently clad, going from office to office with a poem,
or an article on some literary subject, to sell—sometimes simply
pleading in a broken voice that he was ill, and begging for him—
mentioning nothing but that 'he was ill,' whatever might be the reason
for his writing nothing—and never . . . suffering one syllable to
escape her lips that could convey a doubt of him, or a complaint, or
a lessening of pride in his genius. . . ." Through the faith and love
which Poe had been able to inspire, Willis succeeded, in some
measure, in counteracting Griswold's article.

One sentence, in Mrs. Clemm's letter to Willis, soon after her
learning of Poe's death, makes Griswold's article inexplicable except
as the irrational explosion of some deep-seated rancor, for the Mr.
———" whom Mrs. Clemm wished to see, to deliver a message from
Poe, was none other than Griswold himself. The message, already
known to Griswold, was the matter of his appointment as Poe's literary executor. Yet, despite Poe's letter to him and his own answer,
which Poe had shown to the Talleys, Griswold declared he had known
nothing about his appointment until some ten days after Poe's death—
when, by that time, he had already obtained Mrs. Clemm's signature
to a full power of attorney, to edit and publish Poe's works. The document had been drawn up by Sylvanus D. Lewis. In it Mrs. Clemm was
described as the sole owner and possessor of the writings and literary
remains of the late Edgar A. Poe.

Meanwhile a search had been going on for Poe's lost trunk, which
was finally located and sent to Neilson Poe, with whom Griswold
promptly communicated. Neilson Poe informed him that it contained
few manuscripts of value, except for a lecture on the poetic principle
and some random paragraphs. There were, however, some volumes
of Poe's works, full of revisions in his hand, which Neilson Poe felt
the editor should have.

Mrs. Clemm now began to live under the comforting illusion that
she would have the profits from the books and wrote confidently to

Mrs. Richmond that she would realize from two to three thousand dollars. Griswold must have encouraged that hope, for in writing to John R. Thompson, before Poe's trunk had been recovered, he mentioned obtaining full power of attorney from Mrs. Clemm who, he declared, would receive all profits that did not go to the booksellers.

Griswold's communication had an unexpected result. Replying as Rosalie Poe's attorney, Mr. Thompson claimed that she was Mr. Poe's *sole heir* and therefore the rightful recipient of her brother's posthumous earnings. Legally he was right, as the claims of a sister come before those of an aunt, but somewhere justice was lost in the legality. At any rate, it was the first intimation of a course which the "simple" Rosalie was profitably to pursue. As a first measure, Neilson Poe sent the trunk to her at the Mackenzies'.

Griswold duly brought out *The Works of the Late Edgar Allan Poe* through Redfield of New York, 1850–1856. His *Memoir* was not softened by the inclusion of Mrs. Osgood's loving reminiscences, nor by J. R. Lowell's forced and rather stilted introductory biographical sketch of the poet. N. P. Willis' deeply felt article, however, made up for the rancor of the jealous enemy and the coolness of the friend. Still, for many years, Poe's reputation suffered from the blow of the steward who had betrayed his trust.

Mrs. Clemm's expectations proved illusory. She received none of the money that Griswold had led her to expect. She was given, instead, as many copies of the sets as she could dispose of among her friends. Delicacy of feeling, however, kept her from availing herself of the privilege, though a few sympathetic acquaintances bought a few of the sets from her. The *Works* sold well and kept on selling through the years. Someone made money, but it was not Mrs. Clemm nor the *sole heir,* Rosalie.

The Griswold *Memoir* crossed the Atlantic with the *Works.* Soon repercussions were heard in England as well as in France. The English magazine, impressed by the moralistic tone of the Rev. Dr. Griswold, and having little knowledge of the truth, cast their stones upon the pile under which Poe's reputation lay buried. In vain friends of Poe tried to give truth a hearing; its voice scarcely rose above the clamor of vituperation.

Nevertheless, every defense of Poe goaded Griswold to fury. Surely he could not have been in full possession of his senses when he penned an answer to W. J. Pabodie, who, as one of the participants in the romantic interlude in Providence, had tried, through a letter in the *Tribune,* to exonerate Poe of the scandalous behavior which had been given credence by the authority of Griswold's name. Unstoppering the vials of his venom, Griswold poured out their last drops on the man who had been dead for nearly three years. One of his assertions is significant for the malignant interpretation he gave to a sentence in Poe's letter of August 28, 1849, to Mrs. Clemm, an interpretation which reveals the dishonesty and, more, the twisted nature of the man.

"As to Poe's general conduct toward women, it is illustrated in the fact that he wrote to his Mother-in-Law (with whom it is commonly understood and believed, in neighborhoods where they lived, that he had criminal relations), that if he married the woman to whom he was engaged, in Richmond, for her money, he must still manage to live so near a creature whom he *loved* in Lowell, as to have intercourse with her as his mistress. . . ." [9] To Mrs. Whitman and to Lowell, who could not understand his rancor toward the dead man, he justified himself in almost the same words: "I was not his friend, nor was he mine."

Poe had hardly been laid in his grave when a buzz, at first faint, then deafening, arose from erstwhile friends and disciples. Poe had plagiarized their immortal works. From Henry B. Hirst's unremembered "Endymion" he had stolen the goddesses Astarte and Dian for "Ulalume." From Dr. Chivers' "Lily Adair" he had appropriated the whole concept of "Annabel Lee," or so the good doctor claimed, quoting one of his own stanzas:

> She was fairer by far than the Maiden
> The star-bright Cassiope,
> Who was taken by angels to Aiden
> And crowned with eternity.
> For her beauty the Sea-Nymphs offended,
> Because so surpassingly fair;
> And so death then the precious life ended
> Of my beautiful Lily Adair—
> Of my Heaven-born Lily Adair. . . . [10]

Unfortunately for Chivers, an examination of the facts by James A. Harrison gave undisputed precedence to Poe. Dr. Chivers nonetheless attained a certain fame in England, at least in Swinburnian circles, where the red-maned poet would recite with corybantic abandon such gems as the doctor's "Rosalie Lee," ending the recitation with peals of uncontrollable laughter:

[9] MS in Lilly Collection. The letter was first published by Gill, with omission of the above passage, which is quoted in full in Quinn's *Edgar Allan Poe*, p. 680.
[10] Joel Benton, *In the Poe Circle*.

> Many mellow Cydonian Suckets
> Sweet apples, anthosmial, divine
> From ruby-rimmed Berylline buckets
> Star-gemmed, lily-shaped, hyaline—
> Like the sweet golden goblet found growing
> On the wild emerald Cucumber-tree—
> Rich, Brilliant, like Chrysoprase blowing
> I then brought to my Rosalie Lee—
> To my dove-like Rosalie Lee—
> To my beautiful, dutiful Rosalie Lee.[11]

Still Chivers, discounting his poet's vanity, had an abiding affection for his departed friend. In a naïve yet touching gesture, he even reunited Politian, as he called him, to his Lenore, in the rosy bowers of Aiden,

> While the Seraphim all waited
> At the portals congregated
> Of the City Golden gated
> Crying, "Rise with thy Lenore!" [12]

Some of the women whom Poe had loved also defended his fame. Mrs. Osgood, who survived him only a year, contributed the one bright trace in Griswold's sinister portrait. Mrs. Whitman brought out a perceptive study, *Edgar Poe and his Critics,* in 1860. Though still overmystical, she saw deeper than most into the inner man and thus into the motivations of his art. "His proud intellectual assumption of the individual soul was but an expression of his imperious longings for immortality and its recoil from the haunting phantasms of death and annihilation; while the theme of his more imaginative writings is a love that survives the dissolution of the mortal body. . . . His mind indeed was a 'Haunted Palace' echoing to the footfalls of angels and demons. . . ." [13]

In March, 1878, Susan Archer Talley Weiss published her reminiscences of Poe in *Scribner's Monthly* and her *Home Life of Poe* in 1907. Annie Richmond, still serving Poe while helping Mrs. Clemm, held her peace. So also did Mrs. Shelton, except for her candid conversation with E. V. Valentine in 1875.

Poe's fame increased. In England the young Pre-Raphaelites took over not only the new strains of Israfel's lyre but also the traits of his heroines. Lenore's maladive beauty was sung and painted by Dante Gabriel Rossetti, in his "Blessed Damozel." His ballad "Sister

[11] From *Selected Poems* (Monroe, N.C.), July, 1935.
[12] Quoted in Benton, *op. cit.*
[13] Helen Whitman, *Edgar Poe and his Critics.*

Helen" incorporated that link of love and death so dear to Poe. William Morris and, more particularly, Swinburne, later disciples, found in the imaginative tales and poems the perverse atmosphere of their early creations. But it was in France that Poe's influence sank deepest and spread enduring roots with the publication, in 1856 and 1857, of Baudelaire's translation of Poe's tales. The first volume, *Histoires Extraordinaires,* Baudelaire dedicated to Mrs. Clemm, with a translation of Poe's sonnet "To my Mother."

Their impact was immediate, not only upon French literature but on that of Europe and of Russia. Poe's blending of love and death, of yearning intensified by the certainty of loss, and the concomitant of pleasure sharpened by pain now flowed like a subtle poison through the stream of European literature. The neurotic, sybaritic, aesthetic hero came into his own. Egaeus from "Berenice" and Roderick Usher, the exemplar par excellence, soon began to enjoy repeated incarnations, with all their fixations, their absorption in books of religious mysticism and of cruel tortures. Poe explicitly mentioned the *Directorium Inquisitorium* as Usher's favorite reading.

The new hero was by choice a solitary, finding in his imaginative inventions, in his experiments with drugs, in his inducing of suffering, even of insanity, the ultimate satisfaction of his excruciated senses. He was the Marquis de Sade of the soul, recognizable later in the *Contes Cruels* of Villiers de l'Isle-Adam, in the works of Barbey d'Aurevilly, but most of all in the character of des Esseintes, the hero of J. K. Huysman's novel, *À Rebours.*

Here Poe's influence was more than accidental. Huysmans had read and absorbed his Poe. The close family tie, which had implications of incest in Poe's fictional relationships, Huysmans makes explicit from the first in the background of des Esseintes. He was a sybarite, a lover of beauty, of luxury, of curious lore, and of bizarre color schemes. He never read a book without discovering in it a plagiarism from another and, to attract him, the volume "had to possess that quality of strangeness which Poe demanded. . . . He withdrew more and more from reality, particularly from the contemporary world which he held in increasing abhorrence." [14]

Among his books des Esseintes had a specially bound copy of *Arthur Gordon Pym,* for he thrilled to the horrible; but he read everything of Poe's over and over. "In literature under the allegorical title of 'The Imp of the Perverse,' " he said, "Poe was the first to detect those irresistible impulses to which the will submits, without understanding them. . . . He . . . made death more acute; he transformed

[14] *À Rebours,* pp. 237-238. Trans. of passage by F.W.

it. . . . [It was] less the real agony of the dying that he described, than the moral agony of the survivor . . . haunted by the monstrous hallucinations which grief and weariness engender. . . . His women, the Morellas, the Ligeias, were immensely learned. . . . All had the boyish, inert breasts of angels and all were, in a manner of speaking, asexual." [15]

Des Esseintes then draws a striking contrast between Baudelaire and Poe, who have often been compared for their common passion for poetry and their exploration of the maladies of the mind. The two, however, differed radically: "Baudelaire with his unappeasable, iniquitous love, whose cruel disgust made one think of the reprisals of an inquisition; Poe, with his chaste, ethereal loves, wherein the senses had no part, where only the solitary brain found excitement with no relation to those organs which, if they existed, remained forever frigid and virginal. . . ." [16]

It was such heroes, such heroines, and such loves that found their way into French literature in the latter half of the century, crossed the Channel to inspire an Oscar Wilde and an Aubrey Beardsley, and went south to Italy, leaving their last faint traces of corruption on the characters of D'Annunzio's novels and plays. In Russia, Dostoevski was not impervious to the influence of "William Wilson," as evidenced in his *Sosia* nor, in the words of Mario Praz, "of that impotence, elevated to mystical ecstasy, in Myshkin, the protagonist of *The Idiot*." [17]

In French poetry the influence of Poe was even more pronounced, especially after Mallarmé translated "The Raven" and followed it with a volume of Poe's poems done in rhythmic prose, in 1875. Verlaine and Rimbaud, however, had courageously undertaken to read the original, according to a letter of Verlaine's from London, in 1873: "We are learning English . . . Rimbaud and I, in *Edgar Poe,* and in collections of popular songs. . . ." [18] Young Rimbaud certainly profited by his reading, particularly as revealed in the *Bateau Ivre,* which the critic, Seylaz, calls "one of the most magnificent poetic transcriptions of Poe's tales." [19]

Through Poe something extraordinary had happened. Literary Europe had been influenced by an American. It was not that American authors had remained untranslated and unread, for Cooper en-

[15] *Ibid.,* pp. 253-254. Trans. of passage by F.W.
[16] *Ibid.,* pp. 253-254. Trans. of passage by F.W.
[17] Mario Praz, *La Carne, la Morte e il Diavolo,* p. 339.
[18] Quoted by Cambiaire, *Influence of Edgar Allan Poe in France.*
[19] L. Seylaz, *Edgar Poe et les premiers symbolistes français.*

joyed popularity abroad. But it was the first time that one of them—and he by no means a realist—had divined the temper, and felt the pulse, of a century only vaguely aware of the malady of transition.

Meanwhile at home the bones of Poe had been moldering under their unmarked mound. Mrs. Clemm alone grieved at the neglect and tried to raise the money to move the body to Greenwood Cemetery. Nothing came of her efforts. At last, in 1860, Judge Neilson Poe ordered a marble slab at the establishment of Hugh Sisson. It bore the faulty Latin inscription: *Hic tandem felice cunduntur Reliquiae, Edgar A. Poe.* It was lying in the yard with other monuments ready for delivery when a train of the Northern Central Railroad accidentally jumped the track and, of all slabs, shattered Poe's beyond repair.

The years passed. The Civil War came. Lives were shattered; fortunes changed, the rich finding themselves homeless, the poor, poorer. Mrs. Clemm, no longer sheltered by Poe's friends, appealed to everyone who could offer help. Eventually she found sanctuary in the Church Home Infirmary, in Baltimore, in the building that had once been the Washington College Hospital, where Poe had died. It was there that Charles Dickens, on another of his American tours, visited her and, with touching delicacy, gave her $150. It was from there that, in 1871, she made her last journey, to rest not far from Poe's grave.

Rosalie Poe, after the Mackenzie family had been broken and dispersed by the cataclysm, went to live with one of their female relations in the country. It was not the kind of life she enjoyed and, remembering her Baltimore connections, she sought shelter with them there. She had taken with her all the mementos of her brother—photographs, manuscripts—and soon tried to turn to profit, for herself. She had no luck with them at first, nor did she succeed in endearing herself to her relations. For some time she wandered about homeless and without any means of support. Finally, like Mrs. Clemm, she too was received into a charitable institution, the Epiphany Church Home, in Washington.

With the security of a roof over her head, she now went into the business of commercializing Edgar Allan Poe in earnest. With Poe's photographs, or some related item, under her arm she would call on prosperous businessmen, state her poverty-stricken situation and offer them her brother's relics for sale. She seldom left empty-handed and, generally, with her stock intact.

Besides the personal solicitations, she also carried on the work by mail. Few suspected that she had any money, and certainly no one knew where she kept it. Then, on June 14, 1874, after about six years of her gainful business, Rosalie Poe was surprised by death. When found, she was clutching in her hand a letter that she had just received in answer to one of her applications, from George W. Childs, of Philadelphia. It contained a check for $50. No one ever discovered Rosalie's cache or, if it was found, no one ever told. She was buried in the cemetery of the Epiphany Church Home, in a pauper's grave.

It was not until a quarter of a century after Poe's death that a group of Baltimore schoolteachers, aided by the citizenry, succeeded in raising enough money to honor the poet with a monument, and commissioned Sir Moses Ezekiel to execute it. Here, again, contrary destiny intervened. The sculptor had finished his clay model and had sent it to the foundry to be cast into bronze when it was destroyed by fire. He modeled it for the second time, only to have an earthquake demolish it, together with the studio that housed it. The third time Sir Moses managed to get it cast before another intervention.

The dedication ceremony was set for November 17, 1875. Before that, Poe's body was exhumed for reburial in a more appropriate site. Reporters were present at the opening of the grave and recounted the experience. The poplar wood coffin provided by Dr. Moran had not withstood the years. It had split at the sides and the lid at the head was so rotten that it fell to pieces. The *Evening News* man peered in, to report that the skeleton was intact and that hair was still clinging to the skull.

Weird coincidence, that same year, had re-enacted a similar scene at the Fordham cemetery where Virginia Poe was buried. It is best told in the words of the sculptor, James Edward Kelly: "Fearing Gill, on visiting my studio, told me the following: 'Four years after I had written the life of Poe, Dr. Thatcher said, you had better come up with me and visit the tomb of Virginia Poe. We drove up there, and most remarkable to relate, it seemed like a stage setting, etc, [*sic*]

" 'We found the sexton who had buried Mrs. Poe, a Mr. Valentine. As I entered the cemetery from the right, coming towards me from the left, was Mr. Valentine, with the bones of Mrs. Poe on a shovel. His men may have left them. I asked Gill if the skull was there. 'Yes,' answered Gill, 'part of it.' Mr. Valentine said, 'Why don't you take care of it?' (I suppose Mr. Thatcher told him who I was.) 'I buried Mrs. Poe, and they are taking down this cemetery and commencing to make some improvements.' 'Why don't you write to the family?' I said. He said, 'I have written to Mr. Poe in Baltimore, but he has never replied. So I think it is right you should take them and look after them.' Then I took them. Mr. Valentine put them in a paste

board box, such as they put floral pieces in. . . . You know, wreaths
and anchors . . . and I took them home. Some time after, one of the
papers published an article in which it said, Mr. Fearing Gill is such
a Poe enthusiast that he sleeps with the bones under his bed.' He
added, 'Which is almost literally true.' " [20]

At the time of Poe's reburial Mrs. Clemm's remains were also laid
near him. A small bronze box, containing Virginia's bones, joined the
ashes of her husband and her mother in 1885.

Many who had known Poe attended the dedication ceremony in
Baltimore and those who could not be present sent letters. A dis-
sident note, one of the few, came from W. C. Bryant, who could not
find it in himself to say anything good of Poe. "My difficulty arises
from the personal character of Edgar A. Poe, of which I have in my
time heard too much to be able to join in paying especial honor to
his memory. . . . I think . . . that there should be some decided
element of goodness in the character of those to whom a public monument directs the attention of the world." [21] New England had not yet
forgiven the dead poet.

William Fearing Gill recognized many notable figures among those
who came to do Poe honor, among them George W. Childs, who had
contributed generously toward the monument. Near him, his handsome white-maned head rising above the others, was Walt Whitman,
who had not forgotten the famous editor of the *Broadway Journal*
who had accepted the essay of an unknown youth.

Whitman had not come to speak. Nevertheless, after the ceremony,
he joined in the conversation informally, among a group of friends.
For a long time, he said, he had had a distaste for Poe's writings. "I
wanted, and still want for poetry, the clear sun shining, and fresh air
blowing . . . with always the background of the eternal moralities. . . .
Poe's genius has not yet conquered a special recognition for itself,
and I too have come fully to admit it, and appreciate it in him. In a
dream I once had, I saw a vessel on the sea, at midnight, in a storm.
. . . On the deck was a slender, slight, beautiful figure, a dim man,
apparently enjoying all the terror, the murk and the dislocation of
which he was the center and the victim. That figure of my lurid dream
might stand for Edgar Poe, his spirit, his fortunes, and his poems.
. . ." [22]

[20] From original typescript by James Edward Kelly, in the New York Historical Society Library.
[21] S. S. Rice, ed. *E. A. Poe, A Memorial Volume.*
[22] *Washington Star,* Nov. 16, 1875.

Whitman's mystical vision had indeed seen much, yet not enough. The figure in his dream was Poe, but he was also modern Man, conscious of a new dimension: the world within, whose storms, terrible in their revealing flashes, throw light, now more than ever, on the black, hidden regions of the soul.

Bibliography

ALLEN, HERVEY. *Israfel: The Life and Times of Edgar Allan Poe.* 2 vols. New York, 1926; 1-vol. revised edition, 1934.

ASSELINEAU, CHARLES. *Charles Baudelaire, sa Vie et son Oeuvre.* Paris, 1896.

BARRETT, ELIZABETH, and BROWNING, ROBERT. *Letters of Robert Browning and Elizabeth Barrett,* 2 vols. New York, 1898.

BAUDELAIRE, CHARLES. "Edgar Poe, sa vie et ses oeuvres"; preface in *Histoires Extraordinaires.* Paris, 1856.

————. "Notes nouvelles sur Edgar Poe"; preface in *Nouvelles Histoires Extraordinaires.* Paris, 1857.

————. *Les Fleurs du Mal.* (Reference to Poe in preface.) Paris, 1868.

————. *Oeuvres Posthumes. Journaux Intimes.* Paris, 1907.

BAUM, PAUL H. *Dante Gabriel Rossetti; Poems, Ballads and Sonnets.* New York, 1937.

BENTON, JOEL. *In the Poe Circle.* New York, 1899.

BEWLEY, SIR EDMUND. *The Origin and Early History of the Family of Poë or Poe.* Dublin, 1906.

BONAPARTE, PRINCESS MARIE. *Edgar Poe: Étude Psychoanalytique.* Paris, 1933.

————. *The Life and Works of Edgar Allan Poe.* Foreword by Sigmund Freud. Translated by John Rodker. London, 1949.

BRADDY, HALDEEN. *Glorious Incense.* Washington, D.C., 1953.

BRAINARD, CHARLES H. *John Howard Payne. A biographical sketch.* Washington, D.C., 1885.

CAMBIAIRE, CÉLESTIN P. *The Influence of Edgar Allan Poe in France.* New York, 1927.

CAMPBELL, KILLIS. "Some Unpublished Documents Relating to Poe's Early Years." *Sewanee Review.* April, 1912.

————. *The Mind of Poe and Other Studies.* Cambridge, U.S.A., 1932.

CANBY, HENRY S. *Classic Americans.* New York, 1931.

CASSAGNE, ALBERT. *La Théorie de l'Art pour l'Art en France.* Paris, 1906.

Catalogue of Glück Collection of Manuscripts and Autographs. Buffalo Public Library. July, 1899.

CHIVERS, THOMAS HOLLEY. *Selected Poems.* Monroe, N.C., 1935.

COBURN, FREDERICK W. "Poe as seen by the brother of 'Annie.' " *New England Quarterly*. September, 1943.

CRÉPET, JACQUES. *Charles Baudelaire*. Paris, 1919.

DAMON, SAMUEL F. *Thomas Holley Chivers, Friend of Poe*. New York, 1930.

DAVIS, NUEL PHARR. *Life of Wilkie Collins*. Urbana, Illinois, 1956.

DAVIS, RICHARD BEALE, Ed. Chivers' *Life of Poe*. New York, 1952.

ENGLISH, T. D. "Reminiscences of Poe." *The Independent*. October, 1896.

FAGIN, N. B. *The Histrionic Mr. Poe*. Baltimore, 1949.

FIELDS, J. T. *Yesterdays with Authors*. Boston, 1872.

FRENCH, JOHN C. "Poe and the Baltimore Saturday Visiter." *Modern Language Notes*. May, 1918.

GILL, WILLIAM F. *The Life of Edgar Allan Poe*. New York, 1877.

GOURMONT, RÉMY DE. *Promenades littéraires*. Paris, 1922.

GOWANS, WILLIAM. *Catalogue of American Books*. No. 28. 1870.

GREELEY, HORACE. "On Poe's Lecture." New York *Tribune*. March 1, 1845.

GRISWOLD, R. W. "LUDWIG." Obituary of Poe. New York *Tribune*. October 9, 1849.

HANSON, WILLIS T. *Early Life of John Howard Payne*. Boston, 1913.

HARRINGTON, H. F. "Poe not to be Apotheosized." *The Critic*. October 3, 1885.

HARRISON, JAMES A. (ed.). *The Complete Works of Edgar Allan Poe*. 17 vols. New York, 1902.

———. *Life and Letters of Edgar Allan Poe*. 2 vols. New York, 1903.

———, and DAILEY, CHARLOTTE F. "Poe and Mrs. Whitman." *Century Magazine*. January, 1909.

HUXLEY, ALDOUS. *Vulgarity in Literature*. London, 1930.

HYSLOP, LOIS and FRANCIS. (Translators and editors.) *Baudelaire on Poe; Critical Papers*. State College, Pa., 1952.

INGRAM, JOHN H. *Edgar Allan Poe; His Life, Letters and Opinions*. 2 vols. London, 1880.

JACKSON, DAVID K. *Poe and the Southern Literary Messenger*. Richmond, 1934.

KENYON, SIR FREDERICK G. *New Poems by Robert and Elizabeth Barrett Browning*. New York, 1915.

KENYON, JOHN (ed.). *Letters of Elizabeth Barrett Browning*. 2 vols. London, 1897.

KRUTCH, JOSEPH WOOD. *Edgar Allan Poe; a Study in Genius*. New York, 1926.

LANDIS, PAUL, and R. E. FREEMAN. *Letters of the Brownings to George Barrett*. Urbana, Illinois, 1958.

LAUVRIÈRE, ÉMILE. *Edgar Poe. Sa Vie et son Oeuvre*. Paris, 1904.

———. *L'étrange Vie et les étranges Amours d'Edgar Poe*. Paris, 1935.

———. *Le Génie morbide d'Edgar Poe*. Paris, 1935.

LEMONNIER, LÉON. *Edgar Poe et les Poètes français*. Paris, 1932.

―――. "L'Influence d'Edgar Poe sur les Conteurs Français symbolistes et décadents." *Revue de Littérature Comparée*. Paris, 1933.

MABBOTT, THOMAS OLLIVE. "Letters from George W. Eveleth to Edgar Allan Poe." *Bulletin of the New York Public Library*. New York, 1922.

―――. *Merlin, Baltimore, 1827 . . . with Recollections of Edgar A. Poe by Lambert A. Wilmer*. New York, 1941.

―――. *Politian. An Unfinished Tragedy by Edgar A. Poe . . . now first edited with notes and a commentary*. The Edgar Allan Poe Shrine. Richmond, 1923.

MACY, JOHN. *The Spirit of American Literature*. New York, 1913.

MAUCLAIR, CAMILLE. *Charles Baudelaire. Sa Vie, son Art, sa Légende*. Paris, 1917.

―――. *Le Génie d'Edgar Poe*. Paris, 1925.

NEALE, WALTER G., JR. "The Source of Poe's 'Morella.'" *American Literature*. May, 1937.

NICHOLS, MRS. MARY GOVE. "Reminiscences of Edgar Allan Poe." *Sixpenny Magazine*. February, 1863.

OSGOOD, FRANCES S. "Ida Grey." *Graham's Magazine*. August, 1845.

OSTROM, JOHN WARD (ed.). *The Letters of Edgar Allan Poe*. 2 vols. Cambridge, U.S.A., 1948.

OVERMYER, GRACE. *America's First Hamlet*. New York, 1957.

PAYNE, JOHN HOWARD. "Random Scraps and Recollections from the Note Book of a Wanderer." *The Ladies' Companion*, August, 1837.

PHILLIPS, MARY E. *Edgar Allan Poe, the Man*. 2 vols. Philadelphia, 1926.

POPE-HENNESSY, UNA. *Edgar Allan Poe, a Critical Biography*. London, 1934.

QUINN, ARTHUR HOBSON. *Edgar Allan Poe, a Critical Biography*. New York, 1941.

―――, and HART, R. H. *Edgar Allan Poe Letters and Documents in the Enoch Pratt Library*. New York, 1941.

―――. "Marriage of Poe's Parents." *American Literature*. May, 1939.

RICE, MRS. S. S. (ed.). *Edgar Allan Poe. A Memorial Volume*. Baltimore, 1877.

ROBERTSON, JOHN W. *Edgar Allan Poe, a Psychopathic Study*. New York, 1923.

SARTAIN, JOHN. *Reminiscences of a Very Old Man*. New York, 1899.

SEYLAZ, LOUIS. *Edgar Poe et les premiers Symbolistes français*. Lausanne, 1923.

SNODGRASS, J. E. "The Facts of Poe's Death and Burial." *Beadle's Monthly*. March, 1867.

SPANNUTH, JACOB E. *Doings in Gotham*. With an introduction by T. O. Mabbott. Pottsville, 1929.

STANARD, MARY NEWTON. *Edgar Allan Poe Letters till now Unpublished, in the Valentine Museum, Richmond, Virginia*. With an Introductory Essay and Commentary. Philadelphia, 1925.

————. *The Dreamer, the Life Story of Poe.* Philadelphia, 1925.

STARKE, AUBREY. "Poe's Friend Reynolds." *American Literature.* May, 1939.

STEDMAN, E. C. "Edgar Allan Poe." *Scribner's Monthly.* May, 1880.

TICKNOR, CAROLINE. *Poe's Helen.* New York, 1916.

TUSIANI, GIUSEPPE. *Sonettisti Americani.* Chicago, 1954.

VAN CLEEF, AUGUSTUS. "Poe's Mary." *Harper's New Monthly Magazine.* March, 1889.

WALLER, W. E. "Murders in the Rue Morgue." *Notes and Queries.* May 17, 1894.

WEISS, SUSAN ARCHER TALLEY. *The Home Life of Poe.* New York, 1907.

————. "Last Days of Edgar A. Poe." *Scribner's Monthly.* March, 1878.

WHITMAN, SARAH HELEN. *Edgar Poe and his Critics.* New York, 1860.

WHITTY, JAMES A. (ed.). *Complete Works of Edgar Allan Poe.* Boston, 1911.

————. "Poeana." *The Step Ladder.* October, 1927.

WILLIAMS, STANLEY T. (ed.). "New Letters about Poe." *Yale Review.* July, 1925.

WILSON, JAMES S. (ed.). "The Letters of Edgar A. Poe to George W. Eveleth." *Alumni Bulletin, University of Virginia.* January, 1924.

————. "The Young Man Poe." *Virginia Quarterly Review.* April, 1926.

WINSOR, JUSTIN (ed.). *The Memorial History of Boston. 1630–1880.* 4 vols. Boston, 1880–1881.

WOODBERRY, GEORGE E. *Edgar Allan Poe.* Boston, 1885.

————. *The Life of Edgar Allan Poe . . . With his Chief Correspondence with Men of Letters.* 2 vols. Boston, 1909.

————. "The Poe-Chivers Papers." *Century Magazine,* January-February, 1903.

INDEX

-»» • «‹‹-

against U.S., 179; as Poe's refuge from reality, 183; in New York, 186; pleads with Mr. Burton, 207; buys luxuries for house, 213; in Graham's kitchen, 216; sets out to look for Poe, 228; removes to Spring Garden cottage, 229; carries Poe's writings to editors, 231; entertains Hirst at breakfast, 239; hears from Poe in New York, 249-250; sells Philadelphia possessions, 252; at the Brennan house, 254-255; nurses the "deranged" Poe, 281; and the literary women, 288-289; at the Millers', 291-292; and Poe's delirious sieges, 294; and removal to Fordham cottage, 295-296; sews to help family, 297; and the literary intrigues, 299-300; and Rosalie, 302; tries to borrow from W. C. Bryant, 303; and Mrs. Gove, 304; on Catarina, 305; tends Virginia, 308; at her daughter's deathbed, 309-310; and portrait of Virginia, 311; at funeral, 312; her new tea service, 313; encourages Poe's female admirers, 320, 321; and *Eureka*, 323; witnesses contract for *Eureka*, 325; writes to Mrs. Richmond, 346; expects Poe to return with bride, 348; and Poe's "To my Mother," 353; nurses Poe, 355; helped by the Lewises, 358; and Poe's departure, 360-361; returns to Fordham, 363; and Poe's disturbing letters, 364-365, 366; borrows from Griswold, 371; learns of Edgar's death, 380-381; and N. P. Willis' tribute to her, 383; her expectations from Poe's *Works* illusory, 384; maligned by Griswold, 385; dedicatee of Baudelaire's translation of Poe, 387; tries to raise money to move Poe's body to Greenwood Cemetery, 389; visited by Dickens, 389; death, 389; re-buried near Poe, 391

Clemm, Virginia Eliza. *See* Poe, Mrs. Edgar Allan
Clemm, William, 68
Clemm, W. T. D., 377
Coburn, Frederick W., 178n, 334n
Coleridge, S. T., 81, 132, 165
"Coliseum, The," 150, 151, 154, 161, 215
Collier, Edwin, 28; at school, 34, 42-43, 109, 147, 159
Collier, Mrs., 28, 42-43
Collins, Wilkie, 165
Colton, George H., 259, 303, 304
Columbia Magazine, 321, 356
Columbia Spy, 253n
Columbia University, 255n
"Come Rest in This Bosom," 143, 220, 228
Commerce, Le, 212
Conchologist's First Book, 198, 262
Conchologist's Text Book, 198
"Conqueror Worm, The," 196-197
Contes Cruels, 387
Converse, Rev. Mr. Amasa, 176-177
Cooke, Philip P., 205, 235
Cooper, James F., 201, 216, 388

Cooper, Thomas, 11, 16, 21, 22, 23, 65, 66; performs with Mrs. Poe, 19
Cornwallis, 58
Corsa, Richard, 295
Cowper, William, 95
Crocker, Rev. Mr., 348-350
Crump, Edward G., 92
"Cry of the Children, The," 264
Curiosities of Literature, 205
Cushing, Caleb, 284
Cuvier, 142, 198, 199
Cymon and Sylvia, 8

Dailey, Charlotte F., 12, 328n
Daily Madisonian, 233
Dandridge, Dabney, 92
Daniel, John M., 336, 366-367, 370, 372
D'Annunzio, Gabriele, 388
Dante, 124, 264
D'Aurevilly, Barbey, 387
Davis, Andrew Jackson, 322, 323
Davis, Captain, 3
Davis, Nuel Pharr, 165n
Davis, Richard Beale, 219n, 280n
"Dead Daughter, The," 162
De Kalb, Baron, 58
Democratic Review, 305, 356
Démocratie Pacifique, 307
De Sade, Marquis, 387
"Descent into the Maelström, A," 151, 262
Devereaux, Mary, 142, 145-146, 315; on the Poe family mystery, 143; on Poe's passion and jealousy, 143-144; Poe's flight to her, 227-228; at Virginia's deathbed, 310; at the funeral, 312
Devereaux, Mrs., 144-145, 169
"Devil in the Belfry, The," 202
Dewey, Orville, 259
Dickens, Charles, in Philadelphia, 221, 243; derogatory remarks on Poe, 222, 243; helps Mrs. Clemm financially, 389
Didier, Henry, 111
Directorium Inquisitorium, 387
D'Israeli, Isaac, 205
Divina Commedia, 120
Dixon, George, 28
Dixon, John, 27, 35
Doings in Gotham, 254n
Dollar Newspaper, 237
Don Quixote, 68, 91
"Doomed City, The," 132-133
Dorian Gray, 204
D'Ossoli, Marquis Angelo, 275
Dostoevski, 388
Doucet, Father Edward, 303
Douglas, 9
Douglas, Mr., 30, 31
Dow, Jesse E., 233-235
Downey, 124-125
Drama of Exile and Other Poems, The, 263-264
Drayton, Colonel William, 99
"Dream-Land," 257-258, 259
Duane, William, 252
Dubourg, George, 40

of the *Broadway Journal*, 261; his critiques of Elizabeth Barrett, 263-264; dedicates his book to her, 265; his satisfaction in his hoaxes, 267-268; and the "Longfellow War," 268-270; becomes sole owner of *Broadway Journal*, 271; and Walt Whitman, 272; critique of his lecture on American Poetry, 275-276; his amatory exchanges with Mrs. F. S. Osgood, 277; his friendship with T. H. Chivers, 278-281; and the Osgood affair, 282-283; and Boston Lyceum lecture, 283-285; composes "Eulalie," 286-287; his valentine to Mrs. Osgood, 290; lodges with the Millers, 291-292; writes *Literati* for *Godey's*, 292; success of *Literati*, 293; moves to Fordham cottage, 295; complains of his poverty, 297; ridicules T. D. English, 298; his libel suit against the *Mirror*, 299; among the literary women, 300, 301; Virginia as his comforter, 302; and Mrs. Gove's visits, 303-304; his writings, 305; on love of fame, 306; and Baudelaire's absorption in him, 306-307; on honesty as critic, 308; writes Willis about his wife's illness, 308-309; his letter to Mrs. Shew, 310; and Virginia's burial, 311-312; his brain fever, 312; awarded damages in *Mirror* suit, 313; his interest in Mrs. Shew, 314; Poe and the sexual urge, 315; walks to Virginia's grave, 316; and "Ulalume," 317-319; conceives *Eureka*, 322; lectures at Society Library, 323-324; and publication of *Eureka*, 325; his alarming exaltation, 326; comments on "Fable for Critics," 327; receives Mrs. Whitman's valentine, 328; composes "The Bells," 329; makes inquiries about Mrs. Whitman, 330; his second "To Helen," 330-331; lectures in Lowell, 333; meets Annie Richmond, 334; sets out for Richmond for *Stylus* subscriptions, 335; writes to Mrs. Whitman under a pseudonym, 336, 337; visits Mrs. Whitman, 337; their courtship and engagement, 340-341; his flight to Mrs. Richmond and his suicide attempt, 342-343; another attack of brain fever, 344; still divided between the two women he loves, 345; corrects Mrs. Whitman's poem, 346; seeks to interest her in the *Stylus*, 347; his final parting from her, 349; and Annie Richmond as his defender, 350; his last letter to Mrs. Whitman, 351; writes "Hop-Frog," 342; and "For Annie," 353-355; his depression, 356; and "Annabel Lee," 357; and E. H. N. Patterson, 358-359; visits Richmond, 361; his bout of insanity, 361-363, 364; lectures in Richmond, 366-367; renews his addresses to Elmira, 367-368; with Susan Talley, 369; has Elmira's promise of marriage, 370; makes Griswold his literary execu-

tor, 372; his farewell to Elmira, 373; his departure from Richmond and his misadventures in Baltimore, 374-375; his death, 376-377; his burial, 377; no evidence that he had been "cooped," 380; defended by his friends after "Ludwig" attack, 382; accused of plagiarism after death, 385-386; defended by the women he had known, 386; his influence on European literature, 386-388; his exhumation, 390; and dedication of his monument, 391

Poe, Mrs. Edgar Allan (Virginia E. Clemm), 111, 116, 117, 135-136, 139, 142, 144-145, 168-169, 218, 225, 228, 272, 281, 293, 296, 303, 304, 315, 323, 327, 340, 345, 358, 364, 367, 371, 378; her adoration of Edgar, 149; description, 169, 172; secret marriage to Poe, 173; remarried in Richmond, 176-177; and honeymoon, 178-179; in Poe's idealized portrayals, 180-181; in New York, 186-188; her failing health, 199; her singing, 213; her portrait by Thomas Sully, 220; her first hemorrhage, 220-221; her piano sold, 229, 231, 234, 240; in New York with Poe, 249-250; at the Brennan house, 255-257; on brink of death, 258; as "Eulalie," 286; encourages friendship of Mrs. Osgood, 287; at soirées with Poe, 288; and Mrs. Osgood, 289; her valentine to Edgar, 290-291; at the Millers', 291-292; and removal to Fordham, 295; helps to earn money by sewing, 297; critically ill, 299; and Poe's admirers, 300; as Poe's guardian angel, 301; her sickness aggravated, 304-305; dying in extreme poverty, 388; her death and burial, 310-312; reburied near Poe, 391

Poe, Eliza (later Mrs. Henry Herring), 32, 33, 47, 64, 68, 115; writes to Mrs. John Allan, 30-31

Poe, Elizabeth Arnold Hopkins. *See* Poe, Mrs. David

Poe, George, 18, 20, 174

Poe, George Washington, 15, 115

Poe, John, 14

Poe, John Hancock, 15, 31

Poe, Neilson (cousin of E. A. Poe), 138-139; disturbed by Poe's interest in Virginia, 169-170, 171; at hospital to see Poe, 375; at burial of Poe, 377; writes details to Mrs. Clemm, 381; and Poe's trunk, 383; orders marble slab for Poe's grave, 389, 390

Poe, Rosalie, 29, 66-67n, 69, 108, 125, 138, 177, 183, 336; birth, 23; with mother during her illness and death, 24; taken by Mrs. William Mackenzie, 25-26; not mentioned in Eliza's letter, 32; her arrested development, 50-51; as Cupid's messenger, 52; her legitimacy questioned by Mr. Allan, 62-63; and "In a Pocketbook," 63-64; and Virginia, 176; visits to Poes and Mrs.